Governing Natural Resources for Sustainable Peace in Africa

This book examines the dynamics of natural resource conflicts in Africa and explores the different governance approaches for securing sustainable peace.

One of the most prominent challenges facing Africa today is the consequences of natural resource extraction. While these resources hold the potential for economic transformation across Africa, their extraction also comes with a range of environmental, social, and economic consequences, including issues related to governance. This book assembles a unique cohort of peacebuilding, environmental justice, and sustainable development scholars and practitioners from Africa and beyond to examine the dynamics of natural resource conflict and explore the governance approaches that offer pathways for sustainable peace in Africa. Drawing on case studies and empirical lessons from the Horn of Africa, Southern Africa, West Africa, East Africa, and the Central Sahel region, along with the African Union, the multidisciplinary contributors offer fresh insights into the nature of natural resource conflict in Africa, delve deeper into the complexities of natural resource governance, and highlight the interplay between resource governance and sustainable peace. By shedding light not only on Africa's experiences and vulnerabilities but also on the challenges of natural resource governance, this book fills a crucial gap in understanding the connection between natural resource governance, conflict, and pathways for sustainable peace in Africa.

Drawing on a range of disciplinary perspectives, this book will be of interest to students and scholars of natural resource governance, peace and conflict studies, environmental policy and justice, sustainable development, security studies and African studies more widely.

Obasesam Okoi is Assistant Professor of Justice and Peace Studies at the University of St Thomas, USA. He is Charles E. Scheidt Faculty Fellow in Atrocity Prevention at the Institute for Genocide and Mass Atrocity Prevention (I-GMAP), Binghamton University, USA, and Associate Editor of the *African Security* journal.

Victoria R Nalule is an energy and mining professional and consultant with extensive experience working on various projects across the globe. She is the Chief Executive Officer of Nalule Energy and Minerals Consultants (NEM Energy). She is also a lecturer at the University of Bradford, United Kingdom.

Earthscan Studies in Natural Resource Management

Reindeer Husbandry and Global Environmental Change
Pastoralism in Fennoscandia
Edited by Tim Horstkotte, Øystein Holand, Jouko Kumpula and Jon Moen

The bioeconomy and non-timber forest products
Edited by Carsten Smith-Hall and James Chamberlain

Drylands Facing Change
Interventions, Investments and Identities
Edited by Angela Kronenburg García, Tobias Haller, Han van Dijk, Cyrus Samimi, and Jeroen Warner

Blue Flag Beaches
Economic Growth, Tourism and Sustainable Management
Edited by María A. Prats and Fernando Merino

Resource Communities
Past Legacies and Future Pathways
Kristof Van Assche, Monica Gruezmacher, Lochner Marais, and Xaquin Sindin

English Urban Commons
The Past, Present and Future of Green Spaces
Christopher Rodgers, Rachel Hammersley, Alessandro Zambelli, Emma Cheatle, John Wedgwood Clarke, Sarah Collins, Olivia Dee and Siobhan O'Neill

Governing Natural Resources for Sustainable Peace in Africa
Environmental Justice and Conflict Resolution
Edited by Obasesam Okoi and Victoria R. Nalule

For more information about this series, please visit: www.routledge.com/books/series/ECNRM/

Governing Natural Resources for Sustainable Peace in Africa

Environmental Justice and
Conflict Resolution

**Edited by Obasesam Okoi and
Victoria R. Nalule**

First published 2024
by Routledge
4 Park Square, Milton Park, Abingdon, Oxon OX14 4RN

and by Routledge
605 Third Avenue, New York, NY 10158

Routledge is an imprint of the Taylor & Francis Group, an informa business

© 2024 selection and editorial matter, Obasesam Okoi and Victoria R. Nalule; individual chapters, the contributors

The right of Obasesam Okoi and Victoria R. Nalule to be identified as the authors of the editorial material, and of the authors for their individual chapters, has been asserted in accordance with sections 77 and 78 of the Copyright, Designs and Patents Act 1988.

All rights reserved. No part of this book may be reprinted or reproduced or utilised in any form or by any electronic, mechanical, or other means, now known or hereafter invented, including photocopying and recording, or in any information storage or retrieval system, without permission in writing from the publishers.

Trademark notice: Product or corporate names may be trademarks or registered trademarks, and are used only for identification and explanation without intent to infringe.

British Library Cataloguing-in-Publication Data
A catalogue record for this book is available from the British Library

ISBN: 978-1-032-40991-7 (hbk)
ISBN: 978-1-032-40993-1 (pbk)
ISBN: 978-1-003-35571-7 (ebk)

DOI: 10.4324/9781003355717

Typeset in Times New Roman
by Newgen Publishing UK

To all those striving for peace in Africa, may this book inspire and guide your efforts.

Contents

List of Contributors ix
Foreword by Raphael J. Heffron xiii
Foreword by Damilola S. Olawuyi xv
Acknowledgments xvii
List of Abbreviations xviii

Introduction: Natural Resource Governance and Conflicts in Africa in Context 1
OBASESAM OKOI

PART I
Theories and Concepts 13

1 Natural Resource Governance and Sustainable Peace in Africa: A Theoretical Analysis 15
OBASESAM OKOI

2 Gold Mining and Instability in the Central Sahel 38
JOHN SUNDAY OJO AND OLUWOLE OJEWALE

3 Control of Mineral Land by a Para-sovereign Power in the Ethiopia-Djibouti Borderlands 60
GEMECHU ADIAMASSU ABESHU

PART II
Governance Responses 75

4 Addressing Environmental Injustices in South African Artisanal Gold Mining 77
INGA CARRY AND MELANIE MÜLLER

5 The Role of Distributive Justice and Land Law Reforms in
   Tackling Land Inequalities in the Extractive Industries in
   South Africa and Uganda   101
   VICTORIA R. NALULE

6 The Role of the African Union's Panel of the Wise in
   Natural Resource Conflict Resolution   121
   OLAWARI D. J. EGBE AND FIE DAVID DAN-WONIOWEI

PART III
Lessons and Future Directions   **143**

7 Placing the Rule of Law and Environmental Justice in the
   Resource-Conflict Nexus in Nigeria   145
   EGHOSA O. EKHATOR AND GODSWILL AGBAITORO

8 Social Legitimacy as a Sustainable Tool for Resolving
   Mining-Induced Conflicts in Ghana   169
   CHRIS ADOMAKO-KWAKYE AND RICHARD OBENG MENSAH

9 Exploring the Role of Gender and Indigenous Knowledge
   in Peacebuilding and Political Stability in Africa   191
   JONATHAN ROMIC

   Conclusion: Ensuring a Peaceful Africa Based on the
   Sustainable Use of Natural Resources   215
   VICTORIA R. NALULE AND OBASESAM OKOI

   Index   *219*

Contributors

Gemechu Adiamassu Abeshu is a postdoctoral fellow at York University, specializing in refugees and forced displacement. He holds a Ph.D. in Social Anthropology from Bayreuth University in Germany and an M.A. in Governance Studies from Antwerp University in Belgium. Dr. Abeshu's research interests encompass various areas, including forced displacements, the integration of racialized refugees, emerging non-state forms of political power, and natural resource governance. He is affiliated with the Center for Refugee Studies at York University and the Tshepo Institute for the Study of Contemporary Africa at Wilfrid Laurier University. Additionally, he serves as a co-chair of the Racisms and Refugee Subcommittee at the Center for Refugee Studies at York University.

Chris Adomako-Kwakye is Senior Lecturer at the Faculty of Law, Kwame Nkrumah University of Science and Technology (KNUST), Kumasi. He is the Head of the Commercial Law Department and the Acting Dean of the Faculty. His research interest focuses on Natural Resources Law, Transparency and Accountability in utilizing natural resource revenue, Banking and Insurance Law, and Intellectual Property Law. He obtained his master's and doctoral degrees from the University of Bristol, United Kingdom and the University of Cape Town, South Africa.

Godswill Agbaitoro is Lecturer in Law at Essex Law School, University of Essex, United Kingdom. His research focuses primarily on the implementation of the energy justice framework in Africa and the Global South.

Inga Carry Inga Carry is an associate with a focus on environmental governance, socio-environmental conflicts, and natural resources at the German Institute for International and Security Affairs (Stiftung Wissenschaft und Politik, SWP). She works as part of the Research Network Sustainable Supply Chains, funded by the Federal Ministry for Economic Cooperation and Development (BMZ).

x *List of Contributors*

Fie David Dan-Woniowei holds a Ph.D. in International Relations from North-West University in the Republic of South Africa. He is a member of several professional associations, including the Nigeria Political Science Association. Currently, Dr. Dan-Woniowei serves as a teaching staff at Niger Delta University, focusing on research in the areas of International Political Economy (IPE), international organizations, peace and conflict studies, and strategic studies.

Olawari D. J. Egbe is a scholar specializing in international relations and affiliated with the Department of Political Science at Niger Delta University (NDU) in Bayelsa State, Nigeria. He serves as an aAssociate eEditor for the Wilberforce Journal of the Social Sciences and has co-edited the book titled "Nigeria's 2019 Democratic Experience" published by De Gruyter in Berlin in 2022. Dr. Egbe is a member of various professional associations, including the Nigerian Institute of International Affairs (NIIA) and the Nigeria Political Science Association (NPSA). He has obtained degrees from the Universities of Ibadan, Port-Harcourt, and Calabar.

Eghosa O. Ekhator is Senior Lecturer in Law at the University of Derby, United Kingdom. His main research areas include International Environmental Law, African International Legal History, and Natural Resources Governance. Eghosa has published extensively on his research areas and his academic papers have been cited by a plethora of organizations and international agencies.

Raphael J. Heffron is a distinguished Professor of Energy Justice and the Social Contract at Universite de Pau et des Pays de l'Adour, France. He also holds the prestigious EU Jean Monnet Professorship in the Just Transition to a Low-Carbon Economy (2019–2022) and serves as Senior Counsel at Janson in Brussels, Belgium. Professor Heffron has been recognized as a Senior Fellow of the UK Higher Education Academy, a Fellow of the Royal Society of Arts, and a Fellow of the Royal Society of Edinburgh's Young Academy of Scotland. He serves as a Visiting Professor at several esteemed institutions worldwide, including ESCP Business School in London, Paris, and Madrid, Université Paris-Dauphine in France, Queen Mary University of London, Eduardo Mondlane University in Mozambique, Kathmandu University in Nepal, and the University of Brawijaja in Indonesia. He is an Associate Researcher at the Energy Policy Research Group, University of Cambridge, and the Oxford Institute for Energy Studies.

Richard Obeng Mensah is a doctoral researcher at Kwame Nkrumah University of Science and Technology in Kumasi, Ghana, specializing in energy security and clean energy generation. His research interests encompass a wide range of topics, including energy security, renewable energy, climate change, human rights, intellectual property rights, comparative law, natural resources governance, corruption, and good governance. He is an Assistant Law Lecturer with the Faculty of Law at KNUST.

List of Contributors xi

Melanie Müller is Senior Associate with a focus on South Africa/Southern Africa at the German Institute for International and Security Affairs (Stiftung Wissenschaft und Politik, SWP). She heads the SWP component of the Research Network Sustainable Supply Chains, funded by the Federal Ministry for Economic Cooperation and Development (BMZ).

Victoria R. Nalule is an energy and mining professional and consultant, and founder and CEO of NEM Energy. She received her PhD in International Energy Law and Policy from CEPMLP, University of Dundee. She has vast experience in global extractives and energy transition projects and is the founder of the African Energy and Minerals Management Initiative (AEMI). Victoria has published numerous books and articles on energy transitions, climate change, and mining, and has advised governments and organizations worldwide on energy and mining projects.

Oluwole Ojewale serves as the ENACT Regional Organised Crime Observatory Coordinator for Central Africa at the Institute for Security Studies in Dakar, Senegal. He specializes in transnational organized crime, urban governance, security, conflict, and resilience in Africa. Dr. Ojewale has conducted studies and engaged with stakeholders in several countries, including Cameroon, the Central African Republic, the Democratic Republic of Congo, Gabon, Mali, Niger, Nigeria, the Republic of Congo, São Tomé, and Senegal.

John Sunday Ojo is a doctoral researcher at the School of Area Studies, History, Politics, and Literature, University of Portsmouth, United Kingdom. He received his MA in Global Development from the University of Leeds in the United Kingdom. He earned another Master of Science in Urban Management and Development focusing on environment, sustainability, and climate change from Erasmus University Rotterdam in the Netherlands. His research focuses on the intersectionality of climate change and conflict, violent extremism, non-state armed groups, conflict resolution, peace studies, and international security.

Obasesam Okoi is Assistant Professor of Justice and Peace Studies at the University of St. Thomas in Minnesota, USA, Charles E. Scheidt Faculty Fellow in Atrocity Prevention at the Institute for Genocide and Mass Atrocity Prevention (I-GMAP), Binghamton University, New York, and Associate Editor of the *African Security* journal. He is the author of *Punctuated Peace in Nigeria's Oil Region: Oil Insurgency and the Challenges of Post-Conflict Peacebuilding* (Palgrave Macmillan, 2021).

Damilola S. Olawuyi is a professor and holds the UNESCO Chair on Environmental Law and Sustainable Development at Hamad Bin Khalifa University in Doha, Qatar. He also serves as an Independent Expert for the United Nations Working Group on Business and Human Rights.

Jonathan Romic is a researcher specializing in AI, regulation, education, and policy development in an increasingly technology-driven global environment. He recently completed his third master's degree in technology policy at the Judge Business School at Cambridge University and is embarking on a Ph.D. program at the Faculty of Education at the University of Cambridge, with a focus on AI in education and regulation.

Foreword

The world is facing an unprecedented and challenging time, with new realities of climate change hitting the news every day. These stories often dominate the international media, but they tend to heavily focus on developed countries. For instance, Europe's city of Venice in Italy has shifted from yearly floods to a drought in 2023, and extreme weather events in Australia receive continuous attention. However, developing countries receive little coverage, such as the devastating floods in Pakistan in 2022, from which the country is still recovering and needs greater focus. In this context, this short-edited collection that brings attention to Africa is most welcome.

This text focuses on natural resources and their association with conflict, with the overarching aim of promoting peaceful and sustainable use of energy resources. While the book touches upon some African issues, it places specific emphasis on case studies from various countries, including South Africa, Ghana, Uganda, and Nigeria. It is essential to note that Africa comprises 54 countries, and the text provides regional and general perspectives in the opening and concluding chapters, offering a comprehensive outlook on the subject matter.

An important focus of the book is to draw attention to the issue of conflict or in essence pathways of natural resource use where conflict arises. Currently, there is a lack of sufficient literature addressing these conflicts on a global scale, leading to various justice-related issues across the economy. This is even more so the case in terms of Africa and that is why this book should be welcomed.

Normally, the literature always raises the question that instabilities cause economic issues and that is the reason to focus on rectifying them. However, this book presents a diverse range of narratives, highlighting that there are various reasons to address the causes of instabilities. Moreover, these causes are not solely driven by the same factors as in the past, such as solely being an economic governance issue.

This book is a valuable addition to the academic literature, as it delves into topics "beyond economics" while addressing issues related to the use of natural resources in contemporary society. The editors deserve commendation for shedding light on this debate and making efforts to contribute to the path toward achieving a just and sustainable transition to a low-carbon economy for everyone.

Raphael J. Heffron
Biarritz, France

Foreword

It is my greatest pleasure and honor to write a foreword for this important book edited by Dr. Obasesam Okoi and Dr. Victoria R Nalule. The book exhaustively examines natural resources governance and related conflicts, drawing examples from different African countries. All the researchers who have contributed have brought first-hand experiences from different African countries.

Natural resources, including land, minerals, water, energy resources, and related substances, have been the main drivers of economic development in many countries. When effectively managed, these resources have the potential to finance infrastructural development much needed in several African countries. Taking energy resources as an example, which encompass both fossil fuels and renewables, we recognize their vital role in addressing energy access and poverty challenges across Africa. Goal 7 of the United Nations Sustainable Development Goals (UN SDG) focuses on energy access, yet despite the abundance of energy resources on the African continent, reliable data reveals that over 600 million people still lack access to modern energy. This underscores the critical importance of natural resources, such as energy, in addressing energy poverty.

The mining sector equally plays a significant role in African resource-rich countries. The crucial role of minerals is reflected in our everyday lives through the various sectors of the economy. For instance, minerals are used as raw materials in different sectors including construction and transport. The African continent possesses around 30% of the world's mineral reserves, which could potentially contribute to export and tax revenues for the relevant countries. Land and water resources equally play a significant role in every country.

Despite the abundant natural resource wealth and its importance, we cannot overlook the negative impacts associated with such resources. Relevant to this book is the issue of conflicts in resource-rich countries. While natural resources have contributed positively to the economic development of countries such as Botswana and Namibia, they have sadly exacerbated conflicts and instabilities in countries such as the Democratic Republic of Congo (DRC). It therefore becomes crucial to analyze the various approaches to prevent such conflicts in the development and governance of natural resources.

In light of the above facts, this book unpacks some of the key issues relating to the governance of natural resources for sustainable peace. Notable and diverse research analyses are contained in the book, drawing the readers to the various theories of natural resources conflicts, instabilities related to gold mining in the Central Sahel, the influence of para-sovereign powers in the natural resources sector, land-related conflicts, conflicts in artisanal and small-scale mining (ASM), environmental justice and related conflicts, community conflicts and the need for social legitimacy, and the role of gender justice in peacebuilding in resource-rich countries to mention but a few.

The book is timely and relevant, making it an invaluable asset for professionals, government institutions, universities, and a wide range of stakeholders who are interested in understanding sustainable peacebuilding from the perspective of natural resource governance.

Damilola S. Olawuyi
SAN, FCIArb

Acknowledgments

We are profoundly grateful to our colleague, Dr. Ifesinachi Okafor-Yarwood, who has been an invaluable and dedicated member of the editorial team since the inception of this book. Despite facing personal challenges that prevented her from seeing the project through to its completion, she made substantial contributions, including the conceptualization of the book and providing valuable editorial reviews. We extend our deepest appreciation for her invaluable efforts.

We extend our heartfelt gratitude to the three anonymous reviewers for their exceptional reviews and invaluable feedback. We are also deeply indebted to the numerous peer reviewers who promptly responded to our request and provided exceptional comments that greatly enhanced the quality and rigor of the manuscripts. Their insightful feedback and expertise have significantly contributed to the refinement of this book. Furthermore, we would like to express our appreciation to the book contributors for their dedicated work and patience during the publication process. Their efforts have been instrumental in bringing this book to fruition.

We are extremely grateful to Professor Damilola and Professor Raphael Heffron for their prompt response and willingness to contribute the foreword to this book. Their dedication and effort in crafting the foreword have added immense value and significance to the overall content of the book. We truly appreciate their time and expertise in providing these valuable contributions.

Finally, we express our deep gratitude for the unwavering support of our families, whose understanding and encouragement enabled us to dedicate ourselves to this project and successfully bring this book to completion.

Abbreviations

AFED	Association Femmes et Environment au Burundi
AFSA	African Peace and Security Architecture
AMD	acid mine drainage
ANRS	Afar National Regional State
APDP	Afar Peoples Democratic Party
ASF	African Standby Force
ASM	artisanal and small-scale Mining
AU	African Union
BIT	Bilateral Investment Treaty
BME	Bureau of Mines and Energy
CERD	Convention on Elimination of Racial Discrimination
CEWS	Continental Early Warning System
CFU	Carbon Finance Unit
CIT	Corporate Income Tax
CONMESA	Common Market for Eastern and Southern Africa
COP	Conference of the Parties
CPP	Convention People's Party
CSO	Civil Society Organization
CSR	Corporate Social Responsibility
DPCI	Directorate for Priority Crime Investigation
DRC	Democratic Republic of Congo
DSM	Dispute Settlement Mechanism
ECOMOG	Economic Community of West African States Monitoring Group
ECOWAS	Economic Community of West African States
EEZ	Exclusive Economic Zones
EITI	Extractive Industries Transparency Initiative
ESG	Environmental, Social, and Governance
ET	Emission Trading
EU	European Union
FDI	Foreign Direct Investment
FDRE	Federal Democratic Republic of Ethiopia

FG	federal government
FPIC	Free, Prior, and Informed Consent
GDP	gross domestic product
GDPG	gross domestic product growth
GEF	Global Environmental Facility
GHG	greenhouse gases
GRI	Global Reporting Initiative
GSR	Golden Star Resources
HDI	Human Development Index
ICCPR	International Covenant on Civil and Political Rights
ICJ	International Court of Justice
ICMM	International Council on Mining and Metal
ICSID	International Center for the Settlement of Investment Disputes
IFC	International Finance Corporation
ILC	International Law Commission
INDC	intended nationally determined contribution
ISDS	investor-state dispute settlement
ISO	International Organization for Standardization
IUCN	International Union for the Conservation of Nature
KP	Kimberley Process
LDC	least developed countries
LDCF	Least Developed Country Fund
LSM	large-scale mining
MIGA	Multilateral Investment Guarantee Agency
MNC	multinational corporations
MoME	Ministry of Mines and Energy
MOP	Meeting of the Parties
MOSOP	Movement for the Survival of Ogoni People
MOST	Maltese Ocean Space Treaty
MOU	memorandum of understanding
MPRDA	Mineral and Petroleum Resources Development Act
NAAM	National Association of Artisanal Miners
NDBDA	Niger Delta Basin Development Authority
NDCs	Nationally Determined Contributions
NDDB	Niger Delta Development Board
NDDC	Niger Delta Development Commission
NDR	Niger Delta region
NESREA	National Environmental Standards and Regulations Enforcement Agency
NGO	nongovernmental organization
NLM	National Liberation Movement
NNPC	Nigerian National Petroleum Corporation
NOSDRA	National Oil Spill Detection and Response Agency Act
NO_x	nitrogen oxides

NSA	nonstate actors
NYSE	New York Stock Exchange
ODS	ozone-depleting substances
OMPADEC	Oil Mineral Producing Areas Development Commission
PIAC	Public Interest Accountability Committee
POC	people of color
PoW	Panel of the Wise
PRI	Principles of Responsible Investment
PSC	Peace and Security Council
PSC	production sharing contracts
RECs/RMs	Regional Economic Communities/Regional Mechanisms
RST	Rentier State Theory
SA	Republic of South Africa
SADC	Southern Africa Development Community
SASB	Sustainability Accounting Standards Board
SDGs	Sustainable Development Goals
SDR	Sustainable Development Report
SERAP	Socio-Economic Rights and Accountability Project
SLO	the social license
SO_x	sulphur oxides
SPDC	Shell Petroleum Development Corporation
SSA	sub-Saharan Africa
SWX	Swiss Exchange
TCFD	Task Force on Climate-related Financial Disclosures
UAE	United Arab Emirates
UK	United Kingdom
UN	United Nations
UNCLOS	United Nations Convention on the Law of the Sea
UNDP	United Nations Development Program
UNECA	United Nations Economic Commission for Africa
UNEP	United Nations Environment Programme
UNEP	United Nations Environment Programme
UNFCC	United Nations Framework Convention on Climate Change
UNGC	United Nations Global Compact
UNOSOM	United Nations Operation in Somalia
US GAAP	United States Generally Accepted Accounting Principles
US	United States
USD	United States dollar
VIF	Variance Inflation Factor
WHO	World Trade Organisation
WSSD	World Summit on Sustainable Development

Introduction
Natural Resource Governance and Conflicts in Africa in Context

Obasesam Okoi

The abundant natural resources in Africa have the potential to stimulate economic productivity across the continent. The prosperity of African nations and the well-being of their populations are intricately linked to their ability to effectively harness and utilize their resource wealth. However, the exploitation of natural resources has been widely recognized as a catalyst for violent conflicts in Africa since 1990,[1] with a significant percentage of intrastate conflicts in the past six decades having a connection to natural resources.[2] Civil wars in Sierra Leone, Liberia, Angola, and the Democratic Republic of Congo have been fueled by the desire to control natural resources, while tensions in South Sudan, Zimbabwe, and the Horn of Africa have arisen from competition over scarce resources.[3] These tensions have disrupted communities throughout Africa and led to external interventions in affected countries. This paradox underscores the critical role of natural resource governance in fostering stability in Africa. The question is, what types of governance processes can offer pathways for sustainable peace in ways that go beyond conventional thinking?

The institutionalization of the African Union's Agenda 2063 in 2015, as a strategic framework for the socio-economic transformation of Africa over the next 50 years, recognizes the role that natural resources play in Africa's development. It strongly emphasizes natural resource governance as a means to achieve the desired future of shared prosperity on the continent. The moment seems promising for the development of research that recognizes the role of natural resource governance in addressing the root causes of conflicts and contributing to the long-term stability of African societies. While there has been an increase in scholarly development regarding the link between natural resource endowment and instability in Africa over the past few decades,[4] the narrow contextualization of this research reinforces pre-existing assumptions about the negative consequences of natural resources. This gap in the literature restricts our knowledge of the relationship between natural resource governance and sustainable peace. This book presents new research on the connection between natural resources and instability in Africa, as well as a more nuanced understanding of natural resource governance as vital in promoting sustainable peace.

DOI: 10.4324/9781003355717-1

This book is aimed at students, practitioners, policymakers, and scholars of peace and conflict studies, environmental justice, natural resources, energy, mining, and sustainable development. The central theme of the book revolves around the relationship between natural resource governance, conflict, and sustainable peace. The collection of chapters illuminates the complex dynamics of conflicts arising from competition over natural resources in Africa and explores some governance responses to these conflicts. The contributors to this book address three key issues related to this central theme. Firstly, they present new perspectives on the nature of natural resource conflict in Africa, thereby reshaping our understanding of the relationship between natural resources and instability. Secondly, they delve deeper into the multifaceted nature and complexities of natural resource governance, including considerations of the rule of law and justice. They acknowledge the diverse array of factors and dynamics that influence the relationship between natural resources and peace in Africa. Thirdly, they highlight the interplay between resource governance and sustainable peace, emphasizing the importance of environmental justice and conflict resolution. The contributors include scholars and practitioners who are critical of or intimately involved in shaping the intellectual contours of natural resource governance and peacebuilding in Africa. Drawing on case studies from Nigeria, Uganda, Ethiopia, Djibouti, Botswana, Ghana, South Africa, the Central Sahel region, and the African Union, the multidisciplinary contributions critically examine theoretical debates on the dynamics of resource conflict, analyze reforms aimed at improving governance in resource extraction, and explore strategies to address environmental conflicts and injustices, including a focus on gender-related concerns. These perspectives provide frameworks for understanding the new drivers of instability in Africa and for engaging critically with discourses on natural resources governance and sustainable peace on the continent.

The Context of the Book

The African continent is richly endowed with vast deposits of terrestrial and marine resources, including land, oil, gas, water, minerals, forests, fisheries, and timber. Notably, Africa possesses 30 percent of the global mineral reserves, which significantly contribute to exports and tax revenues for most countries on the continent.[5] The region is also rich in various minerals, including gold, diamonds, vermiculite, manganese, cobalt, zirconium, salt, and phosphate rock.[6] Moreover, Africa boasts 65 percent of the world's arable land and 10 percent of the planet's internal renewable freshwater sources. These resources have the potential to drive economic growth, promote development, and uplift the livelihoods of local communities throughout the continent. However, an increasing body of literature has demonstrated that the management and utilization of natural resources have resulted in conflict and instability across the African continent, rather than facilitating the attainment of shared prosperity for Africans.[7]

This book shows that the relationship between natural resource governance and conflicts in Africa is complex and interconnected. Instability can arise due to competition over access to resources and the associated benefits, as well as issues pertaining to control and ownership.[8] The unequal distribution of resource wealth and the marginalization of local communities in decision-making processes can also exacerbate social inequalities and grievances, providing a fertile ground for instability.[9] Moreover, instability itself can have a significant impact on natural resource governance by undermining efforts toward sustainable resource management, which is vital for the achievement of peace. It is worth emphasizing that natural resource conflicts often intersect with territorial issues, as research has shown a clear association between territorial claims and the presence and control of natural resources.[10] A study of the Bakassi Peninsula conflict between Nigeria and Cameroon underlines the relationship between territorial claims, conflict, and the presence of natural resource deposits in disputed territories. It argues that conflicts are more likely to occur when valuable natural resources are at stake in the disputed area.[11] Because of the strategic importance of natural resources in providing a base for conflicts, competition over territorial claims is based primarily on the tangible value of territory.[12] These tensions escalate and manifest in violent conflict when governance institutions are dysfunctional.

In recent years, the mining industry has provided opportunities for foreign corporations to access the abundant mineral reserves found in countries across Africa. However, mining activities elevate the risk of local protests and conflict between mining companies and local communities.[13] Case studies on mining-related conflicts in Africa also reveal that tensions frequently stem from several factors, including loss of settlement and land use for cultivation and grazing, the health effects of mining activities, and lack of compensation or community participation in the process of awarding mining concessions. Other factors include human rights problems linked to forced displacement, the distribution of mining rents, and the demand for employment opportunities for the population living in the mining region.[14] In post-conflict societies such as Liberia and Sierra Leone, conflict developed from the lucrative enterprise around the diamond trade and the undertakings of corrupt government elite and mining companies.[15] Moreover, the growing scarcity of renewable resources, such as land and water, the depletion of marine resources, such as fisheries, and the increasing competition over control and production of onshore and offshore hydrocarbon and other minerals reinforce existing stress factors and motivate actors to resort to violence.[16] These tensions are compounded by proximate factors such as environmental degradation and climate change which threaten to increase the risk of conflicts over natural resources. While these repertoires of contention highlight complex challenges in Africa, concerns about the importance of natural resource governance in ensuring long-term stability within African countries have received limited attention in the peacebuilding literature. Addressing these challenges has been a critical challenge facing

Africa today and will be vital in propelling the continent to achieve its vision of sustainable development by 2063.

The risk of resource exploitation underscores the necessity for effective natural resource governance to provide pathways for sustainable peace in Africa. Although the definition of natural resource governance varies considerably, the concept generally refers to "the norms, institutions, structures, and processes that determine how power and responsibilities over natural resources are exercised, how decisions are taken, and how citizens participate in and benefit from the management of natural resources."[17] Some define natural resource governance as the formal and informal institutions that guide management actions and provide the necessary direction, resources, and structure to achieve the overarching goals of resource governance.[18] In the context of Africa, natural resource governance encompasses the collection of policies, institutions, and practices that govern the extraction, allocation, and utilization of natural resources. It involves addressing concerns regarding ownership, control, the distribution of revenues, environmental sustainability, and social equity. As a condition for sustainable peace, natural resource governance encompasses the range of institutions, policies, and practices employed by societies to achieve sustainable and equitable resource management as well as increase access to and benefit from these resources. The governance processes are influenced by various actors, such as governments, business corporations, local communities, and civil society organizations. The interactions and power dynamics among these actors are instrumental in shaping the outcomes of natural resource management, which can either promote peace or exacerbate instability.

However, the lack of effective institutional frameworks in managing natural resources presents a major challenge in Africa. Weak governance structures create conditions in which resource revenues primarily benefit a small group of individuals, leaving the majority of the population impoverished and prone to conflict. For example, conflict in Nigeria's oil region is mostly attributed to inequities in the "ownership and management of Nigeria's oil wealth and the distribution of oil revenues."[19] The tension arises from Nigeria's constitution, which grants the federal government absolute ownership of oil resources and control over the distribution of oil revenue. However, oil communities assert their entitlement to the wealth generated by these resources, as they believe that the laws governing natural resource management infringe upon their rights.[20] Rotimi Suberu argued that in the Nigerian context, federalism has been manipulated by powerful elites to their advantage, leading to a disregard for national development.[21] He traces the roots of Nigeria's problematic federalism to the competition among regions, groups, and individuals for revenue sharing and control and sheds light on how these issues are connected to the challenges faced by minority groups in the oil region. In doing so, his work underscores the enduring impact of Nigeria's dysfunctional revenue management system. These inefficiencies have arguably contributed to fostering a sense of discontent in the oil region, ultimately leading to conditions that promote instability.

In this context, the achievement of sustainable peace necessitates the creation of effective institutional structures for natural resource governance.

The concept of sustainable peace underscores the absence of both overt and systemic violence, and the presence of social, economic, and political conditions that foster cooperation and well-being among individuals, communities, and nations.[22] It is a state of stability that is characterized by justice, equality, and inclusivity. The pursuit of natural resource governance as a prerequisite for sustainable peace calls attention to the importance of the rule of law. The rule of law stimulates economic growth and socio-economic justice; prevents and deters violent conflict and crime; and strengthens accountability and checks on power, allowing for a more equitable distribution of resources and better environmental protection.[23] This is important because the displacement of land users, disregard for customary rights of ethnic communities, and changes in the distribution of power can occur as a result of legal modifications, institutional reforms, or repressive tactics implemented by state authorities.[24] While some states possess the necessary institutions to ensure the sustainable use of their natural resources, these institutions remain ineffective due to legal limitations. Besides, the corruption of local officials is corrosive, which undermines efforts to improve governance and prevent growing distrust of, and hatred for, the government.[25] Under these conditions, the rule of law remains crucial for translating natural resource governance standards into realistic conflict resolution measures in Africa.

This book presents a unique blend of philosophical and empirical insights, offering fresh perspectives on natural resource governance. It addresses contemporary challenges to natural resource governance, investigates the factors driving instability, analyzes governance frameworks to address natural resource conflicts, and offers valuable lessons and future directions for students, researchers, and practitioners in the field. The chapters are structured logically and integrated around the central theme of natural resource governance and sustainable peace. They progress coherently from a strong theoretical foundation to an analysis of the intricacies of natural resource governance, the spaces of contestation, and strategies for addressing instability. These chapters offer valuable insights and lessons that are applicable to both academic scholarship and practical application.

The Structure of the Book

To provide a deeper understanding of the relationship between natural resource governance and sustainable peace in Africa, this book presents a comprehensive framework divided into three interconnected parts. Each part explores different aspects of this relationship and contributes to the overall analysis. The first part of the framework attempts to contextualize the connection between natural resource governance and instability in its theoretical, political, and philosophical contexts. It also examines the underlying dynamics that fuel conflicts related to natural resources on the African continent. The second part delves into governance and conflict resolution processes aimed at addressing instabilities arising from disputes over natural resources in Africa. The chapters in this section emphasize the significance of the rule of law, including environmental justice, distributive justice, and social justice, in ensuring long-term stability within resource-dependent African countries. The third part documents emerging lessons in natural resource governance and conflict resolution and offers insights and future directions for academics and peacebuilders to consider.

In Part I, the first chapter authored by Obasesam Okoi provides a theoretical overview of the paradox of natural resource abundance and explores the role of governance in resolving resource conflicts and fostering peace in Africa. Okoi's argument implicitly builds on the theoretical foundations of the resource curse debate, highlighting the importance of effective natural resource governance in creating an environment conducive to peace and stability on the African continent. In essence, when natural resource revenues are distributed equitably for the benefit of all citizens, conflicts can be mitigated, and sustainable peace can be attained. The chapter draws evidence from Botswana and South Africa to establish the link between natural resource governance and peace and lay the foundation for the subsequent chapters of the book, which delve deeper into the complexities of these issues.

In the second chapter, John Sunday Ojo and Oluwole Ojewale delve into the resource governance deficit that enables armed groups to finance criminal activities in the Central Sahel. This chapter specifically hones in on the relationship between the illicit economy of gold production, its commercialization, and the resulting regional instability in Burkina Faso, Mali, and the Republic of Niger. Within these countries, armed groups have turned to artisanal mining and illegal gold trading as lucrative means to support their criminal and terrorist endeavors. By closely examining these complex dynamics, Ojo and Ojewale bring to the forefront the urgent issue of resource governance and its implications for stability in the Central Sahel.

The chapter by Gemechu Abeshu examines the emergence of a non-state actor in the Ethiopia and Djibouti borderlands. Capitalizing on the weak state capacity, this actor establishes itself as a para-sovereign power and gained control over the Dobi Salt Lake, thereby assuming authority in regulating mine access, tax collection, and the provision of security in the area. Abeshu utilizes the concept of "heterarchy" to analyze the existence of pluralistic power structures in the Dobi Salt Lake, exemplifying how non-state actors can exert sovereignty over resource-rich territories where the state's legitimacy is compromised. Collectively, these chapters provide the theoretical and conceptual footing for mapping the contours of natural resource governance and its implications.

The chapters in Part II delve deeply into governance responses specifically aimed at addressing conflicts arising from the competition over natural resources. The chapter by Melanie Müller and Inga Carry explores the challenges faced by artisanal miners and the dynamics of environmental, health, and social inequalities prevalent within South Africa's illegal mining communities. In the context of pervasive social inequality and a deeply stratified South African society, certain groups are especially susceptible to vulnerabilities. The illicit nature of artisanal gold mining further exacerbates these power dynamics, as miners operate within a gray zone that the state has struggled to regulate. Melanie and Carry examine these dynamics through the lens of environmental and social justice, highlighting the interconnectedness between vulnerabilities in the gold mining sector, such as race, class-based discrimination, and environmental injustice. The fundamental argument is that the issues faced by artisanal miners in South Africa cannot be separated from the broader context of environmental injustice in postapartheid South Africa. Based on their findings, they propose a comprehensive governance framework aimed at effectively addressing environmental justice concerns in this context.

The chapter by Victoria Nalule takes an interdisciplinary and legal geographic approach to examine the application of distributive justice in land governance. Nalule draws on case studies from South Africa and Uganda to analyze land-related conflicts and law reforms as well as the role of distributive justice in promoting sustainable land use within the extractive industries. Both countries have implemented laws and provisions pertaining to mining closure, land rehabilitation, and decommissioning, reflecting their commitment to environmental protection and energy justice in land governance. These examples provide evidence of how distributive justice can effectively address historical and ongoing land inequalities.

The chapter by Olawari Egbe and Fie Dan-Woniowei focuses on the African Union's Panel of the Wise (PoW) and its role in resolving conflicts arising from natural resources in sub-Saharan Africa. Despite recognizing the natural resource sector as a major catalyst for conflicts in the region, the PoW has shown a decline in attention to this sector, as evidenced by the persisting resource-related conflicts. The chapter highlights key areas that require the PoW's attention, particularly environmental issues, and proposes the need for increased oversight of the natural resource sector to prevent future conflicts and minimize their devastating impact on the continent.

In Part III of the book, the focus shifts to documenting emerging lessons in natural resource governance and conflict resolution, while also offering insights into potential future directions. This section delves deeper into the central theme of the book by exploring case studies and examples that shed light on the complexities of managing natural resources in conflict-affected areas.

The chapter by Eghosa Ekhator and Godswill Agbaitoro examines protracted natural resource conflicts in Africa, with Nigeria as a case study. It highlights the adverse impact of the absence of the rule of law on the economy and environment. Using the environmental justice paradigm, the chapter critically analyzes the rule of law dilemma in natural resource governance. The central argument of this chapter is that the integration of environmental justice principles is crucial for effectively addressing natural resource conflicts in Africa. The implication is that by incorporating environmental justice principles into laws and policies governing resource extraction and use, a more comprehensive and equitable approach can be adopted to address the challenges associated with natural resource conflicts. The proposed practical reform measures, based on the environmental justice paradigm, can guide African countries in improving their natural resource governance and promoting knowledge sharing among nations for more sustainable and equitable outcomes.

The chapter by Chris Adomako-Kwakye and Richard Obeng Mensah examines the concept of social legitimacy as a driver of mining conflicts in Ghana. They argue that the tension between mining companies and host communities arises from the hazardous effects of mining and the lack of development in those communities. Despite initiatives such as corporate social responsibility, aimed at benefiting local communities, disputes in the mining sector have led to international arbitration cases. The lack of consideration for the needs of mining communities in the authorization process and the perception of one-sided benefits have exacerbated the conflicts in the mining sector. By including the communities as stakeholders in negotiations and considering their needs, conflicts can be minimized and social legitimacy for mining operations can be enhanced. The implication for peace is that the development of host mining communities should be integrated into mining laws to foster a more equitable and mutually beneficial relationship between communities and mining companies in Ghana.

The chapter by Jonathan Romic delves into the relationship between indigenous knowledge, gender, and peacebuilding in various contexts. It highlights the role of local women in utilizing their knowledge of resources to promote social, political, and economic stability. Romic introduces a theoretical framework that identifies three explanatory mechanisms for enhancing resource governance practices in support of peacebuilding and uses a case study of Sudanese women to demonstrate the effectiveness of this framework in connecting resource governance, peacebuilding, gender, and indigenous knowledge.

Collectively, the chapters in this section provide valuable insights and recommendations for the future of natural resource governance, emphasizing the importance of environmental justice, stakeholder inclusion, and recognizing the contributions of indigenous knowledge and gender in promoting sustainable peace.

In the conclusion, we draw together the lessons of these chapters for ensuring sustainable peace in Africa based on the theoretical, conceptual, and practical issues raised and reflect on their implications for the sustainable use of natural resources. Collectively, the contributors offer a comprehensive understanding of the relationship between natural resources, conflicts, governance, and peace. The various chapters provide frameworks and perspectives that contextualize these dynamics and present diverse approaches and strategies for effective natural resource governance. These chapters also document emerging lessons in natural resource governance and conflict resolution, offering valuable insights and recommendations for academics and peacebuilders. By incorporating a broad range of perspectives, this book deepens our understanding of the complexity of natural resource governance and provides pathways for promoting sustainable peace.

Notes

1 Michael Ross, "The Natural Resource Curse: How Wealth Can Make You Poor." In *Natural Resources and Violent Conflict*, edited by I. Bannon and P. Collier (Washington, DC: World Bank, 2004); Paul Collier and Anke Hoeffler, "Resource Rents, Governance, and Conflict," *Journal of Conflict Resolution* 49, no. 4 (2005): 625–633; Richard Auty, "Resource Abundance and Economic Development: Improving the Performance of Resource-Rich Countries," *World Development* 29, no. 7 (2001): 1341–1353; Macartan Humphreys, Jeffrey D. Sachs, and Joseph E. Stiglitz, *Escaping the Resource Curse* (New York: Columbia University Press, 2007); Michael L. Ross, *The Oil Curse: How Petroleum Wealth Shapes the Development of Nations* (Princeton, NJ: Princeton University Press, 2012); Terry Lynn Karl, *The Paradox of Plenty: Oil Booms and Petro-States* (Berkeley, CA: University of California Press, 1997).
2 Uppsala Conflict Data Program and Centre for the Study of Civil War, "UCDP/PRIO Armed Conflict. Dataset version 4.0." In Binningsbø, H. and Rustad, S. A. (2008). "PRIO Working Paper: Resource Conflicts, Resource Management and Post-Conflict Peace." Uppsala University and International Peace Research Institute, Oslo.
3 Abiodun Alao, *Natural Resources and Conflict in Africa: The Tragedy of Endowment* (Rochester, NY: University of Rochester Press, 2007).
4 Faith Osasumwen Olanrewaju, Segun Joshua, and Adekunle Olanrewaju, "Natural Resources, Conflict and Security Challenges in Africa," *India Quarterly* 76, no. 4 (2020): 552–568. https://doi.org/10.1177/0974928420961742; Francis O. C. Nwonwu, "The Paradox of Natural Resource Abundance and Widespread Underdevelopment in Africa," *International Journal of African Renaissance Studies – Multi-Inter- and Transdisciplinarity* 11, no. 2 (2016): 52–69. doi:10.1080/18186874.2016.124651; Alao, *Natural Resources and Conflict in Africa*.
5 Victoria R. Nalule, "Introduction to Mining in Africa." In *Mining and the Law in Africa*, 1–17 (Cham: Palgrave Pivot, 2020).
6 Victoria R. Nalule, "Modernisation of the Mining Laws and Key Issues for Consideration in Africa." In *Mining Law and Governance in Africa: Transformation and Innovation for a Sustainable Mining Sector* (UK: Routledge, June 9, 2023).
7 Paul Collier and Anke Hoeffler, "Resource Rents, Governance, and Conflict," *Journal of Conflict Resolution* 49, no. 4 (2005): 625–633; Richard Auty, "Resource Abundance and Economic Development: Improving the Performance of Resource-Rich Countries," *World Development* 29, no. 7 (2001): 1341–1353; Macartan Humphreys, Jeffrey D. Sachs, and Joseph E. Stiglitz, *Escaping the Resource Curse* (New York: Columbia University Press, 2007); Michael L. Ross, *The Oil Curse: How Petroleum Wealth Shapes the Development of Nations* (Princeton, NJ: Princeton University Press, 2012); Terry Lynn Karl, *The Paradox of Plenty: Oil Booms and Petro-States* (Berkeley, CA: University of California Press, 1997).
8 Michael L. Ross, "What Have We Learned about the Resource Curse?" *Annual Review of Political Science* 18 (2015): 239–259. doi:10.1146/annurev-polisci-052213-040359; Paul Collier and Anke Hoeffler, "Greed and Grievance in Civil War,"

Oxford Economic Papers 56, no. 4 (2004): 563–595. doi:10.1093/oep/gpf064; Philippe Le Billon, "The Political Ecology of War: Natural Resources and Armed Conflicts," *Political Geography* 20, no. 5 (2001): 561–584. doi:10.1016/S0962-6298(01)00015-4

9 Richard M. Auty, "The Political Economy of Resource-Driven Growth." *European Economic Review* 45, no. 4–6 (2001): 839–846. doi:10.1016/S0014-2921(01)00146-2; Anthony Bebbington and Jeffrey Bury, "Institutional Challenges for Mining and Sustainability in Peru," *Proceedings of the National Academy of Sciences* 106, no. 41 (2009): 17296–17301. doi:10.1073/pnas.0906096106; Karl, *The Paradox of Plenty*.

10 Wafulu Okumu, "Resources and Border Disputes in Eastern Africa," *Journal of Eastern African Studies* 4, no. 2 (2010): 279–297. Accessed May 19, 2023. https://doi.org/10.1080/17531055.2010.487338; Paul R. Hensel and Sara McLaughlin Mitchell, "Issue Indivisibility and Territorial Claims," *GeoJournal* 64, no. 4 (December 2005): 275–285; Stephen A. Kocs, "Territorial Disputes and Interstate War, 1945–1987," *The Journal of Politics* 57, no. 1 (1995): 159–175. https://doi.org/10.2307/2960275; Paul K. Hutt, *Standing Your Ground: Territorial Disputes and International Conflict* (Ann Arbor, MI: University of Michigan Press, 2001), 4.

11 Obasesam Okoi, "Why Nations Fight: The Causes of the Nigeria – Cameroon Bakassi Peninsula Conflict," *African Security* 9, no. 1 (2016), 43. doi:10.1080/19392206.2016.1132904

12 Paul R. Hensel, "Territory: Theory and Evidence on Geography and Conflict." In *What Do We Know about War?*, edited by John A. Vasquez, 57–84 (Lanham, MD: Rowman and Littlefield, 2000); Hensel, Paul R., and Sara McLaughlin Mitchell, "Issue Indivisibility and Territorial Claims," *GeoJournal* 64 (2005): 275–285.

13 David Szablowski, "Mining, Displacement and the World Bank: A Case Analysis of Compania Minera Antamina's Operations in Peru," *Journal of Business Ethics* 39, no. 3 (September 2002): 247–273.

14 David Szablowski, "Mining, Displacement and the World Bank: A Case Analysis of Compania Minera Antamina's Operations in Peru," *Journal of Business Ethics* 39, no. 3 (September 2002): 247–273. https://doi.org/10.1023/A:1016554512521; Sigismond Ayodele Wilson. "Company – Community Conflicts Over Diamond Resources in Kono District, Sierra Leone." *Society & Natural Resources* 26 (2013): 254–269; Eckart Woertz, "Mining Strategies in the Middle East and North Africa," *Third World Quarterly* 35, no. 6 (2014): 939–957.

15 Abiodun Alao, *Natural Resources and Conflict in Africa: The Tragedy of Endowment* (New York: University of Rochester Press, 2007); Michael D. Beevers, *Peacebuilding and Natural Resource Governance after Armed Conflict: Sierra Leone and Liberia* (Cham: Palgrave Macmillan, 2019).

16 Ifesinachi Okafor-Yarwood, et al. *Stable Seas: Gulf of Guinea* (Broomfield: CO: Stable Seas, 2020).

17 See International Union for the Conservation of Nature (IUCN) at www.iucn.org/our-union/commissions/group/iucn-ceesp-natural-resource-governance-framework-working-group

18 Beatrice Crona, Henrik Ernstson, Christina Prell, Mark Reed, Klaus Hubacek, "Combining Social Network Approaches with Social Theories to Improve Understanding of Resource Governance." In *Social Networks and Natural Resource Management: Uncovering the Social Fabric in Environmental Governance*, edited by Örjan Bodin and Christina Prell, 44–71 (Cambridge, UK: Cambridge University Press, 2011).

19 Rhuks Temitope Ako and Ohiocheoya Omiunu, "Amnesty in the Niger Delta: Vertical Movement towards Self-Determination or Lateral Policy Shift?" *Afe Babalola University: Journal of Sustainable Development Law and Policy* 1, no. 1 (2013): 86–99, p. 87.
20 Ako and Omiunu, "Amnesty in The Niger Delta".
21 Rotimi T. Suberu, *Federalism and Ethnic Conflict in Nigeria* (Washington, DC: United States Institute for Peace, 2001).
22 Johan Galtung, "Violence, Peace, and Peace Research," *Journal of Peace Research* 6, no. 3 (1969): 167–191.
23 Deval Desai and Louis-Alexandre Berg, "Rule of Law and Development: Integrating Rule of Law in the Post-2015 Development Framework: Policy Brief for the Post-2015 Development Agenda" (UNDP, 2013). Accessed May 19, 2023. http://issuu.com/undp/docs/issue_brief_-_rule_of_law_and_the_post-2015_develo
24 Javier Arellano-Yanguas, "Mining and Conflict in Peru: Sowing the Minerals, Reaping a Hail of Stones." In *Social Conflict, Economic Development, and the Extractive Industry: Evidence from South America*, edited by Anthony J. Bebbington, 89–111 (London: Routledge, 2012).
25 Ifesinachi Okafor-Yarwood, et al. "The Blue Economy – Cultural Livelihood – Ecosystem Conservation Triangle: The African experience," *Frontiers in Marine Science* 7 (2020): 586.

Part I
Theories and Concepts

1 Natural Resource Governance and Sustainable Peace in Africa

A Theoretical Analysis

Obasesam Okoi

Natural resources play a significant role in shaping the economic and political landscape of Africa, where many countries are rich in mineral, timber, and oil and gas deposits. The importance of these resources cannot be overstated, as they exert a substantial impact on the developmental trajectory of countries. However, in many African countries, the mismanagement and exploitation of natural resources have often been associated with corruption, environmental degradation, violent conflicts, and instability in many African countries.[1] One of the main challenges of natural resource governance in Africa is the limited capacity of state institutions to manage resource extraction and revenue distribution. In many cases, the revenue generated from natural resource exploitation is captured by a small elite, leading to economic inequality and social unrest.[2] The injustices stemming from the distribution of resource revenue often give rise to grievances that contribute to the escalation of conflicts.

This chapter presents a theoretical overview of the paradox of natural resource abundance, along with a contextual discussion that highlights the importance of natural resource governance in achieving sustainable peace in Africa. It argues that effective natural resource governance can serve as an instrument for reducing the likelihood of conflicts and promoting sustainable peace in Africa by ensuring that natural resource revenues are utilized for the benefit of all citizens. The concept of natural resource governance as used in this book refers to the institutions, policies, and processes, and norms that govern the extraction, allocation, and management of natural resources.[3] Effective resource governance requires the establishment of transparent and accountable institutions that can manage resource extraction, revenue distribution, and environmental protection.[4] It also involves the participation of civil society organizations and local communities in decision-making processes to ensure that their interests are represented.[5] Building on this understanding, this chapter establishes the theoretical groundwork for the subsequent chapters of the book.

DOI: 10.4324/9781003355717-3

Theorizing Natural Resources and Instability

During colonization, African economies were dominated by imperial powers, resulting in the marginalization of local communities and the infringement upon their rights to determine the fate of the natural resources located within their territories. In the aftermath of colonial rule, African countries reliant on natural resources have encountered challenges in diversifying their economies. In the early 1960s, Walt Rostow published a seminal work that established a link between natural resource abundance and development.[6] Rostow argued that the endowment of natural resources is a significant advantage for developing countries, as they facilitate the transition from underdevelopment to industrial take-off, as was the case for developed countries in Europe, North America, and Australia. The rise of neoliberalism in the 1970s and 1980s revived interest in Rostow's thesis, and similar arguments have emerged from several publications by mainstream economists.[7] Although Rostow's argument is persuasive, it fails to explain the reality of resource-rich societies in the developing world. For instance, a growing body of scholarship has demonstrated the strong correlation between natural resource abundance and conflict in developing societies.[8] Therefore, theoretical developments linking natural resources to conflict and underdevelopment can be broadly understood in the context of the "resource curse" debate.

The Resource Curse Debate

The "resource curse" phenomenon is used to describe the disappointing outcomes of economic development and governance in countries that have abundant natural resources compared to those that are less well-endowed. Central to the resource curse debate is the argument that resource-rich countries tend to experience slower economic growth compared to those facing resource scarcity.[9] Several explanations for the "resource curse" have been offered, including Dutch disease, governance challenges, and conflict. For instance, Terry Karl argued that developing countries endowed with abundant natural resources are more likely to experience poverty, poor governance, and violent conflict compared to those without such endowments.[10] In a contribution to an edited volume on the resource curse, Karl asserts that the resource curse is primarily a political and institutional problem, rather than an economic one. Karl argues that the competition for resource rents arising from the scramble for oil resources transforms the resource-producing state into a "honey pot" for external forces to stake their interests in the nation's resources. These external forces often exert significant pressure, which contributes as much to the curse as internal political factors.[11]

A second line of argument posits that while the roots of the resource curse are primarily the result of political and institutional challenges, escaping the curse requires a dedicated effort to strengthen political and institutional agreements.

Such agreements should take the form of a comprehensive fiscal and social contract that creates incentives to discourage rent-seeking behavior in oil-rich economies. This process can be achieved through multi-stakeholder engagement. This thinking aligns with the ideas put forth by Macartan Humphreys, Jeffrey Sachs, and Joseph Stiglitz, who argue that countries endowed with abundant natural resources often exhibit lower economic performance compared to those with fewer resources.[12] They draw empirical evidence from the success of the Asian Tigers, whose economies are less reliant on natural resources, in contrast to African countries abundant in resource wealth but have experienced sluggish economic growth, to strengthen their argument. Jeffrey Sachs, for instance, posits that the "curse" implies that natural resource revenue often fails to translate into long-term development, although he acknowledges that natural resources can also serve as a catalyst for such development. Based on a sample of 95 developing countries, Sachs found a negative correlation between natural resource-based exports and economic growth during the period 1970–1989.[13] His key recommendation is that "oil earnings in low-income countries should be channeled towards public investments rather than increased private consumption."[14]

The Structuralist Argument

The intellectual precursor to the resource curse thesis can be traced back to the seminal publications of some radical economists, particularly Hans Singer and Raul Prebisch, who were the originators of dependency theory. They argued that the structure of the global economy and the nature of the international commodity market create a dependency system that leads to declining terms of trade for developing countries that rely on natural resource exports, compared to developed countries.[15] This structuralist paradigm emerged as a radical critique of the modernization thesis propounded by Walt Rostow, which they argue is seemingly based on benign universal principles that serve to consolidate, rather than dismantle, the exploitative structures that shape relations between developed and developing countries.

In recent decades, a multitude of scholarly publications have emerged to challenge the conventional narrative that countries endowed with abundant natural resources are more prone to negative economic growth. Several publications that emerged after the late 1980s show a negative correlation between natural resource abundance and economic performance.[16] Despite appearing paradoxical, this concept has gained widespread recognition among many researchers. However, the resource curse thesis gained significant attention in 2003 with the publication by Richard Auty, who demonstrated that natural resource endowment is less advantageous for countries undergoing the transition to industrial take-off. Auty's argument is further supported by two key bodies of evidence: the post-war industrialization endeavors of developing countries and the economic performance of resource-rich nations since the 1960s.[17]

The "Dutch Disease" Phenomenon

The "Dutch disease" is a phenomenon that occurs when the discovery of natural resources in resource-rich countries leads to a decline in the existing domestic sectors of the economy. This decline occurs because the foreign exchange earned from the trade of natural resources is predominantly used to purchase goods in the international market, which negatively impacts domestic producers. Consequently, it becomes more challenging for these countries to export nonnatural resource commodities and effectively compete with imports across various sectors.[18] The concept of "Dutch disease" was inspired by the experience of the Netherlands in the 1960s when the natural gas sector boomed, resulting in a decline in the manufacturing sector. As gas exports increased, the exchange rate appreciated against the United States dollar, which led to higher wages but reduced competitiveness in the manufacturing sector and a slowdown in productivity.[19] In other words, the competitiveness of Holland's manufacturing exports declined, while the demand for domestic non-tradable goods increased, leading to inflation and a decrease in savings available for investment. The phenomenon of "Dutch disease" has been employed to elucidate the adverse impacts of resource revenue on a country's economy. According to this explanation, the influx of revenue from natural resources leads to currency appreciation, which in turn causes the contraction of the manufacturing sector.[20]

In the "Dutch disease" model, the economy is divided into three sectors: a tradable natural resource sector, a tradable non-resource sector, and a non-tradable sector. However, as the dependence on natural resources increases, there is a greater demand for non-tradable goods, resulting in a reduced allocation of labor and capital to the manufacturing sector.[21] After the oil boom in the early 1970s, the phenomenon of the "Dutch disease" was evident in oil-rich regions, such as Nigeria, where the agriculture sector began to replace the oil and gas sector. Jayanta Roy and colleagues reviewed a publication by Matsuyama in 1992 that uses empirical examples of agriculture and manufacturing to illustrate the Dutch disease, where a shift from manufacturing to agriculture led to a reduction in the growth rate in manufacturing.[22] They show how this transition exacerbates the resource curse through a heavy dependence on resource revenue, increased spending on non-tradable goods, diversion of labor and capital from agriculture and manufacturing to the booming resource sector, and the subsequent inflation and sluggish growth caused by higher wages. Nigeria serves as a prime example of the Dutch disease phenomenon, as its agricultural sector has suffered a decline since the onset of oil exports, leading to a complete reliance on imported food. Despite the substantial oil export revenues, there have been limited improvements in the overall economy and the well-being of Nigerian citizens.[23] As Otaha notes, the influx of oil revenues often triggers the occurrence of the "Dutch disease," resulting in an appreciation of exchange rates, negative impacts on the balance of payments, and decreased investment in non-oil sectors such as agriculture and manufacturing.[24]

In recent years, scholars have put forth alternative explanations for the "Dutch disease" phenomenon, particularly focusing on the detrimental consequences stemming from the competition for resource rents among various societal groups. These explanations propose that the pursuit of rent from natural resources can be so lucrative that it diminishes the potential incentives for entrepreneurial endeavors, thereby discouraging the development of a thriving entrepreneurial sector in resource-rich economies.[25] By redirecting resources away from productive enterprises, the focus on rent extraction perpetuates a cycle of economic dependency and stifles economic growth. These findings challenge the notion that natural resources inherently promote economic development and underscore the need to address the complex dynamics surrounding resource rents and their effects on economic growth.

Another perspective posits that conflicts and civil wars can arise due to competition among different groups vying for control over natural resources.[26] This competition becomes especially pronounced when elites exploit resource rents for personal wealth accumulation. The diversion of these funds by elites for their own gain can exacerbate social and political tensions, resulting in conflicts and civil wars, while hindering the overall progress and well-being of the nation.[27] In order to retain control and secure their power, these elites may employ repressive tactics to suppress any potential challenges or uprisings from the population.

The Rentier State Approach

Robert Tollison defines "rent-seeking" as the process of converting transfers into social costs by expending real resources and effort to capture them. He argues that engaging in rent-seeking can have substantial economic costs and cause resources to be allocated inefficiently.[28] This has direct relevance to the concept of the resource curse, which suggests that natural resource abundance can impede economic development. While the concept of "rent-seeking" was initially introduced as a theory aimed at explaining the social welfare losses resulting from the establishment of monopolies, tariffs, and subsidies, it has subsequently gained prominence among scholars at the forefront of recent attempts to explain the resource curse phenomenon.[29]

Political scientists have synthesized insights from economics and political science to establish the link between natural resource abundance and underdevelopment, resulting in the development of the "rentier" approach. According to this approach, developing countries endowed with natural resources often engage in rent-seeking behavior, relying heavily on the rent derived from their resources rather than pursuing innovative revenue-generating endeavors.[30] This rent-seeking behavior weakens the capacity of resource-rich governments to address the needs of their citizens, which in turn contributes to the failure of societies to fully harness the benefits derived from natural resource wealth.[31] The underlying premise is that the rent-seeking behavior of political institutions is the main driver of the resource curse, turning natural resources into a "curse" instead of a blessing in societies where property rights are poorly defined or not respected.[32] Therefore, the importance of political institutions in the underdevelopment of society constitutes a fundamental aspect of the rentier approach to understanding the resource curse.

One of the paradoxes of the "resource curse" is the recognition that natural resources are non-renewable products that can be extracted without the participation of large segments of the domestic labor force.[33] Secondly, natural resources are detached from political and economic processes as governments can access them without the cooperation of their citizens or control over political institutions. These two characteristics give rise to political and economic processes that generate detrimental effects on the economy, resulting in what is known as "rent-seeking behavior." In this context, rent refers to the difference between the value of the natural resource and the cost of extracting it.[34] Under such circumstances, political and economic actors have incentives to use political mechanisms to capture the resource rents. Political consequences can arise through the scramble for resources by corporations and their collusion with local elites. As Jacob Chol has shown, the case of South Sudan serves as an example of the challenges involved in effectively managing petroleum resources to promote sustainable development and overcome the common obstacles faced by nations with abundant natural resource wealth.[35] Chol delves into the underlying causes and consequences of the resource curse and the unique circumstances of South Sudan while providing valuable perspectives on potential strategies to prevent its negative consequences.

The Political Economy of Conflict Approach

The scholarship on the resource curse has recently shifted toward theoretical explanations rooted in political economy, driven primarily by the empirical limitations observed in the existing literature. Notably, significant efforts have been made to establish the political economy of conflict, each providing a unique analysis of this phenomenon. For some, the political economy of conflict is "an approach to civil war that focuses on the opportunities and benefits derived from conflict,"[36] or "a complex web of motives and interactions emerging from the interplay of immediate economic agendas, vested interests in prolonging the civil war, widespread destitution, and economically motivated violence."[37] Others like Philippe Le Billon define the political economy of conflict as "the distribution of power, wealth, and destitution during armed conflict, in order to expose the motives and responsibility of those involved, within a historical context."[38] For Achim Wennmann, the political economy of conflict represents the study of the relationship between economics and politics in affecting the dynamics of armed conflict.[39] Wennmann extends his definition beyond economic and political issues to include the connection between material factors and motivations in the organization of conflict.

The political economy approach emerged as an attempt to analyze the main causes of the development or underdevelopment of different countries.

The concern has been to understand whether and how natural resource abundance influences economic growth or contributes to conflict. This renewed theoretical focus is premised on the assumption that natural resource abundance is a curse only when the institutions of governance are initially weak and that a resource curse is most likely to occur in a society where resources are densely concentrated and thus easily appropriated.[40] The political economy approach has sparked a dynamic debate within the resource curse literature. This debate stems from the contention between economists and political scientists over competing theoretical explanations of conflict, including the emergence and growing influence of non-state actors in conflict environments. Since the late 1990s, the political economy literature has evolved significantly with a unique focus on debates surrounding the economic motivations in civil war. The most prominent of these debates has been the "Greed versus Grievance" debate.

The "greed" theory emerged from the rational choice paradigm and gained traction through the influential work of Paul Collier and Anke Hoeffler, who posited that civil wars primarily stem from economic opportunism and the competition among elites for valuable natural resource rents.[41] The central argument is that war is primarily driven by economic greed rather than grievances.[42] According to this theory, rebel groups emerge and engage in violence as a means to accumulate wealth. This situation also creates opportunities for criminal syndicates to participate in looting and illegal trading of primary commodities and minerals.[43]

Based on an empirical study of the impact of resource dependency on armed rebellion in Africa, Collier asserts that oil is a lootable resource that engenders antagonisms amongst competing socio-political forces. For Collier, the predatory nature of these diverse socio-political forces is what produces armed conflict and civil wars. Therefore, people rebel not because of objective grievances but because of the economic opportunities available through rebellion.[44] Collier and Hoeffler found a weak relationship between grievances and civil war, arguing that neither inequality nor political oppression is a determinant of conflict.[45] Thus, rebel groups ignite conflict to continue capturing resource rents. As Stephen Ellis notes, rebel groups are driven by the opportunity to accumulate wealth rather than the desire to fight for a justifiable cause.[46]

In contrast to economic analysis, political scientists have attempted to explain civil conflicts in terms of non-economic motivations and theorize rebellion as the result of accumulated grievances.[47] Grievance theory, developed within the behavioral paradigm in political science, aims to explain rebellion as a result of relative deprivation and grievances stemming from deep-rooted ethnic inequalities that reinforce economic and political divisions between different groups within society.[48] Central to grievance theory is the unique emphasis on non-economic variables such as identity, group marginalization, inequality, and weak state structures.[49] The focus on identity and group formation stems from what Mancur Olson described as the *collective action problem*.[50]

Although mobilizing groups of people for collective action can be challenging due to trust issues, free rider problems and problems with identity can be easily mobilized because ethnic identity itself serves as a more effective force for group formation. According to George Akerlof and Rachel Kranton, an individual's behavior may be influenced by their identity and the relative position of the group they identify with.[51] Groups are assumed to be more readily mobilized when their identity is closely linked to factors such as language, religion, race, and regional distinctions, rather than class divisions based on socioeconomic factors, which are typically the focal point of Marxist analyses of conflict. Consequently, identity and its relationship to inequality are considered fundamental to understanding patterns of conflict behavior. Tamara D'Estree has equally investigated the role of identity in conflict causation, arguing that identity, understood as a struggle over power, resources, and status, does not in itself produce conflict but creates the conditions for the development of conflict.[52] For D'Estree, the interaction between conflict parties is what creates the condition for actual conflict, as it builds on pre-existing conditions and transforms them into either good or bad outcomes. These pre-existing conditions may include differences in identity such as struggles over power, resources, and interests as well as stereotypes and perceived injustice. D'Estree notes, however, that the process by which a conflict moves from animosities to hostilities needs to be taken seriously.

Recently, the political economy debate has evolved beyond the traditional "greed-grievance" concerns, broadening the analytical framework with a renewed theoretical focus on the intersection of need, creed, and greed. Cynthia Arnson and William Zartman conducted a study to understand why conflict and civil war persist in the developing world and whether these conflicts are the result of relative deprivation, identity, or personal gain, which they conceptualized as *need*, *creed*, and *greed*.[53] They argue that while Paul Collier's analysis provides the starting point for this debate, his argument that civil wars are instigated for personal gain and that natural resource abundance predisposes a country to violence is oversimplified.[54] Based on case studies of conflict in Lebanon, Peru, Sierra Leone, Angola, Congo, Colombia, and Afghanistan, Arnson and Zartman contends that wars are not solely motivated by the pursuit of personal gain but rather by a complex interplay of various factors, with greed being just one aspect among many.[55] For example, Idemudia and Ite have traced Nigeria's oil conflict to the complex interplay of social, political, economic, and environmental forces. Their study reveals that while environmental and social factors may act as proximate causes, the root causes of the conflict can be attributed to economic and political factors.[56] While *needs* arise from structural and systemic factors that fuel conflict, *creed* refers to the perception of relative deprivation that fuels intergroup conflicts, and *greed* represents the economic motivations behind participating in acts of violence.[57]

Contextualizing Natural Resource Governance

The International Union for the Conservation of Nature (IUCN) defines natural resource governance as

> the norms, institutions, structures and processes that determine how power and responsibilities over natural resources are exercised, how decisions are taken, and how citizens—including Indigenous Peoples, local communities, people of all genders, and others—participate in and benefit from the management of natural resources.[58]

Governance encompasses a broader understanding of the overall system of decision-making, implementation, and enforcement that governs the management and utilization of natural resources. This includes the creation of government entities responsible for formulating and implementing policies, regulations, and laws as well as the traditional customs and norms governing the management and utilization of natural resources. Throughout Africa, countries with an abundance of natural resource wealth are confronted with the daunting challenge of determining how these resources should be managed, including decisions regarding their optimal utilization for national development. Recognizing that the governance of natural resources has often been plagued by issues such as corruption, mismanagement, lack of transparency, and conflicts over control and distribution of benefits, it is imperative to have institutions and norms that establish the terms for conducting extraction activities and define the roles of different stakeholders. Therefore, the context of natural resource governance in Africa highlights the unique challenges, dynamics, and opportunities that characterize the management of natural resources on the continent.

A significant component of contextualization is understanding the historical and socio-political backdrop within which resource extraction occurs. Recognizing the influence of colonial legacies on extraction-focused economies and their contribution to postcolonial issues like weak institutions, political instability, and governance deficiencies is crucial in analyzing how these factors impact on natural resource governance in Africa. Equally important is the recognition of the interplay between natural resources, governance, and development in Africa. While it has been widely acknowledged that natural resources hold the potential to drive economic growth, they also present significant risks that destabilize the social, political, and economic structures of many resource-rich countries.[59] However, the impact of resource abundance can also vary considerably, and it can be either beneficial or detrimental depending on the quality of governance in place.[60] This calls for a holistic approach to natural resource governance that considers sustainable development, environmental protection, the rule of law, and social justice alongside resource extraction.

The context of natural resource governance in Africa also requires acknowledging the roles, interests, and power dynamics of different stakeholders, including governments, multinational corporations, local communities, civil society organizations, and international actors, as vital factors in shaping governance frameworks that promote transparency, accountability, and the equitable distribution of resource benefits. Additionally, it is crucial to acknowledge the significance of specific country contexts and nuances when contextualizing natural resource governance in Africa. Such recognition stems from the understanding that the challenges, opportunities, and governance structures pertaining to natural resources management vary considerably across individual countries and that these variations are shaped by diverse factors, including but not limited to resource endowments, political systems, and socio-cultural dynamics. By acknowledging these specificities, scholars and policymakers can foster a deeper understanding of natural resource governance in Africa that is both informed and contextually appropriate.

The Prospects and Challenges of Natural Resource Governance in Nigeria

Nigeria is often mentioned as a prime example of the paradoxical nature of natural resource abundance. Consequently, the demand for effective natural resource governance in Nigeria's oil region has prompted numerous development interventions. This effort can be traced back to the establishment of Henry Willink's Commission of Inquiry in 1957, which aimed to investigate the grievances expressed by minority groups and propose solutions to address their concerns. The formation of this commission coincided with the discovery of crude oil in Oloibiri, igniting hopes among Niger Delta people for development in their oil-rich communities. However, as oil extraction commenced in the region, concerns regarding marginalization resurfaced, fueling fears that the Niger Delta would not receive fair benefits from the oil revenue.[61] The failure to implement the recommendations of the Willink's Commission acted as a catalyst for post-independence struggles for self-determination and the pursuit of justice in the oil-rich region.[62] After Nigeria achieved independence in 1960, the government led by Tafawa Balewa recognized the significance of addressing the recommendations presented by the Willink's Commission. This led to the establishment of the Niger Delta Development Board (NDDB) in 1961, with a specific mandate to tackle the various development issues faced by the Niger Delta region. However, the NDDB encountered administrative and political shortcomings, which prompted the military regime to create the Niger Delta Basin Development Authority (NDBDA) through Decree 37 on August 3, 1976. Unfortunately, the NDBDA primarily basically offered palliative solutions rather than effectively addressing the genuine development challenges in the oil-rich region. Consequently, the NDBDA encountered similar issues of political, administrative, and structural difficulties as observed during the era of the NDDB.

In the early 1990s, social movements emerged in Nigeria's oil region with the objective of scrutinizing the image of the Nigerian state and oil multinational companies. These movements were driven by concerns regarding environmental degradation and human rights violations associated with oil extraction activities. The political tensions that emerged in the early 1990s were primarily driven by the failure of oil multinationals and the state to address the demands of ethnic minorities[63] and the growing awareness of the detrimental effects of oil extraction on the environment and ecosystems.[64] Public intellectuals and environmental rights activists played a crucial role in championing these struggles, as they were deeply concerned about the negative impact of multinational oil corporations on the region's underdevelopment. These activists attributed the political tensions in the region to the consequences of oil extraction.[65] The Movement for the Survival of Ogoni People (MOSOP) was the pioneering group in Nigeria's oil region that orchestrated a well-coordinated protest to expose the destructive activities of Shell BP, led by the late Ken Saro-Wiwa.[66] MOSOP's primary demands, outlined in the Ogoni Bill of Rights, included environmental remediation of Ogoniland, political autonomy, resource control, and political representation. Under the leadership of Saro-Wiwa, MOSOP led a transnational campaign that drew global attention to the atrocities committed by Shell in Ogoniland. The campaign highlighted the environmental degradation caused by the oil industry, which posed significant threats to land and water resources, as well as food and health security, undermining the well-being of local communities.

In 1992, General Ibrahim Babangida's military regime established the Oil Mineral Producing Area Development Commission (OMPADEC) in response to the failures of previous development interventions in the oil region, including the NDDB and the NDBDA. OMPADEC had the objective of addressing the environmental devastation caused by oil extraction and facilitating the rehabilitation and development of the oil-producing areas. It was also tasked with increasing the revenue allocation to these areas from 1.5 percent to 3 percent. Moreover, OMPADEC was intended to serve as an institutional framework for mediating between oil multinational companies and the host communities. However, corruption within OMPADEC became prevalent, leading to the awarding of illicit contracts to fictitious contractors and undermining the institution's capacity to effectively address the development challenges in the oil region.[67] These issues, coupled with a lack of accountability and failure to implement long-term development solutions in the region, prompted the federal government to dissolve OMPADEC in 1999. Some studies attributed OMPADEC's failures to inadequate regulatory and monitoring mechanisms.[68]

As a result of these challenges, efforts by the Nigerian regime to respond to MOSOP's agitations with palliative measures sidestepped the main grievances of the Ogoni people, resulting in the Ogoni protest of 1993 seeking the right to "self-determination" and control of their natural resource wealth.[69] The Nigerian regime responded to the protest by unleashing violence against peaceful protesters, including the execution of the environmental rights activist

Ken Saro-Wiwa and his fellow activists in November 1995.[70] While this atrocity brought the image of Nigeria and Shell BP under international scrutiny for human rights violations in Ogoniland, the lack of effective mechanisms for seeking justice was further exacerbated by the close relationship between the repressive state and oil multinational corporations that operated with impunity. Despite the transition of Nigeria's political landscape from military rule to democracy in 1999, the country now confronts a new challenge characterized by a corrupt civilian political elite who disproportionately benefits from oil revenue, leaving the rest of the population deprived. This transfer of power has not addressed the ecological hazards linked to oil and gas extraction, which continue to negatively impact local communities in the oil region. As a result, the region experiences what Obasesam Okoi describes as a state of *punctuated peace*, marked by repeated cycles of insurgency.[71] According to Okoi, punctuated peace in the context of Nigeria's oil region refers to a state of intermittent peace disrupted by periods of insurgency. It signifies the recurring cycles of violence experienced despite occasional periods of relative calm. Despite efforts to address the grievances and challenges in the region, the underlying issues, such as environmental degradation, economic disparity, and political corruption, persist, leading to sporadic outbreaks of conflict.

The failure of OMPADEC prompted the government under President Obasanjo to establish the NDDC in 2000 as a response to the developmental challenges and security issues in the Niger Delta region. The primary objective of the NDDC is to promote sustainable development, economic prosperity, social stability, ecological regeneration, and peace in the nine states that comprise the area. The funding for NDDC is sourced from the federal government, which contributes 15 percent of the oil revenue allocation to the Niger Delta states, and from oil multinationals, who contribute 3 percent of their annual budget and 50 percent of the ecological fund for oil-producing states. With these financial resources, the NDDC has initiated various development projects, including infrastructure, healthcare, education, and sanitation.[72] However, despite its efforts, the NDDC's impact on addressing the developmental challenges in the oil region remains inadequate. To further address these challenges and promote peace, President Musa Yar'Adua created the Ministry of Niger Delta Affairs in September 2008 as part of the Niger Delta peace process. The primary objective of the ministry is to develop and secure the Niger Delta region by formulating and implementing policies related to infrastructure development, environmental protection, and youth employment. The establishment of the ministry was necessary due to the perceived gap between the development programs of agencies like the NDDC and the increasing expectations of the Niger Delta population. However, despite significant financial allocations for development interventions in the region, the ministry has not achieved substantial progress. In other words, the institutional framework for natural resource governance has failed to effectively translate the nation's resource wealth into sustainable development outcomes.

Importantly, concerns regarding natural resource governance in Nigeria raise questions about the equitable distribution and utilization of revenue derived from natural resources. In 1975, Nigeria implemented the derivation principle as a formula for allocating revenue between the central and regional governments. Under this principle, 50 percent of the country's oil revenue was allocated to regions that produced natural resources. However, with the transition to democracy, the derivation principle was revised, resulting in a reduction of the allocation to 13 percent. According to this revised principle, each state in the Niger Delta oil region is entitled to receive 13 percent of the oil and gas revenue generated by the federation. The demand for a revision in the revenue sharing formula raised expectations that the implementation of the 13 percent principle of revenue derivation would lead to an increased allocation of oil revenue to the Niger Delta states.[73] The call for reforms in the Niger Delta region also stressed the importance of abolishing obnoxious laws, restructuring the state, providing reparations for environmental degradation, and undertaking remediation efforts to restore endangered ecosystems in the area.[74]

Avoiding Nigeria's Experience

The Nigerian experience provides important lessons for other African nations that have recently discovered natural resources. In East Africa, countries such as Tanzania and Kenya have made huge discoveries of extractive resources, such as oil, gas, and minerals in recent years. As a result, national governments have developed policies and established regulatory bodies to effectively manage and oversee the extraction, utilization, and revenue generation from these newly discovered resources. While these discoveries hold the potential for economic growth, job opportunities, and increased government revenue, there are also concerns regarding potential adverse impacts on the environment, local communities, and the overall governance of these resources. Florens Luoga has criticized the current trajectory of East African countries, suggesting that without an effective legal framework, their approach to natural resource governance is likely to fail. Luoga emphasizes the need to establish a robust legal framework that promotes democratic governance of natural resources and proposes principles aimed at preventing the unfair disenfranchisement of individuals in their ownership and control of these resources.[75] Simeon Sungi has also investigated the relationship between natural resource extraction and human rights abuses in Tanzania to gain insights into the specific circumstances in which oil and gas extraction intensifies human rights issues within local communities and the importance of implementing governance reform to ensure responsible resource management in Tanzania.[76]

A study by Michael Ross has shown that when natural resources are managed transparently and accountably, it can engender positive outcomes within society by building trust between different groups, ensuring a fair distribution of benefits, and reducing the likelihood of conflicts arising over resource control.[77] Natural resource governance in Africa involves the development of mechanisms and institutions to regulate access and control over these resources. By implementing effective governance mechanisms that prioritize inclusivity and transparency, societies can unlock the potential of natural resources for the benefit of all stakeholders. Ghana serves as a concrete example, demonstrating the feasibility of utilizing natural resources for sustainable development in the African context.[78] This study not only highlights the challenges faced by other resource-rich African countries, such as Nigeria, Angola, and Equatorial Guinea, and how lessons from these countries can be applied to new oil-producing countries like Ghana but also proposes legal and environmental measures that can be used to transform natural resources into valuable assets that can improve the living conditions of Africans.

Ghana has implemented various reforms to govern its natural resources, including efforts to promote transparency, accountability, and sustainable development in the management of its resource sector. One key element of natural resource governance in Ghana is the implementation of legal and regulatory frameworks such as the Minerals and Mining Act and the Petroleum Exploration and Production Act to guide resource extraction, outline the rights and responsibilities of stakeholders, ensure environmental protection, and establish mechanisms for revenue management and benefit-sharing.[79] To enhance transparency and accountability, Ghana has embraced initiatives such as the Extractive Industries Transparency Initiative (EITI).[80] The EITI is a global standard that was established in the early 2000s to address the challenges posed by the resource curse. Its primary objective is to promote transparency, accountability, and anti-corruption measures in resource-rich countries by mandating extractive companies to disclose their payments to the government, while the government is obligated to publish information on the revenues received from resource extraction. Some argue that the EITI has been successful in mitigating the resource curse by improving transparency and accountability in the management of natural resources as well as the specific impact of EITI implementation on different types of resource rents.[81] Ghana has established the Ministry of Lands and Natural Resources to oversee the extractive sector,[82] the Minerals Commission and the Environmental Protection Agency to regulate and monitor extractive activities, the Public Interest and Accountability Committee (PIAC) to monitor the management and utilization of petroleum revenues,[83] and the Community Mining Scheme, to tackle illegal mining and provide local communities in small-scale mining operations with legal frameworks for mining activities, promote sustainable mining practices, and reduce resource conflicts.[84]

Natural Resource Governance and Local Institutions in South Africa and Botswana

Research has shown that African countries have the potential to leverage their abundant natural resources to accomplish sustainable development objectives.⁸⁵ Recent advancements in community-based resource management in South Africa have garnered significant attention, highlighting the potential of local institutions as an alternative to state institutions. In the case of South Africa's Miombo woodlands, Dennis Kayambazinthu and colleagues have conducted research on the institutional arrangements governing the management of these woodlands, the factors that drive institutional change, and how institutions adapt to these changes.⁸⁶ Furthermore, their study revealed the existence of diverse institutions operating at various levels, including national and local, and encompassing both formal and informal structures. This diversity of institutions reflects the socio-cultural and traditional context of the region which underscored the importance of traditional institutions in the governance of natural resources.

Through historical analysis, the study by Kayambazinthu and colleagues reveals that institutions in the Miombo woodlands have been influenced to some extent by shifting state and administrative frameworks from colonial to postcolonial periods.⁸⁷ While some institutions demonstrated weaknesses in effectively governing natural resources, the research identifies crucial factors that contribute to the stability and longevity of specific institutions in the region. Institutions that align closely with traditional socio-cultural norms and incentives, gaining moral and political legitimacy at the local level, were found to be more resilient and enduring.⁸⁸ Notable examples of such institutions include traditional leadership systems, clans, and sacred areas. Recognizing the legitimacy of traditional systems and structures is essential in effectively utilizing local institutions for natural resource governance. Understanding the role of traditional systems can guide policymakers in developing inclusive governance approaches that bridge formal and informal institutions to ensure sustainable and equitable resource management.

Botswana serves as a prime example of an African nation that has effectively utilized its natural resource revenues to bolster the stability of its national institutions. The country's successful transition from a British protectorate to a stable postcolonial democracy has recently attracted the attention of scholars. Despite being one of the world's poorest nations upon gaining independence in 1966, Botswana underwent a remarkable transformation within a few decades, emerging as one of the wealthiest nations in Africa. Subsequently, Botswana gained recognition as Africa's first multi-party democracy, renowned for its peaceful political practices and social stability.⁸⁹ The country's unique position as an exception to the negative impacts typically associated with the resource curse attests to the importance of governance practices, effective institutions, and long-term planning in enabling the country to avoid the resource curse phenomenon.⁹⁰ The study conducted by David Sebudubudu and Keneilwe Mooketsane critically examines the factors that have contributed to the successful management of natural resources in Botswana and offers valuable insights into potential strategies and policies that other resource-rich nations can adopt to address the adverse effects of resource extraction and promote sustainable development.

Research indicates that Botswana has achieved remarkable development by adhering to orthodox economic policies, which have been supported by the presence of robust institutions, particularly those related to private property.[91] They hypothesize several factors that contributed to the emergence of private property institutions in Botswana, setting it apart from other African nations where natural resource abundance has led to negative outcomes instead of development. One of the factors highlighted is that Botswana had inclusive pre-colonial institutions that placed limitations on political elites, creating a more balanced power structure. The presence of inclusive pre-colonial institutions like *kgotla, a* public assembly or traditional community forum for public discussion, debates, and consensus building, played a significant role in Botswana's success.

The *kgotla* is an inclusive institution that has been an integral part of Botswana's governance system for centuries. Its primary function is to provide community members with a space to voice their concerns, express differing viewpoints, and ultimately reach a consensus on a range of issues. By facilitating open dialogue and active participation, the *kgotla* plays a vital role in promoting participatory democracy and ensuring that decision-making processes reflect the interests and perspectives of the community. The *kgotla* functioned as a space in which the Tswana people could freely express their thoughts and opinions, including the ability to openly disagree or criticize, not only among themselves but also in the presence of the chief.[92] As Megan Schoen noted, the *kgotla* system "inspired a form of indigenous democracy in which open dialogue and critical engagement with leadership were possible."[93] This highlights the significance of the *kgotla* as a platform for open and transparent dialogue, enabling individuals to voice their perspectives and engage in discussions without fear of retribution or censure.

Daron Acemoglu and his colleagues have shown that British colonialism had a minimal effect on Botswana compared to other African nations, and this had significant implications.[94] Unlike in many other colonized countries where colonial rule dismantled existing institutions, the pre-colonial institutions in Botswana were relatively preserved, allowing the country to maintain certain aspects of its traditional governance systems that provided a foundation for its later success. By avoiding the destructive consequences of colonialism, Botswana was able to build upon its existing institutional framework, including inclusive institutions like the *kgotla*, which played a crucial role in its long-term development.

After Botswana's independence, the country's elite recognized the economic benefits of maintaining and strengthening private property institutions.[95] This recognition played a pivotal role in shaping Botswana's economic policies and contributing to its remarkable progress over the years. Botswana's diamond reserves also generated substantial revenues, discouraging any groups from challenging the existing system and risking instability. The availability of diamond revenues meant that there was less incentive for interest groups to disrupt the status quo and risk instability as the revenues from diamond exports provided a stable source of income for the government, allowing it to invest in infrastructure development, education, healthcare, and other social programs. This financial stability and the avoidance of resource-related conflicts contributed to the overall political stability and economic growth of Botswana. As Acemoglu and his colleagues argued, the post-independence leaders played a vital role in reinforcing this favorable situation through critical decisions.[96]

Unlike the rest of Africa where natural resource wealth became the impetus for competition among elites for control of political power, the legal framework in Botswana has evolved to promote the optimal use and benefit of resource revenues. In essence, Botswana's diamond reserves played a crucial role in the country's economic landscape as the revenues generated from diamond mining created a financial buffer that discouraged interest groups from challenging the existing political and economic system. Therefore, British colonial rule did not significantly disrupt the pre-colonial system in Botswana because following independence and the subsequent discovery of diamonds, the country's elite staked their vested interests in actively safeguarding traditional democratic institutions to maintain their power and preserve the status quo.

This development is intriguing considering that such policies that seek to preserve pre-colonial institutions are typically challenging to implement in Africa due to political constraints.

Conclusion

This chapter presents a theoretical overview of the paradoxes and contradictions of natural resource abundance and instability in Africa, where different groups are constantly competing for power and economic gains. A clear illustration of this phenomenon can be seen in countries where violent conflicts have arisen from the struggle for control over natural resources, resulting in local communities and some groups feeling marginalized and excluded from the benefits of resource wealth. Considering that large volumes of revenue from natural resources are typically linked to instability in African societies, concerns have been raised regarding the transparency and integrity of the process by which extractive laws and contracts are established. One critical issue is the presence of hidden interests that can influence the distribution of benefits and impede the transparent and accountable management of natural resources. This theoretical foundation is followed by a contextual discussion emphasizing the crucial role of natural resource governance in achieving lasting peace in societies with an abundance of natural resource wealth. This chapter argues that effective natural resource governance is essential for reducing the likelihood of conflicts and fostering sustainable peace in Africa, as it ensures that revenues generated from natural resources are utilized for the collective well-being of all citizens.

Central to this chapter is the recognition that the governance of extractive industries is fundamental in determining whether resource-abundant countries can harness the benefits or experience the harmful consequences of their natural resources. As some scholars have pointed out, the regulatory process of natural resource governance can be susceptible to manipulation by elites with vested interests aiming to shape the regulations in a manner that ensures privileged benefits for themselves to the detriment of broader societal welfare.[97] In light of the significant role played by natural resources in shaping Africa's development and stability, ensuring responsible governance of these resources is critical.

The importance of natural resource governance in attaining sustainable peace in Africa cannot be overstated. It has the potential to alleviate tensions, prevent violent conflicts, and contribute to peacebuilding efforts and economic progress. However, it is crucial to acknowledge that good governance alone cannot resolve all conflicts. Natural resources governance must be integrated into a comprehensive peacebuilding framework that recognizes the importance of harnessing the potential of local institutions and norms in creating the condition for enduring peace and prosperity in resource-rich countries across Africa. Such institutional mechanisms must be evaluated in terms of their inclusivity, transparency, and ability to promote sustainable development. This chapter contributes to the existing literature by theorizing the importance of natural resource governance in promoting sustainable peace in Africa.

Notes

1 Richard M. Auty, *Resource Abundance and Economic Development* (Oxford: Oxford University Press, 1998); Paul Collier and Anke Hoeffler, "Greed and Grievance in Civil War," *Oxford Economic Papers* 54, no. 4 (2002): 563–95.
2 Collier and Hoeffler, *Greed and Grievance in Civil War*.
3 Terry Lynne Karl, *The Paradox of Plenty: Oil Booms and Petro-States* (Berkeley: University of California Press, 1997).
4 Päivi Lujala, "The Spoils of Nature: Armed Civil Conflict and Rebel Access to Natural Resources", *Journal of Peace Research* 47, no. 1 (2010): 15–28.
5 Anthony Bebbington, Denise Humphreys Bebbington, Jeffrey Bury, Jeannet Lingan, Juan Pablo Muñoz, and Martin Scurrah, "Mining and Social Movements: Struggles over Livelihood and Rural Territorial Development in the Andes," *World Development* 36, no. 12 (2008): 2888–905. https://doi.org/10.1016/j.worlddev.2007.11.016
6 Walt W. Rostow, *The Stages of Economic Growth: A Non-Communist Manifesto* (Cambridge: Cambridge University Press, 1960).
7 For example, Bela Balassa, *The Process of Industrial Development and Alternative Development Strategies* (Princeton, NJ: Princeton University, 1980); Anne O. Krueger, "Trade Policy as an Input to Development," *American Economic Review*, 70, no. 2 (1980): 288–292.
8 Robert Kaplan, "The Coming Anarchy," *Atlantic Monthly* (February 1994); Mary Kaldor, *New Wars: Organized Violence in a Global Era* (Cambridge: Polity Press, 2012); Paul Collier and Anke Hoeffler, *Greed and Grievance in Civil War* (Washington, DC: World Bank, 2001); Paul Collier and Anke Hoeffler, "Greed and Grievance in Civil War," *Oxford Economic Papers*, 56, 4 (2004): 563–595. Doi: https://doi.org/10.1093/oep/gpf064; Paul Collier and Anke Hoeffler, "Resource Rents, Governance,

and Conflict," *Journal of Conflict Resolution*, 49, 4 (2005): 625–33. www.jstor.org/stable/30045133.
9. Jeffrey D. Sachs and Andrew M. Warmer, "Natural Resource Abundance and Economic Growth," *NBER Working Papers*, 5398. Harvard Institute of International Development (1995); Terry Lynn Karl, *The Paradox of Plenty* (Berkeley, CA: University of California Press, 1997); Richard M. Auty, *Resource Abundance and Economic Development* (Oxford: Oxford University Press, 2001); Xavier Sala-i-Martin and Arvind Subramanian, "Addressing the Natural Resource Curse: An Illustration from Nigeria," *International Monetary Fund Working Paper* (Washington, DC: IMF, 2003).
10. Karl, *The Paradox of Plenty*.
11. Terry Karl, "Ensuring Fairness: The Case for Transparent Fiscal Social Contract," in *Escaping the Resource Curse*, Macartan Humphreys, Jeffrey D. Sachs, and Joseph E. Stiglitz, eds. (New York: Columbia University Press, 2007).
12. Macartan Humphrey, Jeffrey D. Sachs, and Joseph E. Stiglitz, "What Is the Problem with Natural Resource Wealth?" in *Escaping the Resource Curse*, Macartan Humphreys, Jeffrey D. Sachs, Joseph E. Stiglitz eds. (New York: Columbia University Press, 2007).
13. Jeffrey D. Sachs, "How to Handle the Macroeconomics of Oil Wealth," in *Escaping the Resource Curse*, Macartan Humphreys, Jeffrey D. Sachs, and Joseph E. Stiglitz, eds. (New York: Columbia University Press, 2007), 176–77.
14. Sachs, "How to Handle the Macroeconomics of Oil Wealth," 174.
15. Raul Prebisch, *The Economic Development of Latin America and Its Principal Problems* (Lake Success, New York: United Nations, 1950); Hans Singer, "The Distribution of Trade between Investing and Borrowing Countries," *American Economic Review*, 40 (1950).
16. Sachs and Warner, *Natural Resource Abundance and Economic Growth*; Auty, *Resource Abundance and Economic Development*.
17. As cited in Bimal Chandra Roy, Satyaki Sarkar, and Nikhil Ranjan Mandal, "Natural Resource Abundance and Economic Performance—A Literature Review," *Current Urban Studies* 1, no. 4 (2013): 148.
18. Macartan Humphrey, Jeffrey D. Sachs, and Joseph E. Stiglitz, "What is the Problem with Natural Resource Wealth?" in *Escaping the Resource Curse*, Macartan Humphreys, Jeffrey D. Sachs, Joseph E. Stiglitz, eds. (New York: Columbia University Press, 2007), 5.
19. Roy, Sarkar, and Mandal, Natural Resource Abundance and Economic Performance, 150.
20. W. Max Corden and J. Peter Neary, "Booming Sector and De-Industrialisation in a Small Open Economy," *The Economic Journal* 92, no. 368 (1982): 825–48, accessed May 19, 2023. https://doi.org/10.2307/2232670
21. Roy, Sarkar, and Mandal, *Natural Resource Abundance and Economic Performance*, 150.
22. Roy, Sarkar, and Mandal, Natural Resource Abundance and Economic Performance.
23. Jacob Imo-E Otaha. "Dutch Disease and Nigeria Oil Economy," *African Research Review* 6, no. 1 (2012): 82–90. doi: http://dx.doi.org/10.4314/afrrev.v6i1.7
24. Jacob Imo-E Otaha, *Dutch Disease and Nigeria Oil Economy*.
25. Aaron Tornell and Philip Lane, "The Voracity Effect," *American Economic Review* 89, no. 1 (1999): 22–46. www.aeaweb.org/articles?id=10.1257/aer.89.1.22; Ragnar Torvik, "Natural Resources, Rent Seeking and Welfare," *Journal of Development*

Economics 67, no. 2 (2002): 455–70.https://doi.org/10.1016/S0304-3878(01)00195-X; Halvor Mehlum, Karl Moene, and Ragnar Torvik, "Institutions and the Resource Curse," *Economic Journal* 116, no. 508 (2006): 1–20. https://doi.org/10.1111/j.1468-0297.2006.01045.x

26 Timothy J. Besley and Torsten Persson, "The Incidence of Civil War: Theory and Evidence," *NBER Working Paper* no. 14585 (2008), accessed May 19, 2023, www.nber.org/papers/w14585; Francesco Caselli and Wilbur John Coleman, "On the Theory of Ethnic Conflict," *Journal of the European Economic Association* 11, no. S1 (2013): 161–92. www.nber.org/papers/w12125; Frederick van der Ploeg and Dominic Rohner, "War and Natural Resource Exploitation," *European Economic Review* 56, no. 8 (2012): 1714–35. https://doi.org/10.1016/j.euroecorev.2012.09.003.

27 Francesco Caselli and Tom Cunningham, "Leader Behaviour and the Natural Resource Curse," *Oxford Economic Papers* 61, no. 4 (2009): 628–50. www.jstor.org/stable/27784153

28 Robert D. Tollison. "The Economic Theory of Rent Seeking," *Public Choice*, 152, no. 1/2 (July 2012): 73–82. www.jstor.org/stable/41483753

29 Roy, Sarkar, and Mandal, *Natural Resource Abundance and Economic Performance*, 150.

30 Hazem Beblawi, "The Rentier State in the Arab World," in *The Arab State*, Giacomo Luciani, ed. (Berkeley, CA: University of California Press, 1990).

31 Lisa Anderson, "The State in the Middle East and North Africa," *Comparative Politics*, 20, no. 1 (1987): 1–18. https://doi.org/10.2307/421917.

32 Roger D. Congleton, Arye L. Hillman, and Kai Konrad, "Forty Years of Research on Rent Seeking: An Overview," in *Forty Years of Research on Rent Seeking*, Roger D. Congleton, Arye L. Hillman and Kai Konrad, eds. (Berlin: Springer, 2008).

33 Humphrey, Sachs, and Stiglitz, What is the Problem with Natural Resource Wealth?, 4.

34 Ibid, 4.

35 Jacob D. Chol, "The Reality of Petroleum Resource Curse in South Sudan: Can This Be Avoided?" *The African Review: A Journal of African Politics, Development and International Affairs* 43, no. 2 (2016): 17–50. www.jstor.org/stable/45341720

36 David Keen, *The Economic Functions of Violence in Civil Wars* (Oxford: Oxford University Press, 1998), 11.

37 Mats Berdal and David Malone, *Greed and Grievance: Economic Agendas in Civil Wars* (Boulder, CO: Lynne Rienner Publishers), 2.

38 Phillip Le Billon, "The Political Economy of War: What Relief Agencies Need to Know," Humanitarian Practice Network Paper No.33. Overseas Development Institute, London (2000): 1.

39 Achim Wennmann, "What Is the Political Economy of Conflict? Delimiting a Debate on Contemporary Armed Conflict." Paper Presented at the World International Studies Conference, Ljubljana, 23–26 July 2008, Geneva, 18 July 2008.

40 Roy, Sarkar, and Mandal, *Natural Resource Abundance and Economic Performance*, 150.

41 Paul Collier and Anke Hoeffler, "Greed and Grievance in Civil War," 2004.

42 Collier and Hoeffler, *Greed and Grievance in Civil War*, 2002, 2; Collier, "*Doing Well Out of War*"; William Reno, *Humanitarian Emergencies and Warlord Economies in Liberia and Sierra Leone* (Helsinki: WIDER, 1997).

43 Chris Allen, "Warfare, Endemic Violence and State Collapse," *Review of African Political Economy*, 26, no. 81 (1999): 372.

44 Collier, *"Doing Well Out of War."*
45 Paul Collier and Anke Hoeffler, "Greed and Grievance in Civil War," Working Paper Series WPS/2002-01, Oxford: Centre for the Study of African Economies, Oxford University (2002), 1.
46 Stepen Ellis, "Liberia's Warlord Insurgency," in *African Guerillas*, Christopher Clapham, ed. (Oxford: James Curry, 1998), 162.
47 Laurier Nathan, "The Frightful Inadequacies of Most of the Statistics: A Critique of Collier and Hoeffler on the Causes of Civil Wars," Crisis States Development Research Centre Discussion Paper no.11 (London: Destined Development Studies Institute, 2000), 2.
48 Gurr, *Why Men Rebel*.
49 Francess Stewart, "Horizontal Inequalities as a Cause of Conflict: A Review of CRISE Findings," World Development Report 2011 Background Paper, 1–9 (2011); Mansoob S. Murshed and Mohammad Z. Tadjoeddin, "Reappraising the Greed and Grievance Explanation for Violent Internal Conflict," MICROCON Research Working Paper, 1–41 (2007).
50 Mancur Olson, *The Logic of Collective Action* (Cambridge, MA: Harvard University Press, 1965).
51 George Akerlof and Rachel E. Kranton, "Economics and Identity," *Quarterly Journal of Economics* 115, no. 3 (2000): 715–53. www.jstor.org/stable/2586894.
Tamara D'Estree, "Dynamics," in *Conflict: From Analysis to Intervention* (2nd Edition), Sandra Cheldelin, Daniel Druckman, and Larissa Fast, eds. (New York, NY: Bloomsbury, 2008).
52 D'Estree, "Dynamics."
53 Cynthia J. Arnson and I. William Zartman, *Rethinking the Economics of War: The Intersection of Need, Creed, and Greed* (Washington, DC: Woodrow Wilson Center Press, 2005).
54 Arnson and Zartman, *Rethinking the Economics of War.*
55 Ibid.
56 Uwafiokun Idemudia and Uwem W. Ite, "Demystifying the Niger Delta Conflict: Towards an Integrated Explanation," *Review of African Political Economy* 33, no. 109 (2006): 391.
57 Idemudia and Ite, "Demystifying the Niger Delta Conflict," 315–16.
58 The definition of natural resource governance can be found in the IUCN website at www.iucn.org/our-union/commissions/group/iucn-ceesp-natural-resource-governance-framework-working-group
59 Michael L. Ross, *The Oil Curse: How Petroleum Wealth Shapes the Development of Nations* (Princeton, NJ: Princeton University Press, 2013).
60 Hany Gamil Besada, *Governance, Conflict, and Natural Resources in Africa: Understanding the Role of Foreign Investment Actors* (Montreal and Kingston: McGill-Queen's University Press, 2021).
61 Ikelegbe, "The Economy of Conflict in the Oil Rich Niger Delta Region of Nigeria."
62 Uwafiokun Idemudia, "The Changing Phases of the Niger Delta Conflict: Implications for Conflict Escalation and the Return to Peace," *Conflict, Security and Development* 9, no. 3(2009): 315. doi: 10.1080/14678800903142698
63 Augustine Ikelegbe, "The Economy of Conflict in the Oil Rich Niger Delta Region of Nigeria," *Nordic Journal of African Studies* 15, no. 2 (2006): 105; Richard Aworosegbe, "Petroleum Resource Conflict and the Challenges of Peacekeeping in Nigeria," *Journal of Social Sciences* 21, no. 3 (2009): 583.

64 Ike Okonta and Oronto Douglas, *Where Vultures Feast: Shell, Human Rights, and Oil in the Niger Delta* (New York: Verso Books, 2003); Omolade Adunbi, "Oil Wealth, the Political Economy of Resources and the Niger Delta Crisis," in *The Political Economy of Conflict in the Oil-rich Niger Delta Region of Nigeria*, Cyril Obi ed. (Palgrave Macmillan, 161–75); Augustine Ikelegbe, "The Economy of Conflict in the Oil Rich Niger Delta Region of Nigeria," *Nordic Journal of African Studies,* 14(2), 208–234.

65 Ike Okonta. 2005. "Nigeria: Chronicle of a Dying State." *Current History* 04 (682): 203–208; Okonta and Douglas, "Where Vultures Feast."

66 Okonta and Douglas, "Where Vultures Feast."

67 Osha Sanya, "Slow Death in the Niger Delta," *Africa Review of Books* (2006), accessed March 24, 2023. www.codesria.org/Links/Publication, 06/01/2007; Akeem Ayofe Akinwale and Evans Osabuohien, "Re-Engineering the NDDC'S Master Plan: An Analytical Approach," *Journal of Sustainable Development in Africa* 11, no. 2 (0092): 142–59.

68 Akinwale and Osabuohien, "Re-Engineering the NDDC'S Master Plan."

69 Okonta and Douglas, "Where Vultures Feast, 119.

70 Okonta and Douglas, *Where Vultures Feast*, 119; Cyril Obi, "Oil Extraction, Dispossession, Resistance, and Conflict in Nigeria's Oil-Rich Niger Delta," *Canadian Journal of Development Studies* 27, no. 1 (2006): 96–98; Anthony O. Chukwuemeka, Uche A. Anazodo, and Godwin N. Nzewi, "Environmental Degradation and Oil Corporations' Compliance with Sustainable Development in Nigeria: An Overview of the Niger Delta," *Journal of Sustainable Development in Africa* 13, no. 7 (2011): 336.

71 Obasesam Okoi, *Punctuated Peace in Nigeria's Oil Region: Oil Insurgency and the Challenges of Post-Conflict Peacebuilding* (Cham: Palgrave Macmillan, 2021).

72 J. Sola Omotola, "From the OMPADEC to NDDC: An Assessment of State Responses to Environmental Insecurity in the Niger Delta, Nigeria," *Africa Today* 54, no. 1 (2007): 81–82. doi: www.jstor.org/stable/27666875

73 Uwafiokun Idemudia, "The Changing Phases of the Niger Delta Conflict: Implications for Conflict Escalation and the Return to Peace," *Conflict, Security and Development* 9, no. 3 (2009): 320. doi: 10.1080/14678800903142698

74 Augustine Ikelegbe, "Beyond the Threshold of Civil Struggle: Youth Militancy and the Militia-Ization of the Resource Conflict in the Niger Delta Region of Nigeria," *African Study Monographs* 27, no. 2 (2006): 106. Accessed May 20, 2023. https://repository.kulib.kyoto-u.ac.jp/dspace/bitstream/2433/68251/1/ASM_27_87.pdf

75 Florens D.A.M. Luoga, "Challenges in Setting Up Legal Frameworks for Natural Resources Governance in the East African Countries," *The African Review: A Journal of African Politics, Development and International Affairs* 43, no. 2 (2016): 1–16. www.jstor.org/stable/45341719

76 Simeon P. Sungi, "Extraction of Natural Resources: Is It Fuelling of Human Rights Abuses in the Exploration and Exploitation of Oil and Gas in Tanzania?" *The African Review: A Journal of African Politics, Development and International Affairs* 43, no. 2 (2016): 124–38. www.jstor.org/stable/45341724

77 Michael L. Ross, "What Do We Know about Natural Resources and Civil War?" *Journal of Peace Research* 41, no. 3 (2004): 337–56. www.jstor.org/stable/4149748

78 Kwamina Panford, *Africa's Natural Resources and Underdevelopment: How Ghana's Petroleum Can Create Sustainable Economic Prosperity* (1st Edition). (New York: Palgrave Macmillan, 2017).

79 Minerals and Mining Act, 2006 (Act 703, 2006). Parliament of Ghana. Accessed May 23, 2023. https://resourcegovernance.org/sites/default/files/Minerals%20and%20Mining%20Act%20703%20Ghana.pdf
80 See Ghana Extractive Industries Transparency Initiative. Accessed May 22, 2023. www.gheiti.gov.gh/site/index.php?option=com_content&view=frontpage&Itemid=1
81 Keisuke Okada and Takayoshi Shinkuma, "Transparency and Natural Resources in Sub-Saharan Africa," *Resources Policy* 76 (2022): 102574. https://doi.org/10.1016/j.resourpol.2022.102574
82 See The Ministry of Lands and Natural Resources, Republic of Ghana, Accessed May 24, 2023. https://mlnr.gov.gh/
83 See Public Interest Accountability Committee, Accessed May 24, 2023. www.piacghana.org/portal/
84 Minerals Commission Ghana, "Small-Scale and Community Mining". Accessed May 24, 2023. www.mincom.gov.gh/wp-content/uploads/2021/11/Small-Scale-and-Community-Mining-Operational-Manual-Sep.-2021-1.pdf
85 Kwamina Panford, *Africa's Natural Resources and Underdevelopment*.
86 Dennis Kayambazinthu, Frank Matose, George Kajembe, and Nontokozo Nemarundwe, "Institutional Arrangements Governing Natural Resource Management of the Miombo Woodland," in *Policies and Governance Structures in Woodlands of Southern Africa*. Center for International Forestry Research (2003), accessed May 21, 2023. www.jstor.org/stable/resrep02026.10
87 Kayambazinthu et al., "Institutional Arrangements Governing Natural Resource Management of the Miombo Woodland."
88 Ibid.
89 James Denbow and Phenyo C. Thebe, *Culture and Customs of Botswana* (Westport, CT: Greenwood Press, 2006).
90 David Sebudubudu and Keneilwe Mooketsane, "Why Botswana is a Deviant Case to the Natural Resource Curse," *The African Review: A Journal of African Politics, Development and International Affairs* 43, no. 2 (2016): 84–96. www.jstor.org/stable/45341722
91 Daron Acemoglu, Simon Johnson, and James A. Robinson, An African Success Story: Botswana (July 2001). Available at SSRN: https://ssrn.com/abstract=290791; Daron Acemoglu, Simon Johnson, and James A. Robinson, "The Colonial Origins of Comparative Development: An Empirical Investigation," *American Economic Review* 91, no. 5 (2001): 1369–401.
92 James Denbow and Phenyo C. Thebe, *Culture and Customs of Botswana*. Pauline E. Peters, *Dividing the Commons: Politics, Policy, and Culture in Botswana* (Charlottesvil: University of Virginia Press, 1994).
93 Megan Schoen, "Toward a Rhetoric of Kagiso: Rhetoric and Democracy in Botswana." Constell8cr, November 2018, 5. Accessed May 18, 2023. https://constell8cr.com/wp-content/uploads/2018/11/kairos-botswana-school-.pdf
94 Acemoglu, Johnson, and Robinson, *An African Success Story*.
95 Ibid.
96 Ibid.
97 Farouk Al-Kasim, Tina Søreide, and Aled Williams, "Grand Corruption in the Regulation of Oil," Anti-Corruption Resource Centre, U4 ISSUE 2 (2008). Accessed May 20, 2023. www.u4.no/publications/grand-corruption-in-the-regulation-of-oil.pdf

2 Gold Mining and Instability in the Central Sahel

John Sunday Ojo and Oluwole Ojewale

Introduction

This chapter interrogates the nexus between the illicit economy of gold production, its commercialization, and regional instability in the central Sahel. The chapter explains the resource governance deficit and how it allows armed groups to fund criminal occupations in the Central Sahel. It focuses on the three major countries, Burkina Faso, Mali, and the Republic of Niger. The chapter argues that armed groups have adopted artisanal mining and illegal gold trading as sources of financing criminality and terrorism. Therefore, a recent informal gold rush by non-state armed groups and ineffective state-led resource management measures have contributed to instability in the Central Sahel.

Globally, gold is one of the most treasured mineral resources.[1] It is used to produce various valuable materials such as jewellery, electronic equipment, coinage, and medical appliances, to mention a few.[2] Numerous commodities are manufactured from gold, making this mineral resource a cherished one. Gold mining can be a lucrative business for those who engage in it. Various extractive methods are employed in exploring gold. Gold mining can adopt capital-intensive or small-scale labour-intensive approaches.[3] While the capital-intensive method uses massive mechanical instruments for exploration by companies, the traditional or small-scale labour-intensive method employs simple methods often called *artisanal mining*. It is estimated that about 13 million people are directly engaged in small-scale artisanal mining globally.[4] However, according to a recent World Bank report, more than 40 million people in the global south especially those residing in remote villages engage in artisanal and small-scale gold mining.[5] The International Institute for Environment and Development (IIED) also estimates that between 15 and 20% of global minerals are explored through artisanal mining systems.[6]

Artisanal mining of gold is prevalent in Africa compared to other continents. The Burkinabe mining code defines artisanal *mining* as "any operation which consists of extracting and concentrating mineral substances to obtain marketable products by using traditional or manual methods and procedures".[7] Mali offers a similar definitional perspective, the country defines artisanal mining as

DOI: 10.4324/9781003355717-4

"any operation which extracts and concentrates mineral substances drawn from primary, secondary outcropping or sub-outcropping deposits using manual or traditional methods and procedures to obtain marketable products".[8] Hence, artisanal gold mining can be considered a gold mining operation that employs a non-technological approach.[9] Nevertheless, recent evidence from Ghana demonstrates that artisanal gold mining has been recently mechanized with the use of excavators and pumping machines.[10] Such a mechanism largely depends on the local people for the exploration and mining of gold. Artisanal mining has become a new economic survival for some youths navigating against the tide of unemployment, poverty, and economic hardship in Africa.[11]

Gold mining is a source of livelihood for unemployed youths. For instance, in countries like Burkina Faso, Mali, Nigeria, Niger, Libya, Chad, and Sudan, such an informal gold mining economy has provided youths with employment. Beyond direct engagement in artisanal gold mining, the market supply of necessary equipment for the exploration of gold and food supply to the workers have also enhanced local economies in many extractive communities.[12] In the Central Sahel, artisanal gold mining accommodates between 2 and 3 million employees, with 6 million, directly and indirectly, benefitting from the sector.[13] It was estimated that the largest mining sites in the Central Sahel accommodated tens of thousands of workers during the thriving mining activities. For instance, Djado in northeast Niger hosts 25,000 miners, Komabangou in southwest Niger can employ 30,000 miners,[14] and Taekwondo in Burkina Faso accommodates 10,000 miners.[15] However, despite the large percentage of the population benefiting from artisanal mining, it is considered a complementary occupation for the local people and not a lone-dependent economy for survival. This is because artisanal mining is a seasonal activity, often during the winter, when farming activities are limited. Thus, it cannot replace agricultural-related occupations in rural areas.[16]

To meet the increasing demand for mineral resources, mining companies have engaged artisanal miners to explore gold in many African countries.[17] Several non-state actors engaged in artisanal mining in Africa. However, the informalization of artisanal mining has made it vulnerable to corruption as evident in Ghana,[18] and conflict between diverse non-state armed groups and locals in other African states. Moreover, many of the locations where extractive industries and artisanal miners operate are far from political authority,[19] consequently experiencing weak government presence, making such an environment vulnerable to warlordism and rebel governance system. For instance, artisanal gold miners in the eastern Democratic Republic of Congo (DRC) operate in remote locations far from the country's capital, Kinshasa, controlled by informal actors.[20]

Fundamentally, it is imperative to note that the informalization of gold mining in Africa did not emanate without some policy reforms that took place in the mid-1990s and beyond. In the 1990s, African nations embarked on significant policies affecting mining sectors. These policies are embedded in the privatization and liberalization of the sector.[21] During this period, various guidelines that demonstrated environmental, social, and human rights-related considerations were embedded in the framework. While the primary concern was not jettisoned, attracting foreign investors in the mining sector, these reforms emphasized technical-related issues. However, they abandoned the sector's governance, "the determination of to what end, under whose control, and for whose benefit extractive industries operate".[22] Such an inadequacy in identifying whose responsibility to manage mining industries makes it vulnerable to informal actors, resulting in the ungovernability of the sector in present-day Africa.

Since 2016, in the central Sahelian countries, including Niger, Mali, and Burkina Faso, armed groups and jihadists have taken advantage of ungoverned spaces and weak government presence where resources such as gold are concentrated. The exploration of gold provides a new source of funding to armed groups used to promote their criminal agenda. Moreover, the informal network and booming economy of artisanal mining have triggered intercommunal violence among several competing groups and local actors.[23] The increasing threats posed by artisanal gold mining offer an enabling environment for informal networks in local and international spaces. Such an informal network has facilitated terrorism financing in the region.[24] Consequently, it reinforces transnational organized crime, security threats, and instability in the Sahel region.

The unregulated economy of gold production has encouraged violence perpetrated by the different non-state armed groups in the region. The informal economy of gold production and trading has continued to reinforce transnational organized crime and promote the activities of criminal networks, jihadist groups, and self-defence militias. Several attempts have been made to target the locations of illegal mining by armed groups. This is primarily aimed at acquiring such economic hubs to finance criminal operations by armed groups. At the same time, evidence suggests that proceeds from illegal mining have been used to fund violent extremism in the Central Sahel. The sustainability of illicit gold production and commercialization is central to the ungovernability of mining geographical areas in the Central Sahel. Following this section is an explanation of the scramble for gold mining sites and their attractiveness to armed groups, local and international informal entrepreneurs, resulting in instability. Afterwards, three country case studies are examined, including Burkina Faso, Mali, and Niger. The last part of the chapter is the concluding remarks.

Armed Groups and Instability in the Central Sahel

Gold mining and its historical trajectories are rooted in state formation and political governance of the Sahelian region. The trading of gold shapes the pre-colonial reign of some empires around the 12th century in the Sahel and Africa at large. Such exploitation of gold mining constitutes one of the major opportunities to create affluence, including the 14th-century reign of the

Emperor of Mali, Mansa Musa, considered "the richest man of all time".[25] Currently, state authorities are finding it difficult to govern gold mines in the central Sahel. This results from the ungovernability of the contested mining spaces and inadequate resources to address the security challenges ravaging the region. Due to a lack of capacity to deal with a volatile environment, the formation of local militia and non-state armed groups are encouraged to dominate and manage natural resources.[26]

Existing literature has established a substantial link between artisanal gold mining, violence, and insecurity.[27] Challenges and limitations in encouraging informality of resource governance create an ambience for hybrid security architecture. In this environment, non-state armed groups are empowered to safeguard artisanal mining areas.[28] Due to long-term state disengagement and privatization, armed groups have taken control for economic gain. Informality characterized by non-state actors remains the defining nature of artisanal gold mining in the Sahel.[29] The complexity of such an informal arrangement is entrenched in customary land rights and individual land ownership, which provides an opportunity for unregulated resource governance through which exploitations are promoted within the region.[30]

Another perspective on artisanal gold mining is the network of illegal buyers spread across local and international spaces. These networks include illegal buyers who facilitate the purchase of gold from production sites and transfer it to regional traders and refiners. These networks are used to smuggle gold and evade taxes. It is important to note that these several actors often include corrupt public officials, non-state armed groups, and high-profile individuals. The international dimension of such a criminal network necessitates the movement of gold by air which is facilitated by the corrupt public officials at the airport to its destination. Countries such as China, India, Europe, and the United Arab Emirates (UAE) are considered final destinations of African smuggled gold.[31] Dubai in the UAE is the biggest recipient of African smuggled gold. In the African mining sector, the UAE has been one of the most significant investors. Between 2006 and 2016, the importation of gold to the UAE rose from 16% to 50%. It is believed that the trading of gold forms an essential component of the UAE's economy and constitutes about 20% of its economy.[32]

It is estimated that 95% of gold from Central and East Africa is imported into UAE.[33] Such an estimation emanates from the combination of legal and illegal importation of gold often perfected by non-state actors and transnational criminal networks from Africa to the UAE. The reason it becomes easier to import and sell gold in Dubai revolves around four factors: weak customs control, availability of large cash transactions, inadequate oversight of gold emporiums, and weak oversight of refiners.[34] Notably, illegal gold mining in Africa is made possible through a clandestine criminal network intertwined within the complex conglomerates of politics, business, and crime, exploiting both legitimate and unlawful corridors in achieving their aims.[35] A well and systematic structure involving several criminal actors which play a fundamental role in different levels of the processes, including financing, production, trading, transit, and destination countries dispersed along geographical lines, is concealed from public knowledge.[36] The complex network and its secrecy make it difficult to identify the people involved in such illegal production and trading of gold.

Kalokoh and Kochtcheeva reinforce the above perspective by arguing that the multiplicity of actors and governance struggles among these numerous actors, as well as ineffective monitoring of the gold mining locations by the state, offer an opportunity for corruption, exploitation, human rights abuse, and smuggling of gold.[37] In such an environment, the presence of state and security forces is often non-existence in dealing with non-state armed groups. In most cases, the state accommodates and encourages the formation of armed groups to serve as informal security outfits and safeguard the mining sites. The enabling environment given to the armed groups by the state creates a conducive atmosphere for the armed groups to challenge the legitimacy of the state authority. In this context, armed groups gained a wider autonomy to operate and circumvent the state authorities in controlling and exploiting gold mining and its locational environment. Due to the free-hand operational opportunity provided to armed groups, informal local, regional, and international networks are created for the smuggling of gold, and such proceeds are used to finance criminality and terrorism to sustain and preserve the artisanal gold economy by the armed groups.[38]

Theoretical Underpinning

There have been several attempts to link natural resources with conflict in many fragile countries.[39] These conflicts are fuelled by a desire to capture natural resources such as timber, diamonds, crude oil, gold, and coltan for economic gain.[40] In Africa, natural resources have contended as propellers of war, corruption, poverty, and dictatorship.[41] These narratives have been contextualized as resource curse and leadership curse.[42]

Natural resources play a significant role in the contemporary African political system. The African challenges are not the lack of natural resources such as fertile soil, water, minerals, and land. Syndromes such as the "resource curse"[43] and "paradox of plenty"[44] are considered the most threatening diseases that are suffocating the developmental expedition in Africa. Irrespective of abundant natural resources, African countries have communed with chronic poverty. They remain an epicentre of political instability and economic stagnation, which ensues millions of citizens in an economic nostalgia trap.[45] Hence, resource governance accentuates a critical challenge to African political leadership. Most literature tends to associate the resource curse phenomenon with industrial mining; the exploration and exploitation of mineral resources have continued to trigger violent conflicts among diverse groups that control natural resources in mostly rural or remote African locations.[46]

Resource exploration can be achieved without economic or political governance, unlike other sectors. In this manner, conflicts are more prevalent because of the ungovernability of economic resources.[47] Between 1970 and 2008, about half of global armed conflicts occurred due to competition for natural resources.[48] The recent events in African countries such as Burkina Faso, the DRC, Zimbabwe, Ghana, Nigeria, and Niger have substantiated the nexus between natural resources, criminalities, and violent conflicts.[49] In the Sahelian region, artisanal gold mining resource conflicts have abounded in recent years. Integrating non-state actors into the resource control system has created a hybrid resource governance model that fuels competition among several non-state actors to contend for natural resources, thus necessitating the militarization of the resource environment.[50]

There are three fundamental effects of the resource curse. First, its effect on the political system has been established. Karl explains the resource curse phenomenon using Venezuela as a typical illustration and highlights how its abundant natural resources adversely affect the whole society due to resource governance laxity.[51] Second, Ross establishes the nexus between natural resources and the governance system of resource-rich nations.[52] He argues that natural resources such as oil thwarts democratic governance. Third, Auty further reinforces the perspective that natural resource endowment obstructs economic development, using countries such as Peru, Bolivia, Jamaica, and Chile as typical examples.[53] One fundamental argument of this perspective is the possibility of resource-rich countries experiencing resource governance deficit, especially in mismanaging such economic endowment for profligacy and socio-economic underdevelopment. Thus, natural resources are not determinants of economic growth and development. Such an argument can be validated using several countries worldwide, especially in developing economies with mineral deposits that cannot translate the abundance of natural resources to economic growth and development.

Despite the broader receipt of the resource curse thesis in Africa, a country such as Botswana has been considered a typical progressive country that utilizes its resources for positive change. Due to effective resource governance employed to promote economic growth and development, Botswana has been transformed into a middle-income country based on the World Bank evaluation. Such a new development redefined the resource curse hypothesis that characterized African political and economic equivalences.[54] Botswana's exemplary resource governance provides an enabling environment to repudiate the dominant narrative of the resource curse notion,[55] considered a Eurocentric phenomenon.[56] The curse's impacts on society, politics, and the economy are filtered through a Western perspective that ignores the socio-political and economic realities of African states.

One fundamental perspective to adopt in challenging the resource curse thesis is the one by Sachs and Warner.[57] The perspective has established that resource-rich countries have taken a slow path in growth and development compared to other developing countries without natural resource potential. This raises the question of whether natural resources are a blessing or curse to countries with abundant mineral deposits. Lederman and Maloney conclude that natural resources are neither curse nor destiny. However, the utilization of these natural resources and their translation into growth and development is determined by the quality of governance in such an environment. Hence, it can be argued that effective resource governance remains a relevant factor in resource-rich African states to attain economic prosperity and development.[58]

It is pertinent to note that resources are not solely responsible for conflict. Ungoverned or less governed resources, however, lead to conflict. Several African states have experienced conflict over unregulated artisanal gold mining. South Africa,[59] the Sahel region,[60] and West African states,[61] are among the regions that have documented these conflicts in Africa. It's not uncommon to see conflict in many African states resulting from poor management of resources by the state in resource-rich communities and denial of the dividends derived from such extracted resources, neglecting the areas where these resources are being mined.[62] However, a country like Botswana has taken a departure from the Eurocentric narrative of the resource curse by demonstrating effective governance of natural resources.[63] Based on this Eurocentric reversal, abundant natural resources such as gold mining do not directly cause conflict or crime. However, there is interplay between gold, governance, criminality, and conflict. This is reinforced by informality of gold governance and its appealing nature to armed groups.[64] Artisanal gold mining sites are exploited by criminal armed groups and their collaborators due to poor governance. In most cases, these armed groups initiate conflicts to expel the local population. The objective is to create an environment where terrorist organizations and armed groups are more likely to operate to achieve their economic goals. Such gains are often used to procure arms for their criminal activities. In this sense, the governance curse can be considered the primary challenge rather than the resource curse. In this way, the traditional resource curse hypothesis is invalidated by emphasizing the political and institutional qualities of managing natural resources.[65] Therefore, the following sections offer a glimpse of case studies, including Burkina Faso, Mali, and the Republic of Niger which are central concerns of this chapter.

Burkina Faso

Unlike in other African countries, a long history of gold mining is not present in Burkina Faso. However, the country possesses abundant mineral resources. In the country, 70,000 km^2 of volcanic-sedimentary formations are possessed by the country.[66] Therefore, there is a high concentration of mineral resources, including gold, in such formations. In the past, Burkina Faso was considered a country without mineral resources, while its economy was always concentrated on agricultural productivity. Conversely, gold mining is an exemption to such a claim. The local citizens generally exploited gold mining in the Poura and Gaoua regions. The mining sites were often managed and controlled according to customary law—a decree passed on October 22, 1922, promulgated by the colonial authorities, which reserved and delineated some locations for artisanal mines for the local population. Some companies, such as Equatorial Mining Company and the Mining Company of Upper Volta, carried out mining activities but later abandoned the sites due to the economic crisis of 1932.[67]

Such an account suggests that Burkina Faso has historically engaged in a combination of artisanal gold and industrial mining. However, the pre-1990s era witnessed a state-centred control of artisanal and small-scale gold mining activities in Burkina Faso. Artisanal gold mining started in the 1980s in the Sahel region of the country—the Gangaol region. Today, more than 220 artisanal gold mining sites have been created, providing jobs for 90,000 to 140,000 local citizens, of which 30 to 40% of such a population are women. They often engage in artisanal mining activities between November and May, when agricultural-related activities are unavailable. Thus, artisanal mining accommodates 650,000 employees or at least 1 in 20 local dwellers. The Sahel axis of the north and centre-north, especially those in Soum, Oudalan, Yatenga, and Bam, holds the largest artisanal mining sites.[68]

The October 1997 event witnessed a major reform that provided an opportunity for liberalism, which encouraged foreign investors in the sector. The reform's aim includes creating an enabling environment for large-scale investment in the mining sector.[69] According to the mining code, artisanal miners are not mandated to have a mining license before exploration occurs. The only requirement is the administrative authorization issued for artisanal exploration by the Directorate General of Mines, Geology, and Quarries (DGMGC), which must be complemented by informing the local community about the mining activities to be carried out in the location.[70] Since the implementation of mining reform, the number of private individuals involved in producing and trading gold has risen steeply, dominated by informal actors. From 1987 to 2014, the political regime of Blaise Compaoré encouraged a shift away from neoliberalism that encouraged patrimonialism through state and private ownership of natural resources. This period allowed influential elites and associates close to Blaise Compaoré to get involved in producing and trading gold.[71]

Between 1998 and 2014, an increase in the price of gold led to an economic boom in Burkina Faso, driven by artisanal and industrial gold mining. Consequently, in 2014, 640,800 Burkinabes, representing 4% of the country's population, were estimated to engage in artisanal mining. Following the increase in the price of gold, the country enacted a friendly mining code to attract investors in 2003. As a result, between 2007 and 2014, eight industrial gold mines were created. The creation of these industrial mines influenced the level of gold production and exportation, which constituted 2% of exports in 2007 and 55% in 2014.[72] However, in 2020, gold accounted for 37% of total exports to Burkina Faso.[73] As of 2017, the industrial mining sector employed 9,017 people, most of whom were poorly compensated. It was estimated that more than 1 million local youths, including women, are employed in artisanal gold mining in Burkina Faso.[74]

Burkina Faso experienced a vibrant economy of gold mining, which elicited hope of enhancing the revenue base in the country. However, while artisanal gold mining has continued to expand in Burkina Faso, the violent attacks and conflicts orchestrated by non-state armed groups have increased.[75] Several non-state armed groups have risen around the artisanal gold mining sites in Burkina Faso. For instance, Ansarul Islam terrorist group has been launching attacks around the artisanal gold mining locations in the country. The attack by jihadist extremists on September 24, 2018, involving the abduction of three employees of the Inata gold mine, suggests how artisanal gold mining has become an attraction to terrorists. Additionally, the Ansarul terrorist group operates in several artisanal gold mines, including the Soum region. Besides, transnational organized criminal syndicates, including Libyans and Chadians, have also attacked artisanal gold mines. In September 2016, the Islamic State in Africa attacked the Markoye customs post.[76] On June 4, 2021, jihadist extremists claimed responsibility for the attack at Solhan, a gold mining area, killing more than 130 people.[77]

Regional affiliates of Al-Qaeda and Islamic State engage in an informal economy of artisanal gold mining in Mali, Burkina Faso, and Niger. A source of revenue-generating worth $2bn worth of gold yearly. For instance, in 24 artisanal gold mining sites attacked by insurgents in Burkina Faso, the sites produce more than 700 kg of gold worth more than $35 million yearly. The Jihadists in the central Sahel have taken this opportunity to finance terrorism. Moreover, artisanal mining locations have triggered competition among diverse armed groups, including jihadists. Recent attacks at artisanal gold mining sites demonstrate how competition for gold mining sites exacerbates regional security.[78] There is fierce competition for artisanal gold mining sites between the state, civilians, and armed groups in Burkina Faso. This is evident from the recent killing of more than 60 civilians working in artisanal mining locations. ...[79] Following the attack, the Burkina Faso government banned all artisanal mining sites from operating, having acknowledged the nexus between gold mining and jihadist extremism.[80]

Furthermore, there was a report of the unlawful involvement of state and private security forces in mining locations. For example, in Burkina Faso, security agents have been alleged to have facilitated illegal mining at the Poura site.[81] Furthermore, while security forces were saddled with overseeing and enforcing the closure of mining sites, they were alleged to participate in mining activities and extortion for personal gain.[82] Beside Jihadist groups that have made efforts to control the artisanal gold mines, the emergence of self-defence and vigilante groups known as the *Koglweogo* (guardians of the bush) has contributed to the instability in Burkina Faso. After 2015, the country witnessed the formation of numerous vigilante groups in the rural communities of northern and central Burkina Faso. The rationale behind such a proliferation of informal security is to prevent criminal activities due to state security's weakness to curtail the country's overwhelming security challenges.[83]

After 2018, the informal security outfits were absorbed into counter-terrorism operations. Locally, it is believed that Koglweogo has the backing of the state because of its vital role in resolving local conflicts that revolve around mobility and land-related disputes. However, the struggle between the Koglweogo groups and the Dozo traditional hunters erupted in western Burkina Faso. It is important to note that Dozo traditional hunters have also played an essential role in self-defence under the umbrella of donsoya (hunting) institutions. In central and northern regions, the presence of Fulani nomadic herders has been pronounced due to the drought that swept the Sahelian region. The recent conflict emanated from an attack on Fulani communities by the Koglweogo groups, who have accused Fulani communities of collaborating with jihadist groups. Paradoxically, Koglweogo groups have also been accused of collaborating with gold miners.[84] The escalation of inter-group conflicts was further exacerbated by the extra-judicial killings perpetrated by the military forces. This raises the question of the accountability of state security operatives. This provides a nexus between natural resources and conflict. However, the causal link can be attributed to the nexus and a long-term period of state disengagement, neglect, and security privatization.[85] The accommodation of state-private control of gold mining sites is the foundation of the current woe that bedevilled Burkina Faso.

Mali

While Mali is the fourth largest gold-producing country in Africa, producing more than 71 metric tonnes of gold in 2019,[86] the country is blighted by extreme poverty and poor socioeconomic outcomes. Agriculture is the primary source of income and employment for most Malians, with three-quarters of the country's 18.6 million people relying on agriculture for their food and income.[87] About 42.3% of the country's citizens live in extreme poverty; the adult literacy rate is 30.8%,[88] with a gross domestic product (GDP) of $17.28 billion and a gross national income (GNI) per capita of just $830, making it one of the poorest countries in the world. In addition, Mali's mono-economy depends on gold and cotton, representing 89.6% of the country's exports in 2020.[89]

Corruption, limited infrastructure, poor socioeconomic indicators, human resources deficit, high levels of informality, administrative inefficiency, poor management of ethnic diversity, and worsening insecurity are critical impediments to governance and the viability of the Malian state. Mali has excellent economic potential thanks to sizeable natural resources endowments, energy opportunities, particularly in the renewables sector, and high agricultural potential. However, this has been undermined by political instability and conflict since the 2012 military coup and armed groups' occupation of the north.

Mali's conflict-ridden decade commenced in early 2012 when a Tuareg separatist group, the National Movement for the Liberation of Azawad (MNLA), in the north rebelled and subsequent coup d'état that overthrew Mali's democratically elected government and led the military chain of command to collapse.[90] The 2012 MNLA rebellion developed into a violent extremist insurgency as

Ansar Dine, al-Qaeda in the Islamic Maghreb (AQIM), and the Movement for Unity and Jihad in West Africa joined MNLA and took over several cities and territory in northern Mali. Insecurity in northern Mali has displaced over 350,000 people and worsened regional food insecurity and humanitarian crisis.[91]

Mining and gold have historically been central to the Malian economy, gold officially is Mali's most significant export product, and in 2020, gold worth $4.74 billion was officially exported by the country.[92] Gold mines are located mainly in the southern region, and the largest goldfields are in the Bambouk Mountains in Kayes, western Mali. Gold mining, both artisanal and industrial (medium- and large-scale industrial gold mining), is undertaken in the country. There is a higher level of accountability for industrially mined gold in Mali as there is due diligence and robust compliance with OECD-compliant practices. These processes are controlled by large international mining companies, which include AngloGold Ashanti, Randgold, IAMGOLD, Avion Gold and African Gold Group, Resolute Mining, and Avnel Gold Mining.[93] However, there are doubts about the quantity of gold produced by artisanal mines due to disparate figures adduced by several sources.[94]

It has been observed that after the 2012 insurgency, there has been a spike in artisanal mining. While the exact figure of the Malians involved is unknown, the Malian Chamber of Mines put the number of artisanal miners at a million plus.[95] Furthermore, studies have drawn a link between the post-conflict increase in artisanal mining in Mali and other African countries in conflict in the Sahel. The rationale is that conflicts in the region affect agriculture and employ a substantial percentage of people, forcing citizens to pick up available sources of income to meet their domestic needs. Artisanal mining offers one of these options.[96]

These artisanal miners operate outside government purview, and the gold produced is outside the formal legal value chain of gold in Mali. The informality of the system allows for gold to be traded through various undocumented networks, involving many businesses within and outside Mali before it is eventually exported.[97] Mali has been estimated to lose as much as 15 tons a year, equal to about $860 million, from artisanal gold production smuggled out of the country.[98] The lack of effective government control over the informal gold mining sector has allowed criminal organizations and fundamentalist groups to participate in this multimillion-dollar trade.

Some of Mali's around 350 artisanal gold mining sites are in the border regions, particularly the Kayes region.[99] Criminal groups and networks set up these mining sites to facilitate cross-border trafficking as part of an enlarged regional criminal enterprise. These multiple networks serve as conduits in the illicit gold trade, helping fund the region's violent extremists and transnational crime.[100] Beyond that, there has been an increase in artisanal sites in militant-controlled territories, such as Kidal and Tessalit. Also, Islamist terror groups such as Jama'at Nusrat al-Islam wal-Muslimin (JNIM) have expanded into traditional artisanal mining territories to raise revenue for their terror operations.[101] The insurgents generate revenue by taxing local gold traders in Kidal, located in the far north, and gold mining sites in the west of Niger.[102]

It has been suggested that at the core of the Malian security crisis is a profit-driven organized criminal economy driven and constituted by professional networks of social and family structures.[103] Organized criminal groups involved in gold smuggling and money laundering differ from Islamist fundamentalists and other armed non-state groups operating in the country. However, there are instances where an actor operates in the two categories. Some of the armed non-state actors are involved in the transportation and protection of illicit goods. Some actors are primarily involved because of profit; others secure resources to fund their agitation against the state. Essentially, there is a nexus between the two groups in terms of reliance on the political influence of a group, access to resources, and social networks.[104] This development has become an established pattern accentuating instability in the central Sahel with dominant experiences in Mali, Burkina Faso, and Niger.

Niger Republic

Located at the centre of the Sahel, Niger is one of the poorest countries in the world, with 41.8% of the population living in extreme poverty.[105] The country ranked last on the 2020 Human Development Index.[106] Niger had the fourth lowest gross national income per capita, at $912 in 2017. Furthermore, the United States Agency for International Development estimates that 60% of men worldwide have the lowest education and 58% are illiterate, 72% of women have no education, and 85% are illiterate.[107] These poor socioeconomic outcomes are partly attributable to natural resource constraints amplified by the impacts of climate change. Drought remains the country's most significant risk, and desertification worsens the viability of already scarce land resources.[108]

The security situation in Niger has been very fragile for a long while, with communities, particularly along the borders experiencing attacks from Islamist insurgents and organized criminal groups. In the northwest, the border between Mali and Burkina Faso saw massive deterioration since 2017 with the continuous incursion by the armed non-state actors in the regions of Tillaberi and Tahoua, resulting in repeated attacks against security services and local communities.[109] In the southeast part of the country, particularly the Diffa Region, there has been a subsisting state of emergency since 2015 as a result of the repeated attacks by fundamentalist Islamist insurgents from their positions in Nigeria and northern Mali in western Niger.[110] In addition, in the south region of Maradi bordering the northwestern states of Nigeria, Sokoto, Katsina, and Zamfara have witnessed spillover attacks by armed groups, militias, and unidentified criminal gangs.

While Niger is known customarily for its uranium production, as it is in the list of the global top five producers, there has been an increase in gold production. About 12–15 tonnes of gold is produced every year by Niger's artisanal gold mines.[111] The history of artisanal gold mining in Niger goes back to the

1983–1984 drought and subsequent crop failure. Thus, farmers were forced to look for alternative income-generating activities. As a result, the first gold rush occurred in Koma Bangou in 1984.[112]

Artisanal and small-scale mining activities in Niger are regulated by Law No. 2006–026 of August 9, 2006, and Ordinance No. 2017–03 of June 30, 2017. Artisanal exploitation licenses are granted for a renewable period of two years to artisanal miners' cooperatives, individuals, or groups of economic interests. The artisanal mining permit confers on its holder, within the limits of its perimeter, and up to a depth of 30 m in the case of step mining and 10 m in the case of surface mining, the right to prospect and mine the substances for which it is issued.[113]

Niger's two main gold mining sites are in the Tillabéri region in the western part and the Agadez region in the northern part. More than 69 official gold mining sites are in the region of Tillabéri, and approximately 60 gold mining sites are located in the Djado mountains in the Agadez region. In addition, there are 14 sites in the Tchibarakaten goldfields, and some sites are also present in the southern part of the Maradi region, in the department of Madarounfa, near the Nigerian border. Although artisanal gold mining in Niger is a seasonal income-generating activity, it directly engages 450,000 people, and close to 3 million depend on it.[114]

Analysts have traced the link between the expansion of gold mining and the changes in the security dynamics of the country, highlighting the role of artisanal mining in the deterioration of security in Niger.[115] Mining sites are hubs of conflicts over access, control, and management of mining sites. There are reports of deadly cyclical violence, and an unconfirmed report claims a murder happens every 48 hours in the mining sites in the country.[116] Although, like in other African countries where artisanal mines are operated outside effective government control, the mines in Niger operate at the frontiers of formal institutions of law and order, government control is symbolic rather than effective.

The Nigerien Army, which has a presence across all mining sites, is grossly underrepresented by a singular unit commander managing security in a mining region, even though mining sites are hundreds of miles apart. According to Pellerin, "given the vast distances, the lack of soldiers, and the level of the armament of some miners, it is not unreasonable to conclude that the army cannot control the area in any meaningful way".[117]

This underlines that mines are drivers of insecurity, and the inability of the state to impose itself on the informality that goes on there acerbates insecurity. Artisanal mining combines aspects of licit and illicit commerce. While the state imposes permits, licences, and taxes at the point of extraction, there is no government imposition post-extraction framework, and there is policy instability on access to mines. The operation of the mines has also been linked to an increase in the operation of armed robbers and bandits on the access roads to the mines. Bandits are a loose collection of criminal gangs involved in kidnapping for ransom, armed robbery, cattle rustling, rape and other sexual violence, pillage, and attacks on traders, farmers, and travellers, particularly in Nigeria-Niger corridors of the Sahel.

While the Nigeria-Niger border axis has sites of intense banditry going back to more than a hundred years,[118] one of the aftermaths of the Nigerien Tuareg crisis is the increase in bandit attacks in northern Niger on local communities.[119] Although bandits laid siege to local roads, targeting commuters in time, the attention of these bandits shifted to drug traffickers, who provide a higher revenue source than locals.[120]

However, since the blooming of artisanal mines, bandits have shifted their focus to miners, and it has been projected that bandits' attacks around 30% of commuters from gold mining sites that are escorted by security actors.[121]

Activities of artisanal miners in Niger have seen an increase in arms trafficking in the regions where mining is ascending. This increase is attributable to the increase in wealth by local adjourning communities to mines, worsening regional insecurity and the failure of the Nigerien state to effectively and efficiently police and secure local communities. Trafficking in illicit arms is confined to small arms and ammunition, particularly handguns and AK-pattern rifles, which have become enablers of extractive violence and instability in gold-bearing communities.[122]

There is no direct evidence of an operational nexus between artisanal mining and fundamentalist Islamist groups. There is no evidence of the direct participation of Boko Haram and its many sprawls in gold mining in the country. However, the issue of funding fundamentalist groups from mining proceeds is blurry. Organized criminal groups and former warlords are actively involved in mining. For example, in the Agadez region, the former head of Niger Movement for Justice (MNJ) and well-known criminal economy baron, Saleh Ibrahim, operate artisanal gold mining at the Tchibarakaten site. Also, many mining sites, especially in Tchibarakaten, are believed to be owned by these Nigerien groups of smugglers or by traffickers belonging to Algerian criminal groups.[123]

Armed insurgent groups across the region have targeted gold mines to fund their military operations against the state; this is repeated in Niger to a lesser extent. Azawad Movements (CMA), an alliance of rebel groups with several thousand members formed in October 2014, and to a lesser degree in the Djado area (Niger), home to rebel groups and traffickers moving between Niger, Chad, and Libya, have attempted to seize gold mines for revenue purposes. For instance, in 2014, in the Djado area of northern Niger, a network of militants, mostly Chadians suspected of links to Zaghawa or Toubou rebel groups from southern Libya, seized mining sites, and the Nigerien authorities had to close these sites to expel them.[124] Also, artisanal mining sites are used by human smugglers to hide their human cargo from security services. Smugglers also use mines to move networks of migrants undetected. For instance, Tchibarakaten's mine position as a station on the smuggling routes along Algeria's borders has been a source of diplomatic tensions between Niger and Algeria.[125]

Conclusion

Artisanal mining operations occur across the central Sahel and beyond outside government control, highlighting the fragility of most regional states. The ungovernability of artisanal gold mining by the state thus creates a criminal economy of gold production and commercialization. This raises the question of Africa's resource governance system, entrenched in popular Eurocentric discourses of the resource curse. As an enduring narrative, the resource curse fails to acknowledge the reality created by poorly managed artisanal gold mining sites in the region. Thus, governance and leadership deficits are central to artisanal gold mining in Burkina Faso, Mali, and the Republic of Niger. Rather than a narrative consolidated by a resource curse, effective governance of gold mining represents a critical agenda that should be promoted in the region. In light of gold mining's vulnerability to conflict and security threats in Africa, it should be integrated into the region's peace and security agenda.

Nothing represents the failure of policing across the region more than mining sites, where local and foreign miners operate outside the purview of the state. The sustainability of informal artisanal gold mining is made possible because of multi-layered local and transnational non-state actors (including multi-divergent armed groups, terrorists, local entrepreneurs, informal gold miners, allies, and international collaborators) involved in producing and trading gold in the central Sahel. However, such unregulated artisanal mining has worsened the security situation across the region. Jihadist and non-jihadist groups have exploited such a vacuum to promote their criminal activities in the central Sahel and beyond. Thus, it exacerbates the existing security threats that becloud the region.

Therefore, it has become fundamental for the central Sahel and other African states to formalize artisanal mining across the regional axis. This is necessary to prevent the spillover effect of ungoverned natural resources, which escorts existing security threats, and to thwart jihadist and non-jihadist groups from exploiting artisanal gold mining, considered a prime source of terrorism financing in Africa. Furthermore, to ensure effective governance of artisanal gold mining, it has become crucial for the African Union (AU) to provide collective regional Afrocentric guidelines. Punitive measures must be embedded in the operational guidelines for the deviant local and foreign investors involved in the illegal production and commercialization of gold in the African region.

Notes

1 Butt, Charles, and Robert M. Hough. "Why gold is valuable." *Elements* 5, no. 5 (2009): 277–280.
2 Anand, Amit, Manis Kumar Jha, Vinay Kumar, and Rina Sahu. "Recycling of precious metal gold from waste electrical and electronic equipments (WEEE): A review." In *Proceedings of the XIII International Seminar on Mineral Processing Technology, Bhubaneswar, India*, pp. 10–12. 2013.

3 Ahlerup, Pelle, Thushyanthan Baskaran, and Arne Bigsten. "Gold mining and education: A long-run resource curse in Africa?" *The Journal of Development Studies* 56, no. 9 (2020): 1745–1762.
4 Hentschel, Thomas. *Artisanal and small-scale mining: Challenges and opportunities.* The International Institute for Environment and Development, London (2003),.
5 Word Bank (2019) Shining a light on a hidden sector, June 19.
6 Crawford, Alec, and Christian Ledwell. "Digging Out of Conflict: Can Artisanal Mining Support Peacebuilding?." International Institute for Environment and Development (IIED) September 29, 2017.
7 Gueye, Djibril. *Small-scale mining in Burkina Faso.* London: IIED (2001), p. 4.
8 Ibid, p. 5
9 Bartrem, Casey, Ian von Lindern, Margrit von Braun, and Simba Tirima. "Climate Change, Conflict, and Resource Extraction: Analyses of Nigerian Artisanal Mining Communities and Ominous Global Trends." *Annals of Global Health* 88, no. 1 (2022): 1–17.
10 Ferring, David, Heidi Hausermann, and Emmanuel Effah. "Site specific: Heterogeneity of small-scale gold mining in Ghana." *The Extractive Industries and Society* 3, no. 1 (2016): 171–184.
11 Bartrem, Casey, Ian von Lindern, Margrit von Braun, and Simba Tirima. "Climate Change, Conflict, and Resource Extraction: Analyses of Nigerian Artisanal Mining Communities and Ominous Global Trends." *Annals of Global Health* 88, no. 1 (2022).
12 Global Initiative against Transnational Organized Crime, Observatory of Illicit Economies in West Africa, Risk Bulletin, Issue 2, November 2021.
13 International Crisis Group. Getting a Grip on Central Sahel's Gold Rush, November 13, 2019; Hilson, Gavin, Halima Goumandakoye, and Penda Diallo. "Formalizing artisanal mining 'spaces' in rural sub-Saharan Africa: The case of Niger." *Land Use Policy* 80 (2019): 259–268.
14 Grégoire, Emmanuel, and Laurent Gagnol. "Ruées vers l'or au Sahara: l'orpaillage dans le désert du Ténéré et le massif de l'Aïr (Niger)." *EchoGéo* (2017): 1–23.
15 Guéniat, Marc, and Natasha White. "A golden racket: The true source of Switzerland's "Togolese" gold." *Public Eye Report* (2015): 1–40.
16 Baszillier, Remi., and Girard, Victoire. "The 'natural resource curse' and artisanal mines: The case of Burkina Faso." *The Conversation*, September 23, 2018.
17 Stoop, Nik, and Marijke Verpoorten. "Would you fight? We asked aggrieved artisanal miners in eastern Congo." *Journal of Conflict Resolution* 65, no. 6 (2021): 1159–1186.
18 Crawford, Gordon, and Gabriel Botchwey. "Conflict, collusion and corruption in small-scale gold mining: Chinese miners and the state in Ghana." *Commonwealth & Comparative Politics* 55, no. 4 (2017): 444–470.
19 See Crawford, Alec, and Ledwell. "Digging Out of Conflict," 7.
20 See Crawford, Alec, and Ledwell. "Digging Out of Conflict."
21 Bebbington, Anthony, Leonith Hinojosa, Denise Humphreys Bebbington, Maria Luisa Burneo, and Ximena Warnaars. "Contention and ambiguity: Mining and the possibilities of development." *Development and Change* 39, no. 6 (2008): 887–914.; Campbell, Bonnie. "Introduction", in: Campbell, B. (ed.) *Mining in Africa: Regulation and development* (London and New York: Pluto Press, 2009), 1–24.
22 Campbell, Bonnie K., ed. *Regulating mining in Africa: for whose benefit?* Vol. 26. Nordic Africa Institute, 2004, p. 81.

23 International Crisis Group. Getting a Grip on Central Sahel's Gold Rush, November 13, 2019.
24 Mail & Guardian. Gold rush destabilises central Sahel, November 22, 2019.
25 Mahmoud, Naima. Is Mansa Musa the Richest Man Who Ever Lived? BBC Africa, March 10, 2019.
26 International Crisis Group. Getting a Grip on Central Sahel's Gold Rush, November 13, 2019.
27 Lanzano, Cristiano, Sabine Luning, and Alizèta Ouédraogo. *Insecurity in Burkina Faso–beyond conflict minerals: the complex links between artisanal gold mining and violence*. Nordiska Afrikainstitutet, Uppsala, Sweden, 2021.
28 Bagayoko, Niagale, Eboe Hutchful, and Robin Luckham. "Hybrid security governance in Africa: Rethinking the foundations of security, justice and legitimate public authority." *Conflict, Security & Development* 16, no. 1 (2016): 1–32.
29 OECD. Gold at the Crossroads. Assessment of the Supply Chains of Gold Produced in Burkina Faso, Mali and Niger. The Organisation for Economic Cooperation and Development, Paris, 2018.
30 Guéniat, Marc, and Natasha White. "A golden racket: The true source of Switzerland's "Togolese" gold." *Public Eye Report* (2015); OECD. Gold at the Crossroads. Assessment of the Supply Chains of Gold Produced in Burkina Faso, Mali and Niger. The Organisation for Economic Cooperation and Development, Paris, 2018.
31 Institute of Security Studies, INTERPOL, & Global Initiative against Transnational Organized Crime, (2021). Illegal gold mining in Central Africa, Analytical Report, May 2021.
32 Lezhnev, Sasha, and Megha Swamy. "Understanding Money Laundering Risks in the Conflict Gold Trade from East and Central Africal to Dubai and Onward." *Comprendre les risques de blanchiment d'argent dans le commerce de l'or provenant des zones de conflit en Afrique centrale et de l'Est acheminé vers Dubaï et au-delà), The Sentry* (2020).
33 Smith, P. "Mining in Africa and beyond: Tracking the great gold rush." *The Africa Report* 16 (2020): 1–53.
34 Lezhnev, Sasha, and Megha Swamy. "Understanding Money Laundering Risks in the Conflict Gold Trade from East and Central Africal to Dubai and Onward." *Comprendre les risques de blanchiment d'argent dans le commerce de l'or provenant des zones de conflit en Afrique centrale et de l'Est acheminé vers Dubaï et au-delà), The Sentry* (2020).
35 Ellis, Stephen, and Mark Shaw. "Does organized crime exist in Africa?." *African Affairs* 114, no. 457 (2015): 505–528.
36 Hunter, M. "Pulling at golden webs: Combating criminal consortia in the African artisanal and small-scale gold mining and trade sector." *ENACT Research Paper* 8 (2019): 1–42.
37 Kalokoh, Amidu, and Lada V. Kochtcheeva. "Governing the artisanal gold mining sector in the Mano River Union: A comparative study of Liberia and Sierra Leone." *Journal of International Development* 34 (2022): 1398–1413.
38 International Crisis Group. Getting a Grip on Central Sahel's Gold Rush, November 13, 2019.
39 Collier, Paul, and Anke Hoeffler. "Resource rents, governance, and conflict." *Journal of conflict resolution* 49, no. 4 (2005): 625–633; Alao, Abiodun, and 'Funmi Olonisakin. "Economic fragility and political fluidity: Explaining natural resources

and conflicts." *International Peacekeeping* 7, no. 4 (2000): 23–36; Caspary, Georg, and Verena Seiler. "Extractive industries transparency initiative: Combating the resource curse in fragile and conflict-affected countries" (2011); Alao, Abiodun. *Natural resources and conflict in Africa: The tragedy of endowment.* Vol. 29. University Rochester Press, New York, USA, 2007,.

40 Crawford, Gordon, and Gabriel Botchwey. "Conflict, collusion and corruption in small-scale gold mining: Chinese miners and the state in Ghana." *Commonwealth & Comparative Politics* 55, no. 4 (2017): 444–470; Mehlum, Halvor, Karl Moene, and Ragnar Torvik. "Institutions and the resource curse." *The Economic Journal* 116, no. 508 (2006): 1–20; Ojakorotu, Victor, and Olawale R. Olaopa. "Resource curse and sustainable development in petroleum states of Africa: the case of Nigeria." *Journal of Social Sciences* 49, no. 3–1 (2016): 233–243.

41 Basedau, Matthias, and Jann Lay. "Conceptualising the" resource curse." *Sub-Saharan Africa: Affected Areas and Transmission Channels.* In M. Basedau and A. Mehler (Eds.), *Resource Politics in Sub-Saharan Africa* (2005): 9–24; Kumah, Abraham. "Sustainability and gold mining in the developing world." *Journal of Cleaner Production* 14, no. 3–4 (2006): 315–323.

42 Bannon, Ian, and Paul Collier, eds. *Natural resources and violent conflict: Options and actions.* World Bank Publications, 2003; Diamond, Larry, and Jack Mosbacher. "Petroleum to the people: Africa's coming resource curse-and how to avoid it." *Foreign Affairs* 92 (2013): 86; Duruigbo, Emeka. "The World Bank, multinational oil corporations, and the resource curse in Africa." *University of Pennsylvania Journal of International Economic Law* 26 (2005): 1; Shaxson, Nicholas. "Oil, corruption and the resource curse." *International Affairs* 83, no. 6 (2007): 1123–1140.

43 Auty, Richard. *Sustaining development in mineral economies: The resource curse thesis.* Routledge, Oxfordshire, UK, 2002.

44 Karl, Terry Lynn. *The paradox of plenty: Oil booms and petro-states.* Vol. 26. University of California Press, Berkeley, CA, 1997.

45 Bannon, Ian, and Paul Collier, eds. *Natural resources and violent conflict: Options and actions.* World Bank Publications, Washington, DC, 2003.

46 Kalokoh, Amidu, and Lada V. Kochtcheeva. "Governing the artisanal gold mining sector in the Mano River Union: A comparative study of Liberia and Sierra Leone." *Journal of International Development* 34 (2022): 1398–1413.

47 Humphreys, Macartan, Jeffrey D. Sachs, Joseph E. Stiglitz, Margaret Humphreys, and George Soros. *Escaping the resource curse.* Columbia University Press, New York, USA, 2007.

48 Rustad, Siri Aas, Päivi Lujala, and Philippe Le Billon. "Building or spoiling peace? Lessons from the management of high-value natural resources." In *High-value natural resources and post-conflict peacebuilding*, pp. 587–638. Routledge, Oxfordshire, UK, 2012.

49 Dorner, Ulrike, Gudrun Franken, Maren Liedtke, and Henrike Sievers. "Artisanal and small-scale mining (ASM)." URL: www.polinares.eu/docs/d2-1/polinares_wp2_chapter7.pdf (дата обращения 01.10. 2012) (2012); Bartrem, Casey, Ian von Lindern, Margrit von Braun, and Simba Tirima. "Climate change, conflict, and resource extraction: Analyses of Nigerian artisanal mining communities and Ominous global trends." *Annals of Global Health* 88, no. 1 (2022); Mkodzongi, Grasian. "The rise of 'Mashurugwi'machete gangs and violent conflicts in Zimbabwe's artisanal and small-scale gold mining sector." *The Extractive Industries and Society* 7, no. 4 (2020): 1480–1489; Crawford, Gordon, and Gabriel Botchwey.

"Conflict, collusion and corruption in small-scale gold mining: Chinese miners and the state in Ghana." *Commonwealth & Comparative Politics* 55, no. 4 (2017): 444–470; Ejiofor, Promise Frank. "Beyond ungoverned spaces: Connecting the dots between relative deprivation, banditry, and violence in Nigeria." *African Security* (2022): 1–31; Johnson, McKenzie F. "Who governs here? informal resource extraction, state enforcement, and conflict in Ghana." *Global Environmental Change* 58 (2019): 101959; Ogbonnaya, Maurice. "Illegal Mining and Rural Banditry in North West of Nigeria." A paper published by ENACT (2020).
50 Raineri, Luca. "Gold mining in the Sahara-Sahel: The political geography of state-making and unmaking." *The International Spectator* 55, no. 4 (2020): 100–117.
51 Karl, Terry Lynn. *The paradox of plenty: Oil booms and petro-states*. Vol. 26. University of California Press, Berkeley, CA, 1997.
52 Ross, Michael L. "Does oil hinder democracy?." *World Politics* 53, no. 3 (2001): 325–361.
53 Auty, Richard. *Sustaining development in mineral economies: The resource curse thesis*. Routledge, Oxfordshire, UK, 2002.
54 Sebudubudu, David, and Keneilwe Mooketsane. "Why Botswana is a deviant case to the natural resource curse." *The African Review: A Journal of African Politics, Development and International Affairs* 43, no. 2 (2016): 84–96.
55 Moseley, William G. "Artisanal Gold Mining's Curse on West African Farming." *Al Jazeera English* (July 9, 2014).
56 Yakut, Sarp. "Eurocentrism of the resource curse theory: The case of Saudi Arabia." Master's thesis, Middle East Technical University, 2019.
57 Sachs, Jeffrey D., and Andrew M. Warner. "The curse of natural resources." *European economic review* 45, no. 4–6 (2001): 827–838.
58 Lederman, Daniel, and William F. Maloney, eds. *Natural resources, neither curse nor destiny*. World Bank Publications, New York, USA, 2006.
59 Field, Tracy-Lynn. Artisanal gold mining in South Africa is out of control. Mistakes that got it here, August 3, 2022.
60 Raineri, Luca. "Gold mining in the Sahara-Sahel: The political geography of state-making and unmaking." *The International Spectator* 55, no. 4 (2020): 100–117.
61 Grätz, Tilo. "Moralities, risk and rules in West African artisanal gold mining communities: A case study of Northern Benin." *Resources Policy* 34, no. 1–2 (2009): 12–17.
62 Sini, Snow, A. S. Abdul-Rahim, and Chindo Sulaiman. "Does natural resource influence conflict in Africa? Evidence from panel nonlinear relationship." *Resources Policy* 74 (2021): 102268.
63 Mlambo, Courage. "Politics and the natural resource curse: Evidence from selected African states." *Cogent Social Sciences* 8, no. 1 (2022): 2035911.
64 Hunter, Marcena, Beyond Blood Gold: conflict and criminality in West Africa, The Global Initiative Against Transnational Organized Crimes, November 2022.
65 Boschini, Anne D., Jan Pettersson, and Jesper Roine. "Resource curse or not: A question of appropriability." *Scandinavian Journal of Economics* 109, no. 3 (2007): 593–617.
66 Gueye, Djibril. "Small-scale mining in Burkina Faso." London: IIED (2001).
67 OECD, ALG. "Gold at the crossroads: Assessment of the supply chains of gold extracted in Burkina Faso, Mali and Niger." (2018); Gueye, Djibril. "Small-scale mining in Burkina Faso." London: IIED (2001).
68 Jaques, Eric, Blaise Zida, Mario Billa, Catherine Greffié, and Jean-François Thomassin. "Artisanal and small-scale gold mines in Burkina Faso: today and

tomorrow." *Small-scale mining, rural subsistence and poverty in West Africa.* Practical Action, Warwick, UK, 2006, 115–134.
69 Lanzano, Cristiano, Sabine Luning, and Alizèta Ouédraogo. *Insecurity in Burkina Faso–beyond conflict minerals: The complex links between artisanal gold mining and violence.* Nordiska Afrikainstitutet, Uppsala, Sweden, 2021.
70 Jaques, Eric, Blaise Zida, Mario Billa, Catherine Greffié, and Jean-François Thomassin. "Artisanal and small-scale gold mines in Burkina Faso: today and tomorrow." *Small-scale mining, rural subsistence and poverty in West Africa.* Practical Action, Warwick, UK, 2006, 115–134.
71 Lanzano, Cristiano, Sabine Luning, and Alizèta Ouédraogo. *Insecurity in Burkina Faso–beyond conflict minerals: The complex links between artisanal gold mining and violence.* Nordiska Afrikainstitutet, Uppsala, Sweden, 2021.
72 Côte, Muriel, and Benedikt Korf. "Making concessions: Extractive enclaves, entangled capitalism and regulative pluralism at the gold mining frontier in Burkina Faso." *World Development* 101 (2018): 466–476.
73 North Africa Post, Sahel instability threatens to turn Burkina Faso's gold boom to bust, November 29, 2022.
74 Hunter, Marcena, Beyond Blood: Gold, conflict and criminality in West Africa, Research Report, Global Initiative against Organized Crimes, November 2022.
75 Lanzano, Cristiano, Sabine Luning, and Alizèta Ouédraogo. *Insecurity in Burkina Faso–beyond conflict minerals: the complex links between artisanal gold mining and violence.* Nordiska Afrikainstitutet, Uppsala, Sweden, 2021.
76 Le Cam, Morgane. "Dans le nord du Burkina Faso, les exactions de l'armée contrarient la lutte antiterroriste." *Le Monde* 12 (2018).
77 Demuynck, Méryl. "Civilians on the Front Lines of (Counter-) Terrorism: Lessons from the Volunteers for the Defence of the Homeland in Burkina Faso." (2021); Akinwotu, E, and Agencies. "Suspected extremist attack on Burkina Faso village kills 130 people." *The Guardian*, June 5, 2021.
78 Business & Human Rights Resource Centre. Terrorist gold mining in the Sahel, November 22, 2019.
79 Mail and Guardian. Gold rush destabilises central Sahel, November 22, 2019.
80 Mushi, Neil. "Instability in the Sahel: How a jihadi gold rush is fuelling violence in Africa." *Financial Times*, 27 (2021).
81 OECD. Gold at the Crossroads. Assessment of the Supply Chains of Gold Produced in Burkina Faso, Mali and Niger. The Organisation for Economic Cooperation and Development, Paris, 2018.
82 OECD. Gold at the Crossroads. Assessment of the Supply Chains of Gold Produced in Burkina Faso, Mali and Niger. The Organisation for Economic Cooperation and Development, Paris, 2018.
83 Lanzano, Cristiano, Sabine Luning, and Alizèta Ouédraogo. *Insecurity in Burkina Faso–beyond conflict minerals: The complex links between artisanal gold mining and violence.* Nordiska Afrikainstitutet, Uppsala, Sweden, 2021.
84 Lanzano, Cristiano, Sabine Luning, and Alizèta Ouédraogo. *Insecurity in Burkina Faso–beyond conflict minerals: The complex links between artisanal gold mining and violence.* Nordiska Afrikainstitutet, Uppsala, Sweden, 2021.
85 Lanzano, Cristiano, Sabine Luning, and Alizèta Ouédraogo. *Insecurity in Burkina Faso–beyond conflict minerals: The complex links between artisanal gold mining and violence.* Nordiska Afrikainstitutet, Uppsala, Sweden, 2021.

86 NS Energy. Top five gold mining countries of Africa from Ghana to Burkina Faso, NS Energy, August 28, 2020.
87 United States Agency for International Development. Mali—Agriculture and Food Security (Washington, DC: USAID, 2017).
88 World Bank. The World Bank in Mali, 2022.
89 United States Department of Commerce, Mali Country Commercial Guide, 2022.
90 Arieff, Alexis. Crisis in Mali, US Congressional Research Services, (2013), 2.
91 Stockholm International Peace Research Institute. The European Union Training Mission in Mali: An Assessment. Stockholm International Peace Research Institute, 2022.
92 OEC. Gold in Mali, 2020.
93 Bøås, Morten. "Crime, coping, and resistance in the Mali-Sahel periphery." *African Security* 8, no. 4 (2015): 299–319.
94 Reuters. What is artisanal gold and why is it booming? January 16, 2020.
95 Chambre des. Mines du Mali Une Ambition en Or pour le Mali, 2017.
96 Bøås, Morten. "Crime, coping, and resistance in the Mali-Sahel periphery." *African Security* 8, no. 4 (2015): 299–319.
97 Martin, Alan, and Hélène Helbig De Balzac. "The West African El Dorado: Mapping the Illicit Trade of Gold in Côte d'Ivoire, Mali and Burkina Faso." (2016).
98 Hoije, Katarina. Africa's Crackdown on Informal Gold Miners Spreads to Mali, Bloomberg, November 2, 2021.
99 Hebdo, E. Gold panning in West Africa: Billions of dollars out of control, October 19, 2018.
100 CGTN. Illegal gold mining funding armed groups in Sahel: Interpol, January 16, 2020.
101 Reid, Gabrille. Gold Rush: Artisanal Mining, Crime & Militancy in Africa, SRM, February 1, 2021.
102 Smith, P. "Mining in Africa and beyond: Tracking the great gold rush." *The Africa Report* 16 (2020): 1–53.
103 Scheele, Judith. *Smugglers and saints of the Sahara: Regional connectivity in the twentieth century*. Cambridge University Press, Cambridge, UK, 2012.
104 Bøås, Morten. "Crime, coping, and resistance in the Mali-Sahel periphery." *African Security* 8, no. 4 (2015): 299–319.
105 World Bank. The World Bank in Mali, 2022.
106 United Nations Development Programme. Human Development Report 2020, December 15, 2020.
107 United States Agency for International Development. Niger: Nutrition Profile, 2022.
108 Gambo Boukary, Aboubakr, Adama Diaw, and Tobias Wünscher. "Factors affecting rural households' resilience to food insecurity in Niger." *Sustainability* 8, no. 3 (2016): 181.
109 International Federation of Red Cross and Red Crescent Societies. Operation Update: Niger, Africa, Complex Emergency, MDRNE021, March 31, 2022.
110 Reliefweb, Situation Toumour. Rapport mensuel de monitoring de protection, Région de Diffa (Communes de Diffa, Chétimari, N'guigmi, Gueskerou, Maine-Soroa, Toumour, 2021).
111 Grégoire, Emmanuel, and Laurent Gagnol. "Ruées vers l'or au Sahara: l'orpaillage dans le désert du Ténéré et le massif de l'Aïr (Niger)." *EchoGéo* (2017): 1–23.

112 Abass Saley, A., David Baratoux, Lenka Baratoux, K. E. Ahoussi, K. A. Yao, and K. J. Kouamé. "Evolution of the Koma Bangou gold panning site (Niger) from 1984 to 2020 using Landsat imagery." *Earth and Space Science* 8, no. 11 (2021): 1–25.
113 République du Niger. Ordonnance 2017–03 du 30 juin 2017 portant modification de l'ordonnance n°93–16 du 02 mars 1993 portant loi minière, Vol. 11, 2017.
114 Grégoire, Emmanuel, and Laurent Gagnol. "Ruées vers l'or au Sahara: l'orpaillage dans le désert du Ténéré et le massif de l'Aïr (Niger)." *EchoGéo* (2017): 1–23.
115 Pellerin, Mathieu. *Beyond the'wild West': The gold rush in Northern Niger*. Small Arms Survey, 2017
116 Pellerin, Mathieu. *Beyond the'wild West': The gold rush in Northern Niger*. Small Arms Survey, 2017.
117 Pellerin, Mathieu. *Beyond the'wild West': The gold rush in Northern Niger*. Small Arms Survey, 2017.
118 Rufai, Murtala. "Cattle Rustling and Armed Banditry along Nigeria-Niger Borderlands." *IOSR Journal of Humanities and Social Science* 4, no. 4 (2018): 67.
119 Kisangani, Emizet F. "The Tuaregs' Rebellions in Mali and Niger and the U.S. global war on terror." *International Journal on World Peace* 29, no. 1 (2012): 59–97.
120 Pellerin, Mathieu. *Beyond the'wild West': The gold rush in Northern Niger*. Small Arms Survey, 2017.
121 Pellerin, Mathieu. *Beyond the'wild West': The gold rush in Northern Niger*. Small Arms Survey, 2017.
122 Mackenzie, Knowles-Coursin and Parkinson, Joe. Thousands Flock to Remote, Lawless Sahara in Search of Gold: Miners flock to a remote desert region in impoverished Niger marked by migration, jihadist terrorism and narcotics smuggling, *Wall Street Journal* (October 16, 2018).
123 International Crisis Group. Getting a Grip on Central Sahel's Gold Rush, November 13, 2019.
124 International Crisis Group. Getting a Grip on Central Sahel's Gold Rush, November 13, 2019.
125 Mackenzie, Knowles-Coursin and Parkinson, Joe. "Thousands Flock to Remote, Lawless Sahara in Search of Gold: Miners flock to a remote desert region in impoverished Niger marked by migration, jihadist terrorism and narcotics smuggling." *Wall Street Journal* (October 16, 2018).

3 Control of Mineral Land by a Para-sovereign Power in the Ethiopia-Djibouti Borderlands

Gemechu Adiamassu Abeshu

Introduction

This chapter examines the control of mineral land by As Mohammed Yayo, a non-state actor operating in the Djibouti and Ethiopia borderlands. It raises the following research questions: What are the features of the non-state actor that emerged over a mineral land in Dobi? What was the nature of the relationship between and among the new non-state actor, the state, and the local Afar people? What have been the sources of the non-state actor's legitimacy? Fieldwork for this study was conducted on a mineral land known as Dobi, the second biggest salt mining land in Ethiopia, which was exceeded only by Afdera Salt Lake. Dobi and Afdera salt mining sites are both located in the Afar Region of Ethiopia. The Afar people are predominantly Muslim pastoralists living in the Afar Triangle in Ethiopia, Djibouti, and Eritrea.[1] Following the reorganization of the Ethiopian state along ethnolinguistic lines in 1991,[2] the Afar National Regional State (ANRS) was created, which shares borders with the regional states of Tigray in the North, Amhara in the West, Oromia in the South-West, and Somali in the South.[3] The Afar Region is organized into 5 zones and 32 districts. Based on the 2017 population projections done by the Ethiopian Central Statistical Agency, the population of the Ethiopian Afar state is estimated to be 1.8 million.[4]

Dobi Salt Lake extends over 40 miles across the territories of two countries—Ethiopia and Djibouti—and encompasses territories of two Afar clans, namely the *Lubakubo ke Modaito* clan and the *Wandaba* clan. I conducted fieldwork during three visits to the site between October 2015 and April 2017. I used several data collection techniques including key informant interviews, observations, and a review of secondary sources. I conducted interviews with eight research participants[5] selected from the Afar people and the Ethiopian state. The research participants were individuals who could offer specific, specialized knowledge on a particular issue a researcher wishes to understand better. My role as a researcher was to raise questions and elicit responses from the participants based on informed consent. I used observation to gain first-hand experience with the day-to-day lives of the research participants. This enabled me to understand forms of power at play over Dobi, how actors

DOI: 10.4324/9781003355717-5

acquire access to Dobi, and the land dispute between and among the state, non-state actors (NSA), and the local Afar community. The observation was advantageous in understanding the struggles between actors to establish their control over the mineral land, Dobi. It also helped in understanding whether the actions of the actor groups are in line with their discourses. This was complemented by a review of secondary data sources through land use and policy reports that provided information on forms of ownership and governance of the mineral land, and the geographical, historical, and socio-economic background of the Afar.

For analytical convenience, this chapter is divided into four sections. The first section introduces the research problem and methodology. In the second section, I review the literature regarding the control of minerals lands by NSA. In the third section, I present the rise of a prominent non-state actor named As Mohammed Yayo who controls Dobi salt land located on the Djibouti and Ethiopian border. The chapter concludes with a critical reflection on the implication of para-sovereign power in the Dobi mining site.

Literature Review

The natural resources that are tied to instability, as the proponents of the resource curse argument have shown, are oil and gas, diamonds, columbium tantalite (coltan), gold, platinum, uranium and other gemstones, salt, water, land, grazing pasture, and livestock.[6] Studies have shown that the causal relationship between natural resource endowment and the outbreak of violent conflict (and instability) is complex.[7] In Africa, the resource curse problem intersects with political, social, economic, and ecological factors.[8]

Although natural resources on the continent have played a significant role in many violent conflicts, their character is often embedded in an understanding of the grievance narrative, which underlies social, economic, and political factors.[9] Other studies claim that natural resources are the underlying causal factor in triggering and sustaining instability in Africa.[10] As a result, many see a "resource curse in Africa," whereby easily obtainable natural resources and commodities have essentially hurt the prospects of several African national and regional economies by fostering political corruption and feeding instabilities.[11] Three interrelated dimensions of problems associated with natural resource governance can be distinguishable: slower economic growth, violent civil conflict, types of undemocratic regimes and the rise of non-state forms of political power.[12] This chapter focuses on the last point.

Studies of natural resource extractions in Africa focus mainly on the dominance and mismanagement of the sector by state and multinational companies,[13] and few other studies point to the rise of new forms of NSA. In his research in North Kivu, the Democratic Republic of Congo (DRC), Vogel reveals the convoluted networks of a political and economic order that underpin insecurity in the northwest part of that country.[14] Still, other studies show a resurgence of traditional NSA, such as chieftaincies. In their study in Southern Africa, Capps and Mnwana revealed how chiefly authorities are themselves becoming major shareholders in local mining operations.[15] As a departure from existing studies, this chapter directs attention to the rise of a political power that occupies the state, business, and traditional non-state spheres.

In anthropological analysis, two perspectives attempt to explain the emergence of NSA control over mineral lands in the African borderlands. These are the "substitute argument" and the "deviance argument..[16] The first line of argument, which Utas dubs a "socio-structural explanation," interprets the rise of NSA as substitutes for the declining state power.[17] According to this line of argument, it is the weakness of states (hence a structural void) that opens the space for the rise of NSA in African borderlands. Put differently, a non-state actor exercises power over mineral land where the state has limited sovereignty, or where state authorities do not have sufficient powers.[18] The second line of argument, the "deviance argument," which De Waal calls a "socio-cultural" explanation, advances the proposition that African states deviated from the trajectory of the Weberian model of the modern state after its implantation by colonial powers.[19] This strand of argument suggests that the prevailing forms of power in Africa are embedded in the respective cultures of the societies in which they operate and, as such, create a conducive environment for the rise of NSA over mineral lands and their extraction.

A common thread that runs through both arguments stated above is that non-state actors NSA's control over mineral lands is doomed to disappear as soon as the state rebuilds its structures.[20] A new proposition by the German anthropologist Georg Klute attempts to overcome the limitations of both the substitute argument and the deviance argument. Klute conceptualizes the pluralistic political figuration as *"heterarchy."*[21] Heterarchy underlines the varying distributions of power foci and the fluid and changing relationships between the state and NSA, on a continuum of collaboration and conflict with one another. This study builds on the concept of *heterarchy* to analyze the rise of a *para-sovereign* power that controls mineral land located in the Ethiopia-Djibouti borderlands.

Understanding the nature of the relationship between the state and NSA regarding natural resource governance is crucial. Klute and Trotha introduced the concept of *"para-sovereignty"* to explain the situation of chieftaincy in Mali.[22] They describe a situation in which the local traditional authority appropriates powers and functions from the central Malian state. Another study uses this concept to discuss the takeover of central functions of the state by international development and aid agencies.[23] In this chapter, the concept of para-sovereignty is used to show how NSA appropriated functions of not only the Ethiopian state but also the traditional clan authority in the governance of Dobi salt land, granting permits to salt miners, collection of taxes from salt miners, and providing protection for person and property in Dobi.

The Emergence of a Para-Sovereign over Dobi

Legally, the Ethiopian state is mandated with the governance of natural resources, including minerals. In practice, until 2004, Dobi belonged to two Afar clans (the *Lubakubo ke Modaito* and *Wandaba* clans), and the respective leaders of these two clans had the power to decide who have access to Dobi according to Afar traditional law, known as Afar *Madaha* (which means law in the Afar language). Since 2004, As Mohammed asserted a monopoly over Dobi. The control of a mineral land by a non-state actor, and more importantly outside of the traditional clan authority, is a new phenomenon for the pastoral Afar people.

From the point of view of the Afar people, the rise of a para-sovereign power in the person of As Mohammed (and his networks) as an overlord over Dobi represents a breakaway from the Afar socio-political governance system for two reasons. First, according to Afar *Madaha*, territories belong to clans and respective clan leaders administer clan territories and related natural resources. Second, As Mohammed's control was not limited to the territory of the *Lubakubo ke Modaito*, a clan to whom he belongs, but extended to parts of Dobi that belong to another clan—the *Wandaba*, who live on both sides of the Djibouti-Ethiopia border.

The Constitution of the Federal Democratic Republic of Ethiopia (FDRE) of 1995 authorizes the administration of mineral resources to the state.[24] However, data collected from Dobi shows that this mineral land has fallen under the control of a para-sovereign power in the person of As Mohammed Yayo. In the words of my key informant, Ali Suleyman, from the ANRS's Bureau of Mines and Energy, "As Mohammed is a king over Dobi. He is the one who decides who gets to mine salt on Dobi."[25]

As Mohammed as State Official and Clan Leader

As Mohammed, the para-sovereign power who controls Dobi Salt Lake is both a state official and a clan leader (a non-state authority). Since 2005, As Mohammed has been a state official administrator of Eli Dar District of the Afar Region in Ethiopia. In 2006, he was selected to join the central committee of the Afar Peoples Democratic Party (APDP), which is the ruling party of the ANRS. On top of his state authority, this para-sovereign also has traditional authorities. He is a "leader" of the *Lubakubo ke Modaito* clan. One of my interviewees stated that As Mohammed was handpicked by Ismael Ali Sero, the former president of the Afar Region, to become an intermediary between the Afar Regional State and the clan.[26] My interviews with other members of the *Lubakubo ke Modaito* clan also reveal that As Mohammed is not a legitimate clan leader. For instance, an elder from this clan stated that "As Mohammed is not a legitimate clan leader of the *Lubakubo ke Modaito* clan."[27] While conducting this research, I had the opportunity of meeting the legitimate leader of the clan, and his name is Ibrahim Intibara. He lives in Dichoto, in the Eli Dar District of the Afar Region.

As Mohammed as Para-Sovereign over Dobi Salt Lake

One of the revealing indicators of the rise of a para-sovereign power in the Afar Region may be attested to by investigating who grants permits for salt mining operations on Dobi. For the sake of comparison, let us look at Afdera and Dobi—the first and second biggest salt mining sites in Ethiopia. The FDRE Mineral Proclamation from 2010 states under Article 5(1) "that mineral resources existing in their natural condition on, in, and under the territory of Ethiopia are the property of the Government and all the peoples of Ethiopia."[28] Similarly, Article 11 of the most recent Proclamation (No. 816/2013 Article 11) states

> that the Government, acting through the licensing authority, that is, the Federal Democratic Republic of Ethiopia Ministry of Mines and Energy (MoME) and regional state Bureau of Mines and Energy (BME), shall control and administer mineral resources and grant, refuse and manage licenses.[29]

According to data collected from the Afar Region's Bureau of Mines and Energy, the Bureau gave 1670 licenses to investors in Afdera and none for Dobi. My interviewee from this bureau, an expert who spoke on conditions of anonymity, stated that: "Access to Dobi is off limit to us. I doubt that even you, a researcher, will get access to Dobi. Access to Dobi is granted only by As Mohammed."[30] In the words of Samara University's staff:

> In 2010 Samara University approached the Afar Region's Bureau of Mines and Energy to request a permit to start mining salt in Dobi, but instead of in Dobi the Bureau offered a plot in Afdera. It was clear to us that Dobi was not under the Bureau's control. At that time, as everybody knew, Dobi was under As Mohammed's control. Due to this, Samara University approached As Mohammed. After a lengthy process of pleading with him, we were offered a plot. But As Mohammed did not give us an official letter or permit license.[31]

Since 1991, the FDRE has introduced several proclamations aimed at governing mining operations in the country.[32] Article 11 of the Proclamation set the following obligations on license holders:

> The License Holder reports to the Licensing Authority the quantity and type of mineral mined each month within 10 days from the end of such month and sell the minerals mined every financial quarter within 30 days

from the end of each financial quarter and notify the same to the Licensing Authority.[33]

Furthermore, Article 63 (1) of Proclamation No. 678/2010 states that the holder of a mining license shall pay a royalty based on the sales price of the commercial transactions of the minerals produced by sub-article 2 and 3 of this Article while Article 63 (2) states that the amount of royalty payable by holders of licenses shall be at the rate of 4%.[34] The same Proclamation states:

> Royalty means the payment to the government and the peoples, who are the sole owners of the mineral resources to be made by the licensee for producing minerals from the production site of minerals and the percentage rate of such payment is to be assessed from time to time excluding the price of production and risk expenditures.[35]

According to an interviewee from the Afar Region's Bureau of Mines and Energy, there are 570 active salt mining companies in Afdera Salt mining business, and all have made royalty payments. Data collected from the Afar Region Bureau of Revenue shows that in 2016, the ANRS collected 76 million Birr (about 3.6 million Euros) from Afdera salt producers.[36] By contrast, no royalty has been collected from Dobi ever since commercial salt mining began in 2004. Moreover, in stark contrast to Afdera, Dobi has not become a beneficial resource to the people of the Region. According to Tekola, a senior expert in Afar Region Mining Bureau,

> We hear that Dobi produces from 170,000ql to 250,000ql per month. We also know that As Mohammed collects taxes from all producers at Dobi. But we do not know to whom he pays, or if he pays it. I know he didn't pay a royalty to us.

So, the Afar people are not benefiting from Dobi, as they should. The claim that As Mohammed collects tax payments from salt producers at Dobi is corroborated by evidence from Samara University, one of the actors in Dobi between 2010 and 2014. A review of archives at Samara University reveals that the university paid taxes to As Mohammed during their first year of salt production in 2011.

The Para-Sovereign Amasses Immense Wealth from Dobi

During the time of my fieldwork, I observed that the para-sovereign controls the entire Dobi plain, which extends over 40 miles. Unfortunately, my attempts to inquire from As Mohammed and the Afar Region's Bureau of Revenue about the actual amount of wealth generated from Dobi were unsuccessful. In the alternative, I had to generate an estimate based on the Afar Region's report about the size of salt produced from Dobi.

66 *Gemechu Adiamassu Abeshu*

In 2012, the FDRE Ministry of Trade (MoT) set the prices of salt at the production site at 160 Br ($ 7.30/100 kg), and wholesale prices between 200 Br ($ 9.13/100 kg) and 300 Br ($ 13.7/100 kg).[37] Based on this price, it is possible to estimate the annual wealth generated from Dobi. If all produce is sold at the production site, Dobi may have generated between USD 14.9 million and 21.9 million, while at the wholesale price, it may have fetched between USD 18.6 million and USD 41 million. On average, it may be argued that annually 28 million US dollars were extracted from Dobi. In 2014, the Afar Region received a subsidy transfer from the federal government in the amount of 3.1 billion Ethiopian Birr (which is about US$ 142 million).[38] In comparison, the wealth generated from Dobi amounts to about 19% of the subsidy the Afar Region received during that budget year.

The Para-Sovereign Provides Protection for Persons and Property on Dobi

A para-sovereign power relies on his formal and informal networks not only to build his image but also to protect his business interests. In his seminal anthropological study of forms of authority in a traditional society, Mitchel shows how big men use informal social networks to further their interests and ensure the continuity of their power.[39] Dobi's para-sovereign power uses the local state police force and clan "militia" to protect persons and property in Dobi. As a vice administrator of *Eli Dar* District, As Mohammed is a state authority in charge of the security and justice portfolio of the district. He uses the state's police force to further his interest in Dobi. In particular, he relies on members of the police force stationed in *Dobi* and *Galafi kebeles*. They proved to be As Mohammed's loyal eyes, ears, and hands. Thus, As Mohammed uses the police force to ensure the safety and security of the laborers, investors, and properties on the salt mining site.

In addition to members of the district police force, As Mohammed also relies on the *fihima*, whom he also arms and acts as his militia. The *fihima* constitutes able men who can perform physical duties, such as fights when situations demand. During my extended fieldwork, I observed that the *Lubakubo ke Modaito* clan's *fihima* protects Dobi. As discussed in the previous section, there are two *fihima* around Dobi: *Wandaba* clan *fihima* and *Lubakubo ke Modaito* clan *fihima*. Whereas Mohammed Ibrahim is the leader of the *Wandaba* clan *fihima*, Dawud Mohammed is the leader of the *Lubakubo ke Modaito* clan *fihima*. These leaders estimate the number of their *fihima* at 2300 and 1500, respectively. The author has personally seen the armed *fihima* of the latter clan around Dobi, providing protection and openly declaring that As Mohammed buys AK47s and ammunition for them.

Creed, Greed, Legitimacy, and Conflict

It has been established that As Mohammed generously rewards people in the network. As Mario Kramer noted, this is a classical legitimacy-building technique employed by NSA.⁴⁰ One of the key features of the para-sovereign lord over Dobi is that there is a reciprocal relation between the para-sovereign power, As Mohammed, and the members of his informal networks of mineral resource governance. According to one key informant, "As Mohammed gives salt mining access to whom he chooses, and the recipients of his assistance fight for his interests and image."⁴¹ This reciprocal relationship between the para-sovereign power and members of his network is implicitly acknowledged by As Mohammed himself, as can be seen in the following quotation: "People who have a stake in Dobi salt mining business are like a chicken whose one leg is tied to a rope. Whenever I need something from these people, I just pull the rope."⁴²

As Mohammed's way of evading royalty payments to the state while distributing to the people is partly rooted in Afar traditional morality. During my interview with a participant in Aysaita, I learned that one of the central moral tenets that govern intra-clan relations among the Afar is the obligation to assist each other in defense of their land, people, and livestock and to support each other when their members are entangled in crisis, such as during droughts. Above the clan level, the *Aussa sultanate* also coordinated efforts to aid the Afar people in times of drought. However, the decline of the *Aussa* sultanate created a vacuum in helping the pastoral Afar population affected by recurrent droughts. Traditionally, the Afar relied on a big brother, who provides emergency assistance in times of need, which they call "*Lahu*" (an Afar term describing a response to a distress call or emergency). This responsibility that was shouldered by the *Aussa sultanate* is now undertaken by As Mohammed. Since starting salt mining on Dobi, As Mohammed emerged as a "big man" not only economically and politically, but also socially.

During the 2015 drought, while I was conducting my first fieldwork, I observed As Mohammed delivering fodder and water to the livestock of the *Lubakubo ke Modaito* clan members affected by the drought. I also observed As Mohammed's vehicles transporting emergency food and water assistance to the neediest in the Dobi area. In a biographical interview, Mohammed confirmed that during the 2015 drought, he covered all expenses associated with the emergency assistance provided around Dobi, including transportation with his private trucks.

The actions of As Mohammed speak to Peter Ekeh's argument about morality, in which he identified "two morality spaces," namely, the immoral official public space and the moral primordial space.⁴³ This study corroborates Ekeh's distinction in which he saw morality as shifting resources from the immoral official public space, that is, the state, toward fulfilling their expected moral obligations and benefiting the primordial public, which is perceived to be moral. However, Ekeh's two public spaces are not enough to understand the actions of As Mohammed: his generosity is not limited to his Afar kinsmen alone. According to a key informant, "As Mohammed levies a tax on all salt miners on Dobi. He does not pay taxes to the government, yet he distributes part of it to the people allied to him and his protectors to Afar and non-Afar."[44] Mohammed's generosity to the people in his network and his supporters point to the existence of a third public space, extending Ekeh's two public spaces. The third space, rooted in reciprocal beneficial relations between As Mohammed and the people in his network, seems to be amoral, that is, it is not driven by rights and wrongs, but by greed.[45]

Empirical data presented in this chapter shows how the governance of natural resources, driven by the activities of self-serving political entrepreneurs, creates conflict in the African borderlands. As Mohammed can be seen as one of those entrepreneurs whose greed for personal gain contradicted clan-based communal resource ownership contributing to the creation of the condition for instability. As Mohammed is the exemplification of Zartman's concept of *creed* and *greed*, as he draws on pre-existing ethnic grievances and the historical marginalization of the Afar people as a convenient tool to fend off any competitor coming from other parts of Ethiopia. As Yassin rightly pointed out, the Afar people lived through decades of political marginalization, social exclusion, and economic exploitation.[46] The introduction of multinational federalism in 1995 and the subsequent state reorganization along ethnolinguistic lines created a space not only for the rise of the local ethnic/political entrepreneurs but also for elites such as Mohammed to use historical grievances and ethnic mobilizations to fend off investors from operating in Afar. He is driven by greed—a self-serving private motive for resource accumulation while displacing thousands of the local Afar from the traditional territories. The monopolization of Dobi, a previously communal clan territory created a protracted conflict,[47] which started in 2004 and was still ongoing during the time of fieldwork.

Therefore, there is a heterarchical relationship between the state and the para-sovereign. Heterarchy entails the fluid and changing relationships between and among the different actors, which operate "besides the state" on a continuum of collaboration and conflict with one another. Between 2004 and 2016, As Mohammed granted access to salt mining operations in *Dobi* by taking over the roles of the state and the neotraditional authorities. He collects tax from salt miners on *Dobi*; however, he evades royalty payments to the state. He uses the local state police force and clan "militia" to protect persons and property in *Dobi*. These are some of the core functions of the state that As Mohammed grabbed. Between 2004 and 2016, it may be argued that the state tolerated As Mohammed to perform these central functions of the state. As Mohammed was a "king" and he acted like one.

The standing of As Mohammed and his relationship with the state came under fire beginning in the summer of 2016. With the appointment of a new president of the *Afar* Region, the big man's status and role came under pressure. The new president of the *Afar* Region requested As Mohammed to pay all unpaid taxes and froze bank accounts and assets until it was paid. The relationship between As Mohammed and Afar Regional Government shifted from accommodation to conflict for several reasons. One of the reasons for the new president's big gesture announcement is related to the altercation that took place in the summer of 2016 at the APDP central committee meeting in Aba'ala town. My interviewee, Ali Suleiman, who attended this meeting noted that the big man opposed the nomination for the presidency of Haji Seyoum as the new president of the Afar Region.[48] Not long after his election, the new president ordered the removal of As Mohammed from the APDP central committee and ordered him to pay all the unpaid taxes, which the "big man" has not done until mid-2017. It is not clear whether the state official's announcement is a rhetorical strategy to extract concessions from As Mohammed, or a politics of concern that seeks to redistribute wealth for the sake of the greater public good.

Conclusion

Two important conclusions can be drawn from the discussion in this chapter. The first conclusion is that in the post-2004 period, a para-sovereign emerged over Dobi that took away the power of the state in the governance of mineral resources in the Djibouti-Ethiopia borderlands. This new form of power has unique features, which makes it qualitatively different from the traditional clan authorities. For instance, Dobi's para-sovereign is at the same time a state official, a businessman, and a clan leader. This contradicts the "statist" assumption that state representatives and neotraditional authorities are in opposite relation to one another.

The "para-sovereign," in the person of As Mohammed, took over the functions of traditional authorities and the state. This para-sovereign grants investors access permits for mining salt on Dobi collecting taxes from these investors and protecting persons and property on Dobi. The para-sovereign's functions of granting permits for salt mining on Dobi, collecting taxes from investors, and providing protection relate to Klute's proposition of para-sovereignty.[49] Klute and Trotha introduced the concept of "para-sovereignty" to explain the situation of chieftaincy in Mali. They describe a situation in which the local traditional authority appropriates the powers and functions of the central Malian state. This chapter concludes that this concept may be useful for understanding how big men appropriate some of the functions of the Ethiopian state.

The second conclusion is that the para-sovereign in Dobi constructs and maintains his legitimacy through a redistribution of his wealth to the people in his network and the wider Afar people. In my research, I encountered the dual nature of the para-sovereign overlord over Dobi. On the one hand, he has the appearance of Robin Hood in disguise. He collects taxes from salt producers on Dobi but evades tax payments to the state. He spills some of his wealth to his clan members, an action drawn from the traditional Afar moral space. This is consistent with Ekeh's argument that colonialism in Africa has created two public spaces: the primordial public realm and the civic public realm. These two public realms are governed by different moral codes.

In the primordial public realm, primordial groupings, ties, and sentiments influence and determine an individual's public behavior. This is the moral realm. The civic public realm, by contrast, is historically associated with the colonial administration and based on civil structures: the military, the civil service, the police, etc. Its main characteristic is that this realm has no moral linkages with the private realm. The main theme of Ekeh's article is that most African elites are citizens of these two public spaces within the same society. On the one hand, they belong to a civic public space from which they gain materially but to which they give only grudgingly. On the other, they belong to a primordial public space from which they derive little or no material benefits but to which they are expected to give generously and do (occasionally) give materially. Their relation to the primordial public space is moral, while the one to the civic public space is amoral. Ekeh argues that African elites use the civic public space to gain financially so that they can please their communities. As such, it is regarded as legitimate to be corrupt for one to strengthen the primordial public space. According to him, the civic public space is starved of morality.

The actions of the para-sovereign in evading tax payment from the "civic public space," while distributing financial and material assistance to the primordial space, that is, to his kinsmen during times of need, is "moral." I argue that the fact that the para-sovereign distributes money to members of his network, who are not necessarily members of his clan, points to the existence of a third "space," which differs fundamentally from Ekeh's two public spaces discussed above. The third space, which is rooted in reciprocal beneficial relations between As Mohammed and the people in his network, seems to be amoral, that is, not driven by rights and wrongs, but by mutual reciprocal private interests.

Acknowledgments

This work was supported by the Bayreuth International Graduate School of African Studies (BIGSAS) under the German Research Foundation in the framework of the Excellence Strategy of the German Federal and State Governments.

Notes

1 Yasin Mohammed, "Political History of the Afar in Ethiopia and Eritrea," *African Spectrum* 43, no. 1 (2008): 40.
2 Jon Abbnik, "Ethnic Based Federalism and Ethnicity in Ethiopia: Reassessing the Experiment after 20 years," *Journal of Eastern African Studies* 5, no. 4 (2011): 601, https://doi.org/10.1080/17531055.2011.642516
3 Afar National Regional State Council, *Constitution of the Afar National Regional State* (Samara: Government of Afar Regional State, 1997), 12.
4 Federal Democratic Republic of Ethiopia, *Population Projection of Ethiopia for All Regions at the District Level from 2014–2017* (Addis Ababa: Central Statistical Agency, 2018), 22.

5. All key informant names listed in this chapter are pseudonyms.
6. Richard Auty, *Introduction and Overview. In Resource Abundance and Economic Development* (Oxford: Oxford University Press, 2011), 6; Ibrahim Ahmed Elbadawi and Raimundo Soto, "Resource Rents, Institutions, and Violent Civil Conflicts," *Defence and Peace Economics* 26, no. 1 (2015): 97, doi:10.1080/10242694.2013.848579
7. Michael Ross, "What Have We Learned about the Resource Curse?" *Annual Review of Political Science* no. 18 (2015): 241, https://doi.org/10.1146/annurev-polisci-052 213-040359; Jeffry Sachs and Andrew Warmer, "Natural Resource Abundance and Economic Growth," *Harvard Institute of International Development NBER Working Papers*, 5398 (1995), www.nber.org/papers/w5398.pdf
8. Prince Osei-Wusu Adjei, Abrefa Kwaku Busia, and George Meyiri Bob-Milliar, "Democratic Decentralization and Disempowerment of Traditional Authorities under Ghana's Local Governance and Development System: A Spatio-Temporal Review," *Journal of Political Power* 10, no. 3 (2017): 313, doi:10.1080/2158379X.2017.1382170; Xavier Sala-i-Martin and Arvind Subramanian, "Addressing the Natural Resource Curse: An Illustration from Nigeria," *National Bureau of Economic Research's Working Paper* (2003), doi:10.3386/w9804
9. Cramer Christopher, *Greed versus Grievance: Conjoined Twins or Discrete Drivers of Violent Conflict. In Civil War, Civil Peace*, edited by Joseph Hanlon and Helen Yanacopulos (Oxford: James Currey, 2006), 171.
10. Mamadou Diouma Bah, "Mining for Peace: Diamonds, Bauxite, Iron Ore and Political Stability in Guinea," *Review of African Political Economy* 41, no. 142 (2014): 501, https://doi:10.1080/03056244.2014.917370
11. Rollin F. Tusalem, and Minion K. C. Morrison, "The Impact of Diamonds on Economic Growth, Adverse Regime Change, and Democratic State-Building in Africa," *International Political Science Review* 35, no. 2 (2014): 161, https://doi:10.1177/0192512113496682
12. Francis O. C. Nwonwu, "The Paradox of Natural Resource Abundance and Widespread Underdevelopment in Africa," *International Journal of African Renaissance Studies* 11, no. 2 (2016): 57, https://doi:10.1080/18186874.2016.1246512
13. Agaptus Nwozor, John Olanrewaju, Modupe Ake, and Onjefu Okidu, "Oil and Its Discontents: the Political Economy of Artisanal Refining in Nigeria," *Review of African Political Economy* 47, no. 166 (2020): 667, doi:10.1080/03056244.2020.1835631
14. Christoph Vogel, "The Politics of Incontournables: Entrenching Patronage Networks in Eastern Congo's Mineral Markets," *Review of African Political Economy* 48, no. 168 (2021): 183, https://doi:10.1080/03056244.2021.1886070
15. Gavin Capps and Sonwabile Mnwana, "Claims from below: Platinum and the Politics of Land in the Bakgatla-ba-Kgafela Traditional Authority Area," *Review of African Political Economy* 42, no. 146 (2015): 611, https://doi.org/10.1080/03056 244.2015.1108746
16. Georg Klute and Embalo Bellagamba, *Tracing Emergent Powers in Africa: Introduction* (Cologne: Rudiger Koppe Verlag, 2011), 18.
17. Utas Mats, *Introduction: Bigmanity and Network Governance in African Conflicts. In African Conflicts and Informal Power: Big Men and Networks*, edited by Utas Mats (London/New York: The Nordic Africa Institute & Zed Books, 2012), 16.
18. Capps and Mnwana, *Claims from below*, 611.
19. Alex de Waal, "Mission without End? Peacekeeping in the African Market Place," *International Affairs* no. 85 (2009): 102, www.jstor.org/stable/27694922.

20 Christoph Vogel, "The Politics of Incontournables: Entrenching Patronage Networks in Eastern Congo's Mineral Markets," *Review of African Political Economy* 48, no. 168 (2021): 183, https://doi:10.1080/03056244.2021.1886070
21 Georg Klute and Embalo Bellagamba, *Tracing Emergent Powers in Africa: Introduction* (Cologne: Rudiger Koppe Verlag, 2011), 18.
22 Klute and Bellagamba, *Tracing Emergent Powers in Africa*, 18.
23 Deute Neubert, *Entwicklungspolitische Hoffnungen und gesellschaftliche Wirklichkeit. Eine vergleichende Länderfallstudie von afrikanischen Nicht-Regierungsorganisationen in Kenia und Ruanda* (Frankfurt, New York: Campus Verlag, 1997), 16.
24 Federal Democratic Republic of Ethiopia, "Constitution of the Federal Democratic Republic of Ethiopia," *The House of Peoples Representatives*, June 19, 1995.
25 Suleyman Ali, interviewee, interviewed by Gemechu Abeshu (2016, 13 November). Samara, Ethiopia.
26 Mohammed Aliyo, interviewee, interviewed by Gemechu Abeshu (2016, 1 November), Dobi, Ethiopia.
27 Humed Ali, interviewee, interviewed by Gemechu Abeshu (2018, 24 August), Dichoto, Ethiopia.
28 Federal Democratic Republic of Ethiopia Ministry of Mines and Energy, "Mining Operations Proclamation 678," September 13, 2010.
29 Federal Democratic Republic of Ethiopia Ministry of Mines and Energy, "Mining Operation Proclamation," *The House of People's Representative*, December 19, 2013.
30 Tekola Gebre, interviewee, interviewed by Gemechu Abeshu (2016, 13 November), Samara, Ethiopia.
31 Najash Humed, interviewee, interviewed by Gemechu Abeshu (2016, 19 November), Samara, Ethiopia.
32 Federal Democratic Republic of Ethiopia Ministry of Mines and Energy, "Mining Operation Proclamation".
33 Federal Democratic Republic of Ethiopia Ministry of Mines and Energy, "Mining Operation Proclamation".
34 Federal Democratic Republic of Ethiopia Ministry of Mines and Energy, Mining Operations Proclamation 678.
35 Federal Democratic Republic of Ethiopia Ministry of Mines and Energy, Mining Operations Proclamation 678.
36 Suleyman Ali, interviewee, interviewed by Gemechu Abeshu (2016, 13 November). Samara, Ethiopia.
37 Fortune, "Government Drafts a Directive for Salt Production," *Fortune*, July 14, 2015. https://addisfortune.net/articles/government-drafts-a-directive-for-salt-production-trade/
38 Ethiopian Business Review, "Nation Revises Subsidy Formula, Prepares Close to 179 Billion Birr Budget for 2014–2015," *EBR*, May 11, 2014. https://ethiopianbusinessreview.net/index.php/focuss/item/510-nation-revises-subsidy-formula-prepares-close-to-179-billion-birr-budget-for-2014-15
39 Clyde Mitchell, "Social Networks," *Annual Review of Anthropology* no. 3 (1974): 282. URL: www.jstor.org/stable/2949292
40 Mario Kramer, "The Current Debate on Neotraditional Authority in South Africa-Notes on the Legitimacy and Rise of Intermediaries," In *The Multiplicity of Orders and Practices: A Tribute to Georg Klute*, edited by Thomas Husken et al. (Cologne: Rudiger Koppe Verlag, 2019), 126.

41 Mohammed Aliyo, interviewee, interviewed by Gemechu Abeshu (2016, 1 November), Dobi, Ethiopia.
42 Humed Ali, interviewee, interviewed by Gemechu Abeshu (2018, 24 August), Dichoto, Ethiopia.
43 Peter Ekeh, "Colonialism and the Two Publics in Africa: A Theoretical Statement," *Comparative Studies in Society and History*, no. 103 (1975): 101. www.jstor.org/stable/178372
44 Yayyo Ibrahim, interviewee, interviewed by Gemechu Abeshu (2016, 2 December), Aysaita, Ethiopia.
45 Gemechu Adimassu Abeshu, "The Rise of New Forms of Power in Africa: The Emergence of Big Men in the Afar Region of Ethiopia," *Modern Africa: Politics, History and Society* 7, no. 2(2019): 11. https://doi.org/10.26806/modafr.v7i2.262
46 Yasin Mohammed, "Political History of the Afar in Ethiopia and Eritrea," *African Spectrum* 43, no 1 (2008): 40.
47 Gemechu Adimassu Abeshu, *The Rise of New Forms of Power and Forced Displacement* (Bayreuth University Library, 2022). https://epub.uni-bayreuth.de/5844/1/Gemechu%20PhD%20Thesis%2025%20October%202021.pdf
48 Suleyman Ali, interviewee, interviewed by Gemechu Abeshu (2016, 13 November). Samara, Ethiopia.
49 Georg Klute and Trotha von Trotha, "Roads to Peace: From Small War to Parastatal Peace in the North of Mali." In *Healing the Wounds: Essays on the Reconstruction of Societies after War*, edited by Trotha von Trotha (Oxford: Hart Publishing, 2004), 139.

Part II
Governance Responses

4 Addressing Environmental Injustices in South African Artisanal Gold Mining

Inga Carry and Melanie Müller

Introduction

Artisanal and small-scale mining (ASM) has been an important part of South Africa's mining landscape for years, with an estimated 30,000 men and women working in this sector and around 10 percent of the country's gold production stemming from ASM.[1] Many of these artisanal miners work in and around South Africa's active and abandoned mines. The lack of a clear definition and regulation of ASM as well as the weak governance and oversight of illegal mining activity has created a vacuum of lawlessness and insecurity that has resulted in hundreds of deaths in the past years. Gun violence, child labor and prostitution, water and air pollution, as well as radioactive waste, have made South Africa's artisanal mining sites one of the most violent and hazardous in all of Africa. This has led to a very bad reputation of those who pursue an activity in artisanal mining, even though the range of actors involved in artisanal mining is not homogeneous. On the one hand, artisanal mining is an important element of the subsistence economy in South Africa. On the other hand, the lack of a coherent framework to regulate artisanal mining in South Africa has contributed to the formation of criminal networks that pose a threat, both to the miners and the surrounding communities.

In all of this, artisanal miners and the affected communities surrounding them are emblematic of South Africa's failed transformation from political and economic oppression during apartheid to a landscape of socio-economic inequalities and unaddressed socio-environmental destitution in today's democracy. This chapter examines the situation of artisanal miners and the growing environmental, health, and social crises surrounding South African illegal mining communities within a theoretical framework of environmental and social justice. It argues for an actor-centered approach in order to develop a deeper understanding of the social dynamics and the inequalities in the mining sector in South Africa. Therefore, the chapter examines the inter-linkage between race and class-based discrimination and its intrinsic ideological and material connection to environmental injustice in the gold mining sector by putting a special focus on the role of different actors who are particularly vulnerable. It further investigates key governance challenges in the

South African mining sector and makes recommendations for a framework that could address the issue of environmental justice in the mining sector more systematically.

The findings of this chapter are based on comprehensive desk research and interviews with experts and actors in the artisanal gold mining sector in South Africa, which were conducted in 2021 and in 2022. It is structured as follows: the first section provides a comprehensive introduction to the gold mining sector in South Africa. It investigates the rise of the concept of environmental justice in South Africa and explores how this concept is being used by both academics and civil society activists in order to investigate injustices in the mining sector. The subsequent section provides a comprehensive overview of ASM in South Africa including current legislation governing the sector as well as a differentiation between various actors active in ASM. This is followed by a section examining the environmental and social challenges associated with artisanal gold mining in South Africa and a comparison between those who carry the biggest burden versus those who profit the most from artisanal (illegal) gold mining in South Africa. The final section focuses on the governance of ASM, drawing on and critically examining approaches to regulating ASM in other African countries and ending with a discussion on the viability of these approaches for the South African case particularly in light of the latest developments around formalizing the ASM as proposed by the current South African government.

The Gold Mining Sector in South Africa and Environmental Justice

A Brief Introduction to the South African Gold Mining Sector

Since the Witwatersrand Gold Rush at the end of the 19th century, gold mining has been a key driver of South Africa's economy and a major pillar of its workforce. South Africa's gold sector reached its peak in the 1970s with an annual production of almost 1,000 tons. Since then, the country's gold sector has been on the decline, leveling off at an annual output of around 100 tons in the past few years. Nonetheless, South Africa remains among the world's top 15 gold exporters, accounting for 4.2 percent of global gold production.[2] Domestically, the gold sector contributes roughly R360.9 billion (21.13 billion EUR) to the Gross Domestic Product (GDP) (2019).[3] However, employment in the sector has continuously declined since the 1990s. While South Africa's industrial gold mining sector remains on a downward trajectory, artisanal small-scale mining is booming.

South Africa is one of the countries with the highest levels of social inequality in the world, with inequality having even increased compared to the 1990s.[4] Newer reports, e.g. a comprehensive investigation by the World Bank Group, highlight the lack of employment opportunities—mainly affecting people of color (POC) and women—as the main reason for inequality. The report also revealed cleavages between urban and rural areas: rural residents are disadvantaged in the labor market because of the lack of employment opportunities in their communities.[5] These challenges also particularly affect communities where industrial gold mining used to play an important role but is no longer the central sector. Between 2012 and 2019, industrial gold mining in South Africa lost about 42,000 jobs.[6] Many of these former employees have not found economic alternatives. In a country where youth unemployment—according to official figures—is at 63.9 percent, younger people in particular are trying to earn an income by working in the informal sector.[7]

This explains why artisanal gold mining has become an important source of income in gold mining areas in South Africa. Since the Covid pandemic started, the economic situation in the country has continued to deteriorate, making artisanal gold mining even more attractive. In addition, according to the African Migration Report 2019, South Africa is the country with the highest number of international migrants and hosts 4.2 million people.[8] Many of these people do not have official documents and are therefore also forced to take jobs in the informal sector. This leads to different constellations: in some communities, South Africans and foreign nationals work side by side in the informal gold sector. In other communities, however, violent attacks on foreigners occur. Such tensions and assaults are experienced in different provinces of South Africa, as well as in urban and rural areas. In 2019 and 2020, South Africa experienced violent attacks on non-nationals, mainly from other African countries, but also from Asia. It is not the first time in the history of post-apartheid South Africa, after a first wave of xenophobic attacks in 2008. Since then, many civil society organizations have constantly documented both xenophobic tendencies in South Africa's society and violent attacks on people from other countries. Recent attacks on migrants have triggered an intense debate about the reasons behind them. Some analysts explain these attacks with the apartheid past of South African society, which perpetuated xenophobic stereotypes. Others deny racist motives and instead blame the difficult socio-economic situation of many South Africans.[9]

However, in mining regions, which are particularly affected by poverty and inequality, the effects of the unequal distribution of resources are particularly evident. The illicit nature of artisanal mining increases the problems. In a non-formalized environment, illegally or illicitly mined gold must find its way into the legal market. Due to the high value of gold, smuggling even small quantities is worthwhile. As a consequence, an extensive actor network has formed around artisanal gold mining in South Africa, enabling this trade in gold. Not only illegal actors such as criminal gangs organize and facilitate the trade in illegally or illicitly sourced bold. But also legal actors—such as the police and other security forces or community leaders—profit from these practices.[10] In recent years, this opaque environment has repeatedly given rise to tensions and violent clashes. According to a report from ENACT in 2019, South Africa is not only the "biggest source of illicit gold in Africa" but also "the most lucrative and violent on the African continent".[11]

Environmental Justice in the Gold Mining Sector

Industrial mining sites in South Africa are known to cause significant harm both to the environment and human health. A 2016 report by the South African Human Rights Commission found multiple cases of air and water pollution, nuclear waste and contamination of mining sites, as well as negative impacts for mining communities caused by frequent blasting operations in the vicinity.[12] Other studies have found that (gold) mines, even abandoned ones, are still emitting large amounts of poison, for instance, due to acid mine drainage (AMD) and contaminated dust and soil carrying high levels of heavy metals and radiation.[13] Environmental organizations such as the Mfolozi Community Environmental Justice Network and the Global Environment Trust argue that many of these mining operations have been unlawful because corporations failed to obtain the proper environmental and land use licenses.[14] These allegations weigh particularly heavy as researchers are now pointing to the long-term effects of mining operations for affected communities. Multiple studies have found indications that people living in the proximity of mining sites suffer more often from chronic respiratory diseases than communities further away from active or abandoned mines.[15] Gold dust, in particular, is suspected to be linked to the development of chronic bronchitis, emphysema, and airflow obstruction.[16]

A number of academic articles as well as reports from civil society have investigated not only the role of the gold mining sector in South Africa in general, but also the role of artisanal mining in particular. These articles focus on the development of artisanal mining in South Africa as an illegal or illicit practice and a means of survival. They also investigate the social justice issues in the gold mining sector in South Africa.[17] However, only few connect them to environmental impacts on communities and workers, rarely taking into account that certain groups or individuals are particularly vulnerable and especially affected by environmental destruction.[18] In order to close this gap, the aim of this book chapter is to explore environmental impacts on different social groups and individuals in depth. We will do this by referring to the concept of "environmental justice".

Early approaches to theorize environmental justice focused on the unequal distribution of environmental consequences for certain groups. In particular, the U.S. environmental justice tradition focused on the study of environmental racism, investigating "inequity in the distribution of environmental bads".[19] Schlosberg notes a comprehensive development of the concept of "environmental justice" over the last three decades. It is striking that the academic debate and political practice have repeatedly influenced each other and thus jointly contributed to the further development of the concept. Meanwhile, the environmental justice framework is used by social movements worldwide. The thematic focus has also expanded. Whereas in the beginning the focal point was primarily on the issue of environmental pollution, the concept of "environmental justice" is now used in a variety of other thematic areas for mobilization (e.g. water issues or land rights).[20] In the last decade, a climate justice movement has also emerged.[21]

In South Africa, the concept of environmental justice has a long and important tradition. It has been used by civil society organizations since the late 1980s and became a small, but important component of the struggle against the apartheid regime.[22] By bridging the gap between environmental and social issues, environmental organizations in South Africa also succeeded in highlighting the double discrimination against POC—not only their social and racial discrimination through the apartheid regime, but also the fact that lower classes in both rural and urban areas were very often directly affected by environmental hazards such as air and water pollution, toxic waste, and other forms of environmental destruction.[23]

In the 1990s, an environmental movement developed in South Africa, which explicitly related to the concept of environmental justice.[24] The environmental justice frame has since been used by many different environmental organizations and community organizations in South Africa in order to integrate social issues into their environmental programs and to mobilize local communities.[25] At the same time, Leonard is skeptical about the development of a mass movement in South Africa. While he investigates the potential, he also notes a divide between social issues and environmental issues in terms of political mobilization for a broader environmental justice network.[26] He also shows that "political connections between the mining industry and government, including collusion between mining corporations and local community leadership, have influenced mining approval and development, whilst excluding local communities from decision-making processes".[27]

Nevertheless, there are a number of examples of successful resistance in South African mining: Cock describes mobilization in South African coal mining as a "counter-power" between organized labor, mining affected communities, and environmental justice organizations and investigates the potential for an anti-coal movement.[28] In June 2022, the Makhanda High Court also made an important ruling against Shell, prohibiting the company from seismic surveys and blasting on the Wild Coast that would have had a direct impact on communities in the area. Again, the mobilization of local community organizations and civil society was an important contribution.[29] In artisanal mining, on the other hand, such alliances do not exist. Rather, the landscape of actors is highly fragmented and the unequal distribution of burdens leads to conflicts between different actors. In order to gain a better understanding of the dynamics in the artisanal mining sector, we follow an actor-centric approach that focuses on social and environmental challenges for different groups involved in artisanal gold mining.

Artisanal and Small-Scale Mining in South Africa

There is no universal definition of ASM and its legal status often differs between countries and sectors. Generally, artisanal mining can be understood as any small-scale mining activity that uses traditional methods and rudimentary tools to access mineral ore on the surface or underground.[30] This form of mining is considered labor-intensive but "poor in capital, mechanization, and technology".[31]

According to Traore (1994), "African mining legislation is generally derived from the laws of former colonial powers and does not always draw an obvious distinction between mining concessions for large- and small-scale operations".[32] Although artisanal small-scale mining was legalized in South Africa in 1994 by the newly established democratic government, the 2002 Mineral and Petroleum Resources Development Act (MPRDA)—South Africa's central mining legislation—fails to address the needs of artisanal miners. Current South African mining legislation employs a blanket approach that only loosely defines micro, small, and medium-scale mining but does not adequately accommodate the specific needs and challenges of different types of ASM. For this reason, many artisanal miners are excluded from being legitimate stakeholders by this legislative framework and are consequently classified as illegal.[33] Possible charges range from trespassing, illegal dealing in diamonds and precious metals, corruption, drug dealing, possession of explosives, assault, theft, and environmental damage.[34]

According to the South African Minerals Council, most artisanal mining in South Africa is carried out illegally. The output of illegal mining is estimated to exceed R14 billion (829 million EUR) annually,[35] thus contributing a significant share to South Africa's GDP and making the country one of the biggest sources of illicit gold in Africa. At the same time, ASM creates an enormous financial burden for South Africa's economy. The South African Department of Minerals and Energy estimates that in the gold sector alone more than R70 billion are lost in revenue each year.[36]

Today, around 30,000 artisanal gold miners work in and around South Africa's active and abandoned mines.[37] Locally, these artisanal miners are known as "Zama Zamas", a Zulu phrase meaning "to gamble" or "to keep on trying". Once used to describe the tenaciousness with which they try to make some form of living, often at great risk to their own lives, the term increasingly bears a negative connotation as artisanal miners are stigmatized and associated with illegality, criminality, and violence. In reality, artisanal miners currently lumped together under the term "Zama Zamas" must be further divided into subsistence miners and criminal miners. Subsistence artisanal mining is a form of low-technology mining that provides or supplements income for miners not employed by mining companies. These artisanal and small-scale miners do not possess the necessary licenses or permits to mine legally but, for lack of alternatives, depend on the output of illegal mining to provide food and shelter for themselves and their families.

In South Africa, the boom in subsistence gold mining is in part a direct result of the country's declining industrial gold sector. Many of those once employed by South Africa's biggest mining houses were left jobless and without any alternative income, especially since the country has been grappling with high unemployment rates for decades. Faced with social and financial hardships, many of them try to alleviate their situation by making at least some form of living off mining illegally.[38] Criminal gold mining, on the other hand, is a form of ASM conducted under the auspices of a criminal organization, gang, or network and often comprises a (transnational) web of actors involved in the extraction, processing, export, and smuggling of illegal gold. The leaders of these criminal organizations are in charge of coordinating, financing, and safeguarding the mining operations, connecting with other criminal actors along the illicit supply chain, and maintaining steady relations with corrupt officials and businessmen to uphold illegal mining activities. To safeguard the mining operations against rivaling criminal gangs or law enforcement, the leaders hire security guards to monitor and protect the entrances of mining shafts or to patrol the underground tunnels. According to the South African National Association of Artisanal Miners (NAAM), subsistence artisanal miners increasingly opt to mine above ground and refrain from entering the large mazes of underground mining shafts. This has less to do with potential safety hazards within the unstable and unmaintained shafts, but more to do with dangers posed by the criminal gangs that often comprise ex-soldiers and military-trained personnel with high caliber firearms.[39]

Artisanal small-scale mining includes both surface and deep-level mining. Mining sites are operated by industrial mining houses until they become depleted to the point that large-scale gold exploitation is unprofitable. These then abandoned mining sites create attractive spaces for artisanal miners. While unprofitable for large-scale mining, they still hold small quantities of gold enticing artisanal miners to search for residual minerals. This is what Rosalind Morris calls the difference between "the end of payability of a mine" and the actual end of a mine, and it is within this gap that informal and illegal gold mining most often takes place.[40] Upon ceasing the mining activities, mining companies are supposed to obtain a closing certificate by the authorities and start the rehabilitation process of the mining site. But rehabilitation of these sites is costly and resource intensive and the South African government lacks the "legislative power to force a company to remedy the mine site once such certificate is issued".[41] This has resulted in more than 6,100 abandoned mines scattered across the country with 2,322 of them identified as high risk but only 27 having been rehabilitated since 2009.[42] As a 2022 report of the Mineral Resources and Energy, Home Affairs, and Police Committees on illegal mining reveals, "with the current pace and small budget allocation for the closure and rehabilitation of these mines, it would take Government over 16 years to close these mines".[43] Even when abandoned mines have been sealed off, for example using steel grates and wires or slabs of concrete, a team of researchers investigating the status of abandoned mines across the Sutherland goldfield found that over half of the mines once closed were successfully opened again by illegal miners.[44]

Once illegal miners gain access to a mining site, they proceed with the excavation and processing of gold-bearing material. Because the gold has been retrieved illegally, it cannot be sold on official markets or to legal smelting houses. Instead, artisanal miners sell their loot to known buyers in informal settlements located in the vicinity of the abandoned mines. From there, the gold enters the illicit supply chain but often also ends up mixed into legal supply chains and traded to consumer hubs such as Dubai, Switzerland, or India.[45]

Environmental and Social Challenges Associated with Artisanal Gold Mining

That being said, it has become clear that industrial and artisanal miners, as well as persons living and working close to mining sites, are exposed to a relatively high level of personal health and safety risks. In the case of informal or illegal mining, these risks are often amplified by inappropriate equipment and a lack of environmental and safety regulations.

Environmental, Safety, and Health Risks for Miners and Surrounding Communities

These environmental and health implications linked to mining activities are further amplified in the case of illegal mining. Because this form of mining is conducted with only rudimentary methods and without regard for environmental regulations, it results in significant degradation of the surrounding environment. For one thing, the haphazard digging of shallow pits around the mining site causes the disruption and erosion of soil and contributes to deforestation and the loss of wildlife.[46] Additionally, the use of sluicing sites along the river banks has been found to cause water siltation and a structural alteration of the river morphology.[47] These problems are exacerbated by the nomadic nature of illegal mining, which involves moving the processing sites from one location to another depending on the availability of gold in the mines and water in the river channels.[48] Yet, even more problematic is the use of and exposure to chemicals and toxic metals such as mercury and the high concentration of uranium on the mining sites and the adjacent settlements. Furthermore, it has recently been found that the frequent unregulated practice of underground blasts within close proximity to highly flammable gas and fuel pipelines may pose a significant risk to the surrounding people and infrastructure.[49]

Apart from the ecological impacts, illegal mining activities also create major safety and health issues. Without any protective gear, much less proper equipment, artisanal miners working in underground mines are in constant danger of being killed by rockfall, by inhaling toxic gases, or by drowning as a result of water filling the underground mine voids.[50] As many artisanal miners associated with criminal organizations carry guns as they work below ground, violence and sexual harassment has become a continuous threat. Scores of artisanal miners have fallen victim to fatal shootouts with mine security or rivaling syndicates. Others report being held and raped at gunpoint by superior or rivaling miners with no way of escaping or protecting themselves.[51] According to Sieff (2016), every week one artisanal miner dies in abandoned mine shafts in the Witwatersrand Basin alone.[52]

Around the mining sites, those involved in the washing and processing of the gold-bearing material are regularly exposed to toxic chemicals, particularly mercury, radioactive waste, and AMD, which, if inhaled over long periods of time, can result in chronic illnesses, such as silicosis or asthma. This affects women and children particularly, the former being employed not only for the processing of the gold material but also for cooking and working around the mining sites without any protective gear, and the latter often using the dump sites as playgrounds while their mothers are at work.[53]

Arguably the most dangerous aspect of illegal and artisanal mining in South Africa is the violence and "gangsterism" associated with it. At least 312 artisanal miners have died between 2012 and 2015, although the exact number is believed to be much higher as many deaths are not being reported.[54] Over two-thirds of these deaths were caused by turf wars between rivaling syndicates.[55] In 2017, a criminal syndicate involved in illegal mining murdered 14 artisanal miners on just one day.[56] Rivaling groups patrol the mining sites, always on the lookout for miners resurfacing from the shafts so that they can rob their loot. Reports have also revealed incidents of mining shafts being blasted or sealed to trap the miners underground.[57] Other times, the criminal syndicates send men underground to terrorize other artisanal miners, forcing them to work without providing any food or water and leaving them to die underground only to steal their stones.[58] Above ground, gender-based violence has become a daily reality for those living in nearby settlements. In July of 2022, 8 female members of a film crew working on a music video were raped and robbed at an abandoned mining site by 14 men who are suspected of being illegal miners.[59] Robberies, gang-rapes, beatings, and even murders have become so commonplace in the informal settlements that almost every child will have experienced or witnessed rape or domestic abuse in their years growing up there.[60]

Socio-Economic Challenges: Burdens vs. Profits

The situation of artisanal miners in South Africa is emblematic of the country's changing mining landscape, its systemic socio-economic inequality and persisting high rates of unemployment and poverty. The loss of formal employment in the industrial mining sector both for domestic and foreign workers paired with an influx of migrant workers from other Southern African countries has not been offset by a structural transformation that could provide these workers with alternative legal sources of income. As mineworkers became increasingly retrenched, the rural production shifted toward informal income activities including illegal mining.[61] Wilson (2018), therefore, argues that South Africa's socio-economic context is essentially driving illegal mining activity more than it ever did in the past.[62] The following section will show, however, that not all of those involved in this business are equally vulnerable or disadvantaged. South Africa's illicit mining sector has produced at least some form of income for those who risk their lives in underground shafts; others, meanwhile, exploit their power and the plight of others to profit from an illicit global gold business.

Burdens

Among those that can be counted as the biggest payers of this sub-sector are migrant workers, women, and affected surrounding communities. Around 70 percent of artisanal miners in South Africa are migrant workers from neighboring countries such as Mozambique, Lesotho, and Zimbabwe. They come to South Africa either voluntarily in search for better work opportunities or are recruited directly through criminal organizations and

> transported by syndicate leaders under the impression that they are going to work legally underground, upon their arrival they are kept in safe houses. Their passports get taken away and kept by the syndicates before they are forced underground to work for that specific syndicate.[63]

As such, the large share of non-nationals in South Africa's mining sector is not a new development. Regional migration has been a traditional way of organizing work within the mining sector.[64] Workers from rural areas in South Africa, for instance, migrate to other areas of the country to look for work just as non-nationals from neighboring countries come to South Africa to find employment in the mining sector. Until recently, many countries in southern Africa have served as a "labor reserve" for the South African mining industry.[65] Yet, with the decline of the industrial mining sector and the changing socioeconomic conditions, many of these foreign workers found increasingly fewer and narrowing formal channels of residence and work in South Africa.[66] Upon returning to their home countries, however, they were confronted with high rates of unemployment and a lack of alternative sources of income.[67] This has prompted many of them to return to South Africa, despite the prospect of facing similar problems in the mining sector there.

Highly skilled but with a lack of formal employment opportunities, these migrant workers have become prime targets for criminal syndicates and organized networks of illegal miners. Because South Africa's illegal mining landscape is now largely controlled by these syndicates, artisanal miners are essentially forced to become affiliated with one of these criminal groups, not only to have any chance of an income, food, and equipment but also for personal protection against rivaling gangs as well as law enforcement.

Against this background, migrant workers face yet another burden, consisting in their increasingly negative reputation and xenophobic sentiments from other South Africans. As explained above, the term "Zama Zamas" increasingly bears a negative connotation as it becomes associated with illegality, illegitimacy, and violence.[68] The public perception of artisanal miners in South Africa is thus predominantly shaped by the belief that these people bring violence, social ills, and bad luck to the rest of the country and that human rights organizations such as the South African Human Rights Commission are too concerned with the rights of illegal miners and non-nationals.[69] This portrayal is reinforced by the media and a political discourse that mostly features problems associated with "Zama Zamas" and illegal mining activities but rarely speaks to the relationship between conflict, mobility, and violence.[70] According to Martin, "these perceptions not only breed xenophobic responses to vulnerable people, they also fail to take into account the real criminals behind the Zama Zama phenomenon, thus hampering appropriate policy and enforcement responses".[71] Additionally, the negative press on the social and ecological impacts of artisanal mining (both subsistence and criminal) further prompts the state's adoption of even more repressive laws and policies.[72]

Despite these hardships, artisanal miners are bound by a dependency and stronghold of the criminal syndicates from which it is hard to break free. While there is the odd chance of being lucky and literally "striking gold", for most artisanal miners, the income they make from gold mining in abandoned mines is barely enough to pay for the most basic things like rent and food. In fact, in addition to having to pass on some of their loot to their group leaders, artisanal miners are often paid well below the gold market price, sometimes as little as one quarter of the spot price. Instead, their pay depends on how well they are established within a mine or a community, further reinforcing their dependency on a particular mining group and gang leaders.[73]

Having to live off a meager income for much of the time, most artisanal miners and their families live in informal settlements located in the proximity of the mining sites. As with most townships and informal settlements in South Africa, these communities often lack basic services such as medical and childcare, educational facilities, as well as access to potable water and proper sanitation and drainage, making them vulnerable to environmental hazards and the spread of infectious diseases.[74] Above that, these communities are characterized by high levels of poverty, socio-economic inequality, and violent crime associated with mining syndicates. A poor security infrastructure paired with limited government interventions makes these settlements a breeding ground for criminal activity such as robberies, arms trafficking, beatings, sexual violence, and even murders.[75]

Women, children, and non-nationals are particularly affected by these problems.[76] Traditionally, women, often the wives of artisanal miners going underground, have been in charge of crushing and washing the gold ore at the mining sites. With the introduction of basic forms of mechanization, however, women are forced to search for other ways to make money, mostly by working as prostitutes in the underground mines. Consequently, they are increasingly subjected to sexual and other forms of violence. Their financial dependence, paired with fear of being arrested or deported, prevents many women from seeking medical or legal help.[77] Adding to this is the ambiguous legal status that surrounds illicit mining. The classification of this form of artisanal mining as illegal by the South African state deters victims of mining-related (gender-based) violence and extortion from accessing the criminal justice system. It further prevents both artisanal miners and affected communities alike from forming a critical mass that would enable them to raise awareness for their condition and to meaningfully engage in any process that could improve the situation.[78] Being one of the most impoverished people in South Africa and with public perception against them, artisanal miners have little base for lobbying for their cause. Instead, in the absence of a defined government position or legal clarity as to the distinction between artisanal, informal, and illegal mining, artisanal miners are often categorically postmarked as criminals with no regard for the different motives and roles that exist between artisanal subsistence miners and organized criminal mining networks. As Martin (2019) explains, "the easiest way to 'show results' in the fight against illegal mining is to arrest the miners [at the bottom of the hierarchical chain], not the more elusive criminal bosses".[79]

Profits

It is these illegal mining networks and criminal syndicates that profit most from illegal gold mining and the exploitation of vulnerable communities. Within the criminal groups, those with the most knowledge, experience, and expertise are established as the leaders. They are the ones who act as owners of the abandoned mining sites. As such, they arrange security guards to protect the abandoned mining shafts from rivaling groups, bribe themselves into shafts of active mines, and establish the right connections to get tipped off about imminent security sweeps.[80] They are also the ones who collect the obligatory fee paid by the miners in order to be able to work in their mine and a share of their loot for their own profit.

As leaders of the criminal mining groups, these men constitute the lynchpin between the artisanal miners and the more established criminal syndicates. Apart from illegal mining, these criminal networks are linked to other forms of illicit flows including human trafficking, arms smuggling, tax evasion, and money laundering.[81] It is they who create the means and ways with which illegally mined gold is laundered and eventually introduced into the legal market. Once the gold has left the mines and nearby processing stations, it is sold to licensed scrap-metal dealers, pawnshop owners, or jewelers, who have the legal right to possess and process gold. By mixing and melting in the illicit gold with legal ore and alloys, they disguise its illicit origin, for instance, by making it appear to be recycled gold.[82]

Part of what makes this network of illicit buyers, smelters, and traders possible is an equally established system of corruption with legitimate actors. These include not only local political actors, police officials, and state authorities (such as the Department of Mineral Resources), but also legitimate mining companies. Considering the high financial costs involved in organizing, coordinating, and protecting these criminal mining activities, it seems likely that at least parts of these criminal networks are supported by prominent political figures or business actors.[83] The Directorate for Priority Crime Investigation (DPCI), a South African government organization investigating organized crime and corruption, as well as non-government organizations such as Bench Marks and Global Initiative, has found cases of collusion between South African police officers and the criminal syndicates.[84] According to several artisanal miners, activists, and researchers, local police officers directly profit from the underground economy of illicit gold mining by facilitating access to mining shafts, taking bribes and kickbacks from buyers and syndicates, or by confiscating gold from the artisanal miners to then sell it themselves.[85] According to a recent report by Global Initiative, "[t]hese exchanges are said to be frequent and visible and occur in daylight, showing the brazen nature of such criminality".[86]

The past few years have also seen increased collaboration between artisanal miners groups and members of industrial mining companies. Leaders of criminal groups buy off security guards or shift managers from mining companies to obtain access to active mining sites. A 2015 report by the South African Human Rights Commission further describes how mining companies sometimes use "warehousing"—that is keeping a mining site in limbo between active use and cessation—as a way to incentivize artisanal miners to work in closed mines that are no longer financially viable for large-scale mining. They then collide with the miners to sell their gold through legal channels, thereby evading tax.[87]

Conclusion and Recommendations

This analysis highlights the multi-layered and complex hierarchical relationships in South Africa, which become particularly evident in the example of artisanal mining. Against the background of fundamentally high social inequality and a highly stratified South African society, certain groups are particularly vulnerable. The illegal nature of artisanal gold mining reinforces these complex power relations, as miners operate in a gray zone that the state has so far been unable to regulate. Artisanal miners as well as the surrounding mining communities do not only pay the social but also the environmental costs of illegal mining in South Africa. In many cases, those two aspects go hand in hand.

One of the biggest challenges is that local communities very often lack resources to document these social and environmental consequences and to take measures to fight them.[88] Environmental injustices take place in a very vulnerable social environment, where people are often lacking knowledge of their rights. And even if they are aware, these communities have much else to be concerned about. To be more precise: those who have spent their lives in an informal settlement, without basic social services, often lacking education and primarily struggling to survive, might—understandably—neither have the strength nor the resources to oppose the environmental injustices to which they are being exposed.[89]

As mentioned above, there are a number of environmental organizations in South Africa that are explicitly concerned with justice issues, also addressing the challenges in mining communities. In recent years, some of these organizations have also succeeded in raising serious cases of environmental pollution and even taking these cases all the way to the Constitutional Court. These successes are important. But such lawsuits are usually successful only if social and environmental impacts are so severe that people have already been harmed and, in many cases, carry long-term damages. In that regard, environmental pollution is particularly difficult to identify and mitigate because very often damages show up in the long term, when people have been exposed to hazardous substances over a long period of time and only subsequently develop serious illnesses.

Applying an actor-centered approach, we were able to show that certain groups including non-nationals, women, and children are particularly vulnerable to the impacts of illegal mining. As such, the issue of illegal mining in South Africa is multi-faceted, including environmental, social, and health implications and touching upon the issues of immigration laws, formal and informal work spaces, violence against women and vulnerable groups of society, as well as corruption and security. The question is therefore as follows: how can these multi-faceted problems be solved politically? To this end, much of the current academic and political discussion subscribes to solutions of integrating the ASM sector into the formal economy. Most artisanal mining takes place within the informal sector because the "inflexible regulatory apparatus and rigid policies [...] make securing a license and operating legally exceedingly challenging".[90] The process of formalizing ASM should therefore center on the development and implementation of mining laws and policies that adequately address and accommodate the needs and challenges of artisanal miners. On the side of artisanal miners, formalization would serve to reduce vulnerabilities of miners, particularly with regard to the recruitment and exploitation by illicit and criminal actors. On the state side, formalizing ASM would enable the state to finally capture the revenues of artisanal mining and increase transparency within and about the sector. The newly won financial resources and knowledge could then be used to devise strategies, legal and regulatory frameworks, and regulations that address the needs and challenges of artisanal miners as well as minimize the negative environmental and social impacts of ASM.[91]

In shaping the process of formalization, empirical evidence as well as lessons learnt can be drawn from other African countries, such as Ghana, Zimbabwe, Tanzania, and Mali. Tanzania, for instance, established so-called Centers of Excellence that are integrated into selected governmental Zonal Mining Offices and, among other things, disseminate technologies and provide training to ASM operators. As part of this regulatory framework, artisanal miners are allocated mining rights in designated mining zones or corridors. Even though they are intended to demarcate areas specifically dedicated to artisanal mining, empirical evidence shows that large-scale mining actors have been able to take over mining zones in cases in which large-scale and capital-intensive mining operations have turned out to be more lucrative.[92] This "expropriation and rezoning" of mining areas attests to the "intense resource competition between ASM and large-scale mining operations" and falls under what Hilson describes as the "large-scale mining bias".[93]

Another approach toward regulating the ASM sector is to create strategic partnerships between large-scale mining corporations and actors of ASM. However, here too, researchers point to a power asymmetry between LSM companies on the one side and artisanal miners on the other. According to Hilson et al. (2020), these partnerships are hardly ever altruistic, mostly temporal, and subject to many uncertainties including volatile mineral prices as well as fluctuation in ownership and management of the mining corporations. Hilson therefore suggests a different approach, which he coins "formalization bubbles". The nucleus of this method forms a select group of legal and registered ASM operators that serve as the lynchpin between multiple stakeholders, including informal artisanal miners and prospective licensees, on the one hand, and government officials on different levels on the other hand. A strong argument for such ASM licensees is their local connection and familiarity with both the formalization process and context-specific needs and conditions of artisanal miners and communities, including local languages, demographic and environmental idiosyncrasies, and mining habits. Such a bubble structure would further serve to decentralize and de-bureaucratize the formalization process. By installing local contact points with established lines of communication to both miners and local and national-level government officials, artisanal miners would no longer need to travel vast distances to submit documents, obtain information, or overcome other bureaucratic and financial hurdles all by themselves. Additionally, the development of such formalization bubbles could leverage existing infrastructures such as the abovementioned mining centers as well as national mining associations such as the NAAM in South Africa.

Apart from different methodological approaches, the political and academic discussion surrounding the process of formalization needs to take further note of different concepts of legality and governance. As Lauren Coyle Rosen (2020) explains, the artisanal mining sector is characterized by "informal and shadow governance systems made up of chiefs, elders, ASM sponsors and other local leaders who operate on the authority of customary laws, indigenous spiritualties and informally negotiated arrangements".[94] This might include traditional taxation systems under which artisanal miners pay tribute for their mining output to the local chief.[95] Mensah (2021) adds to this:

> Artisanal miners on their part have also endogenously formulated customs and practices by which they navigate the complex legal plurality of land rights. However, state-centric formalisation as it stands now effectively works to delegitimise any reliance on customary land tenures that are not sanctioned by the state.[96]

Considering this plurality and fragmentation of legal and societal systems, Verbrugge et al. (2015) argue that the development of governance systems for the artisanal mining sector mandates a more open-minded and empirically founded approach to what constitutes "formality" and "legality".[97] In this context, Mensah (2021) discusses the concept of legal pluralism, which as a socio-legal conceptual framework acknowledges the "existence of other legitimising domains besides the state and proposes the use of socio-legal enquiries in unearthing the social interactions, practices and customs that constitute law within these non-state legal systems".[98] Conceding that the concept of legal pluralism and its application to natural resource management and land tenure remains controversial in the political and academic discourse, she argues that

> By embracing a legal pluralist approach to ASM formalisation, governments, donor agencies and researchers can acknowledge that informal artisanal miners who operate predominantly under customary land tenures do not constitute an illegality, but rather a socio-legal field where customary laws, informally negotiated arrangements, customs and spiritualities provide legitimate sources of normative regulation. In so doing, they can retire their perception of informal ASM as an illegality and begin to have the discussion on how best these customary practices can be mapped for a more effective integration into ASM formalisation.[99]

In April 2022, the South African Ministry of Mineral Resources and Energy proposed a new policy on ASM, which drew on many of the concepts and lessons learnt from other African countries outlined above. Conceding that South African legislation so far fails to acknowledge the specific needs of artisanal and small-scale miners, it proposes a legal definition of ASM and SSM separate from large-scale mining, a licensing scheme that includes specific permits and demarcated areas for ASM, a transferability system of mining permits, the creation of regional mining offices and artisanal miners associations, a co-existence system between ASM miners and large-scale miners, as well as the establishment of adequate support mechanisms by the government and relevant policy entities.

At the same time and much more controversially, the proposal envisions artisanal mining permits to be constricted to above-ground mining and reserved for South African citizens only. Considering the influence of non-nationals in South Africa's artisanal mining sector, the attractiveness of underground mines and the centrality of criminal syndicates within the illegal mining sector, critics doubt whether the proposed policy is ultimately able to grab the problem of illegal mining by its roots.[100] As shown in this chapter, any future regulation, framework, or policy regarding ASM, its legalization and integration into the formal economy needs to be organically grown based on the characteristics and context-specific needs of artisanal miners. As shown in this analysis, this must include measures to address underlying structural problems associated with environmental injustices, migration systems, state capture, social equity as much as market-driven incentives for illegal gold extraction and illicit financial flows.

Notes

1 African Minerals Development Centre, "South Africa ASM Profile", n.d., accessed on January 13, 2023. https://knowledge.uneca.org/asm/sa
2 Minerals Council South Africa, "Gold Mining in South Africa", accessed on July 16, 2021. www.mineralscouncil.org.za/sa-mining/gold
3 Ibid.
4 Jeremy Seekings, and Nicoli Nattrass, *Class, Race and Inequality in South Africa* (New Haven/London: Yale University Press, 2005). www.sahistory.org.za/sites/default/files/file%20uploads%20/professor_jeremy_seekings_nicoli_nattrass_classbookos.org_.pdf
5 International Bank for Reconstruction and Development/The World Bank, "Overcoming Poverty and Inequality in South Africa: An Assessment of Drivers, Constraints and Opportunities" (The World Bank, March 2018), xiv. https://documents1.worldbank.org/curated/en/530481521735906534/pdf/124521-REV-OUO-South-Africa-Poverty-and-Inequality-Assessment-Report-2018-FINAL-WEB.pdf
6 Statistics of South Africa, "Mining Industry 2019", 2021. www.statssa.gov.za/publications/Report-20-01-02/Report-20-01-022019.pdf
7 Statistics of South Africa, "South Africa's youth continues to bear the burden of unemployment," *Statistics of South Africa*, June 1, 2022. www.statssa.gov.za/?p=15407
8 International Organization for Migration (IOM), "Africa Migration Report: Challenging the Narrative" (2020): 16. https://publications.iom.int/system/files/pdf/africa-migration-report.pdf
9 Godfrey Mulaudzi, Lizette Lancaster, and Gabriel Herits, "Busting South Africa's myth starts at grassroots: A concerted effort is needed to prevent attacks on foreign-born migrants ahead of this year's local elections", *ISS Africa*, April 2021. https://issafrica.org/iss-today/busting-south-africas-xenophobic-myths-starts-at-grassroots
10 Melanie Müller, "Following the supply chain of "illegal" gold from South Africa" in *Geopolitics of the Illicit* eds. Daniel Brombacher, Günther Maihold, Melanie Müller, and Judith Vorrath (Baden-Baden: Nomos, 2022), 337–360.
11 Alan Martin, *Uncovered. The Dark World of the Zama Zamas* (ENACT, Policy Brief Issue 08, April 2019), 1.
12 South African Human Rights Commission, "National Hearing on the Underlying Socio-economic Challenges of Mining-Affected Communities in South Africa" (September 13–14, September 26 and 28, and November 3, 2016). www.sahrc.org.za/home/21/files/SAHRC%20Mining%20communities%20report%20FINAL.pdf
13 Mike Mwenda, "South Africa, gold mines continue poisoning communities," *Lifegate*, November 8, 2018, www.lifegate.com/gold-mines-poison-south-africa; Cecilia Jamasmie, "South Africa has failed to protect locals from gold mine pollution: Harvard report," *Mining.com*, October 12, 2016. www.mining.com/south-africa-has-failed-to-protect-locals-from-gold-mine-pollution-harvard-report/
14 Katharina Rall, "South Africa: How mining damages communities and the environment," *Human Rights Watch*, August 17, 2018. www.hrw.org/news/2018/08/27/south-africa-how-mining-damages-communities-and-environment

15 Vusumuzi Nkosi, Janine Wichmann, and Kuku Voyi, "Chronic respiratory disease among the elderly in South Africa: Any association with proximity to mine dumps?" *Environmental Health* 14, no. 1 (April 2015): 1–8; see also Olga N. Mayan et al., "Health survey among people living near an abandoned mine. A case study: Jales mine, Portugal," *Environmental Monitoring and Assessment* 123, no. 1–3 (December 2006): 31–40.
16 Olusegun Oguntoke, Matthew E. Ojelede, and Harold John Annegarn, "Frequency of mine dust episodes and the influence of meteorological parameters on the Witwatersrand area, South Africa," *International Journal of Atmospheric Sciences* 3 (2013): 1–10.
17 Pontsho F. Ledwaba, "The status of artisanal and small-scale mining sector in South Africa: Tracking progress," *Journal of the Southern African Institute of Mining and Metallurgy* 117, no. 1 (2017): 33–40; Richard James Roberts, Roger Dixon, and Roland Merkle. "Distinguishing between legally and illegally produced gold in South Africa," *Journal of Forensic Sciences* 61 (2016): 230–236; Robert Thornton, "*Zamazama*, "illegal" artisanal miners, misrepresented by the South African Press and Government," *The Extractive Industries and Society* 1, no. 2 (2014): 127–129.
18 Paidamwoyo Mhangara, Lesia Thomas Tsoeleng, and Willard Mapurisa, "Monitoring the development of artisanal mines in South Africa," *Journal of the Southern African Institute of Mining and Metallurgy* 120, no. 4 (2020): 299–306; Sphiwe E. Mhlongo et al., "Artisanal Gold Mining and its Environmental Stress at Abandoned Louis Moore Mine in the Limpopo Province of South Africa" (ASM Conference "Fostering a Regional Approach of ASM Transformation in Sub-Saharan Africa," 2018); Nicolaas C. Steenkamp, and Vanessa Clark-Mostert, "Impact of Illegal Mining at Historic Gold Mine Locations, Giyani Greenstone Belt Area, South Africa" (Proceedings of the 9th International Mining History Congress, Johannesburg, April 17–20, 2012).
19 David Schlosberg, "Theorising environmental justice: The expanding sphere of a discourse," *Environmental Politics* 22, no. 1 (2013): 37–55.
20 ibid.
21 Brian Tokar, "On the Evolution and Continuing Development of the Climate Justice Movement," in *Routledge Handbook of Climate Justice* (London: Routledge, 2019), 13–25.
22 Jacklyn Cock, *Connecting the Red, Brown and Green: The Environmental Justice Movement in South Africa. A Case Study for the UKZN Project Entitled: Globalisation, Marginalisation and New Social Movements in Post-Apartheid South Africa* (Durban: Centre for Civil Society, University of Kwazulu-Natal, 2004), 1–34.
23 Cock (2004), see EN 1; Melanie Müller, "Adapting Environmental and Climate Justice to Local Political Struggles in South Africa," in *Social Stratification and Movements- Theoretical and Empirical Perspectives on an Ambivalent Relationship*, eds. Sabrina Zajak and Sebastian Haunss (London/New York: Routledge, 2020), pp. 109–125.
24 Llewellyn Leonard, "Bridging social and environmental risks: The potential for an emerging environmental justice framework in South Africa," *Journal of Contemporary African Studies* 36, no. 1 (2018): 23–38.
25 Bobby Peek, "Ground work environmental justice action climate change letter to South African President Cyril Ramaphosa, December 2018," *New Solutions: A Journal of Environmental and Occupational Health Policy* 29, no. 1 (2019): 112–115.

26 Llewellyn Leonard. "Bridging Social and Environmental Risks".
27 Llewellyn Leonard, "Mining corporations, democratic meddling, and environmental justice in South Africa," *Social Sciences* 7, no. 12 (2018): 259. https://doi.org/10.3390/socsci7120259
28 Jacklyn Cock, "Resistance to coal inequalities and the possibilities of a just transition in South Africa," *Development Southern Africa* 36, no. 6 (Sandton, South Africa, 2019): 860–873.
29 Schlosberg.
30 Nalule (2020) further distinguishes artisanal and small-scale mining with the former focusing on subsistence miners and the latter also including enterprises or individuals that employ workers for mining, see Victoria R. Nalule, *Mining and the Law in Africa: Exploring the social and environmental impacts* (Cham, Switzerland: Palgrave Macmillan, 2020), 52.
31 Minerals Council South Africa, "Artisanal and Small-Scale Mining" (Position Paper, 2001), 2; see also Bettina Engels, "Mining Conflicts in sub-Saharan Africa and repertoires of contention" (GLOCON Working Paper Series 2, 2016); Gavin Hilson et al., "Artisanal and small-scale mining (ASM) in sub-Saharan Africa: Re-conceptualizing formalization and 'illegal' activity," *Geoforum* 83 (2017): 80–90; Gavin Hilson et al., "Artisanal and small-scale mining, and COVID-19 in sub-Saharan Africa: A preliminary analysis," *World Development* 139 (2021).
32 Pierre. A. Traore, "Constraints on small-scale mining in Africa," *Natural Resource Forum* 18, no. 3 (1994): 207–212.
33 Kgothatso Nhlengetwa, and Kim Andrea Annafria Hein, "Zama-Zama mining in the Durban Deep/Roodepoort area of Johannesburg, South Africa: An invasive or alternative livelihood?" *The Extractive Industries and Society* 2 (2015): 1–3; see also Michael Kabai, "Illegal Gold Mining Activities in South Africa: 'Zama Zamas'" (The NEWJURIST, March 4, 2020). https://newjurist.com/illegal-gold-mining-activities-in-south-africa.html
34 See, for example, News Agency of Nigeria, "South African police arrest 77 illegal miners," *Peoples Gazette*, April 19, 2022, https://gazettengr.com/south-african-police-arrest-77-illegal-miners/; Reuters, "South Africa lawmakers demand crackdown on illegal mining," *Reuters*, August 2, 2022, www.reuters.com/world/africa/south-africa-lawmakers-demand-crackdown-illegal-mining-2022-08-11/; Mntambo, Nokukhanya, "Case against 21 illegal miners arrested in Stilfontein postponed to 18 October," *Eyewitness News*, October 12, 2022, https://ewn.co.za/2022/10/12/case-against-21-illegal-miners-arrested-in-stilfontein-postponed-to-18-october; see also Report of the Portfolio Committees: Mineral Resources and Energy, Home Affairs and Police on the Joint Oversight visit on Illegal Mining to Five South African Provinces (November 25, 2022): 5.
35 Martin, "Uncovered: The Dark World of the Zama Zamas".
36 Department of Mineral Resources and Energy, "Publication of the Artisanal and Small Scale-Mining Policy 2022 for Implementation" (March 30, 2022): 27.
37 South African Human Rights Commission, "Pfanelo: The South African Human Rights Commission Newsletter" (Newsletter Volume 37, September 2015): 9. www.sahrc.org.za/home/21/files/Pfanelo%20September%202015.pdf
38 Martin, "Uncovered: The Dark World of the Zama Zamas," 4.
39 Report of the Portfolio Committees: Mineral Resources and Energy, Home Affairs and Police on the Joint Oversight visit on Illegal Mining to Five South African Provinces (November 25, 2022): 5, 8.

40 Tamsin Metelerkamp, "The zama zama: Informal mining 'unlike anything else in the world,'" *Daily Maverick*, February 2, 2022. www.dailymaverick.co.za/article/2022-02-02-the-zama-zama-informal-mining-unlike-anything-else-in-the-world/

41 South African Human Rights Commission, "National Hearing on the Underlying Socio-economic Challenges of Mining-affected Communities in South Africa" (November 3, 2016), www.sahrc.org.za/home/21/files/SAHRC%20Mining%20comm unities%20report%20FINAL.pdf, as cited in Sikho Luthango, "Extraterritorial Obligations in the Governance Gap," Policy Paper 1/2022 (Rosa Luxemburg Stiftung, January 2022): 3. www.rosalux.de/fileadmin/rls_uploads/pdfs/Policy_Pa per/Luthango_Policy_Paper_South_Africa_Mine_Closures_1-2022.pdf

42 Human Rights Watch, "The Forever Mines: Perpetual Rights Risks from Unrehabilitated Coal Mines in South Africa" (July 2022): 5. www.hrw.org/sites/defa ult/files/media_2022/07/southafrica0722_web.pdf

43 Report of the Portfolio Committees: Mineral Resources and Energy, Home Affairs and Police on the Joint Oversight visit on Illegal Mining to Five South African Provinces, November 25, 2022.

44 Sphiwe, E. Mhlongo et al., "The impact of artisanal mining on rehabilitation efforts of abandoned mine shafts in Sutherland goldfield, South Africa," *Jàmbá: Journal of Disaster Risk Studies* 11, no. 2, a688 (2019): 6; see also Report of the Portfolio Committees: Mineral Resources and Energy, Home Affairs and Police on the Joint Oversight visit on Illegal Mining to Five South African Provinces, November 25, 2022: 6.

45 Martin, "Uncovered: The dark world of the Zama Zamas"; Marcena Hunter et al., "Illicit Gold Markets: In East and Southern Africa," (Global Initiative Against Transnational Crime, May 2021); United Nations Interregional Crime and Justice Research Institute, "Strengthening the Security and Integrity of the Precious Metals Supply Chain" (Technical Report, 2016).

46 Paiddamwoyo Mhangara, Lesiba Thomas Tsoeleng, and Willard Mapurisa, "Monitoring the development of artisanal mines in South Africa," *The Journal of the Southern African Institute of Mining and Metallurgy* 120 (April 2020): 299–306; Victoria R. Nalule, *Mining and the Law in Africa*, 67.

47 Sphiwe E. Mhlongo et al., "Artisanal Gold Mining and its Environmental Stress at Abandoned Louis Moore Mine in the Limpopo Province of South Africa", 181–193.

48 Nicolaas C. Steenkamp, and Vanessa Clark-Mostert, "Impact of Illegal Mining at Historic Gold Mine Locations, Giyani Greenstone Belt Area, South Africa".

49 Staff Writer, "Parts of Johannesburg could explode or collapse due to illegal mining: Report," *BusinessTech*, November 25, 2018, https://businesstech.co.za/news/government/286804/parts-of-johannesburg-could-explode-or-collapse-report/ ; Felix Njini, Bloomberg, "SA probes illegal miners blast risk under City of Gold," *Fin24*, November 26, 2018, www.news24.com/fin24/companies/mining/sa-probes-illegal-miners-blast-risk-under-city-of-gold-20181126-2; Cheryl Kahla, "Illegal mining brings Johannesburg to the brink of a massive disaster," *The South African*, November 27, 2018. www.thesouthafrican.com/news/illegal-mining-johannesburg-massive-disaster/

50 Sphiwe Mhlongo, and George Oluwole Akintola, "Artisanal and small-scale mining activities as post-mining land use in abandoned mine sites: A case of Giyani and Musina areas, Limpopo Province of South Africa," *Journal of Degraded and Mining Lands Management* 8, no. 3 (April 2021): 2815–2827.

51 Lerato Tshabalala, "Illegal Mining in South Africa: Cash for Gold," Parts 1–2 (CONTACT Series), *YouTube*. www.youtube.com/watch?v=UxETgbBbCqc
52 Kevin Sieff, "South Africa's illegal gold miners forced to scavenge in abandoned shafts in a perilous attempt to survive," *Independent*, March 8, 2016. www.independent.co.uk/news/world/africa/south-africa-s-illegal-gold-miners-forced-scavenge-abandoned-shafts-perilous-attempt-survive-a6919561.html
53 Mhlongo et al., "The Impact of Artisanal Mining on Rehabilitation Efforts of Abandoned Mine Shafts in Sutherland goldfield, South Africa."
54 Cecilia Johnson, "Lethal toll of informal gold mining," *GroundUp*, August 17, 2016. www.groundup.org.za/article/lethal-toll-informal-gold-mining/
55 Martin, "Uncovered: The Dark World of the Zama Zamas", 3.
56 Jan Bornman, Graeme Hosken, Kyle Cowan, and Shenaaz Jamal, "200 die as mine shafts become killing fields in syndicate turf wars," *Times*, March 8, 2017. www.timeslive.co.za/news/south-africa/2017-03-08-200-die-as-mine-shafts-become-killing-fields-in-syndicate-turf-wars/
57 "South Africa's zama zamas: Is this the world's worst job?" *CNN*, August 10, 2015. https://edition.cnn.com/2015/08/10/africa/south-africa-illegal-mining/index.html
58 Lindsey Snell, "Death and destruction in South Africa's 'City of Gold'," *The Investigative Journal* (August 2019), last accessed May 18, 2021.
59 Rédaction Africanews, "South Africa: Fourteen miners charged over rape of eight women," *Africanews*, August 11, 2022. www.africanews.com/2022/08/11/south-africa-fourteen-miners-charged-over-rape-of-eight-women//
60 Statement by Cora Bailey in Lindsey Snell, "Death and destruction in South Africa's 'City of Gold'".
61 Esther Makheta, "Basotho Mineworkers and Zama Zama in Disused Commercial Gold Mines in Gauteng Province, South Africa" in *Borders, Mobility, Regional Integration and Development: Issues, Dynamics and Perspectives in West, Eastern and Southern Africa*, eds. Christopher Change Nshimbi and Innocent Moyo (Cham, Switzerland: Springer International Publishing, 2020), 51–62.
62 Laura-Anne Wilson, "Unshackling South African artisanal miners: Considering Burkina Faso's legislative provisions as a guideline for legislation and regulation" (Master's thesis, University of Cape Town, 2018), 12.
63 Report of the Portfolio Committees: Mineral Resources and Energy, Home Affairs and Police on the Joint Oversight visit on Illegal Mining to Five South African Provinces, November 25, 2022: 9.
64 Esther Makheta, "Artisanal Miners, Migration and Remittances in Southern Africa," in *Migration Conundrums Regional Integration and Development*, eds. Innocent Moyo, Christopher Change and Jussi Laine (Gateway East, Singapore: Palgrave Macmillan, 2020).
65 Ibid.
66 See Jonathan Crush et al., "Migration, remittances, and development in Lesotho," Southern African Migration Programme (SAMP) (2010), www.africaportal.org/publications/migration-remittances-and-development-in-lesotho/; Christopher Change Nshimbi and Lorenzo Fioramonti, "The will to integrate: South Africa's response to regional migration from the SADC region," *African Development Review* 26, no. 1 (2014): 52–63.
67 Makheta, "Basotho Mineworkers," 51–52.
68 Makheta, "Basotho Mineworkers"; Nhlengetwa and Hein, "Zama-Zama mining in the Durban Deep/Roodepoort area of Johannesburg," 2.

69 Report of the Portfolio Committees: Mineral Resources and Energy, Home Affairs and Police on the Joint Oversight visit on Illegal Mining to Five South African Provinces, November 25, 2022: 8.
70 Makheta, "Basotho Mineworkers"; Nhlengetwa and Hein, "Zama-Zama mining in the Durban Deep/Roodepoort area of Johannesburg, South Africa"; Robert Thornton, "Zamazama, "illegal" artisanal miners, misrepresented by the South African Press and Government."
71 Martin, "Uncovered: The Dark World of the Zama Zamas", 4.
72 Andrews Obeng Affum et al., "Influence of small-scale gold mining and toxic element concentrations in Bonsa River, Ghana: A potential risk to water quality and public health," *Journal of Environmenal Health* 75, no. 2 (2016): 178; Kenneth J. Bansah et al., "Socioeconomic and environmental assessment of informal artisanal and small-scale mining in Ghana," *Journal of Cleaner Production* 202 (2018): 465–475 as cited in Linda Mensah, "Legal pluralism in practice: Critical reflections on the formalisation of artisanal and small-scale mining (ASM) and customary land tenure in Ghana," *The Extractive Industries and Society* 8 (2021): 5.
73 Martin, "Uncovered: The Dark World of the Zama Zamas", 5-
74 Amy Weinmann, and Tolu Oni, "A systematised review of the health impact of urban informal settlements and implications for upgrading interventions in South Africa, a rapidly urbanizing middle-income country," *International Journal of Environmental Research and Public Health* 16, no. 19 (September 2019): 1–17; Amy Weimann et al., "Health through human settlements: Investigating policymakers' perceptions of human settlement action for population health improvement in urban South Africa," *Habitat International* 103 (September 2020): 1–11; South African Human Rights Commission, "Response to Questionnaire: Informal settlements and human rights (Submission to the UN Special Rapporteur on the Right to Adequate Housing, May 2018); Lochner Marais, Jan Cloete, and Stuart Paul Denoon-Stevens, "Informal settlements and mine development: Reflection from South Africa's periphery," *The Journal of the South African Institute of Mining and Metallurgy* 118 (October 2018): 1103–1111.
75 see Busisiwe Nkonki-Mandleni et al., "Analysis of the living conditions at eZakheleni informal settlement of Durban: Implications for community revitalization in South Africa," *Sustainability* 13 (February 2021): 1–16; Katharina Rall and Ramin Pejan, "'We Know Our Lives Are in Danger': Environment of Fear in South Africa's Mining-Affected Communities" (Report by Human Rights Watch, groundWork, EarthJustice, Center for Environmental Rights, 2019), www.hrw.org/sites/default/files/report_pdf/southafrica0419_web.pdf; South African Human Rights Commission, "Response to Questionnaire"; Tankiso Makhetha, "Zama-zamas war leaves three dead in revenge attacks," *Sowetan Live*, July 29, 2019, www.sowetanlive.co.za/news/south-africa/2019-07-29-zama-zamas-war-leaves-three-dead-in-revenge-attacks/; Christina Pitt, "4 women, killed in suspected East Rand zama zama turf war," *News24*, January 19, 2018, www.news24.com/news24/SouthAfrica/News/4-women-killed-in-suspected-east-rand-zama-zama-turf-war-20180119; see also Christopher Clark, "'You often get sick': The deadly toll of illegal gold mining in South Africa," *The Guardian*, April 9, 2019. www.theguardian.com/global-development/2019/apr/09/you-often-get-sick-deadly-toll-illegal-gold-mining-south-africa-durban-deep
76 IOM, "African Migration Report" (2020): 16; Catherine Ndinda and Tidings P. Ndhlovu, "Attitudes towards foreigners in informal settlements targeted for

upgrading in South Africa: A gendered perspective," *Agenda: Empowering Women for Gender Equity* 30, no. 2 (August 2016): 131–146.
77 Clark, "You often get sick".
78 See South African Human Rights Commission, "Report of the SAHRC Investigative Hearing: Issues and Challenges in relation to Unregulated Artisanal Underground and Surface Mining Activities in South Africa," (2015). www.sahrc.org.za/home/21/files/Unregulated%20Artisanal%20Underground%20and%20Surface%20Mining%20Activities%20electronic%20version.pdf
79 Martin, "Uncovered: The Dark World of the Zama Zamas," 6.
80 Martin, "Uncovered: The Dark World of the Zama Zamas," 5.
81 Naomi Tite, and Richard Chelin, "Mining and Extractives: South Africa's illegal-mining conundrum," *ENACT*, June 26, 2019, https://enactafrica.org/enact-observer/south-africas-illegal-mining-conundrum; see also Martin, "Uncovered: The Dark World the Zama Zamas."
82 Martin, "Uncovered: The Dark World the Zama Zamas," 5–6; Hunter, Sibanda, Opala, Kaka and Modi, "Illicit Gold Markets," 37; Tite and Chelin, "Mining and Extractives."
83 Interview with Shawn Lethoko, National Association of Artisanal Miners (NAAM), March 3, 2022; see also Report of the Portfolio Committees: Mineral Resources and Energy, Home Affairs and Police on the Joint Oversight visit on Illegal Mining to Five South African Provinces (November 25, 2022): 8.
84 Snell, "Death and Destruction in South Africa's 'City of Gold'"; Parliamentary Monitoring Group, "Illegal Mining: Hawks & Department of Mineral Resources Briefing," August 25, 2017, https://pmg.org.za/page/Illegal%20Mining; Hunter, Sibanda, Opala, Kaka and Modi, "Illicit Gold Markets," 42: see also Report of the Portfolio Committees: Mineral Resources and Energy, Home Affairs and Police on the Joint Oversight visit on Illegal Mining to Five South African Provinces (November 25, 2022): 10.
85 Christopher Clark, "'There's a lot of money down there': The deadly cities of gold beneath Johannesburg," *The Guardian*, October 24, 2019, www.theguardian.com/cities/2019/oct/24/theres-a-lot-of-money-down-there-the-deadly-cities-of-gold-beneath-johannesburg; see also Parliamentary Monitoring Group, "Department of Mineral Resources responses to MP questions: Mine Health and Safety Council on its 2015/16 Annual Performance Plan," April 15, 2015. https://pmg.org.za/committee-meeting/20664/
86 Hunter, Sibanda, Opala, Kaka, and Modi, "Illicit Gold Markets," 42, citing Martin, "Uncovered: The Dark World of the Zama Zamas."
87 South African Human Rights Commission, "Report of the SAHRC Investigative Hearing," 66.
88 Interview with mining activist in South Africa, March 2022.
89 Interview with researcher in South Africa April 2022.
90 Gavin Hilson, "'Formalization bubbles': A blueprint for sustainable artisanal and small-scale mining (ASM) in sub-Saharan Africa," *The Extractive Industries and Society* 7 (2020): 1625.
91 See Patience Singo, and Kady Seguin, "Best Practices: Formalization and Due Diligence in Artisanal and Small-Scale Mining," IMPACT Transforming Natural Resource Management (May 2018): 1–24.

92 Gavin Hilson, "Formalization bubbles", 1624–1638; Patel, K., Rogan, J., Cuba, N., Bebbington, A., "Evaluating conflict surrounding mineral extraction in Ghana: Assessing the spatial interactions of large and small-scale mining," *The Extractive Industries and Society* 3 (2016): 450–463.
93 Gavin Hilson, "Why is there a large-scale mining 'bias' in sub-Saharan Africa?" *Land Use Policy* 81 (2019): 852–861.
94 Lauren Coyle Rosen, *Fires of Gold: Law, Spirit and Sacrificed Labor in Ghana*(Oakland, USA: University of California Press, 2020) as cited in Mensah (2021): 4.
95 Interview with Kgothatso Nhlengetwa, April 1, 2022.
96 Mensah, "Legal pluralism", 4.
97 Verbrugge, B., Cuvelier, J., Van Bockstael, S., "Min(d)ing the land: The relationship between artisanal and small-scale and surface land arrangements in the southern Philippines, eastern DRC and Liberia," *Journal of Rural Studies* 37 (2015): 50–60.
98 Mensah, "Legal pluralism", 7.
99 Mensah, "Legal pluralism", 8.
100 See for example Jason Mitchell, "Opinion: South Africa must regulate artisanal mining carefully," *Mining Technology*, August 11, 2022, www.mining-technology.com/analysis/south-africa-asm-regulation/; Tracy-Lynn Field, "Why illegal artisanal mining in South Africa is out of control," *Mail & Guardian*, August 4, 2022 https://mg.co.za/opinion/2022-08-04-why-illegal-artisanal-mining-in-south-africa-is-out-of-control/

5 The Role of Distributive Justice and Land Law Reforms in Tackling Land Inequalities in the Extractive Industries in South Africa and Uganda

Victoria R. Nalule

Introduction

The crucial role of land in our everyday lives cannot be understated especially as it is essential for agriculture, urbanization, the construction industry, the mining sector and industrialization. Land also provides a habitat for a diverse range of flora and fauna. Despite the crucial role of land, studies show that land is under pressure due to increased population growth, industrialization, deforestation and urbanization.[1] Reliable data shows that up to 40 per cent of the world's land surface has been degraded including 30 per cent of its cropland and 10 per cent of its pastureland.[2] Land degradation has thus been recognized as a major social-economic problem in different parts of the world.[3] Land degradation is attributed to both natural causes and human-driven activities such as urbanization and industrialization.[4]

Moving forward, we note that access to land is key for the successful operation of energy and mining projects and yet the law governing land management and access is ever-changing as reflected in the various land reforms.[5] Land reforms have been experienced in different countries globally to reflect the ever-changing social, economic and political sphere of countries.[6] One might ask, what is the role of justice in land reforms for extractives? This is a question although straightforward and essential; it has received little attention in current literature, which mostly focuses on energy justice in its entirety.[7]

With respect to the energy and mining sectors, it is clear that the land reforms have had various impacts on the extractive industries and on the general economic development in different African countries.[8] For instance, in Uganda, with an estimated 6.5 billion barrels of oil and the various mineral resources, the country has been at the centre of land reforms to tackle the various injustices associated with access to land for extractives.[9] In Zimbabwe, the FastTrack Land Reform Program (FTLRP) positively, and to some extent, negatively impacted the Artisanal and Small-Scale Mining (ASM) sector.[10]

Literature indicates that the FTLRP enabled the newly resettled peasant farmers to access natural resources that were previously enclosed and enjoyed by a minority of white farmers under the dualistic agrarian structure inherited from colonialism: this in essence has driven artisanal gold mining in the

DOI: 10.4324/9781003355717-8

country.[11] Besides Zimbabwe, other countries such as Namibia and South Africa are also still struggling with the land issue. Consequently, these countries have formulated national land policies which are in force in Madagascar,[12] Botswana,[13] Malawi, Mozambique, Namibia, South Africa, Tanzania and Zimbabwe.

There are various drivers for land reforms as stipulated in the examples above, the most common of these being the need to tackle land injustices in different countries.[14] In this book chapter, therefore, we employ the energy justice theory to analyse the impact of land reforms in extractive communities.[15] This theory provides a comprehensive framework for action around five forms of justice, including distributive justice,[16] procedural justice,[17] restorative justice,[18] recognition justice[19] and cosmopolitan justice.[20]

Basically, the energy justice theory and the five justice forms as illustrated above are employed in this chapter with respect to land access for extractives (in the third section). The role of justice has been emphasized in the extractive industries, including in the development of critical minerals[21]; energy justice has also been recognized as being essential for the energy transition[22]; and the development of hydrogen energy.[23]

Taking stock of the above, and applying the energy justice theory to land governance and reforms, we note that injustices have been the source of land conflicts globally.[24] For instance, land conflicts have been documented in Indonesia, where literature has highlighted the problem of resolving agrarian conflicts related to tenure rights over cultivated land in the North Sumatra Provincial government.[25] Besides agrarian land conflicts, literature also suggests that there is increased spatial conflicts related to the increased deployment of renewable energy.[26] It is estimated that required land for energy infrastructure will quadruple in Northern Europe in 2040.[27] In China, a study spotlighted the anticipated land use conflicts influenced by local and policy implementation and the transformation of regional land-use types.[28] The Chinese land conflicts are discussed taking cognizance of the different development policies, which indicate that the accelerated growth and outward expansion of the built-up land area will occupy a large amount of grassland and cultivated land.[29] Furthermore, land use changes, conflicts and vegetation degradation have been linked to the high-refugee population influx in countries such as Uganda.[30]

The land conflicts discussed above have in return been the source of political, social and economic tension between the poor people and the rich people.[31] For instance, industrialization and an increase in large-scale agriculture in Sub-Saharan Africa (SSA) has increased land tension between investors and the local people in many African countries due to the 'land grabbing', with little or no compensation.[32] Goal 1 of the UN Sustainable Development Goal (SDG) is focused on poverty eradication.[33] Over 80 per cent of people in rural Africa rely on agriculture for their livelihood, and yet, most of the extractive activities, including oil, gas and mining explorations, do take place in these rural areas. In this respect, secure land tenures, sound land policies, and better land administration and distribution are key in not only tackling poverty in

SSA, but also in ensuring food security and economic growth.[34] This in essence requires effective and just land reforms, hence the need to incorporate the principle of energy justice in land governance.

Outside Africa, effective land reforms have proved to enhance investment opportunities in different countries. For instance, the 1978 agricultural reforms in China were responsible for reducing poverty and increasing agricultural production in the country.[35] The reforms also dismantled collective farming and conferred land rights on households.[36] In Ethiopia, rural small-holders have been empowered following the land certification programme which started in the late 1990s.[37] The programme is also responsible for reduced land conflicts, increased investments and improved natural resource management.[38] In this respect, therefore, this chapter explores land law reforms in light of the role of energy justice in ensuring the sustainable use of land in the extractive industries.

This book chapter is made up of four sections and this being the introduction. The second section discusses the background and literature review. This section addresses the nexus between land law and the extractives industry. The third section provides the methodology. The fourth section discusses the research analysis in light of the role of energy justice in land access for extractive. The fifth section provides the concluding remarks.

Background and Literature Review

What is Land Law, and How Is It Connected to Extractives?

The increasing importance of land has been a marked feature of the 21st century. Specifically, because land is an assemblage of natural resources including energy resources, minerals, water; and it is also crucial for all social, political and economic human activity.[39] Land, for instance, is instrumental not only in the provision of food and livelihood, but sustainable land use could also contribute to the reduction of greenhouse gas (GHG) emissions.[40] Consequently, land has been recognized as being crucial in addressing climate change, especially given the increasing interest in land-based carbon storage.[41] Because of its surfaces such as forests, land is considered an essential carbon sink. Estimates thus show that in the last decade alone, land-based ecosystems absorbed around 30 per cent of the carbon emissions generated by human activity such as the burning of fossil fuels.[42] Additionally, the energy transition is characterized by a shift from fossil fuels to renewables. Land provides some of these renewable energies, specifically, bioenergy—which is produced from a variety of organic materials such as plant and animal matter.

Consequently, land law, which is also referred to as 'the law of real property', is concerned with land, rights in and over land, and the processes whereby those rights and interests are created and transferred.[43] Understanding the law governing land reforms necessitates an understanding of the term 'land'. Some of the oldest legislation on land law endeavoured to define land. For instance, in England, land is defined in the Law of Property Act 1925, as follows:

104 *Victoria R. Nalule*

> Land includes land of any tenure, and mines and minerals ... buildings or parts of buildings and other corporeal hereditaments; also a manor, an advowson, and a rent and other incorporeal hereditaments, and an easement, right, privilege, or benefit in, over, or derived from land.[44]

Land includes not only the tangible physical property, but also intangible rights in the land such as easements.[45] As such, land law is the study of the creation, transfer, operation and termination of these rights and the manner in which they affect the use and enjoyment of the physical asset.[46]

Access to land is key in the successful operation of various projects across all the sectors of the economy. Consequently, the governance, management and administration of land matters have gone through various reforms in various countries across the globe. For instance, on the African continent, land reforms have been influenced by dissatisfaction among the poor and less privileged people.[47] With the various changes in the social, political and economic aspects of a country, it becomes important to review and reform the statutory land laws, so that they can effectively address these changes.

For instance, socially, we note that many countries in Africa will be at the centre of population growth and urbanization. The International Energy Agency (IEA) data reveals that the African continent will become the world's most populous region by 2023, as one-in-two people added to the world population between today and 2040 are set to be African (more than the combined growth of China and India).[48]

Whereas the increase in population growth requires access to more land to support these people, unfortunately, land is finite and as such, does not increase or decrease depending on external factors. In essence, more people will be competing for the same land and this in return will result in friction and dissatisfaction, especially among the 'have-nots'. Additionally, the global boom in urbanization is projected to increase, as almost 2 billion more people are likely to live in urban centres by 2040 and Africa is projected to contribute one-third of this increasing urbanization.[49] One of the main features of urbanization is infrastructural development, including structured facilities, employment centres, residential buildings, communication and transport networks to mention but a few. All the construction facilities require large chunks of land, not to mention that urban centres are usually densely populated. In this respect, therefore, land issues are not about to end.

In extractive terms, land is key in the establishment of various energy infrastructural projects. For instance, Nigeria is known for its massive oil and gas resources—the country holds the largest natural gas reserves on the continent and was the world's fifth-largest exporter of liquefied natural gas (LNG) in 2018. The country's economy is dependent on the fossil fuels sector; data shows that Nigeria's crude oil and natural gas exports earned US$55 billion in 2018, an increase of US$23 billion from 2016.[50] These massive resources have necessitated the establishment of oil and gas infrastructure. For instance, Mr Dangote, Africa's richest man, has undertaken a project of building the world's largest oil refinery, at an estimated cost of US$12 billion, on 6,180 acres of swampland. Upon completion, the refinery is projected to process 650,000 barrels of crude oil daily. There are various other oil and gas infrastructural projects in different African countries. What is important to note is that all such projects require large pieces of land to be effectively operational. In the acquisition of this land, several social and environmental issues do arise, as will be discussed in this book chapter.

Land Reforms: Case Studies Explored

A. Uganda

Pre-colonial Uganda was characterized by customary or traditional land ownership systems. Before 1888, what is now Uganda (the name didn't exist then) was divided into small kingdoms and a lot of different ethnic groups. Each ethnic group or tribe was ruled by a king or chief. These traditional leaders allocated land to members of their community according to customary law.[51] As in other parts of Africa, customary land tenure emphasized land justice; this was so because it ensured that every single person could access enough land for his own subsistence. Customary land tenure systems are still embraced in Uganda, although these exist alongside other tenure systems such as freehold, leasehold and mailo tenure.[52]

Land legislation in Uganda dates as far back as the early 1900s with the enactment of the Crown Lands Ordinance of 1903. Subsequent to the 1961 Constitutional Conference, the Crown Lands Ordinance was later repealed by the 1962 Public Lands Act (previously Public Lands Ordinance). With the new Act, Crown land was renamed public land and vested in the Uganda Lands Commission. Land Boards were established for every Federal State and every district, which had the same functions with respect to land in the State or district, such functions to be exercised for the benefit of the people of the area.

There have been various land reforms since 1962, the notable ones being as follows. The 1975 Land Reform Decree declared all land in Uganda as public land. The freehold and mailo lands were converted into leases of 99 for individuals and 199 years for public/religious bodies.[53] The 1975 reforms were ineffective and caused massive land conflicts. Consequently, the 1995 Constitution of Uganda recognized the existing land tenure systems and introduced other provisions aimed at addressing the land issues in Uganda. The Land Act was enacted in 1998.[54] The Act provides a legal framework governing land tenure, land administration and the settlement of land disputes. Both the Land Act and the 1995 Constitution have comprehensive provisions with respect to land governance in Uganda. Some of these provisions are highlighted in Table 5.1.

As illustrated in Table 5.1, there are different land tenure systems, some of them being unique to Uganda. For instance, the mailo land tenure system is not available in other African countries.[55] This type of tenure is most common in central Uganda—specifically in the Buganda region. Mailo tenure refers

Table 5.1 Land Regulation and Governance in Uganda

1995 Constitution of Uganda	Constitutional Provision
Article 237 Land ownership	• Land in Uganda belongs to the citizens of Uganda and shall vest in them in accordance with the land tenure systems. • The Government or a local government may acquire land in the public interest. • Non-citizens may acquire leases in land. • Recognized land tenure systems in Uganda include: customary; freehold; mailo and leasehold. • The Government or a local government is to hold in trust for the people and protect natural lakes, rivers, wetlands, forest reserves, game reserves, national parks and any land to be reserved for ecological and touristic purposes for the common good of all citizens. • Landowners under the customary tenure may acquire certificates of ownership. • Land under customary tenure may be converted to freehold land ownership by registration.
Article 238 Uganda Land Commission	• The Uganda Land Commission holds and manages any land in Uganda vested in or acquired by the Government of Uganda. • Consists of a chairperson and not less than four other members appointed by the President with the approval of Parliament.
Article 240 District land boards	• Functions include, among others, to hold and allocate land in the district which is not owned by any person or authority.

Article 243 Land tribunals	• The jurisdiction of a land tribunal includes:
	  o the determination of disputes relating to the grant, lease, repossession, transfer or acquisition of land by individuals, the Uganda Land Commission or other authority with responsibility relating to land;
	  o and the determination of any disputes relating to the amount of compensation to be paid for land acquired.

Article 244 Minerals	• Minerals and mineral ores shall be exploited taking into account the interests of the individual landowners, local governments and the Government.
Article 245 Protection of environment	• Parliament is to enact laws to protect and preserve the environment from abuse, pollution and degradation.

to land holding by a landowner which has its roots from the 1900 Uganda Agreement and 1928 *Busullu Envujjo* Law.[56]

Although the mailo landowners have the same rights as freehold land owners, they must respect the rights of lawful and bona fide occupants and *Kibanja* holders to occupy and live on the land.[57] Section 29(2) of the Land Act defines a bona fide occupant as any person who, before the coming into force of the 1995 Constitution of Uganda, had either occupied and utilized or developed any land unchallenged by the registered owner or agent of the registered owner for 12 years or more; or had been settled on land by the Government or an agent of the Government, which may include a local authority, for instance local council chairpersons.[58]

B. South Africa

Moving on to the political aspects of land reforms on the African continent, it is crucial to understand the history behind the different land law reforms in each country. For instance, before the reforms which commenced in the 1990s, countries were eager to reverse the colonial approach to land law. A cursory look at the case study of South Africa reveals that the country's land reforms, for instance, are mainly driven by the desire to empower farm workers; empower previously unemployed Black people; redress the injustices the Black communities suffered during the apartheid regime, when Black people in urban centres were forcefully removed from their homes that were subsequently declared white. In this respect, land reforms in South Africa can be described as an effort for 'land restitution', aimed at ensuring equality by empowering those who were farm workers under apartheid into owning land and becoming farmers. Land restitution also relates to settling land claims, especially for the Black people who were forcefully removed from their homes as a result of the apartheid government's segregationist Group Areas Act.[59] The Act divided urban areas into 'group areas' in which ownership and residence was restricted to certain population groups. Many Black people were forced to leave their homes in urban areas which were considered white, including Sophiatown, Fietas, Cato Manor, District Six and Greyville.[60] Besides affecting the Black people in urban areas, apartheid land policies also led to the forceful eviction of Black people in rural areas. These brutal policies have had devastating negative impacts on the country, including the social-economic challenges the same people are facing today such as poverty, inequality and landlessness.

The South African example is proof that land reforms are triggered not only by social and economic changes, but also the political history of a country. In this respect, the land reform process in South Africa was mainly characterized by restitution, land tenure reform and land redistribution. These will be expounded on in the next sections. But briefly, under restitution, the government aims at compensating individuals forcefully removed from their land; redistribution occurs where land was bought from its owners (willing seller) by the government (willing buyer) and redistributed, in order to maintain public confidence in the land market. Land tenure systems basically recognized people's right to own land and therefore control the land.[61] For instance, in 1994, approximately 82 million hectares of agricultural land in South Africa was owned by the white minority. The country embraced various reforms aimed at addressing land injustices, and as a result, approximately 4,813 farms had been transferred to Black people and communities between 1994 and 2013.[62]

Scholars have identified two types of land reforms: transformation, and traditional land reforms.[63] The South African example mentioned above would definitely fall under the transformation type. It is also important to contrast transformational and traditional developments: the former aims at change designed to ensure social justice in land laws, and the latter aims to continue the overall thrust of colonial approaches to land laws and land administration. The overall effect of the reforms has been traditional: it was colonial policy to move towards land markets, individualization of land tenure and the demise of customary tenure, all of which have characterized the landscape of the post-1990 reforms.[64] Table 1 shows some of the land reforms in different African countries.

Table 5.2 is not exhaustive. It simply highlights some of the different land Acts and legislation implemented by different countries in different years. However, it is notable that every generation faces different economic, social and political challenges. In responding to these challenges, countries are often obliged to change the legal and fiscal regimes to effectively address the pertinent issues concerning land governance. As discussed previously, access to land is a key aspect not only socially but also economically and politically. In this respect, therefore, countries and politicians often put land matters at the forefront, hence necessitating various land reforms. In the next sub-section, we explore the connectivity between land access and extractives.

Table 5.2 Land Laws in the Era of Land Law Reform

Country	Date	Law
Kenya	1996	Physical Planning Act
	2012	National Land Commission Act
		Land Act
		Registered Land Act
	2016	Community Land Act
Mozambique	1997	Land Law
	2006	Regulation on Urban Soil
Rwanda	2004	Organic Land Law
Tanzania	1999	Land Act
	1999	Village Land Act
	2007	Land Use Planning Act
	2007	Urban Planning Act
Uganda	1924	The Registration of Titles Act (Cap 230)
	1965	The Land Acquisition Act (Cap 226)
	1998	The Land Act (Cap 227) as amended
	2010	Physical Planning Act
	2013	The Uganda National Land Policy, 2013

Land Access and Extractives: Exploring the Environmental Concerns

The negative environmental impacts associated with extractive industries directly affect land use. Petroleum and mining activities, although they are the main source of revenue for the resource-rich countries in Africa, are also a source of pollution and human rights abuses. These sectors are characterized by oil spillages, gas flaring, discharge of heavy metals from mining, chemical pollution, and mine dumps such as tailings and slag material. All these negatively impact on land use, especially farming, fishing and hunting.

For instance, with respect to the petroleum industry and the related environmental and land use issues, Nigeria provides a good example, especially with respect to gas flaring and oil spillage. The local communities in the Niger Delta region have suffered the impacts associated with gas flaring and oil spills, making it hard for them to utilize their land. An 'oil spill' is defined as the accidental release of a liquid petroleum hydrocarbon into the environment due to human activity. In Nigeria, there are several causes of oil spills, and it has been noted that approximately 50 per cent of the spills are attributable to pipeline vandalism and tanker accidents; 28 per cent of spills are due to sabotage; production and operation account for 21 per cent; and the remaining 1 per cent is due to deficient equipment used in production. Additionally, the deliberate blowing up of pipelines by militant groups has also increased oil spillage in the Niger Delta region.[65]

Oil spills are very prevalent in Nigeria and it is estimated that between 1 million and 13 million tons of hydrocarbons have been spilled in the region over the last 50 years. These have led to the destruction of rainforest habitat occupying land equating to 7,400 km^2, the loss of mangrove forests, the destruction of an equivalent of a year's supply of food, and causing diseases afflicting the local people, just to mention but a few.[66]

With respect to the mining industry, the waste generated contains high concentrations of metals and metalloids which have resulted in contamination of ground and surface water. For instance, the mining of gold in the Witwatersrand Basin of South Africa has resulted in environmental degradation. It has been observed that the concentrations of heavy toxic metals—mainly arsenic (As), cadmium (Cd), cobalt (Co), copper (Cu), lead (Pb), uranium (U) and mercury (Hg)—from gold sites are above acceptable levels in South Africa.[67] Other African countries including South Sudan; the DRC and Uganda are also victims of the negative environmental impacts associated with the mining industry.

Method and Conceptual Framework

This research is focused on conceptual review. In the second section, we gave a narrative review of the literature, having in mind that the concept of land justice—which is the subject of our investigation—is vague and unsystematic. Moreover, our analysis is multidimensional (we address interrelated but

110   *Victoria R. Nalule*

different dimensions of justice), and our research question narrowly focuses on how we can employ the energy justice theory in land law reforms for extractive sectors?

Given the gaps in narrative reviews such as lack of transparency,[68] this research spotlights the viewpoint and theoretical framework for the analysis. As such, we employ the energy justice viewpoint and also expound on the JUST framework as a theoretical framework. The analysis and conclusion in the research are therefore relevant taking cognizance of the viewpoint and theoretical framework above.

To understand the main issues associated with land justice through the lens of the energy justice viewpoint, we deploy a qualitative analysis to understand the subject of land justice. Country case studies including Uganda and South Africa are analysed to identify if the JUST theoretical framework is reflected in these countries' land law reforms. Because the concept of land justice is vague, there is only so much that a qualitative analysis can contribute without becoming over complex. As such, the qualitative analysis in this research focuses on identifying the literature on procedural justice in acquiring land for extractive projects. We also look into the aspect of distributive justice in land governance for extractives.

Having in mind the external and internal dimensions of justice, and also having in mind the JUST Framework, the literature has linked the five dimensions of energy justices by relating it to land access in the extractive sector, as illustrated below:

- procedure land justice: this focuses on the legal and regulatory processes for accessing land for energy and mining projects (including relocations of affected communities; fair compensation)
- distributive land justice: concerns the distribution of benefits and also the negatives that accrue from using land for extractive projects (including addressing the environmental damage; sharing the oil and mining revenues equally)
- recognition land justice: entails recognizing and protecting the land rights of the different local communities (for instance, cultural land has to be respected; community and customary land tenures have to be recognized)
- restorative land justice: entails ensuring that the land is rehabilitated at the end of oil and mining activities (this for instance includes mining closures and decommissioning).[69]
- cosmopolitanism land justice: this stems from the notion that we are all citizens of the world, and as such, we should consider the impact of extractives on land use beyond our borders and from a global perspective.[70]

Whereas there is massive literature on the five dimensions of energy justice, in the different energy spheres including in hydrogen development[71]; energy justice in the energy transition[72]; solar energy justice[73]; energy justice in the electricity tariff design[74]; to mention but a few. There is limited literature linking the energy justice theory to access to land for extractives. The review of the literature suggests that papers deal more often with the restorative land justice, which takes into environmental protection by ensuring that the land is rehabilitated at the end of oil and mining activities (this for instance includes mining closures and decommissioning).[75] Energy justice theory has also been deployed to analyse land issues for wind energy projects.[76] However, there is still a gap regarding deploying energy justice theory in the land reforms. This is where the present article contributes.

The energy justice theory is now an accepted tool for investigating the occurrences of (in) justices throughout the energy lifecycle.[77] The justice principles are therefore applied to energy policy, energy production and consumption, energy activism, energy security and climate change.[78] Consequently, in this research, we explore how energy justice principles could be incorporated in land governance and land reforms with a view of ensuring procedural and distributive justice in accessing land for extractive projects.

The energy justice theory as an ethical framework can therefore assist in addressing the injustices reflected with issues concerning little or no compensation for energy project lands. It could also unpack the socio-economic complexities in relocating people from land that is used for extractive projects. This could be achieved taking into consideration the energy trilemma, which seeks to balance the economics, finance, politics—energy security and the environment—climate change.[79] Indeed, the energy trilemma has been recognized for its role in sustainable economic development.[80] This is because the energy trilemma reflects the three pillars of sustainability which include the environmental, economic and social pillar.[81]

Whereas there are different forms of energy justice, the research will focus on the distributive and procedural justice as a way of narrowing down the study, given its exploratory nature and to allow an in-depth understanding rather than broadening the scope with limited contextualized literature. We therefore rely on desktop research, specifically literature review to unpack the distributive and the procedural justice aspects in land reforms. We analysed two country case studies including Uganda and South Africa (in the third and fourth sections).

Analysis

In this section, drawing examples from South Africa and Uganda, we explore the various land law reforms and how these reflect the energy justice theories, specifically distributive and procedural justice. As discussed in the third section, borrowing the energy justice theory to land discussions, we note that procedure land justice focuses on the legal and regulatory processes for accessing land for energy and mining projects (including relocations of affected communities; fair compensation). Distributive land justice on the other hand concerns the distribution of benefits and also the negatives that accrue from using land for extractive projects (including addressing the environmental damage, sharing

112   *Victoria R. Nalule*

the oil and mining revenues equally). This section will unpack the results relating to the application of distributive justice and procedural justice in land governance for extractives.

Procedural Justice

One of the components of procedural justice is to ensure fairness in the processes that allocate resources and resolve disputes. The ILO Convention 169 recognizes Indigenous peoples' right to self-determination within a nation-state, while setting standards for national governments regarding Indigenous peoples' economic, socio-cultural, and political rights, including the right to a land base.[82] Some of the principles covered in the Convention include: the right to be consulted; the right to decide own development priorities; protection of customs and customary law. The findings from this study show key procedural justice issues around communities' participation in the land reform processes.

Communities' Participation in the Land Reform Processes: South African Review

From a JUST theoretical framework, land reforms are focused on promoting equity, reducing poverty and ensuring justice for both the rich and poor with regard to land access. Literature indicates that effective land reforms could benefit the rural households that rely on agricultural for their livelihood including those involved inIndigenous pastoral.[83] Despite their reliance on land, a significant number of farm families estimated at 100 million families, comprising about 500 million people,[84] in less developed countries lack ownership of land, as most of them earn their living as tenant farmers or agricultural laborers.[85]

In light of the above, therefore, procedural justice is essential in ensuring that the poor families and those reliant on agriculture in rural communities are represented and consulted during the processes of land reforms. It is also essential to note that extractive activities including oil, gas and mining extraction are often carried out in rural communities. Consequently, it becomes imperative to involve these communities in the land law reforms that are likely to impact them.

From this study, we found that procedural justice was at the heart of the land reforms experienced in South Africa. The South African example highlights the different struggles of countries such as those in Southern Africa, which up to recently are focused on finding the best solution to ensure land justice. Previous land injustices, as manifested in the 1913 Natives Land Act, characterized the apartheid regime in South Africa.[86] These in turn influenced the current land reforms in South Africa including land redistribution, which indeed reflects the procedural energy justice concept.

However, to date, many Black South Africans remain landless. This has influenced different approaches including a suggestion of expropriation without compensation (EWC).[87] As far back as 2006, the African National

Congress (ANC) mentioned its intentions to enforce expropriation of the various lands that were unjustly taken from the Black Africans.[88] In this respect, in 2017, the ANC-led government made it clear that it would amend Section 25 of the South African Constitution regarding property rights to implement land EWC.[89]

This was followed by the Parliamentary motion in February 2018 aimed at reviewing the property ownership clause of the Constitution, to allow for the expropriation of land in the public interest without compensation.[90] The motion laid the ground for more parliamentary discussions on constitutional land reforms.

Whilst this sub-section does not go into detail on all the various land reforms that have taken place in South Africa, it is clear that these have been influenced by the need for equality and ensuring land justice. The reforms aim not only to correct historical wrongs but also to confront present social and economic inequities and secure an equality-based future for all. This implies that the reforms are transformative in nature and encompass the procedural energy justice theory.

Distributive Justice

Accessing land extractive projects not only leads to relocations, but it also raises questions of the (un)fairness of compensation given to those whose land is expropriated for extractive projects. These indeed raise issues of both procedural and distributive justice. Distributive land justice concerns the distribution of benefits and also the negatives that accrue from using land for extractive projects (including addressing the environmental damage, sharing the oil and mining revenues equally).

There are various land issues in Uganda which cannot be dealt with exhaustively in this section. Rather, the focus here relates to the compensation of local communities for their land in resource-rich areas.

In Uganda, the ultimate ownership of land is vested in the country's citizens. The Constitution, under Article 237(1) and (3), vests the ownership of land in the citizens of Uganda.[91] The article further outlines the different tenure systems under which the land can be held.[92] As such, the owner of the land is entitled to compensation if oil, gas or mining activities are to be carried out on his/her land. The reasoning behind compensation is based on the fact that a mining title does not per se extinguish the rights of the landowner; rather it grants the owner of a mining licence a right to exploit the natural resources present in the subsoil, which definitely requires access to the surface.[93]

With respect to the nexus between land access and extractives, it is worth noting that in Uganda, natural resources, including hydrocarbons and minerals, are held by the government on behalf of the people. In this respect, the state will intervene to ensure that the landowners are fully compensated. If no agreement can be reached, then the state may move to expropriate the land for mining purposes, in which case the landowner will still be entitled to compensation.

Reflecting to the land expropriated for the oil refinery project in Buseruka sub-country in Hoima District, Uganda, research shows that some indigenous people did not benefit from the project.[94] In this scheme, households could choose between cash compensation as a resettlement measure, or a relocation to an established site with a house and some agricultural land.[95] Whereas these options were freely available for every household,[96] research shows that most cash compensated households became more vulnerable and poorer, compared to formally resettled households. This in essence highlights the lack of distributive justice in the compensation and resettlement of affected communities – specifically where inadequate measures such as cash compensation are embraced by the host government and oil companies, to deal with poor people who can barely manage a significant amount of cash for their development.

Conclusion

This research applied the energy justice theory to unpack the land (in)justices associated with extractive projects. In particular, the procedural and distributive justice were employed. Through the analysis of the South African land law reforms, the research revealed that the country has embraced procedural justice to rectify the injustices that for long characterized land access and administration in South Africa. The research demonstrates how energy justice can be used as a tool to reform land laws in different countries.

Distributive justice theory was also employed to analyse the (un)fairness of the measures deployed by host governments and oil companies in compensating and relocating the affected households from land expropriated for extractive projects. The research revealed that households with cash compensation became poorer. This is rooted in the socio-economic challenges faced by these households. It also spotlights a lack of research and representation to ascertain the correct and effective compensatory measures that can be utilized by countries such as Uganda.

This research therefore responds to a question on what should be considered when compensating people in oil-, gas- and mineral-rich areas? Some of the key considerations are outlined below:

- Distributive justice and procedural justice should be at the heart of the compensatory measures for expropriated land intended for extractive projects.
- Considering the fact that most land where mining is carried out is located in rural areas with communities that depend on agriculture, farming and fishing, it becomes imperative to calculate such compensation taking into consideration the livelihood of the local communities, and how they will be negatively impacted if they no longer have access to their land to carry out their daily activities.

- There is a need to ensure that women and children benefit from this compensation. In this respect, policy-makers should ensure that the wife and older children of the landowner take part in the negotiations before the final compensation is agreed upon.
- There is also a need to have a resettlement plan so that the local people have better options for relocating.
- Compensation may also consider disruption caused to the landowner. In Uganda, this is well stipulated under Section 83 of the Mining Act, 2003.

Throughout this book chapter, we have elaborated the role of access to land in ensuring a successful extractive project. Whereas land reforms have been a marked feature of the 21st century, applying the energy justice principles in accessing land for extractives has not been explored. Whereas there are various issues associated with energy justice, the consideration in this book chapter is to ensure the application of distributive justice which concerns the distribution of benefits and also the negatives that accrue from using land for extractive projects (including addressing the environmental damage; sharing the oil and mining revenues equally).

Taking into account the above, it is notable that the land law reforms are focused on ensuring that local people are not unjustly treated in the acquisition of land for energy and mining projects, all of which align with the principles of distributive land justice.

Future research could replicate the methodology used here in other geographical contexts. Also, it could clearly view the application of procedural justice in the land contracts; the application of distributive justice in other forms of compensation utilized by host governments and oil companies in both the developed and developing world.

Notes

1 United Nations: Climate Action. Land the Climate's Carbon Sink, www.un.org/en/climatechange/science/climate-issues/land. Last accessed on 20 March 2023; Martin Dixon. *Modern Land Law* (London and New York: Routledge), 2021.
2 United Nations: Climate Action; Dixon, *Modern Land Law.*
3 Jiang, Liangliang, Anming Bao, Guli Jiapaer, Rui Liu, Ye Yuan, and Tao Yu. "Monitoring Land Degradation and Assessing Its Drivers to Support Sustainable Development Goal 15.3 in Central Asia." *Science of the Total Environment* 807 (2022): 150868.
4 Seifollahi-Aghmiuni, Samaneh, Zahra Kalantari, Gianluca Egidi, Luisa Gaburova, and Luca Salvati. "Urbanisation-Driven Land Degradation and Socioeconomic Challenges in Peri-Urban Areas: Insights from Southern Europe." *Ambio* 51, no. 6 (2022): 1446–1458.
5 Michael Albertus. "The Persistence of Rural Underdevelopment: Evidence from Land Reform in Italy." *Comparative Political Studies* 56, no. 1 (2023): 65–100..
6 Justine M. Williams and Eric Holt-Giménez, eds. *Land justice: Re-imagining Land, Food, and the Commons.* Food First Books, 2017.

7 Benjamin K. Sovacool and Michael H. Dworkin. "Energy Justice: Conceptual Insights and Practical Applications." *Applied Energy* 142 (2015): 435–444; Benjamin K. Sovacool and Michael H. Dworkin. *Global Energy Justice* (Cambridge: Cambridge University Press, 2014); Raphael J. Heffron and Darren McCauley. "The Concept of Energy Justice Across the Disciplines." *Energy Policy* 105 (2017): 658–667.
8 Rob White. "Indigenous Communities, Environmental Protection and Restorative Justice." *Australian Indigenous Law Review* 18, no. 2 (2014): 43–54..
9 Patrick Byakagaba, Bashir Twesigye, and Leslie E. Ruyle, *Dialectics of Conservation, Extractives, and Uganda's 'Land Rush'* (London: Routledge, 2018), p. 7.
10 Lionel Cliffe, Jocelyn Alexander, Ben Cousins, and Rudo Gaidzanwa, "An Overview of Fast Track Land Reform in Zimbabwe: Editorial Introduction," *Journal of Peasant Studies* 38, no. 5 (2011): 907-938, doi: 10.1080/03066150.2011.643387.
11 Grasian Mkodzongi and Samuel Spiegel, "Artisanal Gold Mining and Farming: Livelihood Linkages and Labour Dynamics after land Reforms in Zimbabwe," *Journal of Development Studies* 55, no. 10 (2019): 2145–2161..
12 Perrine Burnod, Nicole Andrianirina, Céline Boue, Flore Gubert, Nelly Rakoto-Tiana, Julia Vaillant, Rado Rabeantoandro, and Raphaël Rotovoarinony, "Land Reform and Certification in Madagascar: Does Perception of Tenure Security Matter and Change?" Annual World Bank Conference on Land and Poverty, World Bank Group, April 2012, Washington, United States, 35p. ..
13 Patrick Malope and Nnyaladzi Batisani, "Land Reforms that Exclude the Poor: The Case of Botswana." *Development Southern Africa* 25, no. 4 (2008): 383–397..
14 Sara Safransky, "Land Justice as a Historical Diagnostic: Thinking with Detroit," *Annals of the American Association of Geographers* 108, no. 2 (2018): 499–512..
15 Raphael J. Heffron, "Applying Energy Justice into the Energy Transition," *Renewable and Sustainable Energy Reviews* 156 (2022): 111936..
16 This concerns the distribution of benefits from the energy sector and also the negatives. For a full discussion, see Raphael Heffron, "Restoring Justice to the Energy Sector and the Economy," Alternative Policy Solutions. 2022 Oct 11.
17 This focuses on legal processes that have to be taken in the energy projects.
18 This focuses on the rectification of any injustices caused by the energy sector.
19 This is concerned with the recognition of rights of different groups and in particular local and/or indigenous communities.
20 This stems from the view that in energy we are all citizens of the same world and therefore, the cross-border effects from the energy activities need to be considered.
21 Indah Dwi Quarbani, Raphael J. Heffron, and Arrial Thoriq Setyo Rifano, "Justice and Critical Mineral Development in Indonesia and across ASEAN," *Extractive Industries and Society* 8, no. 1 (2021): 355–362.
22 Raphael J. Heffron, "Applying Energy Justice into the Energy Transition." .See also, Maciej M. Sokołowski and Satoshi Kurokawa, "Energy Justice in Japan's Energy Transition: Pillars of Just 2050 Carbon Neutrality," *Journal of World Energy Law & Business* 15, no. 3 (2022): 183-192..
23 K. J. Dillman and Jukka Heinonen. "A 'Just' Hydrogen Economy: A Normative Energy Justice Assessment of the Hydrogen Economy," *Renewable and Sustainable Energy Reviews* 167 (2022): 112648.
24 Albert R. Berry. "Reflections on Injustice, Inequality and Land Conflict in Colombia," *Canadian Journal of Latin American and Caribbean Studies/Revue canadienne des études latino-américaines et caraïbes* 42, no. 3 (2017): 277–297.

25 Rahmat Ramadhani, "Endless Agrarian Conflict in Malay Land," in Proceeding International Conference on Language and Literature (IC2LC), November 2020, pp. 256–260.
26 Yi-kuang Chen, Jon Gustav Kirkerud, and Torjus Folsland Bolkesjø. "Balancing GHG Mitigation and Land-Use Conflicts: Alternative Northern European Energy System Scenarios," *Applied Energy* 310 (2022): 118557.
27 Ibid.
28 Qian Zuo, Yong Zhou, Li Wang, Qing Li, and Jingyi Liu. "Impacts of Future Land Use Changes on Land Use Conflicts based on Multiple Scenarios in the Central Mountain Region, China," *Ecological Indicators* 137 (2022): 108743.
29 Ibid.
30 Barasa Bernard, Mwiru Aron, Turyabanawe Loy, Nabalegwa W. Muhamud, and Ssentongo Benard. "The Impact of Refugee Settlements on Land Use Changes and Vegetation Degradation in West Nile Sub-region, Uganda," *Geocarto International* 37, no. 1 (2022): 16–34.
31 Mathilde Fautras. "Land Injustices, Contestations and Community Protest in the Rural Areas of Sidi Bouzid (Tunisia): The Roots of the 'revolution'?," *Justice spatiale-Spatial Justice* 7 (2015). www.jssj.org/article/injustices-foncieres-contestations-et-mobilisations-collectives-dans-les-espaces-ruraux-de-sidi-bouzid-tunisie-aux-racines-de-la-revolution/.ffhalshs-01512398frevolution.
32 Simon Batterbury, and Frankline Ndi. "Land-grabbing in Africa." In *Handbook of African Development*(London: Routledge, 2018) pp. 573–582.
33 Goal one of the United Nations Sustainable Development Goals.
34 Anita Jowitt, "Indigenous Land Grievances, Customary Land Disputes and Restorative Justice," *Journal of South Pacific Law* 8, no. 2 (2004): 1–9
35 The reforms were initiated in 1978 by Deng Xiaoping, the leader of the Communist Party of China at the time.
36 Ibid.
37 Stein T. Holden, Klaus Deininger, and Hosaena Hagos Ghebru, "Impact of Land Certification on Land Rental Market Participation in Tigray Region, Northern Ethiopia," *Northern Ethiopia* (October 1, 2007).
38 See Logan Cochrane and Sebsib Hadis, "Functionality of the Land Certification Program in Ethiopia: Exploratory Evaluation of the Processes of Updating Certificates," *Land* 8, no. 10 (2019), 149.
39 Hannah Wittman and Dana James. "Land Governance for Agroecology," *Elem Sci Anth* 10, no. 1 (2022), 00100.
40 Livia Rasche, Uwe A. Schneider, and Jan Steinhauser. "A Stakeholders' Pathway towards a Future Land Use and Food System in Germany," *Sustainability Science* 18, no. 1 (2023): 441–455.
41 Wayne S. Walker, Seth R. Gorelik, Susan C. Cook-Patton, Alessandro Baccini, Mary K. Farina, Kylen K. Solvik, Peter W. Ellis et al. "The Global Potential for Increased Storage of Carbon on Land," *Proceedings of the National Academy of Sciences* 119, no. 23 (2022): e2111312119.
42 United Nations: Climate Action. Land the Climate's Carbon Sink, www.un.org/en/climatechange/science/climate-issues/land. Last accessed on 20 March 2023.
43 Martin Dixon, *Modern Land Law*.
44 Section 205(1)(ix) of the Law of Property Act 1925.

45 Loka Ashwood, John Canfield, Madeleine Fairbairn, Kathryn De Master, "What Owns the Land: The Corporate Organization of Farmland Investment," *Journal of Peasant Studies* 49, no. 2 (2022): 233–262.
46 Dixon, *Modern Land Law*, p. 4.
47 Damien Beillouin, Rémi Cardinael, David Berre, Annie Boyer, Marc Corbeels, Abigail Fallot, Frédéric Feder, and Julien Demenois. "A Global Overview of Studies about Land Management, Land-Use Change, and Climate Change Effects on Soil Organic Carbon," *Global Change Biology* 28, no. 4 (2022): 1690–1702.
48 IEA, *Africa Energy Outlook 2019* (IEA 2019): www.iea.org/reports/africa-energy-outlook-2019
49 BP, *BP Energy Outlook: 2018 Edition* (BP Plc 2018): www.bp.com/content/dam/bp/business-sites/en/global/corporate/pdfs/energy-economics/energy-outlook/bpenergy-outlook-2018.pdf
50 International Monetary Fund, 'Nigeria: 2019 Article IV Consultation, IMF Country Report no 19/92'.
51 Although land justice was at the centre of customary land tenures in different African countries, it is worth noting that gender equality was never promoted in land ownership. This was so because most of the time land passed from father to son, since lineage is patrilineal in African countries such as Uganda.
52 These three land tenure systems were introduced in Uganda by the British occupiers during the colonial period.
53 This happened in 1975 under the dictatorship of Idi Amin.
54 The Land Act 1998 (No 16 of 1998), Laws of Uganda.
55 Mailo land is as result of the 1900 Uganda Agreement between the British Government and the Kingdom of Buganda. Under this Agreement, the British granted some 8,000 square miles of land (hence known as 'mailo' land) to the Kabaka of Buganda and various other chiefs and notables.
56 Article 237(3) of the 1995 Constitution of Uganda and Section 2 of the Land Act, 1998.
57 Section 3(4) of the Land Act, 1998, Laws of Uganda.
58 A lawful occupant, on the other hand, is defined under Section 29 of the Land Act to include persons occupying land by virtue of the repealed: (i) *Busuulu* and *Envujjo* Law of 1928; (ii) Toro Landlord and Tenant Law of 1937; and (iii) Ankole Landlord and Tenant Law of 1937.
59 The Group Areas Act, 1950 (re-enacted in 1957 and 1966).
60 ibid.
61 Binswanger-Mkhize and Hans Peter. "From Failure to Success in South African Land Reform," *African Journal of Agricultural and Resource Economics* 9, no. 311-2016-5618 (2014): 253–269.
62 Various programmes were used in South Africa to address the land injustices. These include: (i) restitution of land to people who were displaced from their land under apartheid laws; (ii) the Settlement/Land Acquisition Grant (SLAG); (iii) Land Redistribution for Agricultural Development (LRAD) – this programme was initiated in 2001 to make it possible for beneficiaries to acquire larger areas of land for farming; (iv) the Comprehensive Agricultural Support Programme (CASP) was created as a response to the growing crisis in post-settlement support; (v) the Re-capitalisation and Agricultural Development Programme (RECAP) was created to recapitalize failed or poorly performing land reform projects. For a detailed

discussion on this, see Binswanger-Mkhize and Peter, "From Failure to Success in South African Land Reform.".
63 Patrick McAuslan, *Land Law Reform in Eastern Africa: Traditional or Transformative?: A Critical Review of 50 Years of Land Law Reform in Eastern Africa 1961–2011* (London: Routledge, 2013).
64 McAuslan, *Land Law Reform in Eastern Africa*.
65 Prince Emeka Ndimele, ed., *The Political Ecology of Oil and Gas Activities in the Nigerian Aquatic Ecosystem* (Cambridge: Academic Press, 2017); Victoria R. Nalule. *Energy Poverty and Access Challenges in Sub-Saharan Africa: The Role of Regionalism* (Cham: Springer, 2018).
66 Nenibarini Zabby, Kabari Sam, and Adaugo Trinitas Onyebuchi. "Remediation of Contaminated Lands in the Niger Delta, Nigeria: Prospects and Challenges," *Science of the Total Environment* 586 (2017): 952–965.
67 For a detailed discussion, see Damilola Olawuyi, *Extractives Industry Law in Africa* (Cham: Springer International Publishing 2018), p. 270.
68 Benjamin K. Sovacool, Jonn Axsen, and Steve Sorrell. "Promoting Novelty, Rigor, and Style in Energy Social Science: Towards Codes of Practice for Appropriate Methods and Research Design," *Energy Research & Social Science* 45 (2018): 12–42.:
69 Clara Irazábal. "Counter Land-Grabbing by the Precariat: Housing Movements and Restorative Justice in Brazil," *Urban Science* 2, no. 2 (2018): 49.
70 Beitz Charles. Cosmopolitanism and global justice. In *Current Debates in Global Justice* (Dordrecht: Springer, 2005), pp. 11–27.
71 Kevin J. Dillman and Jukka Heinonen. "A 'Just' Hydrogen Economy: A Normative Energy Justice Assessment of the Hydrogen Economy," *Renewable and Sustainable Energy Reviews* 167 (2022): 112648.
72 Raphael J. Heffron. "Applying Energy Justice into the Energy Transition," *Renewable and Sustainable Energy Reviews* 156 (2022): 111936.
73 Benjamin K. Sovacool, Max Lacey Barnacle, Adrian Smith, and Marie Claire Brisbois. "Towards Improved Solar Energy Justice: Exploring the Complex Inequities of Household Adoption of Photovoltaic Panels," *Energy Policy* 164 (2022): 112868.
74 Hafiz Anwar Ullah Khan, Burçin Ünel, and Yury Dvorkin. "Electricity Tariff Design Via Lens of Energy Justice," *Omega* 117 (2023): 102822.
75 Clara Irazábal. "Counter Land-Grabbing by the Precariat: Housing Movements and Restorative Justice in Brazil," *Urban Science* 2, no. 2 (2018): 49.
76 Mejía-Montero, Adolfo, Kirsten EH Jenkins, Dan van der Horst, and Matthew Lane. "An Intersectional Approach to Energy Justice: Individual and Collective Concerns around Wind Power on Zapotec Land," *Energy Research & Social Science* 98 (2023): 103015.
77 Raphael J. Heffron and Darren McCauley. "What Is the 'Just Transition'?," *Geoforum* 88. (2018): 74–77.
78 Raphael J. Heffron and Darren McCauley. "The Concept of Energy Justice Across the Disciplines," *Energy Policy* 105 (2017): 658–667.
79 Luisa Marti and Rosa Puertas. "Sustainable Energy Development Analysis: Energy Trilemma," *Sustainable Technology and Entrepreneurship* 1, no. 1 (2022): 100007; Martínez Viviana and Olga L. Castillo. "Colombian Energy Planning-Neither for Energy, nor for Colombia," *Energy Policy* 129 (2019): 1132–1142.

80 Masoud Shirazi, José Alberto Fuinhas, and Nuno Silva. "Sustainable Economic Development and Geopolitics: The Role of Energy Trilemma Policies," *Sustainable Development* 31, no. 4 (August 2023): 2471–2491.
81 Gomes Silva, Francisco Jose, Konstantinos Kirytopoulos, Luis Pinto Ferreira, José Carlos Sá, Gilberto Santos, and Maria Carolina Cancela Nogueira. "The Three Pillars of Sustainability and Agile Project Management: How Do They Influence Each Other?," *Corporate Social Responsibility and Environmental Management* 29, no. 5 (2022): 1495–1512.
82 ILO, Understanding the Indigenous and Tribal Peoples Convention, 1989 (No. 169), 2013.
83 Roy L. Prosterman and Tim Hanstad. "Land Reform in the Twenty-First Century: New Challenges, New Responses," *Seattle Journal of Social Justice* 4 (2005), 763.
84 Prosterman and Hanstad, "Land Reform in the Twenty-First Century," 763.
85 Ibid.
86 Ibid.
87 Mokoko Piet Sebola. "'Land Expropriation Without Compensation:' Populist Political Charade and Electioneering Slogan in South Africa's 2019 National Elections," *African Journal of Development Studies* 12, no. 1 (2022), 297.
88 Ibid.
89 Mzingaye Brilliant Xaba. "A Review of the Political Economy of South African Land Reform and Its Contested Multifaceted Land Questions," *Africa Review* 14, no. 3 (2022 Jul): 231–52.
90 The reasoning behind this motion is based on the data that 72% of the nation's private farmland is owned by white people, who make up just 9% of the population. As such, in August 2018, the South African Government began the process of taking two white-owned farmlands by filing papers seeking to acquire the farms via eminent domain for one tenth of their estimated value, which, in one case, is based on possible value when the farm is developed into an eco-estate.
91 The Constitution of Uganda, 1995, as amended.
92 Ibid.
93 Victoria R. Nalule. *Mining and the Law in Africa: Exploring the Social And Environmental Impacts* (London: Springer Nature, 2019).
94 Tom Ogwang, Frank Vanclay, and Arjan van den Assem. "Impacts of the Oil Boom on the Lives of People Living in the Albertine Graben Region of Uganda," *The Extractive Industries and Society* 5, no. 1 (2018): 98–103.
95 Caroline Aboda, Pål Olav Vedeld, Paul Musali, Goretti Nabanoga, and Frank Mugagga. "Vulnerability of Households to Resettlement and Compensation Measures for an Oil Refinery Project in the Albertine Region of Uganda," *GeoJournal* 88, no. 3 (2023): 3121–3141.
96 Global Rights Alert. "Acquisition of Land for the Oil Refinery: Tracking Progress in Resettling Project Affected Persons Who Opted for Land for Land Compensation," *Global Rights Alert: Kampala, Uganda* (2015).

6 The Role of the African Union's Panel of the Wise in Natural Resource Conflict Resolution

*Olawari D. J. Egbe and
Fie David Dan-Woniowei*

Introduction

Violent conflicts are widely recognized for their catastrophic implications on countries in the Global South, especially in Sub-Saharan Africa (SSA). Such conflicts stifle, stunt, and even reverse the economic advancement of the continent.[1] Scholarly inquiry into the causes of violent conflicts has revealed that states that are most affected by conflicts are typically those that possess valuable natural resources such as land, diamonds, and crude oil, and whose economies heavily depend on these resources for their economic sustainability through primary commodity exports,[2] and their international relations.[3] Scholarly research has identified crude oil as a primary catalyst for triggering, escalating, and sustaining conflicts, among other natural resources. Land grabbing is also a significant contributor to conflicts in Eastern Africa, primarily driven by dominant actors such as China, India, Saudi Arabia, the United Arab Emirates, Qatar, Bahrain, Kuwait, Libya, Egypt, the United Kingdom, and the United States.[4] The violation of Article 10 of the UN Declaration on the Rights of Indigenous Peoples, which prohibits the forced removal and relocation of Indigenous peoples from their lands without adequate compensation and an option of return, is a result of unregulated land grabbing. This practice serves as an illustration of how natural resources contribute to conflict in sub-Saharan Africa.

The end of the Cold War witnessed an upsurge in violent conflicts associated with natural resources in sub-Saharan Africa.[5] In 2017, there were 52 active conflicts sustained by licit or illicit resource exploitation in 30 sub-Saharan African countries, leading to a landscape littered with conflicts on the continent. Concerned by this pervasive trend, former United Nations Secretary-General Kofi Annan unequivocally stated that "the persistent conflicts and crises of governance and security threaten to derail the hopes for an African Union of peace and prosperity".[6] While the impact of resource-based conflicts on peace and stability in sub-Saharan Africa cannot be overstated, current efforts to address these conflicts remain at a rudimentary stage. The 1990 Liberian crisis and the 1994 Rwandan genocide serve as examples of the lack of political will by the international community, including the African Union (A.U.), United Nations, and Western countries, to confront such conflicts, with

DOI: 10.4324/9781003355717-9

the exception of the deployment of ECOMOG by the Economic Community of West African States (ECOWAS) in Liberia.[7] The lack of intervention by the United Nations and Western countries to prevent the escalation of crises in sub-Saharan Africa is particularly concerning, with some studies suggesting that this may be due to the absence of crude oil in many of the affected countries. The exception to this trend is the case of Somalia, where the UN and United States made three attempts to restore peace and state authority through UNOSOM I (1992–1993), US-led Unified Task Force (1992–1993), Operation Restore Hope, and UNOSOM II (1993–1995). However, the general lack of intervention in most other conflicts highlights two key points. On the one hand, it demonstrates that African countries themselves are primarily responsible for resolving the conflicts that arise within their borders.[8] On the other hand, it shows that the architecture of the Organization of African Unity (O.A.U) has failed.[9] The transformation of the O.A.U into the AU in 2000 and the promotion of the idea of 'African Solutions to African Problems'[10] became essential in promoting peace and security across the continent, as well as improving its socio-economic well-being.

This chapter explores the role of the Panel of the Wise (PoW) in addressing natural resource-based conflicts in Africa. It argues that the PoW can contribute to effective natural resource conflict resolution in Africa by making natural resource governance a running theme. The Fourth Panel of the PoW, created by Article 11 of the PSC Protocol, chose natural resource-based conflicts as its fifth thematic report with the title "Report of the African Union Panel of the Wise on Improving the Mediation and Resolution of Natural Resource-Related Conflicts Across Africa" in October 2017. Through this theme, the PoW may have recognized that unmanaged competition and struggle over natural resources triggers, escalates, and sustains conflicts in the continent.[11] Despite the existence of the PoW, the incidence of resource-based conflicts in Africa has continued to increase. This indicates that the PoW needs to pay more attention to this sector, which is the compelling reason for this chapter. The second section presents the Rentier State Theory (RST) as the theoretical framework. RST argues that resource-rich states' eagerness for economic rents/royalties makes them blind to the environment and hostile to the plight of those whose environments and livelihoods are negatively affected by resource extraction activities. The third section provides a historical overview of the PoW. The fourth section identifies pathways linking natural resource extraction to violent conflicts in Africa. Finally, in the fifth section, the chapter concludes with a call for the PoW to adopt natural resource governance as a running theme in their conflict resolution efforts to promote peace and security on the continent.

Theoretical Background

The RST gained popularity through the works of scholars from North Africa and the Middle East.[12] It is a political economy theory that explains state-society relations in states that generate a significant portion of their income from rents, royalties, and unearned payments. RST assumes that because these states receive their income from external sources and distribute it to society without imposing taxation, they are relieved from making concessions to society such as development or democratic bargains.[13] This phenomenon helps to explain why resource-rich states are often characterized by authoritarian democracies.[14]

Rentier states are countries whose economies are dependent on natural resource rents.[15] These states are characterized by a parasitic economy that violates the fundamental liberal principle of hard work, a rentier mentality where consumption is financed by economic rents, the prevalence of the service sector over agriculture, and autocratic tendencies.[16] This trend is prevalent in Nigeria, where autocratic measures are used to suppress pro-environmental groups and oil-bearing communities that protest against environmental degradation, which affects their livelihoods, as seen in the case of the Ogoni in the 1990s.[17] Thus, a defining characteristic of rentier states is their overreliance on rents/royalties,[18] which compels them to show contempt for the environment. They prioritize economic survival over environmental considerations or interests. Thus, violent conflicts frequently arise where the state's drive for economic sustainability negatively affects the environment, which sustains the economic livelihood of Indigenous peoples.

A Historical Overview of the A.U. Panel of the Wise

At its inception, the AU faced the daunting task of addressing the numerous conflicts ravaging the continent. The organization implemented various measures to address these conflicts, including the creation of the African Peace and Security Architecture (APSA). Through Article 4(h) and (j) of the Constitutive Act of the A.U. (2000), the AU empowered itself to use force as a last resort to prevent war crimes, grave violations of human rights, and genocide. The African-led force's success during this period, spanning from the early 1990s to the late 2020s, was remarkable and encouraged the AU and Regional Economic Communities/Regional Mechanisms (RECs/RMs) to enhance their capacity to conduct peace and security operations (PSOs). This initiative led to the establishment of the African Standby Force (ASF) in 2003, which has contributed to a significant increase in African-led peace operations capacity for almost two decades.

The ASF was developed by African leaders with the aim of generating capabilities for African peace support operations and enhancing African capacity to prevent, respond to, and manage civil wars and other security challenges that had plagued the continent in the post-Cold War period. These institutionalized measures were established by the AU to ensure a conflict-free continent or at least drastically reduce conflicts. Under the PSC Protocol, these institutions include the PoW (Article 11), the now inactive Continental Early Warning System (CEWS) (Article 12), the ASF (Article 13), and the Peace Fund (Article 21). All these institutions were established by the AU.[19]

The rationale behind these institutionalized measures was that timely warnings could help prevent or mitigate the onset, duration, intensity, and effects of deadly conflicts.[20] The AU, through the 2003 Protocol on the Establishment of the Peace and Security Council (PSC Protocol), mandated the PSC to initiate measures for the early resolution of deadly conflicts in the continent. The PSC is composed of 15 elected member states, and Article 11 of the PSC Protocol birthed the PoW to strengthen the PSC's work in advising on peace, security, and stability in Africa. The PoW also had the autonomy to address critical issues of peace and security.[21] The A.U.'s PoW has its roots in several sources, including the A.U.'s deployment of an African Elders Council for Peace. This vision was realized through two main sources: the 1991 conference on "Towards a Conference on Security, Stability, Development, and Co-operation in Africa (CSSDCA)", and the ECOWAS' Council of the Wise. The vision of the PoW was based on traditional African influences, where the concept of "the wise" refers to the importance of age, elderliness, and experience, which provide the necessary ingredients for wisdom and counseling to resolve conflicts between opposing parties.[22]

The merit of the PoW lies in its composition of five distinguished African personalities with exceptional experience, which they bring to bear in anticipating and resolving conflicts.[23] In essence, the PoW draws the attention of decision-makers to circumstances or policies in a given country that can threaten the fragile peace of the continent. The PoW is a recognition by the A.U. of the significance of traditional conflict resolution methods in Africa. The Panel convenes at least three times a year, or more frequently as necessary, at the discretion of the Chairperson of the Commission. The Panel's meetings are usually closed-door and last between one and three days, or longer if necessary. During its regular meetings, a chairperson is elected on a rotational basis for a term of one year to preside over the Panel's deliberations.[24]

The first membership of the PoW was constituted on January 29 and 30, 2007, during the A.U.'s Eighth Ordinary Session of the Assembly. Membership of the PoW has consisted of five panels since 2007 (see Table 6.1), with each panel satisfying the following criteria:

a Composed of highly respected eminent Africans who have made outstanding contributions to the cause of peace, security, and development on the continent;
b Members have high integrity, moral authority, and independence;
c Members are not holding an active political office;
d Equal representation is given to each of the five subregions in Africa; and
e Gender representation is ensured on a ratio of 3:2.

The PoW has a dedicated secretariat that is located within the Political Affairs, Peace and Security Department (previously called Peace and Security) of the A.U. It is guided by a mandate and modalities of action such as, amongst others, to:

Table 6.1 A.U. Panels of the Wise since 2007

Member's Name	Country of Origin	Regional Representation
5th Panel of the Wise, March, 2022		
H.E. Amre Moussa, former Foreign Minister of Egypt and former Secretary-General of the League of Arab States	Egypt	North Africa
H. E. Domitien Ndayizeye, former President of Burundi	Burundi	Central Africa
Hon. Lady Justice Effie Owuor	Kenya	East Africa
Professor Babacar Kante	Senegal	West Africa
Pending		Southern Africa
4th Panel of the Wise, 2018–2021		
Amr Moussa, former Arab League Secretary-General; former Minister of Foreign Affairs	Egypt	North Africa
Mrs. Honorine Nzet Bitéghé, former Minister of Social Affairs	Gabon	Central Africa
Dr. Specioza Wandira Kazibwe, former Vice President of Uganda	Uganda	East Africa
Hifikepunye Pohamba	Namibia	Southern Africa
Ellen Johnson Sirleaf, former President of Liberia; 2011 Nobel Peace Prize laureate	Liberia	West Africa
3rd Panel of the Wise, September, 2010–2016		
Lakhdar Brahimi, former UN and Arab League envoy for Syria, former Minister of Foreign Affairs	Algeria	North Africa
Albina Pereira Faria de Africano, former Minister of Petroleum	Angola	Central Africa
Dr. Specioza Wandira Kazibwe, former Vice President of Uganda	Uganda	East Africa
Dr. Luisa Diogo	Mozambique	Southern Africa
Dr. Edem Kodjo, former Prime Minister of Togo, former OAU Secretary-General	Togo	West Africa
2nd Panel of the Wise, December, 2010–September, 2014		
Ahmed Ben Bella, former President of Algeria	Algeria	North Africa
Marie Madeleine Kalala-Ngoy	DRC	Central Africa
Dr. Salim Ahmed Salim, former Secretary-General of the O.A.U.	Tanzania	East Africa
Kenneth Kaunda, former President of Zambia; former Secretary-General of the Non-Aligned Movement	Zambia	Southern Africa
Mary Chinery Hesse, former Deputy Director-General of the International Labour Organization; former Chancellor of the University of Ghana	Ghana	West Africa
1st Panel of the Wise, 2007–2010		
Ahmed Ben Bella, former President of Algeria	Algeria	North Africa

(*Continued*)

Table 6.1 (Continued)

Member's Name	Country of Origin	Regional Representation
Miguel Trovoada, former President of São Tomé and Príncipe	Sao Tome and Principe	Central Africa
Dr. Salim Ahmed Salim, former O.A.U Secretary-General	Tanzania	East Africa
Mme Brigalia Bam, former Chairperson of the Independent Electoral Commission of South Africa	South Africa	Southern Africa
Mme Elisabeth Pognon, former President of the Constitutional Court of Benin	Benin	West Africa

Source: The Author.

advise the Council and/or the Chairperson of the Commission on all matters within their respective competences pertaining to the promotion and maintenance of peace, security and stability in Africa; facilitate the establishment of channels of communication between the Council and the Chairperson of the Commission, on the one hand, and parties engaged in a dispute, on the other hand, in order to prevent such dispute from escalating into conflict; carry out fact finding missions as an instrument of conflict prevention in countries and/or regions where the Panel considers there is a danger of conflict either breaking out or seriously escalating.[25]

The Panel adopts yearly themes as its focus. Since the formation of the PoW in 2007, it has focused on the following five themes: (a) Election-Related Violence in 2008; (b) Non-Impunity, Truth, Justice, and Reconciliation in 2009; (c) Women and Children in Armed Conflict in 2010; (d) Strengthening Political Governance for Peace, Security, and Stability in 2011[26]; and (e) Improving the Mediation and Resolution of Natural Resources-Related Conflicts Across Africa in 2017.[27]

Pathways of Natural Resource-Induced Conflicts in Sub-Saharan Africa

As previously mentioned, numerous African nations are currently involved in violent and often protracted conflicts that are triggered by the abundance of natural resources,[28] the extraction of these resources,[29] and the governance surrounding them.[30] Given the large number of conflicts on the continent that stem from natural resources, there is an urgent need for effective governance measures to control them.[31] While the Fourth Panel of the PoW has already set the pace by choosing natural resources as their theme, the ongoing violent conflicts on the continent suggest that the PoW needs to exercise greater oversight on this critical sector. It is evident that the desire for rents/royalties by African states plays a significant role in exacerbating the numerous violent conflicts in the continent, as demonstrated in the identified pathways.

State-Induced Environmental Spoliation

Rebecca Bear Reed, a member of the Crow Tribe in Montana, United States, who receives a coal payment of about $225 every four months, was widely quoted as saying, "I care for the environment; I really do. But when you see that money, then you do not care. Because you are getting the thing you need".[32] This woman's dilemma is similar to the dilemma faced by rentier states in Africa. They are confronted with two distinct problems. First, the fact that some level of environmental degradation is inevitable due to the extraction of resources from the environment, which is necessary for human survival.[33] Second, the challenge of the environmental dialectic, which suggests that resource extraction causes environmental degradation, but at the same time, African states need revenue from resource extraction to cope with environmental challenges.[34] However, how much resource extraction or consumption is in excess? However, it is essential to determine the extent of resource extraction or consumption that exceeds planetary boundaries. It is crucial to exercise restraint while enjoying the bounty of nature to stay within these limits.[35]

The need for restraint is further reinforced by the fact that the quality of the environment is heavily dependent on how this salient resource is managed, considering our relationship not only with other humans, but also with the fauna and flora that complete the intricate web of our Earth family.[36] However, the extraction of natural resources to satisfy human needs risks overexploitation and extinction.

The environment in most resource-rich states in SSA is pitifully degraded, resulting from unbridled natural resource expropriation. This degraded environment is home to Indigenous peoples who not only live next to but also rely on the environment for their sustenance. Resource overexploitation ensues where there is unbridled resource extraction, reckless alteration of ecosystems, reprogramming of nature, careless pollution, and so on. The sum of these practices induces violent conflicts (see Table 6.2). When these conflicts occur, they reaffirm the fact that natural resources are an established source of conflict in the 21st century.[37] They also bolster the green war hypothesis, which suggests that pristine forests, marine and terrestrial life are threatened to the extent that they can cause violent conflicts.[38]

Natural resources are not only the root cause of many conflicts in sub-Saharan Africa but also the means to sustain them. These conflicts result in countless human suffering, deaths in the thousands, and displacement requiring humanitarian aid.[39] Much of the human suffering on the continent is induced by natural resources. This is a concerning issue, but it is nearly unavoidable, given that the political economy and international relations of most sub-Saharan African states are reliant on natural resource extraction.[40]

This incident reinforces the narrative of environmental degradation in sub-Saharan Africa, which violates human rights and contributes to the onset of conflicts. The community of Okoroba, near Nembe in Bayelsa State, Nigeria, is situated between fresh and saltwater streams. Each stream serves a specific purpose for the community, with the fresh water used for cooking and drinking, while the saltwater is a source of seafood such as periwinkles and snails. The Niger Delta region, where Okoroba is located, is known for its challenging terrain. However, in 1991, Royal Dutch Shell discovered crude oil in the community and to transport their heavy drilling equipment to exploit this new resource, they dredged a canal connecting the salt and freshwater streams. This action went against the basic geographical principle that salt and fresh water should not mix. The unfortunate result was the death of aquatic life in both streams.[41] As seen in Table 6.2, this single action by Shell Nigeria had adverse effects on the economy, well-being, and ecosystem of the Okoroba community.

Table 6.2 Natural Resources as Conflict Inducers

Causes of Conflict	Manifestations	Locations	Ecological Effects	Effects on Subsistence Rights
Extraction of raw materials	Mining, oil, deforestation, overfishing	Rainforest, mountainous areas, coastal areas	Loss of biodiversity	Displacement from living space, loss of livelihood, pollution of living space
Alteration of Ecosystems	Plantations, dams, prawn farms	Farmland, river valleys, coastal areas	Monoculture, pesticides, loss of biodiversity, increased water consumption	Displacement from living space, loss of livelihood
Reprogramming of nature	Hybrid plants, genetic seeds, optimized livestock	Monocultures	Water consumption, loss of species	Loss of free access to cultivated plants and animals, dependence on money and corporations, concentration in agricultural sector
Pollution of urban living space	Harmful chemicals in drinking water, air and soil, unregulated waste water	Urban slums	Poisoning of Environment	Diseases, especially among women and children

Source: Wolfgang Sachs, "Environment and Human Rights," *Development*, 47, no. 1 (2004): 42–49, 44.

The preceding narrative validates the fact that if the basic capabilities of people are endangered to the extent that they cannot sustain themselves with dignity, then their fundamental rights are violated, and this could potentially trigger violent conflicts. In such situations, the blame lies on the rentier interests of resource-rich African states and the corporate interests of various oil Transnational Corporations (TNCs) that work in tandem with them, disregarding the environment and the livelihoods of Indigenous peoples.

Land Grabbing in Africa

The unbridled extraction of renewable resources, such as land, which is commonly referred to as "green grabbing" or transnational land acquisitions, involves the forceful acquisition of land without the valid consent of the dispossessed and without consideration for their future survival.[42] Land grabbing is on the rise in Africa, causing conflicts as communities feel unjustly treated and resort to resistance. This trend is often described as "Africa is for sale, there is a land grab underway",[43] highlighting the economic motive of exploiting Africa's ecosystems for profit.[44]

Since 2009, there has been intense commodification of nature, where external interests have acquired millions of hectares of land in Africa for the purpose of industrialized agriculture (see Table 6.3).[45] The global rush for land grabbing in Africa is rationalized on two fronts: first, the notion that Africa's lands are empty, available, underutilized, and ripe for commercialization; and second, that land is so cheap and almost free.[46]

Most African governments have exacerbated these conflictual trends. In Ethiopia, Indigenous communities of the Gambella region are victims of

Table 6.3 Land Grabs in Africa

Country	Hectares Transferred	Major Investor
Benin	263,300	Italy
Ghana	210,461	United Kingdom
Guinea	106,415	United Kingdom
Côte d'Ivoire	47,000	Singapore
Liberia	689,800	Singapore/Malaysia
Mali	473,334	Libya, Saudi Arabia
Mauritania	52,000	Saudi Arabia
Niger	15,922	Saudi Arabia
Nigeria	362,292	United Kingdom
Senegal	375,570	India, China
Sierra-Leone	705,450	Vietnam, Portugal

Source: Tana High-Level Forum for Security in Africa (TLHFSA), Background Paper on Natural Resource Governance in Africa: Conflict, Politics and Power, accessed 5 May 2022, www.google.com/search?client=firefox-bd&q=Background+Paper+on+Natural+Resource+Governance+in+AfricaConflict%2C+Politics+and+Power, p. 11.

land alienation through the "villagilization" program.[47] Additionally, land allocations in Ethiopia are recorded at the National Investment Promotion Agency as wastelands without prior users. However, such classifications do not represent the situation on the ground for a country with over 75 million people.[48] These lands are not free; instead, they are owned and have been occupied and farmed by Indigenous peoples.[49]

In Cameroon, the government in Yaoundé has authorized Cameroon Vert SARL (Camvert) to clear ancestral lands belonging to the Indigenous Bagyeli people, in a region known for its biodiversity hotspot and occupied by 28 local communities that cultivate palm oil plantations. To achieve the state's objectives, Prime Minister Joseph Dion Ngute illegitimately removed the region in question from the "permanent" forest estate, paving the way for State Property Minister Henri Eyebe Ayissi to authorize the first phase of clearing 2,500 hectares of the 60,000 hectares that Camvert is eager to acquire for a plantation. In addition, in Cameroon, land-dependent communities of the Baka people are being evicted by Sud-Cameroun Hévéa (Sudcam), a Cameroonian subsidiary of Halcyon Agri Corporation Limited, which has over 10,000 hectares of tropical land rubber plantation.[50]

Instead of providing fair compensation for their lost land, Camvert is attempting to appease the Bagyeli aborigines with short-term gifts such as canned tomatoes, bags of rice, and soap.[51] However, these superficial gifts are not a sustainable replacement for the land that is so vital to their way of life. This situation is a potential precursor to hunger, starvation, and conflict. The consequences of such practices are far-reaching, resulting in the disruption of social and economic ties within land-dependent communities in Tanzania, DR Congo, Madagascar, Zambia, Sudan, Mozambique,[52] and elsewhere, leading to displacement and violent conflicts.[53]

The inevitable eruption of these conflictual situations stems from the fact that while Africans desire a transformed agricultural sector and diversified economies, external interests in African lands are driven by the necessity to meet future food security.[54] This asymmetry of interests makes the prospects of accruable benefits a mirage in sub-Saharan Africa (SSA). The benefits remain elusive because the existing asymmetries between external interests in land acquisitions and local community needs are not only inconsistent but also never addressed at all. For instance, there are contentious issues such as the need to compensate for local community land rights, inconsistent external investor proposals, and inadequate economic, social, and environmental assessments of project impacts on local people. Addressing these salient structural impediments cavalierly has resulted in violent conflicts.[55]

The foreign countries that dominate the business of large-scale land acquisition, as noted earlier,[56] are not oblivious to the fact that the lands in question are occupied and farmed by local communities in several African countries, including Ethiopia, Kenya, Malawi, Tanzania, Zambia, Mozambique, DR Congo, and Cameroon.[57] The result is often forceful displacements and the ensuing regrettable resistance, as seen in Sierra Leone.[58] For instance, a land lease agreement with Daewoo in Madagascar ignited political unrest due to the large population living in abject poverty and the heightened level of food insecurity in the country.

The 2007 Declaration of Nyeleni, which was issued by the La Via Campesina, an international peasant movement, and the aborigines of Nyeleni Village, Selingue, in Mali, was prompted by the complications arising from land grabbing. The declaration boldly states that "Our land is our identity, it is not for sale…We need to fight against all forms of expulsion of peoples from their territories and against mechanisms that favor remote, corporate or centralized control of territories…"[59] Despite such a declaration, Indigenous land defenders in Africa have continued to lose their lives in the process of defending their land against powerful external interests.[60]

Bank-Assisted Projects in Africa

Several multilateral development banks, including the World Bank, have made the environment a part of their approach to development in Africa. However, these institutions fail to consider the environment as a holistic element of the development trajectory, and as more than just a burden.[61] Specifically, the World Bank has been accused of facilitating land grabs in Africa, which could exacerbate food shortages, displace entire communities, and perpetuate rural deprivation.[62]

The World Bank's involvement in facilitating land grabs in Africa is a cause for concern as it could worsen food shortages and rural deprivations.[63] One such program that has led to the eviction of peasant farmers and the confiscation of their landholdings without compensation is the World Bank's financialization policy of food and agriculture in Southern Africa.[64] In addition to this, Southern Africa is suffering from land grabs through the "villagization" program, particularly in Ethiopia's Gambella region, where Indigenous communities are experiencing land alienation.[65] In Kenya and Zambia, peasant farmers have been displaced without adequate resettlement schemes.[66]

The World Bank has a track record of financing large dam projects in Africa for hydroelectricity generation. However, the supposed beneficiaries, Indigenous peoples,[67] often end up suffering, while the actual beneficiaries are commercial logging and commercial agriculture businesses.[68] This has earned the World Bank a notorious reputation. Previously, the World Bank had committed to not financing large dam projects after receiving extensive criticism for the ill-fated Polonoroeste dam project in Brazil and the Sardar Sarovar dam project in India.[69]

Following a short hiatus, however, the World Bank has resumed the financing of large dam projects through businesses in SSA where it felt there are untapped potentials.[70] The implications therefrom is that the World Bank's resumption has been controversies surrounding pre- and post-project Environmental Impact Assessments (EIA) exercises. The World Bank has been accused of failing to conduct, or inadequately conducting, assessments to determine the environmental effects of large dams and the physical and health impacts of projects on Indigenous communities and regions downstream of most dam projects.[71]

The World Bank has designed involuntary resettlement guidelines that take into account the potential negative effects of the projects it finances. The guidelines state that if displacement is necessary, affected persons should be compensated, supported in their move, assisted during the transition period in the resettlement site, helped to maintain a standard of living similar to their previous living standards, and even have the opportunity to improve their earnings and production levels.[72] Unfortunately, the World Bank has failed to adequately observe these guidelines, if at all.[73] Despite this, the World Bank has been involved in several dam projects in Africa, including the Lesotho Highlands Water Project (LHWP), which involves the construction of five dams,[74] the DR Congo Inga 1, 2 and 3 dam projects, and the Lom Pangar Dam in Cameroon.[75], [76] Although these projects were intended for development, they primarily served the interests of the elite and had negative impacts on the forests, fisheries habitats, and game reserves of Indigenous peoples.[77]

Thus, programs that aim to solve one problem, such as electricity generation through dam projects, can exacerbate other challenges, such as the food crisis, which is a more pressing need for local communities. The displacement resulting from these projects is also a violation of Article 32 of the International Covenant on Economic, Social and Cultural Rights.[78] It is important to prioritize the needs of local communities and to ensure that their rights are respected and protected in any development project. This requires that the prior consent and cooperation of Indigenous peoples be obtained in good faith before the approval and execution of any project affecting their lands, territories, and resources, particularly those relating to the development, utilization, or exploitation of mineral, water, or other resources. Failure to do so can lead to violent conflicts in the continent.

Another arena where the World Bank has adversely impacted on Africa's Indigenous peoples is their forests. Although the importance of rainforests to the well-being of Indigenous communities is widely acknowledged,[79] the World Bank's perspective on forests differs from that of the Indigenous peoples. Instead of viewing forests as essential to the survival of local communities, the World Bank has financed projects such as mining, dams, oil and gas, modern agriculture, and soft commodities (e.g., logging) that are purported to help African countries become richer but have caused deforestation and displacement.[80] The forest-risk companies involved in these projects prioritize profit overpaying royalties, rents, and taxes to the owners and shareholders.[81]

The World Bank's financing of various projects in Africa has negative implications for forests and peasant farmers alike.[82] For instance, the effects of colossal dam projects on downstream communities, regions, and countries are evident from the forceful migrations/displacements that occur. This migration often leads to the survival of individuals through engaging in slash and burn agriculture, which indirectly triggers deforestation.[83] Additionally, extensive logging operations undertaken by several businesses through bank financing in parts of Africa, such as Cameroon's Ebo forest, originally occupied by over 40 million local Banen communities,[84] instigate deforestation, conflict,[85] and organized corruption which adversely impacts resource governance.[86]

The PoW has a tremendous amount of work to do in Cameroon if it is genuinely determined to reduce conflicts resulting from illegal logging of timber. Vietnamese companies are heavily involved in carrying out these criminal mass logging operations. Moreover, the World Bank has supported forestry in the DR Congo, including the design of the country's new forestry code. However, the Bank has failed to ensure the implementation of key components of the code, failed to comply with several safeguard policies, and disregarded the 40 million forest-dependent communities in the DR Congo, particularly the Pygmy community.[87]

In addition to the risk of deforestation-induced conflicts in Africa, forest mortality through forest dieback is also a concern.[88] While soft commodity companies have deforested pristine forests in Cameroon and the Congo basin, oil and gas operations have also caused the loss of extensive forests in the Niger Delta, Nigeria.[89] Deforestation in the Mayombe forest in the Cabinda region of Angola is also worrisome.[90] The resulting consequences are better imagined, especially the impacts on forests that cause deforestation and contribute to global warming.[91]

Multilateral financial institutions, including the World Bank, have acted as close allies to oil and gas TNCs and commodities companies involved in logging activities.[92] Despite the salience of forests and the environment in Africa, the World Bank and other sister banks have displayed an unbridled blindness toward these issues due to the uncritical support they receive from industrialized nations.[93] Therefore, the PoW must not only mediate conflicts arising from unsustainable resource exploitation on the continent but also negotiate sustainable resource exploitation pathways with resource-rich African states and their external collaborators, such as TNCs, banks, and agribusinesses.

Conclusion

The RST demonstrates that resource-rich African states are overly dependent on natural resources for rents and royalties for their economic sustenance. However, this avidity has unintended consequences. Firstly, it compels resource-rich African states to exhibit a disdain for the environment, even when they feel compelled or desirous to protect it. Secondly, it unavoidably triggers diverse resource-based violent conflicts, also known as the green war hypothesis, resulting from environmental degradation, resource inaccessibility, inequitable distribution of wealth, exclusion of resource-bearing communities from participation in planning and decision-making on matters that affect them, and more.

134 *Olawari D. J. Egbe and Fie David Dan-Woniowei*

This chapter examined the causes of resource-induced conflicts in Africa under three themes: state-induced environmental spoliation, instances of land grabbing in the continent, and bank project financing in Africa. The theme of state-induced environmental degradation asserts that African states' reliance on resource extraction as a means to economic survival. The RST places the environment at risk and, by extension, impoverishes the livelihoods of land-dependent Indigenous communities. Land grabbing as a theme examines local and external interests in agribusinesses or investments that use up a substantial portion of virgin lands or forests without adequate compensation. This sometimes involves the forceful displacement of entire communities. The chapter supports land acquisitions for food security, as long as all stakeholders benefit from the arrangement. The theme on bank-assisted project financing, like land grabbing, involves foreign banks providing loan facilities to agribusinesses or investors in Africa who are mainly interested in harvesting timber (i.e., commercial logging)—an act that contributes to deforestation in the continent and loss of farmlands.

This chapter contends that the prevalence of such conflict triggers in the continent makes third-party intervention an essential component. In this context, the chapter recognizes the efforts of the PoW in conflict resolution. However, the enormity of violent ongoing conflicts in the continent dampens the efforts invested by the PoW so far—a daunting task that places extraordinary demand on the PoW to further engage on the theme of resource-based conflicts if it must retain its usefulness in the conflict resolution architecture of the Peace and Security Architecture of the A.U. Though the PoW has no power whatsoever to enforce its ideas, it can draw attention to important topics, set the agenda, and then rely on the A.U. Assembly, the AU Executive Council of the PSC to take action.

Behind the several blaring headlines of conflicts in sub-Saharan Africa reflect agitations over underdevelopment, poverty, and unbridled degradation of the environment. The many ongoing conflicts do not respond to emergency reliefs but require sustainable human development that is pro-people, pro-poor, pro-nature and increases the choices and opportunities of ordinary people to participate in making decisions that affect them.[94]

Notes

1 Paul Collier and Nicholas Sambanis, *Understanding Civil War: Evidence and Analysis, Vol.1 Africa.* (Washington, DC: The World Bank, 2005).
2 Ian Bannon and Paul Collier, *Natural Resources and Violent Conflict: Options and Actions* (Washington, DC: The World Bank, 2003); Paul Collier, *The Bottom Billion: Why the Poorest Countries are Failing and What Can Be Done about It* (Oxford: Oxford University Press, 2007).
3 Tim Murithi, *Handbook of Africa's International Relations* (New York, NY: Routledge, 2015).
4 Ernest Aryeetey and Zenia Lewis, African Land Grabbing: Whose Interests are Served? Retrieved July 24, 2022, https://www.brookings.edu/articles/african-land-grabbing-whose-interests-are-served/; Lorenzo Cotula, "The International Political

Economy of the Global Land Rush: A Critical Appraisal of Trends, Scale, Geography and Drivers," *The Journal of Peasant Studies*, 39, nos. 3–4 (2012): 649–680.
5. Robert D. Kaplan, *The Coming Anarchy: Shattering the Dreams of the Post-Cold War* (New York, NY: Vintage, 2001), 7.
6. David-Ngendo Tshimba, "A Continental Conflict Prevention Mechanism on the Horizon? An Assessment of the Early Warning System in Africa," *NAP* no. 5, (2014), 2.
7. Sandle G. Gwexe, "Prospects for African Conflict Resolution in the Next Millennium: South Africa's View," *African Journal of Conflict Resolution*, 1, no. 1 (1999): 103–124; Jakkie Cilliers, "Peacekeeping, Africa and the Emerging Global Security Architecture," *African Security Review*, 12, no. 1. (2003): 111–114; Tor Sellstrom and Lennart Wohlgemuth, The International Response to Conflict and Genocide: Lessons from the Rwanda Experience—Study 1: Historical Perspective: Some Explanatory Factors. Joint Evaluation of Emergency Assistance to Rwanda.
8. William I. Zartman, *Cowardly Lions: Missed Opportunities to Prevent Deadly Conflict and State Collapse* (Boulder, CO: Lynne Rienner Publishers, 2005).
9. Sarjoh Bah, Elizabeth Choge-Nyangoro, Solomon Dersso, Brenda Morfa and Tim Murithi, *The African Peace and Security Architecture: A Handbook* (Addis Ababa: Friedrich-Ebert-Stiftung, 2014).
10. Ericka A. Albaugh, "Preventing Conflict in Africa: Possibilities of Peace Enforcement," in *Peacekeeping and Peace Enforcement in Africa: Methods of Conflict Prevention*, ed. Robert Rotberg (Washington, DC: Brookings Institution Press and World Peace Foundation, 2000), 111–210; Gilbert M. Khadiagala, *Meddlers or Mediators? African Interveners in Civil Conflicts in Eastern Africa* (Leiden: Brill, 2007).
11. James G. Stewart, *Corporate War Crimes: Prosecuting the Pillage of Natural Resources* (New York, NY: Open Society Foundations, 2011).
12. Theda Skocpol, "Rentier State and Shi'a Islam in the Iranian Revolution," *Theory and Society*, 11, (1982): 293–300; Hazem Beblawi, "The Rentier State in the Arab World," *Arab Studies Quarterly*, 9, no. 4 (1987): 383–398; Douglas A. Yates, *The Rentier State in Africa: Oil Rent Dependency and Neo-Colonialism in the Republic of Gabon* (Trenton, NJ: Africa World Press, 1996).
13. Matthew Gray, "A Theory of Late Rentierism in the Arab States of the Gulf," Qatar Centre for International and Regional Studies Occasional Paper No. 7, 2011; p. 1.
14. Michael L. Ross, "Does Oil Hinder Democracy?" *World Politics*, 53, no. 3 (2001): 325–361.
15. Hossein Mahdavy, "The Patterns and Problems of Economic Development in Rentier States: The Case of Iran," in *Studies in the Economic History of the Middle East: From the Rise of Islam to the Present Day*, ed. Michael A. Cook (London: Oxford University Press, 1970), 428–467.
16. Douglas A. Yates, *The Rentier State in Africa: Oil Rent Dependency and Neo-Colonialism in the Republic of Gabon* (Trenton, NJ: Africa World Press, 1996), 18.
17. Darren Kew and Peter M. Lewis, "Nigeria," in *Introduction to Comparative Politics: Political Challenges and Changing Agendas*, eds. Mark Kesselman, Joel Krieger and William A. Joseph, (Boston, MA: Cengage Learning, 2016), 495–543.
18. Charles Issawi, *An Economic History of Middle East and North Africa* (Columbia: Columbia University Press, 1982); Andre Elias Mazawi, "The Contested

Terrain of Education in the Arab States: An Appraisal of Major Research Trends", *Comparative Education Review*, 43, no. 3 (1999): 332–352.
19 African Union. Protocol Relating to the Establishment of the Peace and Security Council of the African Union (Durban: Adopted by the 1st Ordinary Session of the Assembly of the African Union, July 9, 2002).
20 Laurie Nathan, "Africa's Early Warning System: An Emperor with No Clothes?" *South African Journal of International Affairs*, 14, no.1 (2007): 49–60; African Centre for the Constructive Resolution of Disputes (ACCROD), The African Union Panel of the Wise: Strengthening Relations with Similar Regional Mechanisms. A Report Based on the High-Level Retreat of the African Union PoW, held in Ouagadougou, Burkina Faso, on 4 and 5 June 2012 (Durban: ACCORD, 2013).
21 Joao G. Porto, and Kapinga Y. Ngandu, *The African Union's Panel of the Wise: A Concise History* (Durban: ACCORD, 2015).
22 Henrietta Didigu, "Developing a Common Agenda for Subregional Organizations for Peace, Security and Conflict Prevention in Africa: A View from ECOWAS," (ISS, 2001, www.iss.co.za/pubs/Books/Unesco/didigu.html.); Joao G. Porto and Kapinga Y. Ngandu, *The African Union's Panel of the Wise: A Concise History* (Durban: ACCORD, 2015).
23 Laurie Nathan, Mediation and the African Union's Panel of the Wise. Discussion Paper No.10 (Crisis States Development Research Centre, 2005).
24 Jamila El-Abdellaqui, The Panel of the Wise: A Comprehensive Introduction to a Critical Pillar of Environmental Investigation Agency, ISS Paper 193 (Pretoria Institute for Security Studies, 2009); Environmental Investigation Agency, Tainted Timber, Tarnished Temples-How the Cameroon-Vietnam Timber Trade Hurts the Cameroonian People and Forests (Washington, DC: EIA, 2020).
25 African Union, Modalities for the Functioning of the Panel of the Wise as Adopted by the Peace and Security Council at its 100th Meeting Held On 12 November 2007 (Addis Ababa: The A.U., 2007); Sarjoh Bah, Elizabeth Choge-Nyangoro, Solomon Dersso, Brenda Morfa and Tim Murithi, *The African Peace and Security Architecture: A Handbook* (Addis Ababa: Friedrich-Ebert-Stiftung, 2014).
26 Bah, Choge-Nyangoro, Dersso, Morfa and Murithi, *The African Peace and Security Architecture*.
27 African Union, Report of the African Union Panel of the Wise on Improving the Mediation and Resolution of Natural Resource-Related Conflicts Across Africa. The 5th Thematic Report of the African Union Panel of the Wise (Addis Ababa: African Union Commission, 2019).
28 John H. Bodley, *Victims of Progress* (New York, NY: AltaMira Press, 2008).
29 Nils Peter Gleditsch, "Armed Conflict and the Environment: A Critique of the Literature," *Journal of Peace Research*, 35, no. 3 (1998): 381–400.
30 Wirirana Brilliant Masara, "Environment-Conflict Nexus: The Relevance of Thomas Homer-Dixons Environmental Conflict Theory in Africa", *African Journal of Empirical Research*, 2, no. 2 (2021): 170–175.
31 Tana High-Level Forum on Security in Africa (TLHFSA). Background Paper on Natural Resource Governance in Africa: Conflict, Politics and Power, p. 11. www.google.com/search?client=firefox-bd&q=Background+Paper+on+Natural+Resource+Governance+in+AfricaConflict%2C+Politics+and+Power; Abdelhak Bassou, *Africa's Natural Resources and Geopolitical Realities* (Rabat: OCP Policy Centre, Policy Brief PB 17/19, 2017).
32 New York Times, April 2, 2017.

33 Richard J. Lazarus, "Human Nature, the Laws of Nature and the Nature of Environmental Law," *Virginia Environmental Law Journal*, 24, no. 3 (2005): 231–261, 234.
34 Yale H. Ferguson and Richard W. Mansbach, *Globalisation: The Return of Borders to a Borderless World?* (New York, NY: Routledge, 2012).
35 Daniel W. O'Neill, Andrew L. Fanning, William F. Lamb and Julia K. Steinberger. "A Good Life for All Within Planetary Boundaries," Nature Sustainability 1, no. 1 (2018): 88–95; Holmes Rolston III. *A New Environmental Ethics: The Next Millennium for Life* (New York, NY: Routledge, 2020).
36 Winona LaDuke, *All Our Relations: Native Struggles for Land and Life* (Brooklyn, NY: South End Press, 1999).
37 Robert D. Kaplan, "The Coming Anarchy," *The Atlantic Monthly*, 273, no. 2 (1994): 58.
38 Frances Stewart, "Root Causes of Violent Conflict in Developing Countries," *British Medical Journal*, 324 (2002): 342–345.
39 Amnesty International, Oil, Gas and Mining Industries, accessed 12 May 2022, www.google.com/search?client=firefox-b-d&q=Oil%2C+Gas+and+Mining+Industries
40 Human Rights Watch, Oil, Mining, and Natural Resources, accessed 15 June 2022, www.google.com/search?client=firefoxbd&q=Oil%2C+Mining%2C+and+Natural+Resources
41 Jack Doyle, *Riding the Dragon: Royal Dutch Shell and the Fossil Fire* (Boston, MA: Environmental Health Fund, 2002), 166.
42 Fred Pearce, *The Land Grabbers: The New Fight Over Who Owns the Earth* (Boston, MA: Beacon Press, 2012); Tony Allan, Martin Keulertz, Sojamo Suvi and Jeroen Warner, *Handbook of Land and Water Grabs in Africa: Foreign Direct Investment and Food and Water Security* (London: Routledge, 2013).
43 Ruth Hall, "Land Grabbing in Southern Africa: The Many Faces of the Investor Rush," *Review of African Political Economy*, 38, no. 128 (2011), 193–214, 1.
44 James Fairhead, Melissa Leach and Ian Scoones, "Green Grabbing: A New Appropriation of Nature?" *The Journal of Peasant Studies*, 39, no. 2 (2012): 237–261.
45 World Bank, Rising Global Interest in Farmland: Can It Yield Sustainable and Equitable Benefits? (Washington, DC: The World Bank, 2010); Olivier De Schutter, "How Not to Think of Land-Grabbing: Three Critiques of Large-Scale Investments in Farmland," *Journal of Peasant Studies*, 38, no. 2 (2011): 249–279.
46 Ruth Hall, "Land Grabbing in Southern Africa: The Many Faces of the Investor Rush," *Review of African Political Economy*, 38, no. 128 (2011): 193–214.
47 Human Rights Watch, *Waiting Here for Death: Forced Displacement and 'Villagization' in Ethiopia's Gambella* Region (Washington, DC: Human Rights Watch, 2012); Human Rights Watch, *What Will Happen If Hunger Comes: Abuses Against the Indigenous Peoples of Ethiopia's Lower Omo Valley* (Washington, DC: Human Rights Watch, 2012).
48 Ruth Hall, "Land Grabbing in Africa and the New Politics of Food" (Future Agricultures, Policy Brief 041, 2011).
49 Fouad Makki, "The Political Ecology of Land Grabs in Ethiopia," in *From Biocultural Homogenization to Biocultural Conservation* eds. Ricardo Rozzi, Roy H. May Jr., F. Stuart Chapin III, Francisca Massardo, Michael C. Gavin, Irene J. Klaver, Aníbal Pauchard, Martin A. and Nuñez, Daniel Simberloff (Switzerland: Springer, 2018), 83–95.

50 Greenpeace, Halcyon Agri's (Sudcam): Ruinous Rubber, accessed 5 August 2022, https://m.gsearch.co/search/?search_term=Halcyon%2520Agri%2592s%2520Ruinous%2520Rubber&brand=g2; Greenpeace, *Sudcam's Assault on Human Rights* (Johannesburg, SA: Greenpeace Africa, 2019).
51 Tal Harris, Greenpeace Africa and Rainforest Rescue: Joint Statement Following the Suspension of Logging Plans for Ebo Forest, August 13, 2020.
52 Lorenzo Cotula, Vermeulen Sonja, Rebecca Leonard and James Keeley, *Land Grab or Development Opportunity? Agricultural Development and International Land Deals in Africa* (London: International Institute for Environment and Development & Rome: Food and Agricultural Organization; Rome, International Fund for Agricultural Development, 2009).
53 Chris de Wet, *Development-Induced Displacement: Problems, Policies and People* (Oxford: Berghahn Books, 2005); Claire Provost, Global Land Grab Could Trigger Conflict, Report Says, accessed 3 July 2022, www.theguardian.com/global-development/2012/feb/02/global-land-grab-trigger-conflict-report
54 Klauis Deininger, "Challenges Posed by the New Wave of Farmland Investment," *Journal of Peasant Studies*, 38, no. 2 (2011): 217–247; Klauis Deininger and Derek Byerlee, "The Rise of Large Farms in Land Abundant Countries: Do They Have a Future?" Policy Research Working Paper No. 5588 (Washington, DC: World Bank, 2011).
55 Ayodele F. Odusola, Land Grab in Africa: A Review of Emerging Issues and Implications for Policy Options, Working Paper No. 124 (International Policy Centre for Inclusive Growth, 2014).
56 Ernest Aryeetey and Zenia Lewis, African Land Grabbing: Whose Interests are Served? Retrieved July 24, 2022, https://www.brookings.edu/articles/african-land-grabbing-whose-interests-are-served/; Lorenzo Cotula, "The International Political Economy of the Global Land Rush: A Critical Appraisal of Trends, Scale, Geography and Drivers," *The Journal of Peasant Studies*, 39, nos. 3–4 (2012): 649–680.
57 Emmanuel Sulle and Fred Nelson, Biofuels, Land Access and Rural Livelihoods in Tanzania (London: International Institute for Environment and Development, 2009).
58 Claire Provost and Paige McClanahan, Sierra Leone: Local Resistance Grows as Investors Snap Up Land, accessed 5 August 2022, www.theguardian.com/global-development/poverty-matters/2012/apr/11/sierra-leone-local-resistance-land-deals; Frederic Mousseau, *Understanding Land Investment Deals in Africa: Socfin Land Investment in Sierra Leone, Land Deal Brief* (Oakland, CA: The Oakland Institute, 2012).
59 Adwoa Yeboah Gyapong, "Land Grabs, Farmworkers, and Rural Livelihoods in West Africa: Some Silences in the Food Sovereignty Discourse," *Globalisations*, 18, no. 3 (2021): 339–354, 339.
60 Jonathan Watts, Murders of Environment and Land Defenders Hit Record High, accessed 3 May 2022; www.theguardian.com/environment/2021/sep/13/murders-environment-land-defenders-record-high
61 Caroline Thomas, *The Environment in International Relations* (London: RIIAs, 1992).
62 Chris de Wet, *Development-Induced Displacement: Problems, Policies and People* (Oxford: Berghahn Books, 2005); Mabusetsa Lenka Thamae and Lori Pottinger, *On the Wrong Side of Development: Lessons Learned from the Lesotho Highlands Water Project* (Lesotho: Transformation Resource Centre, 2006).

63 Vidal John and Provost Claire, Campaigners Claim World Bank Helps Facilitate Land Grabs in Africa, accessed 5 August 2022, www.theguardian.com/global-development/2012/apr/23/world-bank-land-grabs-africa
64 Patricia Adams, "The World Bank and the IMF in Sub-Saharan Africa: Undermining Development and Environmental Sustainability," *Journal of International Affairs*, 46, no. 1 (1992): 97–117; Patricia Adams, "The World Bank's Finances: An International Debt Crisis," in *Globalisation and the South*, eds. Caroline Thomas and Peter Wilkin (New York: St. Martin's Press, Inc., 1997), 163–183.
65 Human Rights Watch, *Waiting Here for Death: Forced Displacement and 'Villagization' in Ethiopia's Gambella* Region (Washington, DC: Human Rights Watch, 2012); Human Rights Watch, *What Will Happen If Hunger Comes: Abuses Against the Indigenous Peoples of Ethiopia's Lower Omo Valley* (Washington, DC: Human Rights Watch, 2012).
66 Marion Couldrey and Tim Morris, *Dilemmas of Development-induced Displacement* (Oxford: Forced Migration Review, January 12, 2002).
67 Willem van Genugten, *The World Bank Group, the IMF and Human Rights: A Conceptualized Way Forward* (Cambridge: Intersentia, 2015); Daniel D. Bradlow, "The World Bank, the IMF, and Human Rights," *Transnational Law and Contemporary Problems*, 6, no. 47 (1996): 47–90.
68 John Madeley, *Big Business, Poor Peoples: How Transnational Corporations Damage the World's Poor*, 2nd ed. (London: Zed Books Ltd, 2008).
69 Susanna Hecht and Alexander Cockburn, *The Fate of the Forest: Developers, Destroyers, and Defenders of the Amazon* (New York, NY: The Penguin Group, 1990); Peter Bosshard, "World Bank Returns to Big Dams," *World Rivers Review*, September 5, 2013.
70 International Rivers, The World Bank and Dams. Part 1: Lessons Not Learned (Berkeley, CA: International Rivers, 2015).
71 Ans Kolk, Forests in International Environmental Politics: International Organisations, NGOs and the Brazilian Amazon (Utrecht,: International Books, 1996); Jennifer C. Veilleux, "The Human Security Dimensions of Dam Development: The Grand Ethiopian Renaissance Dam," *Global Dialogue*, 15, no. 2 (2013): 1–15.
72 Ibrahim F. I. Shihata, "The World Bank and the Environment: A Legal Perspective," *Maryland Journal of International Law*, 16, no. 1 (1992): 1–42.
73 International Rivers, African Dams, Rivers and Rights: A Guide for Communities to be Impacted by the Inga 3 Dam (Pretoria: International Rivers Africa Programme 2012).
74 Ryan Hover, Pipe Dreams: The World Bank's Failed Efforts to Restore Lives and Livelihoods of Dam-Affected People in Lesotho (Berkeley, CA: International Rivers Network, 2021).
75 Peter Bosshard, "World Bank Returns to Big Dams," *World Rivers Review*, September 5, 2013.
76 Raul M. Sanchez, "To the World Commission on Dams: Do Not Forget the Law, and Do Not Forget Human Rights: Lessons from the U.S.-Mexico Border," *Inter-American Law Review*, 30, no. 3 (1999): 629–657.
77 Mabusetsa Lenka Thamae and Lori Pottinger, *On the Wrong Side of Development: Lessons Learned from the Lesotho Highlands Water Project* (Lesotho: Transformation Resource Centre, 2006); Thayer Scudder, "Social Impacts of Large Dam Projects," in *Large Dams: Learning from the Past, Looking at the*

Future, eds. Tony Dorcey, Achim Steiner, Michael Acreman and Brett Orlando (Washington, DC: The World Bank, 1997), 41–68.
78 United Nations, *International Covenant on Economic, Social, and Cultural Rights* (New York, NY: United Nations, 1966).
79 Norman Myers, "The Anatomy of Environmental Action: The Case of Tropical Deforestation," in *The International Politics of the Environment: Actors, Interests and Institutions*, eds. Andrew Hurrell and Benedict Kingsbury (Oxford: Clarendon Press, 1992), 430–454.
80 Chris de Wet, *Development-Induced Displacement: Problems, Policies and People* (Oxford: Berghahn Books, 2005).
81 Anna Maria Caldara, *Endangered Environments: Saving the Earth's Vanishing Ecosystems* (New York, NY: Mallard Press, 1991); BakTrack, Soft Commitments, Hard Lessons: An Analysis of the Soft Commodities Compact. BankTrack Report (Nijmegen, 2020). www.banktrack.org/download/soft_commitments_hard_lessons_an_analysis_of_the_soft_commodities_compact/201130_scc_report_3.pdf
82 John H. Vandermeer and Ivette Perfecto, *Breakfast of Biodiversity: The Truth about Rain Forest Destruction* (Oakland, CA: The Institute for Food and Development Policy, 1995).
83 Tamar Gutner, "World Bank Environmental Reform: Revisiting Lessons from Agency Theory," *International Organization*, 59, no. 3 (2005): 773–783.
84 Tal Harris, Greenpeace Africa and Rainforest Rescue: Joint Statement Following the Suspension of Logging Plans for Ebo Forest, accessed 7 June 2022, www.greenpeace.org/africa/en/press/11908/greenpeace-africa-and-rainforest-rescue-joint-statement-following-the-suspension-of-logging-plans-for-ebo-forest/.
85 BankTrack, Soft Commitments, Hard Lessons: An Analysis of the Soft Commodities Compact..
86 Environmental Investigation Agency, Rotten to the Core: How to Tackle the Corrupt Networks Facilitating Wildlife and Forest Crime. Prepared for the UN General Assembly Special Session on Corruption, New York, 2–4 June, 2021.
87 Bretton Woods Project, Deforestation and Double Standards, accessed 5 June 2022, www.brettonwoodsproject.org/2007/10/art-557184/
88 Paul D. Manion, *Tree Disease Concepts* (Bergen County, NJ: Prentice Hall, 1981); William M. Ciesla and Edwin Donaubauer, *Decline and Dieback of Trees and Forests: A Global Overview* (Rome: FAO, 1994).
89 Ayansina Ayanlade and Nicolas Drake, "Forest Loss in Different Ecological Zones of the Niger Delta, Nigeria: Evidence from Remote Sensing," *GeoJournal*, 81, no. 5 (2016):717–735; Glory O. Enaruvbe and Ozien P. Atafo, "Analysis of Deforestation Pattern in the Niger Delta Region of Nigeria," *Journal of Land Use Science*, 11, no. 1 (2014): 113–130.
90 John M. Mendelsohn, "Landscape Changes in Angola," in *Biodiversity of Angola. Science and Conservation: A Modern Synthesis*, eds. Brian J. Huntley, Vladimir Russo, Fernanda Lages and Nuno Ferrand (Cham: Springer Nature, 2019), 123–137; Jose Kundy, Over Logging Threatens Key Forest in Angola's Cabinda, accessed 22 November 2022, www.africanews.com/2022/10/27/over-logging-threatens-key-forest-in-angolas-cabinda//
91 Editorial Nature, "A Warning from the Forests of Africa and the Amazon: Carbon Analysis Suggests Faster Emissions Reductions are Needed," *Nature*, 579, (2020): 7–8, 8.

92 Roger Perman, Ma Yue, McGilvray James, Maddison Davis and Common Michael, *Natural Resource and Environmental Economics* (Harlow: Pearson Education Ltd, 2003).
93 Marcus Colchester and Larry Lohmann, *The Struggle for Land and the Fate of Forests* (New York, NY: Zed Books, 1993); Odin K. Knudsen, "The World Bank's Forest Policy and Strategy", *The International Forestry Review*, 2, no. 3 (2000): 169–170; Nigel Sizer and Dominiek Plouvier, *Increased Investment and Trade by Transnational Logging Companies in Africa, the Caribbean, and the Pacific: Implications for the Sustainable Management of and Conservation of Tropical Forests* (Belgium: World Wide Fund for Nature International, 2000).
94 James Gustave Speth, "Foreword," in *Human Development Report 1994* (United Nations Development Programme, 1994), iii.

Part III
Lessons and Future Directions

7 Placing the Rule of Law and Environmental Justice in the Resource-Conflict Nexus in Nigeria

Eghosa O. Ekhator and Godswill Agbaitoro

Introduction

Africa is blessed with vast natural resources which, if well-managed, could translate into significant economic growth and development. Regrettably, a series of protracted conflicts with links to natural resources have negatively affected the much-needed development of the continent. More so, the impact and/or damage from natural resource conflicts in Africa have been extended to the environment and, in most cases, the impact goes beyond the immediate people and is further passed on to future generations. The damage from natural resource extractions to the environment includes the reduction of the air quality and water supply, negative impact on biodiversity, and conservation hotspots amongst others. These damages are known to be some of the root causes of resource conflicts. Undoubtedly, natural resource conflicts remain a good example to describe some of the developmental challenges in Africa. This is true to the extent that African countries have suffered extreme levels of incessant conflicts, poor policymaking and decisions, deforestation and desertification, pollution of water, air, land, environmental degradation, and generally bad governance,[1] all of which are in some way linked to natural resources.

Over the years, it has been observed that many internal conflicts have been linked to natural resources in Africa. For example, the United Nations Environmental Programme (UNEP) study found that over the last 60 years, at least 40% of all internal conflicts have been linked to the exploitation of natural resources such as diamonds, oil, and other mineral resources.[2] From Nigeria to Angola, to the Democratic Republic of Congo (DRC), and from Sierra Leone to Liberia and the Great Lakes region of Africa, conflicts have been perpetuated through the exploitation of natural resources. Consequently, the exploitation of natural resources in Africa has generated a lot of controversies which have translated into major conflicts with serious impacts on Africa's environment and economy.

Against the background above, this chapter seeks to deploy the instrumentality of the environmental justice paradigm towards addressing natural resource conflicts in Africa. This is because conflicts linked to natural resource

DOI: 10.4324/9781003355717-11

exploitation in Africa have their roots in the lack of adherence to the rule of law and environmental justice. For instance, it is observed that poor environmental practices leading to injustices in the Niger Delta Region (NDR) of Nigeria have exacerbated the environmental challenges faced by members of oil host communities. Furthermore, the absence of the rule of law worsens environmental injustices and exacerbates resource conflicts in many developing countries. The point is that access to and/or ownership of natural resources by the inhabitants of the NDR are the underlying factors in the environmental justice paradigm in Nigeria.[3] This is in addition to poor implementation of the rule of law—that is the lack of enforcement of the legal regime for environmental protection. Undoubtedly, there are a plethora of laws and environmental regulations protecting the Nigerian environment.[4] Some of the laws include legislative enactments on gas flaring, the Environmental Impact Assessment Act 1992, National Oil Spill Detection and Response Agency Act (NOSDRA Act) 2006, the National Environmental Standards and Regulations Enforcement Agency (Establishment) Act 2007, the National Environmental Policy, the Criminal Code, Oil in Navigable Waters Act 1968, and the recently revised Petroleum Industry Act 2021, amongst other laws and regulations. Arguably, Nigeria environmental protection regime is adequate but buffeted by implementation challenges including environmental problems in the Niger Delta such as oil spills and pollution, gas flaring, and human rights violations.[5] This is against the backdrop of the lack of political will of the Nigerian government to enforce or implement laws on environmental protection in the oil and gas industry.[6] Arguably, the causes of instability in the Niger Delta can also be traced to the lack of implementation of the environmental protection regime in Nigeria.

This chapter is divided into five parts including this introduction. The second part explores the contextual framework of environmental justice and further argues that proper implementation of the environmental justice paradigm potentially remains a viable strategy for addressing natural resource conflicts in Africa. Part of the analysis is centred on how environmental justice is situated within African scholarship. More specifically, the section analyses how the lack of the implementation of environmental justice principles in the environmental protection legal regime (including the rule of law) in Africa exacerbates natural resource conflicts. The third part focuses on natural resource conflicts in Africa. This section highlights the challenges posed by resource conflict to Africa's economy and the environment. It provides some analyses of the challenges through the lens of selected African countries (using Nigeria as the main case study) that have experienced natural resource conflicts. Furthermore, it discusses how these conflicts have impacted their environment and economy at large. The fourth part focuses on some principles embedded in environmental justice that could be used to address natural resource conflicts. Using Nigeria as a case study, this section provides an analysis on the effectiveness of environmental justice principles in the context of resolving natural resource conflicts in other African states. We argue that guaranteeing the enforcement of the rule of law would then depend on the integration of environmental justice principles into the laws governing resource extraction and use. The fifth section is the conclusion.

Conceptual Frameworks

Environmental Justice

The historical evolution of the concept of environmental justice is traced to the United States (US) where it served as a counterbalance to the dissatisfaction for racist government policies in parts of the country in the 1960s and 1970s.[7] A plethora of studies have analysed the disproportionate burden of differential environmental harms on minorities.[8] Therefore, environmental justice "...is the first paradigm to link environment and race, class, gender and social justice in an explicit framework."[9] Environmental justice is understood to have different meanings from the perspectives of developed and developing countries.[10] In Africa, environmental justice could be described as a concept that mainly encompasses access to natural resources, while in countries like the US and the UK, it focuses on maintaining the planet's well-being, particularly through public participation.[11] For example, environmental justice advocates in the US have for many years focused on the continuous challenge to the current environmental protection apparatus and offer their framework for addressing environmental inequities, disparate impact, and unequal protection.[12] The environmental justice framework in the US incorporates other social movements that seek to eliminate harmful practices in housing land use, industrial planning, health care, and sanitation services.[13] For the UK, the concept is tailored to an understanding of socio-economic parity.[14] Arguably, the nature of the challenges it creates and the impact on people do not differ, i.e., there are no significant differences in the controversies and impact on peoples' lives that environmental injustice generates in the US and UK.[15] However, it should be noted that environmental justice has varied meanings, strategies of access, and implications in various contexts.[16]

For Africa, access and/or control and ownership of natural resources, as earlier stated, by the inhabitants of the NDR of Nigeria (where the oil and gas industry is located) are the underlying factors in the environmental justice paradigm.[17] In the African country context, environmental justice is defined as "the equitable distribution of environmental amenities, the rectification and retribution of environmental abuses, the restoration of nature, and the fair exchange of resources."[18] Others view environmental justice as any undue imposition of environmental burdens on innocent bystanders or communities not parties to the activities generating such burdens.[19] The concept as defined by African scholars shares similarities with the framing from the perspective of Western countries. The conception from Western countries includes ensuring public participation in environmental decision-making, accountability, equality and non-discrimination, access to information, and access to justice in environmental issues. These same issues have led to protracted conflict in the NDR of Nigeria as armed groups continue to struggle for the control and ownership of natural resources.

The inequitable distribution of environmental benefits and disadvantages (i.e., environmental injustices) in Nigeria is a source of conflict and the resultant violence has threatened the Nigerian state, the oil industry, and the host communities.[20] This is in addition to contributions from the Multinational Corporations (MNCs) and the Federal Government (FG) of Nigeria which has exacerbated the environmental injustices.[21] Notwithstanding the various efforts from the FG and MNCs operating in the NDR, which take the form of militarization, increased spending on community development, and the amnesty programmes and other corporate social responsibility programmes, the NDR remains susceptible to natural resource conflicts due largely to environmental injustices.[22]

Interestingly, there have been arguments put forward by scholars that challenges posed by environmental injustice are also borne out of the failure of the legal framework for the protection of the environment to adequately hold the oil industry accountable for environmental problems.[23] This challenge is somewhat attributed to the difficult position of the government, particularly in developing countries. For instance, Nigeria's joint and conflicting role as an operator and regulator of the oil industry puts the Nigerian government in a position to prioritize the protection of economic interest at the expense of its mandate to ensure effective regulation of the oil industry.[24] Regrettably, this approach which translates into environmental injustice has consistently led to environmental pollution and degradation, human rights abuse, and violent conflicts with further impact on the economy.

The next section discusses the rule of law concept.

Rule of Law

Historically, the rule of law concept has no commonly accepted definition but is often described as encompassing a clear system of laws and requirements, widely accepted and advanced by all levels of society and its governance.[25] Scholars have described the rule of law as a broad concept that includes the accountability of the government under the law; the clarity, stability, fairness, and public nature of laws; the accessibility, fairness, and efficiency of the process by which laws are enacted, administered, and enforced; and the competence, independence, and ethics of adjudicators, attorneys, and judicial officers.[26] Furthermore, Ako and Uddin suggest that notwithstanding that the rule of law lacks a precise definition that there are

> three elements of the rule of law which makes its presence crucial for any legal system; these are the supremacy of the law and the absence of arbitrariness, equality before the law, and constitutional law as part of the ordinary law of the land.[27]

The rule of law is said to be a stimulating factor for economic growth and socio-economic justice, prevents and deters violent conflict and crime, and strengthens accountability and checks on power, allowing for more equitable distribution of resources and better environmental protection.[28] Furthermore, the rule of law concept remains crucial for translating natural resource governance standards into realistic conflict resolution measures in Africa. This is mainly achieved through strict implementation of the legal frameworks designed to protect the environment by designated authorities.

Furthermore, the rule of law is one of the key principles of effective natural resource management. For example, Ako and Uddin suggest that one definition of good governance phenomenon in the context of natural resource management in Africa is said to encapsulate the four cardinal principles of rule of law, accountability, and transparency, management of revenues, and democracy.[29] Through strict adherence to environmental justice, in particular, those relating to the rule of law, resource-rich countries with years of protracted natural resource conflicts can begin to enforce legal protection mechanisms to ensure that the environment is sufficiently protected. This, in turn, will significantly resolve underlying environmental challenges such as lack of accountability for the exploitation of natural resources and, therefore, reduce abuses of power and corruption that exacerbate resource conflicts in many African countries.

Natural Resource Conflicts in Africa: Challenges and Impacts

As has been mentioned, Africa is endowed with different types of natural resources, including bitumen, gold, oil, timber, and water amongst others. Unfortunately, except for a few countries on the continent, many African states (especially its citizens) have not reaped or benefited from the abundance of natural resources in their countries. Ordinarily, the exploitation and exploration of natural resources are expected to develop African economies, as has been replicated in some parts of the world, but in some African states this has led to what has been termed "resource curse" or "paradox of plenty".[30] Resource curse "refers to the failure of many resource-rich countries to benefit fully from their natural resource wealth, and for governments in these countries to respond effectively to public welfare needs."[31] The "resource curse" debate gained theoretical influence following the intervention by prominent economists such as Humphreys, Sachs, and Stiglitz who argued that countries endowed with abundant natural resources tend to experience economic underperformance compared to countries with fewer resources.[32]

Notwithstanding, the notion of "resource curse", the availability of natural resources has led to economic growth and development in some African states.[33] Also, it should be noted that the resource curse phenomenon is not without its critics. For example, the African Progress Panel Report 2013 argues that Africa has never suffered from "resource curse" thesis and goes to suggest that:

> What the region has suffered from is the curse of poor policies, weak governance and a failure to translate resource wealth into social and economic progress. The favorable market conditions created by global resource constraints provide no guarantee that the growth of extractive industries will lead to improvements in the lives of people. But if governments seize the moment and put in place the right policies, Africa's resource wealth could potentially transform the continent's prospects.[34]

It is important to note that scholars have stridently criticized the resource curse theory. For example, Obi suggests that

> explaining such conflicts on the basis of the ways natural resources either act as an incentive/motive for rebel groups or erode and weaken states, does not adequately capture the complex histories, dimensions and transnational linkages to civil conflict in Africa.[35]

Furthermore, Cusato alludes to the inherent shortcomings or contradictions in the resource curse theory in clarifying the roots and dynamics of resource conflicts in the Global South.[36] Cusato further suggests that the resource curse theory's "simplistic and generalizing appeal resulted in widespread and often uncritical acceptance of the resource curse thesis by international organizations, civil society, and scholars across disciplines."[37] Notwithstanding the valid criticisms, the resource curse theory provides a lens to look at the various conflicts in Africa exacerbated by the presence of mineral resources. Hence, scholars should be more nuanced in their analysis of the contribution of the presence of mineral resources to the conflicts in Africa.

On the other hand, the presence of natural resources in African states has also exacerbated environmental pollution, human rights violations, corporate abuses, and natural resource conflicts amongst other issues arising from the activities of MNCs and other firms (including other non-state actors) operating in African states. It is not in doubt that many of the intrastate conflicts in resource-rich African states have been heavily linked to natural resources. For instance, it is observed that less than a quarter of peace agreements for conflicts with links to natural resources mainly address natural resource management and governance.[38] According to Alao,

> natural resources can be linked to conflicts in Africa in three ways. These include (1) cases in which natural resources constitute a direct or remote cause of conflict; (2) situations in which natural resources fuel and/or sustain conflicts; and (3) instances in which resources have come into consideration in efforts to resolve conflicts.[39]

It is pertinent to note that one of the reasons for the protracted conflicts in resource-rich countries in Africa is the injustices attributed to the government's failure to adopt a holistic framework within which it can assess the problems and develop a strategy that addresses them.[40] Additionally, the alliance and/or joint operation between MNCs and host governments for the exploitation of natural resources often tend to exclude public participation of host communities. According to Amusan, the interest of MNCs to operate in dangerous zones of Africa would be accorded a blank cheque for their operations.[41] This may explain some of the reasons why some of the MNCs are effective in countries such as South Sudan, Sudan, and Nigeria and continue to scramble for the exploitation of hydrocarbons despite the conflict.[42] Regrettably, this approach is also used in the management of the oil industry and has thus remained a factor that contributes to environmental injustice in resource-rich countries. This long-standing approach breeds the ground for resource conflict as members of host communities where oil and gas operations are conducted often feel neglected. The efforts of MNCs in extractive industries to obtain oil and mineral resources from developing countries in the Global South have often caused serious environmental harm and intense conflicts with local communities or populations.[43]

A defining feature of the many recent conflicts of the last three decades in Africa, especially those in Angola, Sierra Leone, Liberia, and more recently the Great Lakes region, is the fact that they have been perpetuated through illegal exploitation of extractive resources.[44] The illegal exploitation of resources tends to instigate conflicts as often members of host communities feel neglected—as per not being allowed to publicly participate in the use and management of the resources. This often leads to access and control problems which may allow rebels and other militant groups to generate conflict financing.[45] Charles Taylor (the former rebel leader turned President of Liberia) had financed his insurrection by using revenue engendered by the sale of natural resources.[46] Even when the source of Taylor's access to diamonds was curtailed by a United Nations imposed embargo, he turned his attention to illicit logging of timber and forest resources to fund his activities.[47] The diamond trade financed wars in different parts of Africa including Sierra Leone, Congo, Liberia, and Angola.

The DRC is one of the poorest countries in the world notwithstanding its rich natural resource wealth. It is a country that is known to be rich in minerals including diamonds, coltan, tantalum, tin, and gold amongst other natural resource endowments. These mineral resources are desired for their prevalent use in modern technologies, like semiconductors for vehicles and mobile phones.[48] Since the 1990s, a succession of bloody armed conflicts or wars in the DRC have had damaging effects on flora and fauna populations.[49] The DRC is said to be the greatest exemplar of a resource-fuelled war.[50] Hence, these minerals originating in the DRC have financed one of the world's most complicated and long-lasting prolonged wars or conflicts.[51] However, it should be noted that not all the armed or militia groups operating in the DRC (and other conflict zones in Africa) occupies or have access to mining sites.[52] Some of the armed groups operating in the DRC fund their activities in a plethora of ways including taxes from the local communities, funds from political sponsors or running roadblocks on trade channels amongst other strategies.[53]

Hence, not all "natural resource" conflicts in Africa are actually funded from the sale of natural resources.[54] The ongoing tensions or conflicts in the DRC have cost the lives of over 5 million people.[55] DRC is a country rich in natural resources and it is said to be a "textbook forum for natural resource-induced conflicts at both; local and national levels."[56] Cuvelier et al suggest that in the last two decades, there has been a remarkable rise in the number of armed conflicts in the Global South wherein "many of which are believed to have been caused, prolonged or intensified by the abundant availability or lack of natural resources."[57]

Over the years, a plethora of international mechanisms have emerged to regulate conflicts associated with natural resources. For example, due to the atrocities arising from the conflict diamond trade, a certification process known as the Kimberley process (KP) was developed in 2003 and the KP Certification Scheme is said to be one of the first significant international responses to the resource conflict issue.[58] The KP is a global governance-led scheme that was set up to counteract the trade in conflict diamonds. The KP Certification Scheme "is an innovative, voluntary system that imposes extensive requirements on participants to ensure that shipments of rough diamonds are not illegally obtained by rebel movements to finance wars against legitimate governments."[59] Notwithstanding the positive impacts of the KP (such as improving the economies of the different mineral-producing African countries), some scholars have argued that it has not had major impact in the reduction of the conflict diamonds trade in different parts of Africa.[60] Furthermore, in many parts of Africa, ordinary citizens are yet to benefit from the various international initiatives on responsible sourcing initiatives or programmes. For example, scholars have argued these initiatives have had detrimental impacts on local artisanal miners in the DRC.[61] This next section will now focus on how principles derived from environmental justice could be used to address conflicts arising from resource extraction and use in Africa.

Recommendations

Embedding Principles of Environmental Justice into the Laws and Policies Governing Resource Extraction and Use in Africa

This section focuses on addressing the natural resource conflicts in Africa through principles derived from the environmental justice paradigm. We note here that natural resource conflicts in Africa are a result of the general weakness of the rule of law and the minimization of environmental justice in resource governance. Hence, a key part of the argument advanced in this section is a call to redefine the environmental protection legal regime in Africa. We, therefore, propose some reform measures that include the use of non-governmental organizations (NGOs), improved access to environmental justice, environmental rights, and good resource governance practices to address underlying challenges that lead to natural resource conflicts. These measures, if well

Non-Governmental Organizations (NGOs) and Access to Environmental Justice

As was mentioned earlier, the implementation of environmental justice in African countries with huge deposits of natural resources is akin to having access to justice.[62] The use of NGOs remains a viable strategy for the implementation of the environmental justice paradigm towards resolving natural resource conflicts. According to Ikelegbe, activities of civil society (i.e., NGOs) in the NDR of Nigeria have reconstructed their agitation into a broad, participatory, highly mobilized, and coordinated struggle and redirected it into a struggle for self-determination, equity, and civil and environmental rights.[63] This approach could be further leveraged to address conflicts characterized by the exploitation of natural resources.

In practice, one of the major impediments to access to environmental justice in Nigeria is the principle of *locus standi*. This is an obligatory requirement for claimants or plaintiffs to be coated with *locus standi* (sufficient interest) as a pre-requisite to institute public interest suits in regard to environmental damage in the oil industry where direct wrong or harm to the plaintiff or litigant has not occurred.[64] In *Senator Adesanya v The President of Nigeria*,[65] the Supreme Court of Nigeria held that "standing will only be accorded to a plaintiff who shows that his civil rights have been or are in danger of being violated or adversely affected by the act complained of." The *locus standi* principle affects the ability of CSOs (and non-governmental organizations—NGOs) to institute action in Nigerian courts.[66] Arguably, the rigid rule of *locus standi* is changing in Nigeria. Scholars have argued that some recent developments have led to the liberalization of the *locus standi* rule in Nigeria. For example, scholars have argued that the rigid *locus standi* rule has been abolished in Nigeria by virtue of Preamble 3(e) of the new Fundamental Rights Enforcement Rules 2009 (FREP Rules).[67]

Okafor and Effoduh argue that the actual abolishment of the strict standing requirement will "have to be done via an operative provision of one of the following, the Constitution, a statute, or the FREPRs."[68] Most of the environmental litigation in Nigeria arises from the oil and gas industry and environmental NGOs play major roles in various activities geared towards improving environmental justice for victims (including women) and communities in the Niger Delta. However, the *locus standi* doctrine affects the ability of NGOs to institute action in Nigerian courts.[69] Fortunately, there have been recent judicial pronouncements on the requirement of *locus standi* for environmental NGOs in instituting legal action on behalf of victims of environmental injustice in Nigeria. For example, the Nigerian Supreme Court in the *Centre for Oil Pollution Watch v. Nigerian National Petroleum Corporation* held that environmental NGOs have the legal standing or *locus standi* to institute environmental cases in Nigeria.[70] This case has liberalized *locus standi* of NGOs in environmental matters in Nigeria, thereby improving access to environmental justice and promoting sustainable development for litigants, victims (including women), and communities in Nigeria.[71] Notwithstanding some of the criticisms[72] of this judgement, particularly that it will lead to a floodgate of cases in courts, this judgement will aid and promote the ability of environmental NGOs in Nigeria to file or institute cases on behalf of victims of environmental injustices in Nigeria.

NGOs have played major roles in elevating the plights of victims of environmental degradation in the NDR of Nigeria from local to international recognition and awakening of the international community.[73] This was especially evidenced by the Ogoni crisis, where a community-based organization (MOSOP—in coalition with both local and international CSOs) brought to the attention of the world the human rights violations and environmental degradation in that part of Nigeria. This action by MOSOP also influenced the major MNC (Shell) operating in Ogoni. Shell revised its code of conduct to include human rights and also Shell (and other MNCs) now regularly organize training and consultation with stakeholders in the Nigerian oil sector.[74] It should be noted that MOSOP's nonviolent protests have had a massive impact on Shell's operations in Ogoniland; for almost 30 years, Shell has not operated any of its facilities in Ogoniland due to its rejection by the Ogoni people.[75] This is notwithstanding that under Nigerian laws, Shell has the right to operate in the region.

Environmental Rights

Over the years, some environmental advocates have consistently called for the use of environmental rights as a critical approach to improving environmental outcomes.[76] This approach is supported by existing literature which indicates that constitutional recognition of environmental rights is indeed correlated with superior environmental performance at the national level.[77] Many countries have embedded enforceable and justiciable environmental rights provisions in their constitutions or laws. Hence, "Human rights provisions, particularly constitutional environmental rights, are essential to promoting environmental justice."[78] However, because countries have enforceable environmental rights provisions do not necessarily correlate to positive environmental justice outcomes for their citizens or address environmental problems that degenerate into conflicts. For example, countries such as Egypt, South Africa, and Senegal have constitutionally recognized environmental rights but arguably have poor environmental performance.[79]

In Nigeria, ordinarily, socio-economic rights are not enforceable because the socio-economic rights are not provided in the Nigerian constitution per se.[80] Chapter II deals with fundamental objectives and directive principles of state policy, which are not enforceable against the state by citizens of Nigeria.

This is epitomized by Section 20 of the Nigerian Constitution, which seeks to promote and protect the environment as provided in Chapter II of the Constitution and therefore neither justiciable nor enforceable.[81] However, in a recent decision of the Nigerian Supreme Court in Centre for Oil Pollution Watch v NNPC, the court specifically relied on the provisions of Article 24 of the African Charter on Human and Peoples' Rights and Section 33 (1) of the Nigerian Constitution and Section 17 (4) of the Oil Pipelines Act to hold that the right to the environment can be justiciable in Nigeria, thus stipulating that these instruments recognized the fundamental rights of Nigerians to a clean and healthy environment.[82]

Therefore, the judgement in the Centre for Oil Pollution Watch v. Nigerian National Petroleum Corporation has arguably made the right to the environment (a socio-economic right) justiciable in Nigeria. Furthermore, this judgement can serve as a launchpad to further develop the emergent jurisprudence around economic and social rights (ESR) in Nigeria.[83] This decision has implications for individuals and communities suffering from environmental injustices arising from extractive industries in Nigeria. Thus, the decision in the Centre for Oil Pollution Watch v. Nigerian National Petroleum Corporation can be used to enhance the rule of law by ensuring that the government and multinational companies (and other relevant stakeholders) adhere to environmental regulations and policies in Nigeria.

Improving Access to Environmental Justice

Scholars including Okogbule[84] and Ugochukwu[85] have argued that the concept of access to justice can be looked at from two major dimensions: the narrow and the wider perspectives. In its narrow conceptualization, access to justice can be said to be in tandem with access to the courts, while in its wider conceptualization or meaning, it embraces access to the political order in society and sharing in the benefits arising from the social and economic developments in the state.[86] As highlighted earlier, there has been a systemic failure by the Nigerian authorities to adequately regulate the oil and gas industry. Also, there have been countless incidents of environmental injustices arising from the activities of oil MNCs in Nigeria (especially in the NDR). Unfortunately, achieving environmental justice in Nigeria has been quite difficult. Some of these challenges militating against access to environmental justice (including environmental litigation) include

> limited resources of litigants, delays in the judicial process, the strict requirement of locus standi proof, and the over-reliance on common law torts such as trespass, negligence and nuisance in suits by litigants (in the absence of an effective framework on oil pollution control or litigation), amongst others. These factors have hindered access to justice, especially environmental justice in Nigeria.[87]

Due to the difficulties associated with access to environmental justice in Nigeria, victims, individuals, litigants, NGOs, and other relevant stakeholders from the NDR are now using national, sub-regional, regional, and other foreign jurisdictions to enhance access to environmental justice.[88] For instance, while *Gbemre v. SPDC* was initiated in a Federal High Court in Nigeria, *Bowoto v. Chevron* and *Wiwa v. Shell* were filed in the US, *Akpan v. Shell* was litigated at The Hague, The Netherlands, and *Bodo Community v SPDC* was heard in the UK.[89] Additionally, there is a plethora of cases in several foreign jurisdictions by Nigerian litigants who allege that they are victims of environmental injustices perpetuated or arising from the activities of oil MNCs in Nigeria.[90]

Furthermore, litigants from Nigeria and other African countries are now relying on principles of environmental justice via the prism of sub-regional and regional litigation in Africa.[91] For example, in the *Social and Economic Rights Action Centre & Centre for Economic and Social Rights v. Nigeria* (SERAC Case),[92] the African Commission on Human and Peoples' Rights held that the Nigerian Government and its agencies (and not the MNCs) were in violation of the African Charter on Human and Peoples' Rights. However, recommendations by the African Commission are non-binding on states.[93]

NGOs and victims of environmental injustices in Nigeria have also relied on the Economic Community of West African States (ECOWAS) Court of Justice (the West African sub-regional court), to seek redress for victims of environmental injustice in Nigeria.[94] For example, in *SERAP v Federal Republic of Nigeria*,[95] the plaintiffs averred that the FG of Nigeria has been culpable for environmental degradation in the Niger Delta. The ECOWAS Court of Justice held that Nigeria has violated Articles 1 and 24 of the African Charter on Human and Peoples' Rights and ordered the Nigerian government to take effective measures within the shortest possible period to restore or remediate the environment of the Niger Delta.[96] Some scholars argue that Nigeria is yet to implement or enforce this judgement.[97] However, scholars including Okafor et al argue that the SERAP judgement has had modest impacts on different stakeholders including the executive, judicial, and legislative branches of government in Nigeria.[98] Thus, it can be contended that the SERAP decision has had modest impacts on the promotion of rule of law by some environmental agencies in Nigeria.

For example, as a direct aftermath of the SERAP decision, during the consultations that took place between the Nigerian Ministry of Environment and other relevant stakeholders as part of the efforts to clean up the spills or pollution in Ogoniland, the National Environmental Standards and Regulations Enforcement Agency (NESREA) conducted a thorough review of the impact of the SERAP case (and other relevant foreign and local cases relating to the Niger Delta) in Nigeria.[99] Hence, Okafor et al argue that the SERAP case has contributed immensely to the executive branch's decision-making processes on the means of dealing with the oil spillage and clean-up issues in the Niger Delta. It was also one of the factors that shaped the executive branch's thinking about the issue at hand. This consultation's emphasis on the need for the government's policy and action to conform with its international law duties in this area is related to the impact that the ECOWAS Court judgement made on the government's decision-making processes.[100]

A major challenge inherent in the ECOWAS Court of Justice is the enforceability of its decisions in the Member States.[101] Notwithstanding the conundrum involving the implementation or domestication of the cross-border judgements in Nigeria, the recent cross-border or transnational human rights judgements involving litigants from the NDR (including sub-regional and regional judiciaries in Africa) have created opportunities for victims of environmental injustice in Nigeria to by-pass the justice machinery and attempt to get justice, for victims of environmental injustice, thus enhancing the rule of law in natural resource management in Nigeria. Hence, scholars have argued the SERAP judgement and similar litigation has enhanced the protection of the environment and improved access to justice in Nigeria with implications for natural resource conflict resolutions.[102] Therefore, the Nigerian government and its agencies have "become more sensitive to the environmental and social responsibilities of oil companies."[103]

Good Resource Governance and Management

There is general acknowledgement within the Western world—and in the Global South—that "the rule of law provides the foundation for predictability in the law and that government is subordinate to the law not superior to it."[104] This implies that an effective rule of law framework should be underpinned by the presence of strong institutions, security, human rights, and good governance.[105] Unfortunately, these manifestations of the rule of law are lacking or inadequate in Nigeria and similar resource-producing countries in Africa. This is worsened by existing environmental injustices plaguing resource-producing communities which have been exacerbated by ineffective or natural resource governance practices in many African states.

One strategy of improving good governance in the oil and gas industry is for the Nigerian government (and regulators) to exhibit the political will to enforce laws and regulations, remediate environmental degradation in the NDR, and compel oil MNCs to live up to their legal responsibilities. It is universally agreed that the rule of law is essential to sustainable development and serves as the nucleus of an efficient environmental rule of law in different jurisdictions or countries.[106] Furthermore, Goal 16 (Peace, Justice, and Strong Institutions) of the Sustainable Development Goals (SDGs) framework provides explicit connections to access to (environmental) justice, sustainable development, and the rule of law.[107] Thus, environmental justice and effective rule of law is germane to the actualization of the SDGs and many of its targets.[108]

Furthermore, as highlighted earlier, Ako and Uddin suggest that one conceptualization of good governance phenomenon in the context of natural resource management in Africa is said to encapsulate the four cardinal principles of rule of law, accountability, and transparency, management of revenues, and democracy.[109] In reality, these are underlying issues that have consistently been the basis for the emergence of resource conflicts in Africa. It is contended that African countries that meet these four criteria above (amongst other similar criteria or indexes) arguably have effective resource governance.[110] Thus, the overarching view is that the principles of environmental justice and the "…rule of law, well-designed laws are implemented by capable government institutions that are held accountable by an informed and engaged public that leads to a culture of compliance that embraces environmental and social values."[111]

Conclusion

This chapter sets out to establish how the environmental justice paradigm can be used as one of the strategies to address natural resource conflicts in Africa. To do so, it has provided analyses that focus on the introduction of some reform measures drawn from the concept of environmental justice to address the underlying root causes of natural resource conflicts. The analysis which is mainly based on the Nigerian experience as discussed in this chapter could be extrapolated and applied to other African countries.

This chapter discusses some of the barriers afflicting the rule of natural resource conflicts in Africa from the prisms of environmental justice using Nigeria as a case study. The key argument made is that countries suffering from resource conflicts in Africa should embed principles derived from environmental justice into their laws and policies. Also, African leaders should also ensure that laws enacted for environmental protection are respected and implemented in their various countries. This chapter argues that reliance on environmental justice principles in tandem with other existing strategies can serve as systemic approaches to fight against the scourge of natural resource conflicts in Africa.

Notes

1 Funmi Abioye, "Advancing Human Rights Through Environmental Rule of Law in Africa," in *Human Rights and the Environment Under African Union Law*, eds. Michael Addaney and Ademola O. Jegede (Cham: Palgrave Macmillan, 2020): 81–105.
2 United Nations Peacekeeping. n.d., "Conflict and Natural Resources." Accessed March 1, 2022. https://peacekeeping.un.org/en/conflict-and-natural-resources .
3 Eghosa O. Ekhator, "Improving Access to Environmental Justice under the African Charter on Human and Peoples' Rights: The Roles of NGOs in Nigeria," *African Journal of International and Comparative Law* 22, no. 1 (2014): 63–79; John B. Ejobowah, "Who Owns the Oil? The Politics of Ethnicity in the Niger Delta of Nigeria," *Africa Today* 47, no. 1 (2000): 29–47.
4 Generally, see Adebola Ogunba, "An Appraisal of the Evolution of Environmental Legislation in Nigeria," *Vermont Law Review* 40 (2015): 673; Damilola S. Olawuyi, *The Principles of Nigerian Environmental Law* (Ukraine: Business Perspectives 2013); Eghosa O. Ekhator, "Environmental Protection in the Oil and Gas Industry

in Nigeria: The Roles of Governmental Agencies," *International Energy Law Review* 5 (2013): 196–203.
5 Generally, see Olawuyi, *Principles of Nigerian Environmental Law.*
6 Generally, see Enabulele, Osamuyimen and Eghosa O. Ekhator, "Improving Environmental Protection in Nigeria: A Reassessment of the Role of Informal Institutions," *Journal of Sustainable Development Law and Policy (The)* 13, no. 1 (2022): 162–199.
7 Eghosa O. Ekhator, "The Role of Non-Governmental Organisations in the Environmental Justice Paradigm," *Nnamdi Azikiwe University Journal of International Law and Jurisprudence* 8, no. 2 (2017): 28–37, 28.
8 Robert D. Bullard and Glenn S. Johnson, "Environmentalism and Public Policy: Environmental Justice: Grassroots Activism and Its Impact on Public Policy Decision Making," *Journal of Social Issues*, 56, no. 3 (2000): 555–578; Ryan Holifield, Jayajit Chakraborty, and Gordon Walker, eds., *The Routledge Handbook of Environmental Justice* (Oxon, New York: Routledge); J. Timmons Roberts, David Pellow, and Paul Mohai, "Environmental Justice," in *Environment and Society: Concepts and Challenges*, eds. Magnus Boström and Debra J. Davidson (Cham: Palgrave Macmillan, 2018), 233–255.
9 Dorceta E. Taylor, "The Rise of the Environmental Justice Paradigm: Injustice Framing and the Social Construction of Environmental Discourses," *American Behavioural Scientist* 43, no. 4 (2000): 508–580, 542. Also see, Julian Agyeman and Bob Evans, "'Just Sustainability': The Emerging Discourse of Environmental Justice in Britain?" *Geographical Journal* 170, no. 2 (2004): 155–164.
10 Rhuks Ako and Damilola Olawuyi, "Environmental Injustice in Nigeria: Divergent Tales, Paradoxes and Future Prospects," in *The Routledge Handbook of Environmental Justice*, eds. Ryan Holifield, Jayajit Chakraborty, and Gordon Walker (Oxon and New York: Routledge, 2018), 568. Also, Professor Gonzalez espouses a four-part definition of "environmental justice consisting of distributive justice, procedural justice, corrective and social justice. Distributive justice calls for the fair allocation of the benefits and burdens of natural resource exploitation among and within nations. Procedural justice requires open, informed, and inclusive decision-making processes. Corrective justice imposes an obligation to provide compensation for historic inequities and to refrain from repeating the conduct that caused harm. Social justice, the fourth and most nebulous aspect of environmental justice, recognises that environmental struggles are inextricably intertwined with struggles for social and economic justice." See Carmen G. Gonzalez, "Environmental Justice and International Environmental Law," in *Routledge Handbook of International Environmental Law*, eds. Shawkat Alam, Jahid Hossain Bhuiyan, Tareq M. R. Chowdhury, and Erika J. Techera (London: Routledge, 2013), 78–79.
11 Rhuks Ako, "Nigeria's Land Use Act: An Anti-thesis to Environmental Justice," *Journal of African Law* 2, no. 53 (2009): 289–304.
12 Robert D. Bullard, "Environmental Justice in the 21st Century: Race Still Matters," *Phylon* (1960-) 49, no. 3/4 (2001): 151–71.
13 Bullard, 153.
14 Rhuks Ako, *Environmental Justice in Developing Countries: Perspectives from Africa and Asia-Pacific* (Oxfordshire: Routledge, 2013).
15 However, generally see Gordon Mitchell, "The messy challenge of environmental justice in the UK: evolution, status and prospects." (2019): 1–14 Natural England Commissioned Reports, Number 273; Agyeman and Evans, *Just Sustainability.*

16 Shauntice Allen, Michelle V. Fanucchi, Lisa C. McCormick, and Kristina M. Zierold, "The Search for Environmental Justice: The Story of North Birmingham," *International Journal of Environmental Research and Public Health* 16, no. 12 (2019): 2117. For the argument for the decolonization of environmental justice studies from the Global South (especially Latin America and Caribbean) theoretical perspective, see Lina Álvarez and Brendan Coolsaet, "Decolonizing Environmental Justice Studies: A Latin American Perspective," *Capitalism Nature Socialism* 31, no. 2 (2020): 50–69.

17 Caroline Ifeka, "Oil, NGOs & Youths: Struggles for Resource Control in the Niger Delta," *Review of African Political Economy* 28, no 87 (2001): 99–105.

18 Obiora, L. Amede, "Symbolic Episodes in the Quest for Environmental Justice," *Human Rights Quarterly* 21, no. 2 (1999): 464–512; Eghosa O. Ekhator, "Public Regulation of the Oil and Gas Industry in Nigeria: An Evaluation," *Annual Survey of International & Comparative Law* 21 (2016): 43–49; Ikechukwu Umejesi, "Collective Memory, Coloniality and Resource Ownership Questions: The Conflict of Identities in Postcolonial Nigeria," *Africa Review* 7, no. 1 (2015): 42–54.

19 Francis O. Adeola, "Cross-National Environmental Injustice and Human Rights Issues: A Review of Evidence in the Developing World," *American Behavioral Scientist* 43, no 4 (2000): 686–706, 688.

20 Ako and Olawuyi, *Environmental Injustice in Nigeria*, 567.

21 Ibid, 569.

22 Ibid, 568.

23 Ibid, 569.

24 Ibid, 569.

25 Alexandra D. Dunn and Sarah Stillman, "Advancing the Environmental Rule of Law: A Call for Measurement," *Southwestern Journal of International Law* 21 (2014): 283, 284.

26 Jessica Scott, "From Environmental Rights to Environmental Rule of Law: A Proposal for Better Environmental Outcomes," *Michigan Journal of Environmental & Administrative Law* 6 (2016): 203.

27 Rhuks Ako and Nilopar Uddin, "Good Governance and Resource Management in Africa," in *Natural Resource Investment and Africa's Development*, ed. Francis Botchway (Cheltenham: Edward Elgar, 2011), 21–48 at 24.

28 Louis-Alexandre Berg and Deval Desai. 2013. "Background Paper: Overview on the Rule of Law and Sustainable Development for the Global Dialogue on Rule of Law and the Post-2015 Development Agenda." (August 2013). Accessed March 1, 2021. www.researchgate.net/publication/276409489_Overview_on_the_Rule_of_Law_and_Sustainable_Development_for_the_Global_Dialogue_on_Rule_of_Law_and_the_Post-2015_Development_Agenda.

29 Ako and Uddin, *Good Governance*.

30 Jeffrey D. Sachs and Andrew Warner, "Natural Resource Abundance and Economic Growth." (Cambridge, MA: NBER, 1995); Terry Lynn Karl, *The Paradox of Plenty* (Berkeley: University of California Press, 1997); Eddy Wifa, "The Paradox of Plenty: An Analysis of The Environmental and Socio-Economic Symptoms of The Resource Curse in The Niger Delta Region of Nigeria," in *The Challenge of Justice: Contemporary Legal Essays in Honour of BM Wifa*, eds. Worika Ibibia and Sylvester Popnen (Port Harcourt: PAP, 2017), 576–601; Godswill Agbaitoro, "Legal Strategy for Resolving the Socio-Economic and Environmental Symptoms of the Resource Curse in Nigeria: The Role of Impact and Benefit Agreements

(IBAs)," *Commonwealth Law Bulletin* 44, no. 3 (2018): 381–399; Eghosa E. Osaghae, "Resource Curse or Resource Blessing: The Case of the Niger Delta 'Oil Republic' in Nigeria," *Commonwealth & Comparative Politics* 53, no. 2 (2015): 109–129.
31 NRGI Reader, "The Resource Curse: The Political and Economic Challenges of Natural Resource Wealth" (March 2015). Accessed March 1, 2022. nrgi_Resource-Curse.pdf (resourcegovernance.org).
32 Macartan Humphreys, Jeffrey D. Sachs, and Joseph E. Stiglitz, "Future Directions for the Management of Natural Resources," *Escaping the Resource Curse* 1 (2007): 322–336.
33 Generally, see United Nations Conference on Trade and Development (UNCTAD), Reaping the benefits of the African Free Trade Area for Inclusive Growth: Economic Development in Africa Report 2021 (2021) https://unctad.org/system/files/offic ial-document/aldcafrica2021_en.pdf; Daniëlla Dam-de Jong, *International Law and Governance of Natural Resources in Conflict and Post-conflict Situations* (Cambridge: Cambridge University Press, 2015).
34 African Progress Panel Report (2013) *Equity in Extractives: Stewarding Africa's Natural Resources for All.* Available at: https://reliefweb.int/report/world/africa-progress-report-2013-equity-extractives-stewarding-africa-s-natural-resources. World | ReliefWeb. Accessed March 1, 2022, at 92. Also see Angela Gapa, "Natural Resources and African Economies: Turning Liability to Asset," in *The Palgrave Handbook of African Political Economy*, eds. Samuel Ojo Oloruntoba and Toyin Falola (Palgrave Macmillan, 2020), 679–697.
35 Cyril Obi, "Oil as the 'Curse' of Conflict in Africa: Peering through the Smoke and Mirrors," *Review of African Political Economy* 37, no. 126 (2010): 483–495, 483; Zainab Usman, "The "Resource Curse" and the Constraints on Reforming Nigeria's Oil Sector," in *The Oxford Handbook of Nigerian Politics*, eds. Carl Levan and Patrick Ukata (Oxford: Oxford University Press).
36 Eliana Cusato, "International Law, the Paradox of Plenty and the Making of Resource-Driven Conflict," *Leiden Journal of International Law* 33, no. 3 (2020): 649–666.
37 Eliana Cusato, "Diamonds Are Forever: Law, Conflict Theories, and Natural Resource Governance in Africa." 20 November 2020. AfronomicsLaw. Accessed March 1, 2022, www.afronomicslaw.org/2020/11/20/diamonds-are-forever-law-confl ict-theories-and-natural-resource-governance-in-africa
38 See Christian Nellemann, Henriksen Rune, Arnold Kreilhuber, Davyth Stewart, Maria Kotsovou, Patricia Raxter, Elizabeth Mrema, and Sam Barrat, *The Rise of Environmental Crime: A Growing Threat to Natural Resources, Peace, Development and Security.* United Nations Environment Programme (UNEP), 2016.
39 Abiodun Alao, *Natural Resources and Conflicts in Africa: The Tragedy of Endowment*, Vol 29 (Boydell and Brewer: University of Rochester Press, 2007): 5.
40 Ako and Olawuyi, *Environmental Injustice in Nigeria*, 572. However, this book chapter will not undertake an extensive analysis of militant groups in the Niger Delta. For an extensive analysis of the maritime piracy and criminality in the NDR, see Katja Lindskov Jacobsen, *Pirates of the Niger Delta: Between the Blue and Brown Water* (Denmark: UNODC, 2021).
41 Lere Amusan, "Multinational Corporations' (MNCs) Engagement in Africa: Messiahs or Hypocrites?" *Journal of African Foreign Affairs* 5, no. 1 (2018): 41–62.
42 Generally, see Amusan ibid.

43 Robert V. Percival and Jingjing Zhang, "Transnational Environmental Accountability," *Natural Resources & Environment* 35, no. 2 (2020): 8–12.
44 Phoebe Okowa, "Environmental Justice in Situations of Armed Conflict," in *Environmental Law and Justice in Context*, eds. Jonas Ebbesson and Phoebe Okowa (Cambridge: Cambridge University Press, 2009).
45 Clementine Burnley, "Natural Resources Conflict in the Democratic Republic of the Congo: A Question of Governance," *Sustainable Development Law & Policy* 12 (2011): 7.
46 Generally, see Okowa, *Environmental Justice in Situations*.
47 Ibid.
48 Generally, see Peer Schouten, "Why responsible sourcing of DRC minerals has major weak spots" (Conversation 22 April 2019). Accessed March 1, 2022. https://theconversation.com/why-responsible-sourcing-of-drc-minerals-has-major-weak-spots-115245] ; Michael Addaney and Emma Charlene Lubaale, "An Unintended Legacy: The External Policy Responses of the USA and European Union to Conflict Minerals in Africa," *Laws* 10, no. 2 (2021): 50.
49 Generally, see Burnley, *Natural resources conflict*, 7.
50 Burnley *ibid*.
51 Christoph Vogel and Timothy Raeymaekers, "Terr (it) or (ies) of Peace? The Congolese Mining Frontier and the Fight Against "Conflict Minerals"," *Antipode* 48, no. 4 (2016): 1102–1121.
52 Schouten, *Responsible Sourcing*.
53 Ibid.
54 Furthermore, Jeroen Cuvelier, Koen Vlassenroot, and Nathaniel Olin, "Resources, Conflict and Governance: A Critical Review," *The Extractive Industries and Society* 1, no. 2 (2014): 340–350, 341 states that "The accounts that resources produce a key explanation for the behaviour of armed groups or that cutting access to minerals reduces the risk of violence and warfare, often lack sufficient empirical support but have become so dominant that little room is left for alternative approaches."
55 BBC News Website "Q&A: DR Congo Conflict." 2 November 2012. Accessed March 1, 2022, www.bbc.co.uk/news/world-africa-11108589. BBC News; Schouten, *Responsible Sourcing*.
56 Burnley, *Natural Resources Conflict*.
57 Cuvelier et al, *Resources, Conflict and Governance*, 340. Also see, Jesse S. Ovadia, "Natural Resources and African Economies: Asset or Liability?" In *The Palgrave Handbook of African Political Economy*, eds. Samuel Oloruntoba, Samuel Ojo, and Toyin Falola (Cham: Palgrave Macmillan, 2020), 667–677.
58 Pricillia Schwartz, "Corporate Activities and Environmental Justice: Perspectives on Sierra Leone's Mining," in *Environmental Law and Justice in Context*, eds. Jonas Ebbesson and Phoebe Okowa (Cambridge: Cambridge University Press, 2009), 429–446. According to Cusato, *Paradox of Plenty*, 650–651, some of the most prominent examples of the international framework for regulating conflict minerals include commodity and targeted sanctions adopted by the United Nations Security Council (UNSC) and multi-stakeholder initiatives, such as the Kimberley Process Certification Scheme for Diamonds, the Extractive Industry Transparency Initiative, and the OECD Due Diligence Guidance on Responsible Supply Chain of Minerals.
59 Schwartz ibid, 429.

60 Meike Schulte and Cody Morris Paris, "Blood Diamonds: An Analysis of the State of Affairs and the Effectiveness of the Kimberley Process," *International Journal of Sustainable Society* 12, no. 1 (2020): 51–75; Schwartz, *Corporate activities*.
61 See Schouten, *Responsible Sourcing*; Mancini, Lucia, Nicolas A. Eslava, Marzia Traverso, and Fabrice Mathieux, "Assessing Impacts of Responsible Sourcing initiatives for cobalt: Insights from a Case Study," *Resources Policy* 71 (2021): 102015; Vogel and Raeymaekers, *Congolese Mining*.
62 Ekhator, *Improving Access*.
63 Augustine Ikelegbe, "Civil Society, Oil and Conflict in the Niger Delta Region of Nigeria: Ramifications of Civil Society for a Regional Resource Struggle," *The Journal of Modern African Studies* 39, no. 3 (2001): 437–469.
64 Ekhator (n 3).
65 *Senator Adesanya v The President of Nigeria,* 2 NCLR 258 (1981).
66 Miriam C. Anozie and Emmanuel O. Wingate, "NGO Standing in Petroleum Pollution Litigation In Nigeria—Centre For Oil Pollution Watch V Nigerian National Petroleum Corporation," *The Journal of World Energy Law & Business* 13, no. 5–6 (2020): 490–497.
67 Femi Falana, *Fundamental Rights Enforcement in Nigeria*, 2nd edn (Lagos: Legaltext Publishing, 2010); Onyeka K. Anaebo and Eghosa O. Ekhator, "Realising Substantive Rights to Healthy Environment in Nigeria: A Case for Constitutionalisation," *Environmental Law Review* 17, no. 2 (2015): 82–99. Generally, see Emeka P. Amechi, Uzuazo Etemire, and Agent Ihua-Maduenyi, "Access to Justice through Environmental Public Interest Litigation: Exploring Contemporary Trends in Nigeria," *VRÜ Verfassung und Recht in Übersee* 54, no. 3 (2021): 398–414.
68 Obiora C. Okafor and Okechukwu J. Effoduh, "The ECOWAS Court as (Promising) Resource for Pro-Poor Activist Forces," in *The Performance of Africa's International Courts: Using Litigation for Political, Legal, and Social Change*, ed. James T. Gathii (Oxford: Oxford University Press, 2020). Furthermore, Justice Nweze in the Oil Pollution case stated that Section 6(6)(b) of the Constitution did not lay set down rules of standing but simply delineated the exercise of judicial power. Also see Anozie and Wingate, *NGO Standing*.
69 Generally, see Anozie and Wingate, *NGO Standing*.
70 *Centre for Oil Pollution Watch v. Nigerian National Petroleum Corporation* [2019] 5 NWLR 518.
71 Ayodele Babalola, "The Right to a Clean Environment in Nigeria: A Fundamental Right," *Hastings Environmental Law Journal* 26 (2020): 3.
72 See Adeniyi Olatunbuson and Kingsley O. Onu, "The Liberalisation of Locus Standi in Environmental Cases in Nigeria: An Appraisal of the Supreme Court's Decision in Centre for Oil Pollution Watch v NNPC," *The Gravitas Review of Business & Property Law* 11, no. 2 (2020): 1–11.
73 Rhuks Ako, "Enforcing Environmental Rights under Nigeria's 1999 Constitution: The Localisation of Human Rights in the Niger Delta Region," in *The Local Relevance of Human Rights*, eds. Koen de Feyter et al (New York: Cambridge University Press, 2011).
74 Evaristus Oshionebo, *Regulating Transnational Corporations in Domestic and International Regimes: An African Case Study* (Toronto: University of Toronto Press, 2009).

75 Generally, see Eghosa O. Ekhator, "Regulating the Activities of Oil Multinationals in Nigeria: A Case for Self-Regulation?" *Journal of African Law* 60, no. 1 (2016): 1–28; Joseph I. Uduji, Elda Nduka Okolo-Obasi, and Simplice A. Asongu, "Oil Extraction in Nigeria's Ogoniland: The Role of Corporate Social Responsibility in Averting a Resurgence of Violence," *Resources Policy* 70 (2021): 101927.
76 Scott, *Environmental Rights*.
77 Scott *ibid*.
78 Rhuks Ako, "Mainstreaming Environmental Justice in Developing Countries: Thinking Beyond Constitutional Environmental Rights," in *Nigerian Yearbook of International Law 2017* (Cham: Springer, 2018), 269–289; Anaebo and Ekhator, *Realising Substantive Rights*.
79 Generally, see Caiphas Soyapi and Louis J. Kotzé, "Environmental Justice and Slow Violence: Marikana and the Post-Apartheid South African Mining Industry in Context," Verfassung und Recht in Übersee/LAW AND POLITICS IN AFRICA| ASIA| LATIN AMERICA (2016): 393–415. Also see Godswill Agbaitoro, "Enforcing Constitutional Environmental Rights in Court: A Comparative Analysis of Nigeria and India," *Miyetti Quarterly Law Review* 3, no. 1 (2018): 119–150.
80 Generally, see Ekhator, *Improving Access*, 66.
81 Ekhator, *Improving Access*, 70.
82 *Centre for Oil Pollution Watch v. Nigerian National Petroleum Corporation* [2019] 5 NWLR 518.
83 Generally, see Eghosa Ekhator, "Sustainable Development and the African Union Legal Order" in *The Emergent African Union Law: Conceptualization, Delimitation, and Application*, eds. Femi Amao, Michele Olivier, and Konstantinos Magliveras (Oxford: Oxford University Press, 2021).
84 Nlerum Okogbule, "Access to Justice and Human Rights Protection in Nigeria: Problems and Prospects," *It's Over. International Journal of Human Rights* 2 (2005): 100–119.
85 Basil Ugochukwu, "Engendering Access to Justice in Nigeria" in *Gender, Poverty and Access to Justice: Policy Implementation in Sub-Saharan Africa* eds. David Lawson, Adam Dubin, and Lea Mwambene (: London: Routledge, 2020).
86 Ugochukwu ibid; Okogbule, *Access to Justice*.
87 Ekhator, *Improving Access*, 68. Also see, Olanrewaju Fagbohun and Godwin U. Ojo, "Resource Governance and Access to Justice in Nigeria: Innovating Best Practices in Aid of Nigeria's Oil Pollution Victims," *NIALS Journal of Environmental Law* 2 (2012): 257, 271–302.
88 Eghosa Ekhator, "International Environmental Governance: A Case for Sub-Regional Judiciaries in Africa," in *Human Rights and the Environment under African Union Law*, eds. Michael Addaney and Ademola O. Jegede (Cham: Palgrave Macmillan, 2020), 209–231.
89 Generally, see Rhuks Ako and Eghosa O. Ekhator, "The Civil Society and the Regulation of the Extractive Industry In Nigeria," *Journal of Sustainable Development Law and Policy (The)* 7, no. 1 (2016): 183–203.
90 Amnesty International (2020, February 10). *On Trial: Shell in Nigeria: Legal actions against the oil multinational*. Nigeria: www.amnesty.org/en/documents/afr44/1698/2020/en/. Amnesty International.
91 Generally, see Abioye *Advancing Human Rights*; Ekhator, *International Environmental Governance*.
92 Communication No. 155/96(2001).

93 However, Frans Viljoen, "The African Human Rights System and Domestic Enforcement" in *Social Rights Judgments and the Politics of Compliance: Making it Stick*, eds. Malcom Langford et al (Cambridge: Cambridge University Press, 2017), 339, suggests that the recommendations are final and binding if they are contained in the Activity Reports of the African Commission and are approved by the OAU/AU Assembly or Executive Council.
94 Generally, see Ekhator, *Improving Access*; Ekhator, *International Environmental Governance*.
95 *SERAP v Federal Republic of Nigeria*, Judgement No ECW/CCJ/JUD/18/12.
96 *ibid* at 29.
97 Rahina Zarma, "A Role for the ECOWAS in Addressing the Challenges of Ineffective Regulation of Transnational Oil Corporations in Nigeria," *Asper Review of International Business and Trade Law* 19 (2019): 303–374; Ekhator, *Improving Access*.
98 Obiora Chinedu Okafor, Udoka Owie, Okechukwu Effoduh, and Rahina Zarma, "On the Modest Impact of West Africa's International Human Rights Court on the Executive Branch of Government in Nigeria," *Harvard Human Rights Journal* 35 (2022): 169–232; Obiora Chinedu Okafor, Udoka Ndidiamaka Owie, Okechukwu Effoduh, and Rahina Zarma, "The ECOWAS Court and Civil Society Activists in Nigeria: An Anatomy and Analysis of a Robust Symbiosis," *African Journal of Legal Studies* 14, no. 4 (2022): 491–521.
99 Generally, see Obiora Chinedu Okafor, Udoka Owie, Okechukwu Effoduh, and Rahina Zarma, "On the Modest Impact of West Africa's International Human Rights Court on the Executive Branch of Government in Nigeria," *Harvard Human Rights Journal* 35 (2022): 169–232 for an incisive review of the impacts of the SERAP decision in Nigeria.
100 Okafor et al ibid, 194.
101 Generally, see, Amos A. Enabulele, "Reflections on the ECOWAS Community Court Protocol and the Constitutions of the Member States," *International Community Law Review* 12 (2010): 111–138; Enyinna Nwauche, "Enforcing ECOWAS Law in West African National Courts," *Journal of African Law* 55, no. 22 (2011): 181; Ekhator, *Improving Access*; Ekhator, *International Environmental Governance*.
102 Obiora. C. Okafor, "Modest Harvests: On the Significant (But Limited) Impact of Human Rights NGOs on Legislative and Executive Behaviour in Nigeria," *Journal of African Law*, 48, no. 1 (2004): 23–49; Ikelegbe, *Civil Society*, 460; Ekhator, *Improving Access*.
103 Ikelegbe, *Civil Society*.
104 Arthur H. Garrison, "The Traditions and History of the Meaning of the Rule of Law," *Georgetown Journal of Law & Public Policy* 12 (2014): 565; Scott, *Environmental Rights*.
105 Scott, *Environmental Rights*.
106 Generally, see Scott, *Environmental Rights*; Environmental Rule of Law: First Global Report (2019). www.unep.org/resources/assessment/environmental-rule-law-first-global-report?_ga=2.226675739.766941567.1631031712-747452028.1624543330.
107 Environmental Rule of Law: First Global Report *ibid*.
108 Ibid 228.
109 Ako, and Uddin, *Good Governance*.

110 Francis Botchway, "Good Governance: The Old, the New, the Principle, and the Elements," *Florida Journal of International Law* 13 (2000): 159.
111 Environmental Rule of Law, *First Global Report*, 1.

Bibliography

Adeola, Francis O. 2000. "Cross-National Environmental Injustice and Human Rights Issues: A Review of Evidence in the Developing World." *American Behavioral Scientist* 43, no. 4: 686–706

Abioye, Funmi. 2020. "Advancing Human Rights Through Environmental Rule of Law in Africa." In *Human Rights and the Environment under African Union Law*, edited by Michael Addaney and Ademola O. Jegede, 81–105. Cham: Palgrave Macmillan.

Agbaitoro, Godswill. 2018. "Enforcing Constitutional Environmental Rights in Court: A Comparative Analysis of Nigeria and India." *Miyetti Quarterly Law Review* 3, no. 1: 119–150.

Agbaitoro, Godswill. 2018. "Legal Strategy for Resolving the Socio-economic and Environmental Symptoms of the Resource Curse in Nigeria: The Role of Impact and Benefit Agreements (IBAs)." *Commonwealth Law Bulletin* 44, no. 3: 381–399.

Agyeman, Julian, and Bob Evans. 2004. "'Just Sustainability': The Emerging Discourse of Environmental Justice in Britain?" *Geographical Journal* 170, no. 2: 155–164.

Ako, Rhuks. 2013. *Environmental Justice in Developing Countries: Perspectives from Africa and Asia-Pacific*. Abingdon Oxon: Routledge.

Ako, Rhuks, and Damilola Olawuyi. 2018. "Environmental Injustice in Nigeria: Divergent Tales, Paradoxes and Future Prospects." In *The Routledge Handbook of Environmental Justice*, edited by Ryan Holifield, Jayajit Chakraborty and Gordon Walker, 567–576. Abingdon, Oxon: Routledge.

Ako, Rhuks, and Nilopar Uddin. 2011. "Good Governance and Resource Management in Africa." In *Natural Resource Investment and Africa's Development*, edited by Francis Botchway, 21–48. Cheltenham: Edward Elgar.

Amechi, Emeka P., Uzuazo Etemire, and Agent Ihua-Maduenyi. 2021. "Access to Justice through Environmental Public Interest Litigation: Exploring Contemporary Trends in Nigeria." *VRÜ Verfassung und Recht in Übersee* 54, no. 3: 398–414.

Álvarez, Lina, and Brendan Coolsaet. 2020 "Decolonizing Environmental Justice Studies: A Latin American Perspective." *Capitalism Nature Socialism* 31, no. 2: 50–69.

Bullard, Robert D. 2001. "Environmental Justice in the 21st Century: Race Still Matters." *Phylon* (1960) 49, no. 3/4: 151–71.

Bullard, Robert. D., and Glenn Johnson. S. 2000. "Environmentalism and Public Policy: Environmental Justice: Grassroots Activism and Its Impact on Public Policy Decision Making." *Journal of Social Issues*, 56, no. 3: 555–578.

Cusato, Eliana. 2020. "International law, the paradox of plenty and the making of resource-driven conflict." *Leiden Journal of International Law* 33, no. 3: 649–666.

Cusato, Eliana. "Diamonds Are Forever: Law, Conflict Theories, and Natural Resource Governance in Africa." 20 November 2020. AfronomicsLaw. Accessed March 1, 2022 www.afronomicslaw.org/2020/11/20/diamonds-are-forever-law-conflict-theories-and-natural-resource-governance-in-africa

Dam-de Jong, Daniëlla. 2015. *International Law and Governance of Natural Resources in Conflict and Post-conflict situations*. Cambridge: Cambridge University Press.

Ejobowah, John B. 2000. "Who Owns the Oil? The Politics of Ethnicity in the Niger Delta of Nigeria." *Africa Today* 47, no. 1 (Winter): 29–47.

Ekhator, Eghosa O. 2013. "Environmental Protection in the Oil and Gas Industry in Nigeria: The Roles of Governmental Agencies." *International Energy Law Review* 5: 196–203.

Ekhator, Eghosa O. 2014. "Improving Access to Environmental Justice under the African Charter on Human and Peoples' Rights: The Roles of Ngos in Nigeria." *African Journal of International and Comparative Law* 22, no. 1: 63–79.

Ekhator, Eghosa O. 2016. "Public Regulation of the Oil and Gas Industry in Nigeria: An Evaluation." *Annual Survey of International & Comparative Law* 21: 43–49.

Ekhator, Eghosa O. 2017. "The Role of Non-Governmental Organisations in the Environmental Justice Paradigm." *Nnamdi Azikiwe University Journal of International Law and Jurisprudence* 8, no. 2: 28–37.

Ekhator, Eghosa O. 2020. "International Environmental Governance: A Case for Sub-Regional Judiciaries in Africa." In *Human Rights and the Environment under African Union Law*, edited by Michael Addaney and Ademola Jegede, 209–231. Cham: Palgrave Macmillan.

Ekhator, Eghosa O. 2021. "Sustainable Development and the African Union Legal Order." In *The Emergent African Union Law: Conceptualization, Delimitation, and Application*, edited by Femi Amao, Michele Olivier, and Konstantinos Magliveras, 335–358. Oxford: Oxford University Press.

Enabulele, Osamuyimen, and Eghosa O. Ekhator. 2022. "Improving Environmental Protection in Nigeria: A Reassessment of the Role of Informal Institutions." *Journal of Sustainable Development Law and Policy (The)* 13, no. 1: 162–199.

Fagbohun, Olanrewaju, and Godwin U. Ojo. 2012. "Resource Governance and Access to Justice in Nigeria: Innovating Best Practices in Aid of Nigeria's Oil Pollution Victims." *NIALS Journal of Environmental Law* 2: 257–301.

Gonzalez, Carmen G. 2013. "Environmental Justice and International Environmental Law." In *Routledge Handbook of International Environmental Law*, edited by Alam Shawkat, Jahid Hossain Bhuiyan, Tareq M. R. Chowdhury, and Erika J. Techera, 77–97. Abingdon, Oxon: Routledge.

Holifield, Ryan, Jayajit Chakraborty, and Gordon Walker, eds. 2018. *The Routledge Handbook of Environmental Justice*. Abingdon, Oxon: Routledge.

Ifeka, Caroline. 2001. "Oil, NGOs & Youths: Struggles for Resource Control in the Niger Delta." *Review of African Political Economy* 28, no. 87: 99–105.

Ikelegbe, Augustine. (2001). "Civil Society, Oil and Conflict in the Niger Delta Region of Nigeria: Ramifications of Civil Society for a Regional Resource Struggle." *The Journal of Modern African Studies*, 39, no. 3: 437–469.

Karl, Terry L. 1997. *The Paradox of Plenty*. California: University of California Press.

Obi, Cyril. 2010. "Oil as the 'Curse' of Conflict in Africa: Peering through the Smoke and Mirrors." *Review of African Political Economy* 37, no. 126: 483–495

Obiora, L. Amede. 1999. "Symbolic Episodes in the Quest for Environmental Justice." *Human Rights Quarterly* 21, no. 2: 464–512.

Ogunba, Adebola. 2015 "An Appraisal of the Evolution of Environmental Legislation in Nigeria." *Vermont Law Review* 40: 673–694.

Okafor, Obiora C. 2004. "Modest Harvests: On the Significant (But Limited) Impact of Human Rights NGOs on Legislative and Executive Behaviour in Nigeria." *Journal of African Law* 48, no. 1: 23–49.

Okafor, Obiora C., and Okechukwu J. Effoduh. 2020. " The ECOWAS Court as a (Promising) Resource for Pro-Poor Activist Forces: Sovereign Hurdles, Brainy Relays, and "Flipped Strategic Social Constructivism"" In *The Performance of Africa's International Courts: Using Litigation for Political, Legal, and Social* Change, edited by James T. Gathii. 106–148. Oxford: Oxford University Press.

Okafor, Obiora Chinedu, Udoka Owie, Okechukwu Effoduh, and Rahina Zarma. 2022. "On the Modest Impact of West Africa's International Human Rights Court on the Executive Branch of Government in Nigeria." *Harvard Human Rights Journal* 35: 169–232

Okafor, Obiora Chinedu, Udoka Ndidiamaka Owie, Okechukwu Effoduh, and Rahina Zarma. 2022. "The ECOWAS Court and Civil Society Activists in Nigeria: An Anatomy and Analysis of a Robust Symbiosis." *African Journal of Legal Studies* 14, no. 4: 491–521.

Olawuyi, Damilola S. 2013. *The Principles of Nigerian Environmental Law*. Ukraine: Business Perspectives.

Osaghae, Eghosa E. 2015. "Resource Curse or Resource Blessing: The Case of the Niger Delta 'Oil Republic' in Nigeria." *Commonwealth & Comparative Politics* 53, no. 2: 109–129.

Sachs, Jeffrey D., and Andrew Warner. 1995. "Natural Resource Abundance and Economic Growth." Working Paper 5398, National Bureau of Economic Research. www.nber.org/papers/w5398

Scott, Jessica. 2016. "From Environmental Rights to Environmental Rule of Law: A Proposal for Better Environmental Outcomes." *Michigan Journal of Environmental & Administrative Law* 6: 203.

Taylor, Dorceta E. 2000. "The Rise of the Environmental Justice Paradigm: Injustice Framing and the Social Construction of Environmental Discourses." *American Behavioral Scientist* 43, no. 4: 508–580.

Umejesi, Ikechukwu. 2015. "Collective Memory, Coloniality and Resource Ownership Questions: The Conflict of Identities in Postcolonial Nigeria." *Africa Review* 7, no. 1: 42–54.

Usman, Zainab. 2019 "The "Resource Curse" and the Constraints on Reforming Nigeria's Oil Sector." In *The Oxford Handbook of Nigerian Politics*, edited by Carl Levan and Patrick Ukata, 520–544. Oxford: Oxford University Press.

Wifa, Eddy. 2017. "The Paradox of Plenty: An Analysis of the Environmental and Socio-Economic Symptoms of the Resource Curse in the Niger Delta Region of Nigeria." In *The Challenge of Justice: Contemporary Legal Essays in Honour of BM Wifa*, edited by Worika Ibibia and Sylvester Popnen, 576–601. Port Harcourt: PAP.

Zarma, Rahina, 2019. "A Role for the ECOWAS in Addressing the Challenges of Ineffective Regulation of Transnational Oil Corporations in Nigeria." *Asper Review of International Business and Trade Law* 19: 303–374.

8   Social Legitimacy as a Sustainable Tool for Resolving Mining-Induced Conflicts in Ghana

*Chris Adomako-Kwakye and
Richard Obeng Mensah*

Introduction

This chapter examines the principle of social legitimacy in mining and assesses its influence on the increasing number of mining disputes and conflicts in Ghana's host communities. It examines the gaps in the implementation of social legitimacy norms in mining contracts, which have contributed to the escalation of disputes, and proposes ways to address these gaps. While natural resources are usually controlled by the state, their exploitation should benefit both the mine operator and the broader society. However, the contentious issue of who should bear the burden of the harmful effects of mining remains unresolved.[1] Mineral extraction has increased over the years, leading mining companies to expand and explore new commodity frontiers.[2] During the extraction process, soil, forest cover, and even river bodies are often affected, posing environmental risks and potential harm.[3] The depletion of resources disrupts the ecological balance of mining communities, resulting in displacements, the denial of livelihoods, and various social inequalities.[4] Consequently, conflicts have arisen between mining companies and the communities hosting them.[5] The primary factors behind the resistance include a lack of trust between local communities, mining companies, and the state, limited involvement of locals in mining community decision-making processes, and perceived marginalization.[6] Recognizing these challenges, mining companies have come under pressure to improve their environmental practices and prioritize the social and economic well-being of their host communities.[7]

A study by Abuya has recorded six examples of mining conflicts.[8] They include land ownership,[9] 'unfair' compensation packages,[10] inequitable resource distribution,[11] environmental degradation,[12] mine-induced poverty,[13] and conflict on human rights abuse.[14] Erb, on the other hand, argues that mining conflicts in the Nusa Tenggara Timur Province of Indonesia stem from the clash of values of justice, democracy, sustainability, environmental conservation, and cultural tradition between tourism and mining.[15] These examples illustrate diverse reasons for conflicts in the relationship between companies and communities in the mining sector. Some of these reasons are common across various jurisdictions. As Ayling and Kelly noted, conflicts

DOI: 10.4324/9781003355717-12

over natural resources expose inequalities in society, underscoring the importance of finding solutions that minimize conflict and ensure equitable resource management through potential resolution methods.[16] Until these issues are addressed, the conflict between mining companies and mining communities will persist, adversely affecting the relationship between the companies and the host communities.

This chapter is organized into six sections. Following the introduction, the second section examines the ongoing debate surrounding social legitimacy in mining and evaluates its impact on mining companies. This section emphasizes the significance of incorporating development provisions in mining laws. The third section delves into the conflicts between mining communities and mining companies in Ghana, exploring the methods used to resolve these disputes. In the fourth section , the legal regime governing the negotiation of mining agreements in Ghana is discussed. The state's responsibility for negotiating mining leases with companies through its ministries and agencies leads to challenges in mining operations due to the exclusion of mining communities. Fifth section provides recommendations to address these issues, aiming to foster a harmonious relationship between mining communities and companies and enhance social acceptance of mining operations. Finally, the chapter concludes in the sixth section with a comprehensive review of the issues raised throughout the various sections.

The Search for Social Legitimacy in Mining Operations

In the domain of natural resource governance, the concept of 'social license to operate lacks a universally agreed-upon definition in the literature. However, in broader terms, it pertains to the ongoing approval of an operation by stakeholders within local communities who are directly impacted by it, as well as those stakeholders who have the capacity to influence its profitability.[17] According to Gunningham et al., a social license to operate refers to a collection of demands and expectations held by local stakeholders and broader civil society regarding how a business should conduct its operations.[18] Harvey also views the social license as a process wherein the industry must 'fit in' and adapt to the prevailing social norms.[19] These definitions underscore the increasing awareness among communities concerning the exploitation of natural resources and its consequences on their well-being. It is now evident that the community holds the power to grant a social license to operate. Thus, the social license to operate has evolved into an implicit social contract between companies and communities. In this regard, the social license to operate has become an unwritten social contract between companies and communities[20] that cannot be granted by formal authority.[21] In this context, this chapter argues for the codification of the social license to operate.

The principle of social legitimacy postulates that mining companies should not solely be interested in acquiring mining leases; instead, they must equally obtain a license from the communities in which they intend to operate. The social legitimacy obtained in this process will create a conducive atmosphere for mining activities in those communities to progress without facing community resistance. To that extent, mining companies' interests ought to be twofold. First, they should secure a legal license from national authorities, and second, they should engage with the host community to confirm their social legitimacy to operate. The social license to operate should not be considered a soft law but rather requires the force of the law to be effective. Therefore, one can reasonably conclude that there is a strong relationship between social license and legitimacy in the context of mining operations.[22] Once the mining company's activity is accepted, it gains legitimacy, and as a result, the community grants the social license and legal authorization for the company to operate. Herein lies the significance of the social license, as it plays a pivotal role in reducing mining disputes.

The underlying issue associated with conflicts in mining communities revolves around the imbalance between the impacts of mining and the derived benefits. These imbalances are evident in the harmful effects experienced by mining communities. For example, an official from Newmont in Peru stated,

> we have the concession, and we have the land. I do not understand what a social license means. I expect a license from the authorities, from the minister of mines, and from the regional government. I don't expect a license from the whole community.[23]

The inability to obtain a social license often comes at a significant cost to mining companies.[24] The principle of social legitimacy postulates that mining companies should not only focus on acquiring mining leases but must also obtain a license from the communities in which they intend to operate. By obtaining social legitimacy, a conducive atmosphere for mining activities in these communities is created, allowing for progress without community resistance.

The mining communities believe that the resources mined from their areas disproportionately benefit the mining companies, leaving the communities impoverished. The social license to operate functions as an informal social contract, aiming to bridge the gap between the perspectives of the key stakeholders involved in mining.[25] The crucial issue at hand is whether the social license requires codification to ensure a peaceful and conducive mining atmosphere. The chapter argues that codification would address community concerns, which have become the focal point of conflicts in mining communities. Although a social license to operate is not permanent and can be withheld or withdrawn, codification will help mitigate conflicts and bring harmony between international mining companies and the host community. This suggestion for codification finds support in the stance of Golden Star Resources, a mining company in Ghana, which acknowledges that mining companies need local legitimacy in their areas of operation for their business to thrive.[26] Embedded in this acknowledgment is the recognition of the necessity to prioritize the interests of mining communities to prevent future conflicts.

Joyce and Thomson explain that a 'social license to operate exists when a mineral exploration or mining project is seen as having the approval and broad acceptance of society to conduct its activities.' Such acceptability must be achieved on multiple levels, but it primarily begins with and must be firmly grounded in the social acceptance of resource development by local communities.[27] This explanation highlights that mining companies' engagement in mining activities within host communities must win the hearts of the local population. It is essential for mining companies not to obtain licenses and begin operations without consulting and involving the mining communities. Gehman et al. describe three varieties of social license, namely the pyramid, the three-strand, and the triangle model. The pyramid model was developed through articles, papers, and presentations by mining industry consultants between 2000 and 2013.[28] In 1997, the challenges faced by industry players in the mining sector were compiled and shared with World Bank officials, emphasizing the importance of obtaining a social license to operate. Subsequently, these findings were circulated by World Bank officials during a conference on mining and the community.[29] This model emerged as an industry response to opposition and a mechanism to ensure the viability of the mining sector.[30]

The second model, known as the three-strand model, stipulates that mining activity must encompass three licenses: the legal license, the social license, and the economic license. Therefore, the granting of a mining lease (legal license) must be accompanied by obtaining both economic and social licenses. Without these additional licenses, the mining company could face challenges during its operations. The third model is the triangle model, which emphasizes that social acceptance builds confidence, familiarity, and trust.[31] Social acceptance is essential for garnering support from policymakers to implement the financial and regulatory incentives needed to overcome entrenched interests and the path dependency of conventional fossil fuel energy systems.[32] It comprises three levels of acceptance: sociopolitical/legal acceptance, community acceptance, and market acceptance.[33] This model acknowledges the importance of obtaining a legal license and the necessity of gaining acceptance from the community. The key question is how these models or concepts can be effectively applied in mining communities. The essence of the social license to operate lies in mining industries engaging in negotiations with communities and other stakeholders concerning the costs and benefits of mining.

Moffat and Zhang have assessed the components of the social license and argued that the manner in which mining companies interact with communities will greatly impact the level of trust community members place in the mining company, as well as their acceptance of mining operations within the community. Subsequently, they delve into the key aspects of their model, encompassing trust, the effects on social infrastructure, interactions between local community members and mining companies, and procedural fairness.[34] Under the United Nations Declaration on the Rights of Indigenous Peoples and the International Labour Organization Convention 169, the state is obligated to obtain the consent of indigenous communities before approving mining activities. This principle is known as Free Prior and Informed Consent (FPIC). However, it appears that the state has neglected its responsibility by not consulting mining communities before granting mining leases. As a result, mining communities are excluded from negotiations, enabling mining companies to disregard the interests of the host communities.

The social license (SLO) is also interpreted as the social acceptance of mineral exploration and mining activities.[35] In the last two decades, the principle has become increasingly necessary, putting pressure on mining companies to contribute more to the development of host communities. By examining the concept of social legitimacy in mining, conflicts can be addressed through meaningful engagement between the state, mining companies, and host communities during negotiations. Such an approach ensures that host communities become an integral part of the process and do not feel ignored. Therefore, this chapter advocates for a paradigm shift that includes mining communities in the negotiation stage.

Company-Community Conflict in Ghana's Mining Communities

Formerly known as the Gold Coast, Ghana is rich in natural resources, including gold, diamonds, manganese, and bauxite, which are the major minerals mined in the country. Additionally, Ghana possesses untapped deposits of iron ore, copper, chrome, nickel, limestone, quartz, and mica. These valuable reserves have attracted 20 large-scale mining companies, engaged in the production of gold, diamonds, bauxite, and manganese. Furthermore, there are more than 300 registered small-scale mining groups and 90 mine support service companies operating in the country. Mining has played a significant role in Ghana's political economy for centuries, but, like many industries, it has both positive and negative effects on the host community. Aboka et al. argue that environmentally, mining impacts on host communities include noise pollution caused by heavy trucks from mining locations and pollution of water bodies due to the use of chemicals such as arsenic, mercury, and cadmium during the refining of mined minerals. Moreover, agricultural soils become contaminated with heavy metals and other pollutants, leading to the depletion of agricultural land and a reduction in food production due to infertile land. Furthermore, mining activities contribute to the depletion of wildlife habitats, as forests are cleared to make way for mining operations, resulting in a decline in various animal species.[36] These negative effects adversely impact host communities' livelihoods and have contributed to disputes in mining communities to the extent that host communities see little or no improvement in their living standards.

On the social front, inhabitants of mining communities have faced a multitude of challenges. The social impacts of mining activities are diverse, spanning various indicators such as unemployment, population growth, migration, economic and business development, prostitution, crime, conflict, poverty issues, infrastructural development, and prices of goods and services. Mining communities generally recognize and accept the significant influence of mining activities on their community in these various ways.[37] These challenges also give rise to frustrations within host communities, leading to disputes between the company and the community, as little effort is seen to address these issues.

Economically, mining has made significant contributions to the Ghanaian economy. Mining companies pay royalties, corporate taxes, and also provide employment opportunities. The sector employs 28,000 people in the large-scale mining industry, while over 1,000,000 individuals are engaged in the small-scale gold, diamond, sand winning, and quarry industries.[38] For example, in 2015, gold made a substantial contribution to Ghana's economy, accounting for 96.68% of the total earnings from exported minerals. In comparison, diamond, bauxite, and manganese accounted for 0.31%, 1.24%, and 1.95%, respectively.[39] The mining sector currently contributes around 41% of total export earnings, 14% of total tax revenues, and 5.5% of Ghana's gross domestic product (GDP). Despite the impressive economic returns from Ghana's minerals, host communities have very little to show for the wealth generated by the sector, which remains an underlying cause of mining disputes.

Mining-related conflicts have been present since the pre-colonial era. Buah argues that regions abundant in gold were susceptible to the jealousy and malevolence of other states in pre-colonial Ghana. The possession of gold symbolized power, wealth, and influence for those areas fortunate enough to possess it.[40] Therefore, in pre-colonial times, communities rich in gold sought to establish their supremacy through conquest, making them a natural target during times of war. Before Ghana's independence, another resistance emerged concerning the management of natural resources. President Kwame Nkrumah opted for a unitary state, but soon after the elections, the National Liberation Movement (NLM) opposed it, advocating for a federal form of governance. These struggles mentioned above can be traced back to the economic activity of gold mining.

The post-colonial mining conflicts primarily involve social disputes arising from land-use conflicts, unfair compensation schemes for displaced communities, distribution of mining rent, and conflicts between large and small-scale mining operations leading to environmental degradation. Furthermore, the lack of development in mining communities has further contributed to disputes. After gaining independence in 1957, the government of the Gold Coast established a Commission in 1958 to provide advice on the exploitation of timber and minerals.[41] After its work, the Commission recommended the state's ownership of natural resources and proposed that a percentage of mining royalties be paid to the landowners as outlined in the law.[42] The recommendations led to the enactment of a series of statutes concerning land and minerals. Some of the laws passed included the Minerals Act, which vested ownership of minerals in the 'President on behalf of the Republic and in trust for the people of Ghana.'[43] Connected to this constitutional mandate is the question of whether the subsequent laws passed adequately address the interests of Ghanaians who are the 'owners' of natural resources, especially the mining communities that bear the adverse effects of mining activities.

The aspirations of the mining communities revolve around the state taking over natural resources to utilize them for the development of mining communities, ensuring they are not left worse off. However, the prevailing conditions in mining communities reflect a state of neglect, evidenced by numerous conflicts between mining companies and host communities. In light of these challenges, this chapter advocates for legal support for stakeholder consultation during negotiations for mining leases, aiming to balance the interests of the state, mining companies, and the indigenous people of the mining communities. By engaging stakeholders in frank discussions about the needs of the host community and the mining companies, a consensus can be built, creating a congenial atmosphere for mining operations and thus avoiding mining disputes. Stakeholder consultation without legal backing remains mere rhetoric, unable to effectively resolve conflicts between companies and communities.

The mining sector involves various stakeholders, such as mining companies, state authorities, service contractors, and mining communities. These companies hold either a mining lease or a prospecting license issued by the state. In Ghana, mining companies operate in locations like Obuasi, Tarkwa, Prestea, Bibiani, Abirem, Kenyase, Dunkwa-on-Offin, Nsuta, Bogoso, Damang, Akwatia, Chirano, Ahafo, Konongo, Wassa, Terbrebie, Kyebi, Anhwiaso Bekwai, and recently some towns in the Northern Region. Mining activities predominantly take place in the Ashanti, Eastern, Ahafo, Central, Western North, and the Northern regions of Ghana.

The deplorable conditions in these mining communities have led to conflicts. The issues contributing to these conflicts are diverse and numerous, such as the lack of social amenities, high unemployment rates, increased illegal mining, pollution of river bodies, destruction of forest cover and farmlands, deprivation of land for farming, destruction of livelihoods, brutalization and harassment of artisanal miners by security services, and the loss of national heritage. For instance, one artisanal miner stated:

> We have disagreements with Golden Star Resources (GSR) because we've been deprived of our rich lands. You see, this situation has affected our cultural heritage, and many of our people have been socially dislocated. I believe you have heard about the destruction of our livelihoods. GSR should know that if they contend all the suitable parcels of land are their concession, there is no way we will understand because this is where we come from. We will mine with all the force because we must make ends meet, and they can bring in security forces, and that would not stop us from mining here.[44]

The statement above highlights the frustrations experienced by mining communities regarding the legal process of granting licenses to exploit minerals in Ghana. The neglect of these communities has given rise to bold challenges from artisanal miners, questioning the authority of the state and the peaceful operations of mining companies. The conflict between the mining companies and the small-scale miners serves as an example of the ongoing disputes within the sector.

Literature exists documenting the conflict between Ghana's large-scale and small-scale miners as one part of the problem.[45] Patel et al. give detailed instances of conflicts existing in mining communities in Ghana.[46] The conflicts encompass the invasion of mining concessions, demonstrations against mining companies, and the use of guard dogs to deter 'galamsey' activities.[47] The conflicts involve miners, violent clashes between artisanal miners and mining companies, as well as the use of state security against 'galamsey' operators.[48] These are the manifestations of a lack of social legitimacy, which greatly influences the conflicts. In the following section, this chapter examines several examples of conflicts in mining communities in Ghana, their underlying causes, and the efforts made to resolve these disputes. The discussions primarily center on prevalent issues in mining communities, challenges that cut across all mining areas and will be addressed accordingly. It is evident that the conflicts in mining communities can largely be attributed to the lack of social legitimacy to operate in these communities, serving as a significant driver of mining conflicts in Ghana.

The prevailing agreement in the literature is that natural resource conflicts vary based on the type of mineral being extracted, the process of extraction, and the specific deposit area involved.[49] It is essential to distinguish between the conflicts associated with natural resources. Scholars like Collier and Hoeffler,[50] Collier and Sembane,[51] and Aspinal[52] argued that the wars in Sierra Leone, Angola, and the Democratic Republic of Congo related to diamonds are economically motivated, with underlying greed driving rebels to seize control of mining areas and launch insurgencies against the state.[53]

Nevertheless, conflicts related to gold resources exhibit distinct dynamics, as proposed by Ross[54] and Humphrey,[55] who argue that grievances in gold mining areas primarily revolve around an unequal distribution of resource rents, land expropriation, and environmental pollution.[56] These conflicts have been attributed to the reforms in the mining sector in sub-Saharan Africa, which resulted in an increase in mining activities by multinational mining firms.[57] The reforms introduced new favorable mining laws that attracted foreign private investment into the mining industry, fueling large-scale mining in impoverished mining communities. These developments have led to company-community conflicts in locations like Obuasi in Ghana.[58] However, these reforms failed to address the developmental challenges of the mining communities, hence the disputes.

In Obuasi and numerous other mining communities, conflicts arise from a variety of challenges. One of the primary tensions lies in the relationship between small-scale miners and large-scale mine operators.[59] Small-scale miners express grievances rooted in the legal framework. According to them, the legal regime is biased in favor of multinational mining companies, granting them extensive land and license permits for prolonged periods, while restricting the opportunities available to small-scale miners.[60] Another significant conflict arises between 'galamseyers' and AngloGold Ashanti, primarily driven by the lack of land for their livelihood, which compels them to resort to illegal mining to sustain themselves. This behavior of the 'galamseyers' has resulted in extensive encroachment on AngloGold concessions, leading to numerous violent clashes between AngloGold security officers and the illegal miners.[61]

Conflicts between company and community stem from the harmful effects and cost of mining on the environment[62] in the mining community. Several studies conducted by research institutions and non-governmental organizations have explored this subject. The findings reveal adverse effects, such as water pollution, land contamination, and land degradation.[63] One significant harmful effect of mining is water pollution.

The pollution arises from the leakage of chemicals used in mineral washing, which finds its way back into water bodies. This contamination affects both water quality and the suitability of water for human, livestock, and agricultural purposes. Many streams have dried up and are now unfit for human consumption. Consequently, community members are left with no choice but to search for alternatives in their surroundings. As Mensah and Okyere propose, these concerns are intricately tied to the daily lives and livelihood capabilities of the communities.[64] Such stacked denial of a basic necessity of life inflames passion, hence the conflict between company and community.

Mining activities have led to a decrease in the available land for farming in mining communities. Additionally, the use of chemicals has resulted in land contamination, negatively impacting the quality and productivity of farmland. According to Mensah, farmers in mining communities suffer losses in harvest and the fertility of their land due to these mining activities.[65] Of particular significance is the further deterioration of soil quality for farming as a result of the chemicals used in mining activities.[66] Puja contends that mining has adverse effects on soil quality and leads to fertility degradation, is closely linked to land degradation, and poses toxic risks.[67] The mining activities have a detrimental impact on the environment, leading to the loss of land and reduced harvest for the indigenous communities. Meanwhile, the mining companies extract wealth without providing any tangible benefits in return.

On the economic front, the negative impacts include the loss of farming activities, delays or lack of payment for farms taken over by mining companies, and an increase in living costs due to the influx of workers into the mining community.[68] Indeed, gold has played a transformative role in many mining communities worldwide, but the same cannot be said for Prestea in Ghana. Despite a century of mining, the town continues to struggle as a poor community.[69] At the heart of mining conflicts in communities lies the lack of economic, social, and environmental well-being for the local populations.[70] If left unaddressed adequately, these issues will persist and lead to ongoing conflict between mining companies and the communities where they operate. It has been argued that to obtain the social license to operate, mining companies must actively listen, engage, and seek consent for the participation of locals in some of the company's decision-making processes.[71] Their relationship relies on mutual understanding without legal enforcement. This chapter argues for legal support in stakeholder relationships, with penalties for mining companies in case of non-compliance. In Prestea, land-use conflicts dominate, highlighting the state's compulsory acquisition of land and its subsequent leasing to large-scale mining companies, with compensation paid by the state.[72]

The activities of mining companies can lead to the displacement of entire communities, forcing them to relocate to new areas and severing their livelihoods and social connections. This relocation process often brings about stress, insecurity, and unequal treatment.[73] The World Bank emphasizes that the relocation of communities should not leave the settlers worse off in terms of their work and income opportunities after the relocation process.[74] The responsibility for implementing programs to restore these communities is left on the shoulders of the companies by the government, which lacks the capacity to execute these initiatives.[75] The neglect creates challenges for both the indigenes and the mining company's operations, exacerbating conflicts between the community and the company.

In Wassa West, surface mining has significantly impacted water quality, leading to ongoing conflicts between local communities and mining companies.[76] The grievances of the mining communities revolve around concerns related to water quality and health. These issues are exacerbated by the pollution of water bodies resulting from mining activities.[77] Previous studies conducted in the area indicate elevated levels of water contamination caused by toxic elements such as mercury, arsenic, lead, cadmium, and cyanide spillage. These issues have led to residents harboring animosity toward mining companies.[78] In general, there is a lack of legal instruments to protect community rights. Community expectations often go unmet as mining companies prioritize increasing production at a minimal cost. Consequently, mining communities demand community investment, leading to conflicts arising from the profit motive of the companies and the needs of the communities.[79]

Evidence indicates that many farmers have been displaced due to large-scale farming operations, receiving inadequate compensation for their losses. Some notable cases have occurred in Tarkwa, where mining activities resulted in the destruction of houses, schools, and religious institutions in the area.[80] In some instances, mine security combines with state security, leading to violence against illegal miners, resulting in injuries and sometimes fatalities. The unresolved problem of poverty and deprivation faced by the local inhabitants presents a significant challenge. Without addressing these concerns, mining companies may find it difficult to gain social legitimacy to operate in these communities. The existing inequality between the communities and the mining companies requires urgent attention. Attempts by state security and mine security to suppress conflicts have not succeeded in fostering harmony between the community and the company. Therefore, a new approach is needed to effectively resolve this tension.

The lack of trust has become a source of conflict between mining companies and the local communities. The mining community perceives collusion between the state and the mining company, resulting in the depletion of resources to benefit the state while neglecting the mining communities. The activities of various mining companies have led to the displacement of indigenes from their farmlands, and the compensations offered often prove inadequate to satisfy the local community members. The mining industry has come to realize the significance of fostering lasting relationships with the communities to gain their trust. Without such relationships, tensions between the company and the community are likely to persist.[81] Most of the disputes have been resolved through various means, including negotiations, dialogue, mediation, litigation, out-of-court settlements, campaigns, and training and education of community members. These efforts are geared toward holding the companies accountable, with the assistance of civil society organizations[82] in mining.[83] These manifestations clearly indicate that the absence of social legitimacy is a significant factor contributing to the conflicts between mining companies and host communities.

The Legal Framework for Negotiating Mining Agreements in Ghana

The legal regime governing the exploitation of natural resources has not adequately addressed the challenges identified in the previous section. Consequently, conflicts have arisen when mining companies failed to adhere to responsible mining practices, resulting in environmental damage and inequitable distribution of benefits.[84] Since gaining independence, the various mining laws enacted to regulate the exploitation of minerals did not include provisions specifically aimed at developing mining communities.[85] To address this gap, the government of Ghana passed the Minerals Development Fund Act in 2016. The objective of this act is to provide financial resources for the benefit of various stakeholders, including mining communities, holders of an interest in land within a mining community, traditional and local government authorities within a mining community, and institutions responsible for the development of mining.[86] The implementation of this law in 2016 signified a significant step for Ghana, recognizing the need to proactively develop mining communities after more than a century of mining gold and other natural resources.

However, despite its clear intentions, the law has been ineffective in creating meaningful development in these communities due to a lack of funding.[87] This deficiency motivated the government to pass the Minerals Income Investment Fund Act in 2018. The objective of this act is to maximize the value of the income due to the Republic from its mineral wealth for the benefit of its citizens, monetize the minerals income in a beneficial, responsible, transparent, accountable, and sustainable manner, and develop and implement measures to reduce the Republic's budgetary exposure to minerals income fluctuations.[88] Upon closer examination of the fund's objectives, it becomes evident that any revenue generated will be distributed equally, and mining communities will not receive special treatment to ensure sustained development in their areas. Furthermore, the law allows the Minister of Finance and Economic Planning to enter into a stability agreement with the fund and establish a special purpose vehicle, subject to Parliament's approval, which will receive minerals income assigned by the fund and attract investments from investors.[89]

An analysis of the Minerals Income Investment Fund Act reveals that the prompt development of mining communities, which would foster a conducive environment for mining companies to operate, might not happen in the near future. One of the responsibilities of the Fund, as stated in the law, is to allocate 20% of minerals income received to the Minerals Development Fund.[90] The disbursement formula of the Minerals Development Fund Act has been a subject of comment in a previous article, which suggests that the Act requires an amendment to effectively achieve the Fund's objectives.[91] The Minerals Income Investment Fund Act has not adequately addressed the issues raised in the article. The existing problems that hinder the development of mining communities remain unresolved, which is unsatisfactory for the affected communities. Given these challenges, it raises questions about whether the President of Ghana, who holds natural resources on behalf of and in trust for the people of Ghana, has utilized resource revenues to benefit all citizens, especially the mining communities who bear the risks associated with mining.

The preceding discussion highlights the deficiencies in Ghana's mining agreements and laws, leading to a lack of social legitimacy and subsequent disputes in mining communities. Empirical evidence indicates that mining agreements are often crafted without involving the mining communities. Addressing this lack of community engagement is essential to counteract conflicts in mining communities. The proposed engagement aims to create a win-win situation that tackles the challenges identified in these communities.[92] The process enables the mining company and the community to exchange ideas and discuss issues related to the development of mining communities. However, the provision of amenities by mining companies through corporate social responsibility (CSR) has not been sufficient to ensure peace, as conflicts still persist between the companies and the communities, as discussed earlier.

The implementation of sustainable development strategies in mining communities involved a collaboration between the state and mining companies. However, this collaboration faced challenges as mining companies were reluctant to allocate additional funds beyond corporate tax, royalties, and other payments. The alternative livelihood programs introduced to alleviate poverty in mining areas have had limited success in Ghana, contributing to the conflicts in mining communities. Community members perceive little hope for their future beyond the continued exploitation of natural resources by mining companies.

Mining companies sometimes contribute to the construction of social amenities under their CSR programs. However, since CSR is considered a soft law, it lacks the binding force of legislation. The existing mining agreements and legislation have not incorporated the social license to operate as a legally binding requirement. This flaw in the legal regime leads to a failure in addressing the interests of mining communities, ultimately exacerbating conflicts within these communities.

Another issue of concern in mining agreements and laws in Ghana pertains to the handling of mineral revenues, which are now included in the consolidated fund.[93] As a result, the allocation of mineral revenue for development projects in mining communities has become impractical, leading to a perceived dilution of mining's contribution in the eyes of the public. The legislative attempts in Ghana to foster development in mining areas have been hindered by the lack of financial commitments. The state has not designated any specific funds for the development of mining communities, despite the ongoing conflicts in these areas. Furthermore, the legal regime has shown minimal effort in establishing a dedicated body responsible for the development of mining communities. The limited initiatives undertaken by central government through district, municipal, and metropolitan assemblies have proven insufficient in addressing the developmental needs of mining communities. The absence of a coordinating body for community development has acted as a catalyst for conflicts in the mining sector.

An equally significant gap in mining laws and agreements is the lack of accountability concerning the treatment and utilization of money generated from Ghana's mineral resources. This revenue includes royalties and corporate tax, which are funneled into the consolidated fund. Accountability is reflected in the ability of mining communities to identify and implement development projects within their host communities using these resources. The absence of such projects, despite the accrued revenue, contributes to the rise of disputes between mining companies and host communities. This chapter shows that in many resource-rich countries, mining communities are excluded from the negotiation of mining agreements due to shortcomings in the legal regime. As a result, the interests of mining communities are often neglected in contracts related to the exploitation of natural resources. Since mining communities are not involved in the negotiation process, they do not reap the full benefits from the mining activities, except for what is allocated through the national budget in a general sense. As demonstrated in this chapter, the issues related to mining are diverse and multifaceted.

The undeniable truth is that conflicts over ownership of natural resources have persisted from pre-colonial times until independence. The Convention People's Party (CPP), led by Kwame Nkrumah, aimed to vest natural resources in the state and have them held in trust by the President of the Republic. However, the NLM vehemently opposed this proposition, leading to confrontations and even loss of lives. Nonetheless, the government remained resolute, and natural resources were eventually taken under state ownership and held in trust for the citizens, as confirmed by various constitutions of Ghana. Despite this state ownership, the government failed to take substantial action to address the challenges faced by mining communities, even after more than a century of mining in Ghana. Consequently, these unresolved issues have caused ongoing turbulence and conflicts in the mining sector. The existing mining laws and agreements have not sufficiently incorporated development-oriented programs in mining communities, leading to legitimacy concerns for mining companies and exacerbating conflicts.

Recommendations

This chapter has explored the challenges that give rise to conflicts between mining companies and host communities. The mining communities argue that despite being granted mining leases and authorizations to operate, mining companies still need to gain social legitimacy from the host community. The absence of this social legitimacy often leads to conflicts. According to the constitutional provision that vests all natural resources in the President to hold in trust for the benefit of Ghanaians, the state is obligated to make financial commitments toward developing mining communities. However, the lack of such commitments has contributed to the conflicts in these communities.[94] The state's inability to fulfill these obligations arises from the gaps in the mining laws and agreements, which, in turn, have contributed to the escalation of conflicts between mining companies and host communities. The following section provides recommendations aimed at mitigating the conflicts between mining companies and host communities in Ghana.

The stakeholder consultation process is enhanced by prioritizing the interests of mining communities in mining agreements. Currently, the law involves the state and mining companies, but it overlooks the inclusion of host communities. To facilitate meaningful engagement, the legal framework for negotiating mining agreements should be amended to recognize mining communities as stakeholders. This would enable host communities to actively contribute their input and address their needs, considering the risks associated with mining companies' operations. Mining communities' active involvement in the negotiation process for mining agreements is a key step in addressing the multitude of problems related to company-community conflicts. Alongside amending the law to include the community as a party in negotiations, it is crucial to codify the social license to operate based on mutual agreement. This codification enables the host community to assert its specific fundamental requirements, taking into account the development needs of the mining communities. Attaining such an agreement will foster a favorable environment for mining companies to operate without facing resistance from the host communities.

If the legal provision addresses this request, it would entail creating a dedicated financial allocation specifically for the development of mining areas, aiming to generate employment opportunities and address the developmental challenges outlined in this chapter. Establishing a fund that receives a portion of the royalties paid to the state, dedicated to projects benefiting the mining communities, becomes essential. This recommendation arises from the fact that the revenue from exploiting natural resources is currently managed by the state, which has not adequately invested in the development of mining communities. Setting up such a fund is crucial for fostering peaceful operations of mining companies, as the funds would be solely utilized for the benefit of the mining communities, unlike the present scenario where the funds are used centrally with limited impact on the mining communities.

Establishing such a fund requires a transparent and accountable approach to fulfill the development aspirations of the mining communities. The chapter proposes the formation of a body comprising representatives from the state, mining communities, and mining companies to ensure the responsible and efficient utilization of the funds for the benefit of the mining communities. The utilization of the fund would be directed toward development projects that have been mutually agreed upon by the community. This body would be responsible for overseeing the progress of these development projects and reporting back to all involved parties. As a result, the mining communities would witness tangible development in their areas. This intervention would foster a harmonious environment for the mining companies to operate without facing confrontations with the community, ultimately granting them the social legitimacy needed to conduct their business activities.

Conclusion

This chapter delves into the concept of social legitimacy in the mining sector and its impact on conflicts and disputes within mining communities in Ghana. It examines the existing gaps in implementing social legitimacy principles in mining contracts, which have contributed to the escalation of disputes, and proposes legal reforms to address these deficiencies. If mining communities witness visible development that addresses the challenges discussed, it would foster a conducive and peaceful atmosphere for mining companies, leading to the social acceptance of their activities and granting them social legitimacy. It is important for Ghana to review its legal framework for natural resource exploitation and incorporate the codification of the social license to operate, following the recommendations outlined in this chapter.

The implementation of such reforms would involve allocating a portion of the revenue accruing to the state and contributions from mining companies to establish a fund supervised by representatives from the host community, the state, and the mining companies. This approach would mitigate suspicion and empower mining communities to plan and execute their development initiatives, resulting in a harmonious coexistence between the communities and mining companies. Emphasizing the importance of equitable treatment and meaningful engagement between mining companies and communities, the concept of a social license to operate underscores the need for mitigating operational impacts to secure and maintain social legitimacy.[95]

Notes

1 Håkan Tarras-Wahlberg, Freek Cronjé, Suzanne Reyneke, and Susanne Sweet, 'Meeting Local Community Needs: The Cases of Iron Ore Mining in Sweden and South Africa', *The Extractive Industries and Society*, Vol. 4, (Elsevier

BV, 2017): 652–660; Damiola Olawuyi, *Extractives Industry Law in Africa* (Cham: Springer 2018): pp. 1–25.
2 Marta Conde, and Philippe Le Billon, 'Why Do Some Communities Resist Mining Projects While Others Do Not?', *The Extractive Industries and Society*, Vol. 4, (2017): 682.
3 Timothy Prior, Damien Giurco, Gavin Mark Mudd, Leah Mason, Johannes Behrisch, 'Resource Depletion, Peak Minerals and the Implications for Sustainable Resource Management,' *Global Environmental Change*, Vol. 22, (2012): 577–587.
4 Martinez-Alier, Joan, Isabelle Anguelovski, Patrick Bond, Daniela Del Bene, Federico Demaria, Julien-Francois Gerber, Lucie Greyl, Willi Haas, Hali Healy, Victoria Marín-Burgos, Godwin Ojo, Marcelo Porto, Leida Rijnhout, Beatriz Rodríguez-Labajos, Joachim Spangenberg, Leah Temper, Rikard Warlenius, and Ivonne Yánez, 'Between Activism and Science: Grassroots Concepts for Sustainability Coined by Environmental Justice Organisations,' *Journal of Political Ecology*, Vol. 21, (2014): 19–60.
5 Daniel M. Franks, Rachel Davis, Anthony J. Bebbington, Saleem H. Ali, Deanna Kemp, and Martin Scurrah. "Conflict Translates Environmental and Social Risk into Business Costs." Proceedings of the National Academy of Sciences, U.S.A. 111, no. 21 (2014): 7576–7581. doi: 10.1073/pnas.1405135111
6 Conde, and Le Billon, "Why Do Some Communities Resist Mining Projects While Others Do Not?", 682.
7 Bruce Harvey, 'Social Development Will Not Deliver Social License to Operate for the Extractive Sector', *Extractive Industries and Society*, Vol. 1, Issue 1, (2014): 7–11. Also Lynda Cheshire, 'A Corporate Responsibility? The Constitution of Fly-In, Fly-Out Mining Companies as Governance Partners in Remote Mine-Affected Localities', *Journal of Rural Studies*, Vol. 26, (2010): 12–20 and Stuart L. Hart, 'Beyond Greening: Strategies for a Sustainable World', *Harvard Business Review*, (1997): 66–76 (January–February).
8 Willice O. Abuya, 'Mining Conflicts and Corporate Social Responsibility: Titanium Mining in Kwale, *Kenya*', *The Extractive Industries and Society*, Vol. 3, (2016): 485–493.
9 Wisdom Akpalu, and Peter J. Parks, 'Natural Resource Use Conflict: Gold Mining in Tropical Rainforest in Ghana', *Environment and Development Economics*, Vol. 12 (01), (2007): 55–72.
10 Gavin Hilson, 'An Overview of Land Use Conflicts in Mining Communities', *Land Use Policy*, Vol. 19, (2002): 65–73.
11 Jedrzej George Frynas, and Geoffrey Wood, 'Oil and War in Angola', *Review of African Political Economy*, Vol. 28 (90), (2001): 587–606.
12 Jock McCulloch, 'Beating the Odds: The Quest for Justice by South African Asbestos Mining Communities', *Review of African Political Economy*, Vol. 32 (103), (2005): 64–66.
13 Seth Opoku Mensah, and Seth Asare Okyere, 'Mining, Environment and Community Conflicts: A Study of Company-Community Conflicts over Gold Mining in the Obuasi Municipality of Ghana', *Journal of Sustainable Development Studies*, Vol. 5 (1), (2014): 64–99.
14 William N. Holden, 'Indigenous Peoples and Non-ferrous Metals Mining in the Philippines', *The Pacific Review*, Vol. 18 (3), (2005): 417–438.
15 Maribeth Erb, 'Mining and Conflict over in Nusa Tenggara Timur Province, Eastern Indonesia', *The Extractive Industries and Society*, Vol. 3 (2), (2016): 370–382.

16 Ron D. Ayling, and Kimberly Kelly, 'Dealing with Conflict: Natural Resources and Dispute Resolution', *Commonwealth Forestry Review*, Vol. 76 (3), (1997): 182.
17 Kieren Moffat, Justine Lacey, Airong Zhang, and Sina Leipold, 'The Social License to Operate: A Critical Review', *Forestry*, Vol. 89, (Oxford Academic, 2016): 480. For more on social license to operate see the following, Susan A. Joyce and Ian Thomson, 'Earning a Social License to Operate: Social Acceptability and Resource Development In Latin America', *Canadian Mining Metallurgical Bull*, Vol. 93, (2000): 45–93; ; Rose Dakin, James D Van Alstine, and Matthew Gitsmam, 'Managing Risk and Maintaining License to Operate: Participatory Planning and Monitoring in the Extractive Industries'. (2008). World Bank and Ian Thomson and Robert Boutilier, 'Social License to Operate'. In *SME Mining Engineering Handbook*, 3rd edition, edited by P. Darling. Society for Mining, Metallurgy Explorations, (2011): pp. 1779–1796.
18 Neil Gunningham, Robert A. Kagan, and Dorothy Thornton, 'Social License and Environmental Protection: Why Businesses Go beyond Compliance', *Law and Social Inquiry*, Vol. 29, (2004): 307–341.
19 Harvey Bruce, 'SIA from a Developer's Perspective: Forward'. In *New Directions in Social Assessment*, edited by Frank Vanclay and Ana Maria Esteves. Cheltenham: Edward Elgar Publishing, (2011): pp. xxxvii–xxxiii.
20 Minerals Council of Australia (MCA). (2005), Enduring Value: The Australian Minerals Industry Framework for Sustainable Development (Guidance for implementation), MCA. Available at www.minerals.org.au/file_uploads/files/resources/enduring_value/EV_GuidanceForImplementation_July2005.pdf [Accessed on 15th February 2022].
21 Daniel M. Franks, and Tamar Cohen, 'Social License in Design: Constructive Technology Assessment within a Mineral Research and Development Institution', *Technological Forecasting and Social Change*, Vol. 79, (2012): 1229–1240.
22 Joel Gehman, Lianne Lefsrud, and Stewart Fast, 'Social License to Operate: Legitimacy by Another Name?', *Canadian Public Administration*, Vol. 60 (2), (2017): 304–305.
23 J. Perlez, and L. Bergman, 'Tangled Strands in Fight over Peru Gold Mine', *The New York Times*, 25 October 2005 (2010).
24 C. L. Reichardt, 'Due Diligence Assessment of Non-Financial Risk: Prophylaxis for the Purchaser', *Resources Policy*, Vol. 31, (2006): 193–203.
25 Konstaninos Komnitsas, 'Social License to Operate in Mining: Present Views and Future Trends', *Resources*, Vol. 9, (2020): 79.
26 Obed Adonteng-Kissi, and Barbara Adonteng-Kissi, 'Living with Conflicts in Ghana's Prestea Mining Area: Is Community Engagement the Answer?', *Journal of Sustainable Mining*, Vol. 16, (2017): 197.
27 Susan A. Joyce, and Ian Thomson, 'Earning a Social Licence to Operate: Social Acceptability and Resource Development in Latin America', *CIM Bulletin* Vol. 93 (1037), (2000): 52.
28 Joel Gehman, Liame M. Lefsrud, and Stewart Fast, 'Social Licence to Operate: Legitimacy by Another Name', *Canadian Public Administration*, Vol 60 (2), (2017): 295.
29 Robert Boutilier, and Ian Thomson, 'Social License to Operate'. In *SME Mining Engineering Handbook*, 3rd edition, edited by Peter Darling. Englewood, CO: Society for Mining, Metallurgy, and Exploration, (2011): pp. 779–796.

30 John R. Owen, and Deanna Kemp, 'Social Licence and Mining: A Critical Perspective', *Resources Policy*, Vol. 38, (2013): 29–35.
31 John R. Owen, and Deanna Kemp, 'Social Licence and Mining: A Critical Perspective', *Resources Policy*, Vol. 38, (2013): 299.
32 Owen and Kemp, 'Social Licence and Mining, 299.
33 John R. Owen, and Deanna Kemp, 'Social Licence and Mining: A Critical Perspective', *Resources Policy*, Vol. 38, (2013): 299–300.
34 Kieren Moffat, and Airong Zhang, 'The Paths to Social Licence to Operate: An Integrative Model Explaining Community Acceptance of Mining', *Resources Policy*, Vol. 39, (2014): 62–64.
35 Tapio Litmanen, Tuija Jartti, and Eoro Rantale, 'Refining the Preconditions of Social Licence to Operate (SLO): Reflections on Citizens' Attitudes towards Mining in Two Finnish Regions', *The Extractive Industries and Society*, Vol. 3, (2016): 782.
36 Aboka Yaw Emmanuel, Cobbina Samuel Jerry, and Doke Adzo Dzogbodi, 'Review of Environmental and Health Impacts of Mining in Ghana', *Journal of Health and Pollution*, Vol. 8(17), (2018): 43–52.
37 Jones Opoku-Ware, 'Social Impact Analysis of Mining Operations in Kenyasi and Surrounding Communities of Ghana: The Case of Newmont Gold Mining Company in Ghana', *Developing Country Studies*, Vol. 4(18), (2014): 54.
38 Benjamin Nii Aryee, 'Contribution of the Minerals and Mining Sector to National Development: Ghana's Experiment', *Great Insights*, Vol. 1(5), (2012) available at https://ecdpm.org/great-insights/extractive-sector-for-development/contribution-minerals-mining-sector-national-development-ghanas-experiment/#:~:text=The%20sector%20directly%20contributed%2038.3,sand%20winning%20and%20quarry%20industries [Accessed on 24 March 2021].
39 Alexander Aryertey Odonkor, and Emmanuel Amoah Darkwah, (2019), Ghana: Economic Impact of Mining in Ghana, available at https://allafrica.com/stories/201906110359.html [Accessed on 24 March 2022].
40 Frank K. Nyame and Joseph Blocher, 'Influence of Land Tenure Practices on Artisanal Mining Activity in Ghana', *Resources Policy*, Vol. 35(1), (2009): 47-53.
41 Chris Adomako-Kwakye, 'Neglect of Mining Areas in Ghana: The Case for Equitable Distribution of Resource Revenue', *Commonwealth Law Bulletin*, Vol. 44 (4), (2018): 645. The article devotes a section that discusses the legal ownership of natural resources in Ghana and the implication of the constitutional provision which vest natural resources in Ghana in the President to hold same in trust for the people of Ghana.
42 Chris Adomako-Kwakye, 'Neglect of Mining Areas in Ghana: The Case for Equitable Distribution of Resource Revenue', *Commonwealth Law Bulletin*, Vol. 44 (4), (2018): 645.
43 Chris Adomako-Kwakye, 'Neglect of Mining Areas in Ghana: The Case for Equitable Distribution of Resource Revenue', *Commonwealth Law Bulletin*, Vol. 44 (4), (2018): 645.
44 Obed Adonteng-Kissi, and Barbara Adonteng-Kissi, 'Living with Conflicts in Ghana's Prestea Mining Area: Is Community Engagement the Answer?', *Journal of Sustainable Mining*, Vol. 16, (2017): 200.
45 Kayla Patel, John Rogan, Nicholas Cuba, and Anthony Bebbington, 'Evaluating Conflicts Surrounding Mineral Extraction in Ghana: Assessing the Spatial Interactions of Large and Small-Scale Mining', *The Extractive Industries and Society*, Vol. 3, (2016): 450. For more discussion on conflicts between Ghana's

large and small-scale miners see the following works; Gavin Hilson, 'An Overview of Land Use Conflicts in Mining Communities', *Land Use Policy*, Vol. 19 (1), (2002): 65–73, Gavin Hilson, and Natalia Yakovleva, 'Strained Relations: A Critical Analysis of the Mining Conflict in Prestea, Ghana', *Political Geography*, Vol. 26 (1), (2007): 98–119, Sadia Mohammed Banchirigah, 'Challenges with Eradicating Illegal Mining in Ghana: A Perspective from the Grassroots', *Resources Policy*, Vol. 33 (1), (2008): 29–38, Anthony Aubynn, 'Sustainable Solution or a Marriage of Convenience? The Coexistence of Large-Scale Mining and Artisanal and Small-Scale Mining on the Abosso Goldfields Concession in Western Ghana', *Resources Policy*, Vol. 34 (1–2): (2009), 64–67 among others.

46 Kayla Patel, John Rogan, Nicholas Cuba, and Anthony Bebbington, 'Evaluating Conflicts Surrounding Mineral Extraction in Ghana: Assessing the Spatial Interactions of Large and Small-Scale Mining', *The Extractive Industries and Society*, Vol. 3, (2016): 452–453.

47 Galamsey loosely refers to individuals who engage in illegal mining in forests, river beds, and concession of mining companies.

48 Kayla Patel, John Rogan, Nicholas Cuba, and Anthony Bebbington, 'Evaluating Conflicts Surrounding Mineral Extraction in Ghana: Assessing the Spatial Interactions of Large and Small-Scale Mining', *The Extractive Industries and Society*, Vol. 3, (2016): 452–453.

49 Paivi Lujala, 'The Spoil of Nature: Armed Civil Conflict and Rebel Access to Natural Resource', *Journal of Peace Research*, Vol. 47 (1), (2010): 15–28.

50 Paul Collier, and Anke Hoeffler, 'Greed and Grievance in Civil War', *World Bank Policy Research Paper* (2002): 2355.

51 Paul Collier, and Nicholas Sambanis, '*Understanding Civil War: Evidence and Analysis*', Vol. 1. Washington, DC: IBRD/World Bank, (2005).

52 Edward Aspinall, 'The Construction of Grievance: Natural and Identity in A Separatist Conflict', *Journal of Conflict Resolution*, Vol. 5: 950.

53 Godfred Appiah Okoh, 'Grievance and Conflict in Ghana's Gold Mining Industry: The Case of Obuasi', *Futures*, Vol. 62, (2014): 52.

54 Michael L. Ross, 'How Do Natural Resources Influence Civil Conflict? Evidence From 13 Cases', *International Organisations*, Vol. 58 (1), (2004): 35–67.

55 Macartan Humphreys, 'Natural Resource Conflict and Conflict Resolution: Uncovering the Mechanism', *Journal of Conflict Resolution*, Vol. 47(1), (2005): 508–537.

56 Godfred Appiah Okoh, 'Grievance and Conflict in Ghana's Gold Mining Industry: The Case of Obuasi', *Futures*, Vol. 62, (2014): 52.

57 Godfred Appiah Okoh, 'Grievance and Conflict in Ghana's Gold Mining Industry: The Case of Obuasi', *Futures*, Vol. 62, (2014): 52.

58 Godfred Appiah Okoh, 'Grievance and Conflict in Ghana's Gold Mining Industry, 52.

59 Theresa Gavin, Tara K. McGee, Karen E. Smoyer-Tomic and Emmanuel Ato Aubyn et al., 'Community-Company Relations in Gold Mining in Ghana', *Journal of Environmental Management*, Vol. 90, (2009): 571–586.

60 Andrew, (note 68), 117–130.

61 Godfred Appiah Okoh, 'Grievance and Conflict in Ghana's Gold Mining Industry: The case of Obuasi', *Futures*, Vol. 62, (2014): 52. According to Okoh, some of the reported clashes are as follows: first, in 1994, AngloGold security with the military and the police killed three artisanal miners. Second, in 1996, the

company suffered damage of over $10 million of company property during a violent clash between artisanal miners and the company and state security forces. Third, in 1997, AngloGold security was brutalized who set out their security dogs on 16 artisanal miners. Fourth, in 2000, artisanal miners burnt a poultry farm belonging to AngloGold and sold valuable items of the company and livestock. Fifth, in 2010, artisanal miners attacked and wounded two company security who went on patrol on the company's concession. Sixth, in 2011, company security shot and killed artisanal miners. Seventh, in 2011, a massive demonstration against AngloGold for the arrest of 150 artisanal miners by the military and police which violent. The narration reveals that despite the death of artisanal miners seeking to make ends meet, the operation of illegal mining is very rife in Ghana. The picture shows the unbalanced nature of mining leases which has nothing in it for citizens. This creates problems for mining companies exacerbating their legitimacy to operate in host communities.

62 Theresa Gavin, Tara K. McGee, Karen E. Smoyer-Tomic and Emmanuel Ato Aubyn et al., 'Community-Company Relations in Gold Mining in Ghana' *Journal of Environmental Management,* Vol. 90, (2009): 580. The authors argue that environmental impacts are twofold, one positive and two negative. The positive effect refers to new facilities provided by the mining companies, namely, housing, educational facilities, access to water, health facilities, improved transportation networks. The negative effect includes noisy environment, disrupted water, air, and land decreasing the environmental quality, and increase in disease. Some of the health problems associated with mining raised include tuberculosis, catarrh, skin irritations, boils, eye problems, chronic coughs, and malaria. The effect of these diseases contributes to the conflicts between host communities and mining companies.

63 For a more detailed discussion on the environmental effect of mining on Obuasi, see Mensah and Okyere, (note 13), 74–81.

64 Seth Opoku Mensah, and Seth Asare Okyere, 'Mining, Environment and Community Conflicts: A Study of Company-Community Conflicts over Gold Mining in the Obuasi Municipality of Ghana', *Journal of Sustainable Development Studies,* Vol. 5 (1), (2014): 75.

65 Elvis Owusu-Mensah, 'The Role of Corporate Social Responsibility on Sustainable Development: A Case Study of the Mining Community in Obuasi Municipality— Unpublished Thesis. Available at http://hdl.handle.net/11250/135139 [Accessed on 24 March 2022].

66 Seth Opoku Mensah, and Seth Asare Okyere, 'Mining, Environment and Community Conflicts: A Study of Company-Community Conflicts over Gold Mining in the Obuasi Municipality of Ghana', *Journal of Sustainable Development Studies,* Vol. 5 (1), (2014): 78.

67 Puja, Mondal '9 Adverse Effects of Mining on Environment', Available at www.yourarticlelibrary.com/environment/9-adverse-effects-of-mining-on-environment/12334 [Accessed on 4th February 2022].

68 Theresa Gavin, Tara K. McGee, Karen E. Smoyer-Tomic, and Emmanuel Ato Aubyn et al., 'Community-Company Relations in Gold Mining in Ghana', *Journal of Environmental Management,* Vol. 90, (2009): 577–578.

69 Obed Adonteng-Kissi, and Barbara Adonteng-Kissi, 'Living with Conflicts in Ghana's Prestea Mining Area: Is Community Engagement the Answer?', *Journal of Sustainable Mining,* Vol. 16, (2017): 196.

70 Uwafiokun Idemudia, 'Corporate Social Responsibility and Development in Africa: Issues and Possibilities', *Geography Compass,* Vol. 8 (7), (2014): 421–435.

71 Obed Adonteng-Kissi, and Barbara Adonteng-Kissi, 'Living with Conflicts in Ghana's Prestea Mining Area,196.
72 Article 20 (1) and (2) of Ghana's 1992 Constitution.
73 Nesar Ahmad, and Kuntari Lahiri-Dutt, 'Engendering Mining Communities Examining the Missing Gender Concerns in Coal Mining Displacement and Rehabilitation in India', *Gender Technology and Development*, Vol. 10 (3), (2006): 313–339. Also, Theodore E. Downing, (2002), 'Avoiding New Poverty: Mining-Induced Displacement and Resettlement', International Institute for Environment and Development, London, United Kingdom.
74 David Szablowski, *Transnational Law and Local Struggles': Mining Communities and the World Bank*. Oxford and Portland: Bloomsbury Publishing, (2007). Also John R. Owen and Deanna Kemp, 'Mining-Induced Displacement and Resettlement: A Critical Appraisal', *Journal of Cleaner Production*, Vol. 87, (Elsevier, 2015): 478–488.
75 John R. Owen, and Deanna Kemp, 'Mining-induced displacement and resettlement: a critical appraisal', *Journal of Cleaner Production*, Vol. 87, (2015): 486.
76 Nandita Singh, John Koku and Berit Balfors, (2007), 'Resolving Water Conflicts in Mining Areas of Ghana Through Public Participation: A Communication Perspective', *Journal of Creative Communication*, Vol. 2 (3), (2007): 362.
77 Avotri et al., (2002) '*The Health Impact of Cyanide Spillage at Goldfields Ghana Limited*, Tarkwa, Report.
78 Nandita Singh, John Koku, and Berit Balfors, Resolving Water Conflicts in Mining Areas of Ghana Through Public Participation: A Communication Perspective', *Journal of Creative Communication*, Vol. 2 (3), (2007): 362. The authors refer to works undertaken by Amonoo-Neizer and Amekor, 'Determination of Total Arsenic in Environmental Samples from Kumasi and Obuasi', *Ghana Environmental Health Perspectives*, Vol. 101 (1), (1993): 46–49, A K. Armah, G. A. Darpaah, and D. Carboo, 'Heavy Metal Levels and Physical Parameters of Drainage Ways and Wells in Three Mining Areas in Ghana', *Journal of the Ghana Science Association*, Vol. 1 (1), (1998): 113–117, Gavin Hilson, 'Promoting Sustainable Development in Ghanaian Small-Scale Gold Mining Operations', *The Environmentalist*, Vol. 22, (2002): 51–57 and Pauline L. Smedley, 'Arsenic in Rural Groundwater in Ghana', *Journal of African Earth Sciences*, Vol. 22 (4), (1996): 459–470.
79 Cynthia Kwakyewah, and Uwafiokun Idemudia, 'Canada-Ghana Engagements in the Mining Sector: Protecting Human Rights or Business as Usual', *Transnational Human Tights Review*, Vol. 147 (4), (2017): 1–26.
80 Gavin Hilson, and Frank Nyame, 'Gold mining in Ghana's Forest Reserves: A Report on the Current Debate', *Area*, Vol. 38 (2), (2006): 175; Jerry Mensah-Pah, 'Demolished Ghanaian Village Wins Court Decision', Oxfam America available at www.oxfamamerica.org/explore/stories/demolished-ghanaian-village-wins-court-decision/ [Accessed on 31 January 2022].
81 Brooke Dawn Barton, *A Global/Local Approach to Conflict Resolution in the Mining Sector: The Case of the Tintaya Dialogue Table*. Boston: Fletcher School, 2005. Also, A. R. Parker et al., *Managing Risk and Maintaining License to Operate: Participatory Planning and Monitoring in the Extractive Sector*. (2008), Washington, DC: World Bank Group.
82 They include, Wassa Association Communities Affected by Mining (WACAM), Third World Network, CEPIL.

83 Cynthia Kwakyewah, and Uwafiokun Idemudia, 'Canada-Ghana Engagements in the Mining Sector: Protecting Human Rights or Business as Usual', *Transnational Human Tights Review*, Vol. 147 (4), (2017): 1–26.
84 World Commission on Environment and Development (WCED), Report, 1987. Also MMSD, 'Report of the Workshop on Indigenous Peoples and Mining, Minerals and Sustainable Development', Perth (4–6 February), International Institute for Environment Development (IIED), London, 2002b.
85 These include the Concession Ordinance, 1900 Cap 14, the Concessions Ordinance Act of 1939, Cap 136, the Minerals Act 1962, Act 126, the Minerals and Mining Law 1986, P.N.D.C.L. 153, Minerals and Mining (Amendment) Act, 1994, Act 475, the Minerals and Mining Act, 2006, Act 703, and Minerals and Mining (Amendment) Act, 2015, Act 900.
86 The Minerals Development Fund Act, 2016 (Act 912).
87 Chris Adomako-Kwakye, and Emmanuel Adjei Bediako, (2019), 'Is the Mineral Development Fund Act the Panacea for Development of Mining Areas in Ghana?', *KNUST Law Journal*, Vol. 8, (2019): 165. The authors argue that the royalties paid and the manner they are applied cannot ensure the development of the mining areas due to little or no accountability regime under the law as well as the quantum paid.
88 Minerals Income Investment Fund Act, 2018 (ACT 978).
89 See section 40 and the interpretation section of Act 978.
90 Section 4 of Act 978.
91 Chris Adomako-Kwakye, and Emmanuel Adjei Bediako, (2019), 'Is the Mineral Development Fund Act the Panacea for Development of Mining Areas in Ghana?', *KNUST Law Journal*, Vol. 8, (2019): 165.
92 Obed Adonteng-Kissi, and Barbara Adonteng-Kissi, 'Living with Conflicts in Ghana's Prestea Mining Area: Is Community Engagement the Answer?' *Journal of Sustainable Mining*, Vol. 16, (2017): 204.
93 ICMM, (2015), 'Mining in Ghana-What Future Can We Expect?', 9 available at www.icmm.com/website/publications/pdfs/mining-partserships-for-development/mining-in-ghana_what-future-can-we-expect [Accessed on 24 March 2022].
94 Article 257 (6) of Ghana's 1992 Constitution.
95 Kieren Moffat, and Airong Zhang, A. 'The Paths to Social Licence to Operate: An Integrative Model Explaining Community Acceptance of Mining', *Resources Policy*, Vol. 39, (2014): 61.

9 Exploring the Role of Gender and Indigenous Knowledge in Peacebuilding and Political Stability in Africa

Jonathan Romic

Introduction

This chapter explores the role of gender and indigenous knowledge in peacebuilding and political stability in Africa. In indigenous African communities, there exist traditional knowledge systems, practices, and wisdom passed down through generations, which encompass a profound understanding of natural resource governance. These knowledge systems have been shown to offer sustainable and culturally appropriate solutions to conflict resolution and peacebuilding. This chapter shed light on how gender and indigenous knowledge can contribute to peacebuilding and political stability. By exploring case studies and empirical evidence from specific countries, the chapter seeks to showcase the ways in which local women have mobilized indigenous knowledge to foster peace, mitigate conflicts, and promote stability. The chapter is structured in three sections.

The first section explores the complex relationship between natural resources and political instability in Africa. Natural resources have far-reaching impacts on social, political, and economic dynamics, going beyond their environmental significance. Contrary to popular belief, natural resources alone do not inevitably lead to socio-political conflict and instability. There are several additional explanatory variables that play a crucial role in shaping the outcomes. These variables include corrupt leadership, the influence of external actors such as corporations, and the erosion of socio-cultural knowledge and practices related to resource management. Understanding these dynamic factors is essential for comprehending the functioning of contemporary African states. By drawing on the historical socio-religious perspectives on natural resources, this section analyzes the rise and fall of Great Zimbabwe during A.D. 1420–1550. The analysis in this section is guided by the following questions: What spiritual lessons can Africans teach us about natural resource management? Are there historical examples of resource mismanagement leading to socio-political instability? Do these historical examples mirror the experiences of modern African states? The case of Great Zimbabwe is particularly relevant as it shares parallels with contemporary socio-political experiences in modern African states, demonstrating the persistence of underlying variables that cause instability. Identifying these

DOI: 10.4324/9781003355717-13

key variables can provide valuable insights for academics, practitioners, and policymakers to address the root causes of socio-political instability.

In the second section, I explore the connections between gender, indigenous knowledge, resource management, and localized peacebuilding with the aim to establish a theoretical and practical foundation for advancing future peacebuilding initiatives. I ask, what role do local women play in resource management? Are there specific cases of women utilizing their indigenous knowledge to promote social, political, and economic stability? If so, can these examples pave the way for improving socio-political relations through resource management? By examining case studies from Burundi and Liberia that showcase the positive impact of local women on resource management and their use of indigenous knowledge for peacebuilding, this chapter aims to highlight opportunities for implementing similar practices in different contexts to promote stability and peace across Africa.

The final section introduces a theoretical construct proposed by Krampe, Hegazi, and VanDeveer, which includes three mechanisms supporting peacebuilding efforts through enhanced resource governance: contact hypothesis, diffusion of international norms, and state service provision.[1] Two central questions frame this analysis: Do the concepts of gender and indigenous knowledge align with this theoretical framework? If so, do they provide additional explanatory support for improving peacebuilding and resource governance? I utilize a case study of local Sudanese women to assess the potential of this framework for peacebuilding and its explanatory mechanisms. This approach allows for an analysis that highlights practical applications to local peacebuilding while examining how gender and indigenous knowledge might further strengthen the framework and its mechanisms. This chapter contributes to a nuanced understanding of the role of gender and indigenous knowledge in peacebuilding and political stability.

Contextualizing Natural Resources

The governance of resources is aptly described as a contested space with multiple stakeholders that include citizens, communities, corporations, nations, and international organizations.[2] This dynamic has given rise to a continent rife with violence and governance structures chronically characterized by corruption and instability. Therefore, these interconnections necessitate a conception of peacebuilding that is sensitive to its interlocking modalities. However, peacebuilding as a functional concept can be described as amorphous. This is due to multiple actors, agencies, organizations, and institutions providing conceptual constructions that vary in structural capacities.[3] Boutros Boutros-Ghali, the UN Secretary-General defined peacebuilding as an: 'action to identify and support structures which will tend to strengthen and solidify peace in order to avoid relapse into conflict'.[4] This definition was selected as the basis for analysis because it is conceptually expensive enough to incorporate multiple explanatory variables including governance structure, indigenous knowledge, and gender with its analytical ambit. If the definition selected was too narrow, it could miss out on key contextual variables that possess explanatory powers.

At this juncture, it is essential to link the concept of indigenous knowledge explicitly with its capacity for peacebuilding. There is a plethora of potential explanations why peacebuilding efforts have not been successful. One explanation is that the epistemological foundations of peacebuilding are predicated upon conceptions of conflict resolution that are entrenched in Western ideological frameworks.[5] This is precisely why indigenous knowledge is invaluable to peacebuilding processes; it provides information and perspectives that are contextually sensitive.[6] Contextually, African societies have a different conception of knowledge from Western societies.[7] Western conceptions of peacebuilding and conflict resolution are not sensitive to African cultural contexts in which they are expected to operationally function. For example, local charms play a significant role in local land conflicts, a variable often overlooked by Western researchers.[8] This is one potential contextual reason why peacebuilding and peacekeeping efforts have floundered. Like peacebuilding, there are multiple categorizations and definitions of indigenous knowledge. Conceptual clarity is further exacerbated by each categorization having multiple definitions.[9] Therefore, the chapter will employ 'indigenous knowledge' as an umbrella term, holistically encapsulating competing conceptualizations. There are two reasons why this approach was selected. First, this approach lays the foundation for conceptual cooperation.[10] Second, it provides a basis for consensus building.[11] For peacebuilding initiatives to move forward, there is a desperate need for consensus building among stakeholders to address larger issues.

Natural Resources and Political Instability

To understand the relationship between natural resources and political instability, it is indispensable to trace their connective roots historically. This section will begin by exploring the historical role of natural resources within socio-religious worldviews and practices. Highlighting how this system of indigenous knowledge enriched the responsible use of resources and created stable socio-political relationships. This will be followed by exploring the rise of Great Zimbabwe and the reasons for its eventual downfall. Purposely, focusing on political leadership and resource management practices. Supplemented by exploring how shifts in governance structure also shifted resource management practices. This case was selected for two reasons. First, it connects indigenous knowledge with socio-religious resource management practices through the genealogical lens of governance. Second, it acts as a segue into a comparative analysis, exploring the similarities between Great Zimbabwe and current African states. The comparative analysis serves as a method to highlight several similarities. Emphasizing the parallel formation of political elite hierarchies and the subsequent mismanagement of resources. Exploring the various stakeholders who benefit from the mismanagement of resources and socio-political instability will function as a supportive analysis structure. The aim here is to identify commonalities among competing explanatory variables to better understand the socio-political dynamics that reduce stability.

Traditionally, natural resources represented sacred spiritual objects imbued with power, this sacred perspective provided the prescriptive foundation for their judicious consumption. For example, Shona spirits were ancestorial spirits that manifested themselves in rocks, water, and animals like lions and eagles.[12] In Great Zimbabwe, these ancestor spirits were found in anthropomorphized soapstone bird carvings.[13] Gumo et al. state that this spiritual view led to prudent conservation and responsible consumption practices.[14] However, this is not an isolated phenomenon, LaDuke identifies similar Native American practices that produced social harmony, political stability, and economic progress.[15] Naturally, there are examples of conflict within cultures that had this social worldview. This includes the continual contestation of land claims in Zimbabwe between the Nemanwa and Mugabe tribes.[16] However, the point here is that these indigenous knowledge systems were also contextually the basis for long periods of social, political, and ecological stability. Holistically, these values and practices gradually dissipated during colonization. Eneji et al. concluded that the religious components of natural resource protection eroded through the 'acculturation and enculturation' of Western spiritual traditions.[17] Modern-day Zimbabwe is experiencing 'intra-state' conflict and political instability due in part to the lack of a system of deeply held and shared values.[18] It is worth stating contextual sensitivity to indigenous historical practices and cultural values is an important part of peacebuilding.

The rise and fall of Great Zimbabwe illustrates several practical connections between shifts in socio-religious and political governance structures leading to destabilization. The birth of Great Zimbabwe is rooted in small agrarian farming communities that over time became highly hierarchical and aristocratic.[19] Amassing power and wealth through herds of cattle, taxation systems, and the trade of valuable resources such as ivory and gold across the East African coast.[20] This culture practiced a form of nature worship holding its land and resources to be sacred.[21] One question that flummoxed scholars was what caused the demise of this great power. It was hypothesized that it was the result of environmental degradation. However, recent scholarship suggests that the decline was not strictly environmental. The social, political, and economic mismanagement of resources by the ruling elite was also a significant contributing factor.[22] Strang states that when cultures become increasingly hierarchical over time, they humanize their view of nature and their right to exercise dominion over it.[23] It could be hypothesized that the veneration of natural resources was a cementing bond among the inhabitants. However, with the introduction of colonialism, veneration was replaced by avarice, eroding the foundational pillars supporting socio-political stability.

Natural resources are frequently framed as a detriment to political stability. However, it has been argued that the negative impacts are actually the result of poor governance, corruption, and weak institutions.[24] African countries have a history of systemic political and economic corruption.[25] One method employed to secure power and protect against corrupt practices is through the creation of political alliances and elite hierarchies. For example, modern African leaders have developed a system of coalitions and hierarchies to defuse key individuals at senior levels of government.[26] Ibrahim and Cheri argue that poor leadership has exacerbated instability, conflict, corruption, and environmental degradation.[27] The Great Lakes conflict exemplifies instability stemming from political and economic control and natural resources.[28] Mozambique provides another operational example where the economic benefits of foreign investors, seeking to extract natural resources, are monopolized through elite coalitions.[29] These examples of elite hierarchies strategically controlling resources parallel the experience of Great Zimbabwe. Holistically, these examples illustrate how resources that once unified people slowly became the wedge that divided them. Ultimately leading to intra-state and inter-state conflicts to exploit resources for economic gain and political power.

Historically, external actors also affected political stability. For example, Mutapa rulers sought the assistance of private Portuguese traders to secure political stability in exchange for land and minerals.[30] However, this ended up weakening the state and giving the Portuguese a degree of dominion over state affairs.[31] This Faustian exchange is currently operating in Africa with private mining corporations replacing the Portuguese. Corporations often exercise control over decision-making processes by influencing government officials.[32] With the wealth from resources distributed among the political elite and government officials. Furthermore, the extraction of minerals has resulted in human rights abuses, including slavery and child labor.[33] Additionally, neighboring states benefit economically from the exploitation of resources. A prime example would be the pilfering of Congo's resources by presidents Kagame of Rwanda and Museveni of Uganda.[34] In summation, there are three entities that economically benefit from corruption and instability. First, there are incentives for elites, public officials, and civil servants to exploit resources for personal enrichment.[35] Second, corporations have economic incentives to support corruption to secure lucrative government contracts.[36] Third, external political actors are incentivized to foment instability to exploit resources for profit.

The purpose of this section was not to suggest a return to ancient religious practices. Rather that we once again view natural resources as something to be cared for and utilized with diligence. Connecting historical examples with their current expressions illustrated that several variables producing instability have remained constant over time. This analysis emphasized the link between corrupt leadership and the mismanagement of resources. In both historical and modern contexts, the formation of elite political hierarchies to control resources led to the gradual breakdown of socio-political relations. Furthermore, elite mismanagement of socio-political relationships and economic opportunities has produced conflict, corruption, and instability. This includes the bifurcation of social structures through hierarchies, nepotism, and corrupt economic practices. The analysis also illustrated how cultural practices and indigenous knowledge applied to resource management were ignored in favor of economic gain. Finally, the importance of leadership was highlighted for augmenting the social, political, and economic health of a state. This connection acts as a segue into the following section that explores the role of local leadership. Specifically, how women act as community leaders, exercising their indigenous knowledge to secure economic opportunity, socio-political stability, and peacebuilding initiatives. Holistically, the analysis provides an opportunity to identify and explore common variables, in order to address root causal factors. This is a necessary step in the development and implementation of supportive peacebuilding solutions.

Ideology Shift: From International to Local

The concept of peacebuilding has undergone several dynamic conceptual transitions. For example, one transition is a shift in the scale of analysis from international projects toward localized prospects.[37] As a result, local actors and communities have taken center stage in peacebuilding. This shift in the scope of focus is one supportive trend emphasizing the importance of gender analysis in peacebuilding. However, this transition is not without criticism. One methodological issue that has arisen is what exactly constitutes local analysis.[38] A response to this methodological uncertainty has been the specific focus on urban centers.[39] This is in part due to their clear geographical delineations. However, it may be argued that the concept of 'local' can also be framed epistemologically to represent a specific targeted rural area. For example, a distinct geographical location, like a forest, mountain, or river, could also be conceptually framed as a localized space. This transition necessitates a shift in variables for analysis. The following variables will be explored: gender, indigenous knowledge, and resource management practices. One connecting characteristic of indigenous knowledge is that it is intrinsically a local concept.[40] This conceptualization anchors its inclusion and application to local peacebuilding. Indigenous knowledge is not strictly patriarchal in nature; it is possessed and transmitted by women as well.[41]

United Nations Inclusion of Gender in Peacebuilding

Gender analysis has increasingly become an important lens through which new peacebuilding opportunities have presented themselves. Peacebuilding efforts in Africa represent an eclectic mix of entities including international and regional organizations, non-state actors such as NGOs, and government agencies.[42] In the year 2000, the United Nations Security Council passed Resolution 1325, accentuating the importance of women in peacebuilding. However, this Resolution has drawn criticism because women are largely ignored in peacebuilding processes.[43] One explanation for their omission is that peacebuilding often operates in a top-down process.[44] Nonetheless, other conceptualizations focus on bottom-up perspectives, centered on personal experiences and cultural contexts. For example, Lederach emphasizes the significance of socio-cultural and socio-economic components, with local individuals providing contextually sensitive knowledge.[45] It is often the responsibility of community elders to transmit socio-cultural knowledge ensuring resources are responsibly distributed. It is a common misconception that cultural knowledge and distribution practices are strictly transmitted generationally via patriarchal systems. In Kenya, for example, there is a long history of women functioning as community sages transmitting cultural practices and ecological knowledge.[46] Moreover, recent evidence suggests that the involvement of women in negotiations increases the quality and durability of peacebuilding efforts.[47] Halle argues that without incorporating gender dimensions to resolve conflict, long-run peacebuilding initiatives are severely limited.[48] The role of women as community leaders employing indigenous knowledge toward peacebuilding and socio-political stability will be explored further hereunder.

The shift in scope from international to local necessitates the increased importance of local community actors. Once again, community leaders are often thought of as male; however, women liaise with local communities and international organizations in peacebuilding efforts.[49] The following analysis will specifically examine the roles of local women and the tools they employ to actively engage in peacebuilding. The application of indigenous knowledge to peacebuilding efforts represents one tool utilized by local women. These connections were emphasized for two reasons. First, it may be accurately stated that all indigenous knowledge is local in nature.[50] Second, women have employed local indigenous knowledge to achieve positive community impacts, ranging from food security to sustainable development.[51] For example, women in Kenya's Sotik/Borabu cross-border conflict have adopted indigenous conflict mitigation techniques to quell disputes.[52] This ideational outline firmly situates local women within the spheres of resource management, utilization of indigenous knowledge, and peacebuilding initiatives. Furthermore, it secures the role of local women in future peacebuilding operations due to their ability to provide contextually and culturally sensitive information ensuring peacebuilding enterprises operate effectively within local environments.

Two operational peacebuilding cases where women take leadership roles will be explored. This is a necessary step in order to secure a nuanced understanding of the potential explanatory powers and connections between those variables. The cases link indigenous knowledge with the promotion of sustainable consumption practices, equitable access to resources, and positive local economic growth. In addition, the cases offer models of how local women practice inclusive decision-making and develop strategic partnerships in post-conflict regions. Offering a unique perspective view of how women actively engage in peacebuilding initiatives within different socio-political contexts. The cases will be separated into two categories predicated upon the landscape. The first case will explore peacebuilding activities in rural environments. The second case will explore similar activities within an urban context. The purpose of this format is to provide examples that are sensitive to their socio-political and cultural contexts. This methodological delineation was chosen because social and political structures can vary greatly from urban centers to rural villages. Therefore, any explanatory variables such as gender and indigenous knowledge should operate in both rural and urban contexts and environments.

Rural Case: Burundi

Burundi is a country marred by decades of social conflict and political instability. During the height of the civil war, many citizens fled to the Kibira forest, seeking safety and refuge.[53] As a result of this mass exodus from conflict zones, sections of the forest and its ecosystem were severely damaged.[54] The Kibira forest restoration case was selected because it illustrates how local women acted as peacebuilding leaders through the application of indigenous knowledge to guide the regeneration of the ecosystem. This case represents a local level of analysis because it occurs within specific locations of the forest. As noted herein, conceptually local peacebuilding analysis has favored urban settings because of its clear geographical delineations. One objection that may be presented with this case is that the Kibira forest is very large geographically. However, the specific areas ruined by fleeing citizens represent a specific localized geographical target for analysis. Therefore, the identification and selection of a specific forest section constitutes a valid localized analysis. It is this isolated and damaged area that these women have begun to regenerate through the application of their indigenous ecological knowledge, in conjunction with the support of multiple NGOs.

There are four key lessons that can be drawn from this case. Each provides a fruitful foundation for future peacebuilding and comparative studies. First, these women actively developed strategic partnerships with Association Femmes et Environnement au Burundi (AFEB), Global Environmental Facility (GEF), and the United Nations Development Program (UNDP).[55] The ability to successfully develop strategic partnerships, aimed at resource management, is a step in the right direction toward reducing resource-based conflict. Second, they marshaled their indigenous knowledge of local vegetation to restore the ecological systems by planting eucalyptus trees.[56] This serves as a practical example of how the application of indigenous knowledge can serve as the basis for successful resource management. Third, they facilitated local opportunities for economic growth and stability through negotiating strategic business agreements. Specifically, these contracts stipulated that 70% of generated income from eucalyptus harvesting would be reinvested into the community.[57] This example illustrates how local women created profitable business agreements, benefiting local communities through the equitable distribution of wealth. Fourth, this initiative secured a stable socio-political platform to reduce resource conflict and support future peacebuilding initiatives.[58] Moving forward, the ability to promote ecological conservation, create strategic partnerships, and ensure the local redistribution of economic profit will go a long way in reducing socio-political and resource conflicts.

Urban Case: Liberia

Liberia is a Western African nation that has seen violence and political power struggles, culminating in civil war and periods of severe famine. Recently, urban roadside gardens in the capital of Monrovia have begun to spring forth. This development has brought a sense of hope, optimism, and personal empowerment.[59] All of which would not be possible without indigenous agricultural knowledge of local plants and soil. This section will examine how local women utilize these urban gardens to provide several familial and communal benefits. Specifically, urban gardens enhance socio-political stability, increase economic opportunities, and provide psychological benefits through personal empowerment. This case fulfills the criteria of local peacebuilding constructs because it offers clear geographical bounding within an urban setting. Urban gardens foster socio-political stabilization by breaking cycles of food insecurity and stimulating self-sustainable practices through the production of fresh produce. Urban agricultural developments present local communities with the opportunity to break famine-driven conflict cycles.[60] This is contextually important because Liberia has relied on international humanitarian food aid for over 20 years.[61] Naturally, breaking this pernicious cycle is a positive step in the stabilization of post-conflict regions. These developments are important contextually because of their potential application to African states that have experienced similar periods of conflict, starvation, and socio-political instability.

These women in Monrovia implemented their indigenous ecological knowledge to create numerous economic opportunities. It may be argued that food insecurity and poverty acted as catalysts for creative agricultural solutions. For example, the cost of rice is often outside the capability of citizens to purchase.[62] As a result, these industrious women created roadside gardens as a solution to high food prices. This stable economic production reduced communal poverty and socio-political instability originating from food insecurity. Moreover, these women have engaged in entrepreneurial practices through the sale of excess food surplus. For example, one woman who runs a roadside garden was able to feed her children and use the excess funds to support them throughout their education.[63] Additionally, there are numerous psychological benefits to the local community. Urban gardening has been shown to enhance social integration of diverse communities, improving psychological and physical health.[64] The successful integration of diverse communities is contextually important to large urban centers, like Monrovia, for successful peacebuilding. Moreover, these women have empowered themselves by lifting economic yokes that restrain their ability to support families and provide educational opportunities.[65] For these women, each new harvest provides an opportunity to manifest a new destiny, one far removed from civil war, poverty, and famine.

Summation of Cases

These cases provided several important lessons and examples of local peacebuilding. This section answered the first research question by providing two operational examples where women took leadership positions in the management of resources, whilst facilitating peaceful cohabitation. Second, the cases provided practical examples of how local women utilized their indigenous knowledge to promote economic opportunities and sustainable practices. This in turn created an environment that was conducive to socio-political stability. Third, these cases provided examples that illustrated an actionable path forward through the utilization of indigenous knowledge to manage resources. Specifically, the Burundi case illustrated how women developed strategic partnerships to implement tactical resource management plans. They utilized their ecological knowledge to reverse environmental damage and equitably redistribute income through sagacious business agreements. The Liberian case provided an example of how local women were able to empower themselves through creative economic enterprises. Urban roadside gardens are an excellent example of local entrepreneurial practices. Exemplifying how women were able to break cycles of poverty and hunger through their indigenous agricultural knowledge. These creative actions promoted socio-political stability by reducing the likelihood of hunger-driven conflict and providing economic opportunities. Holistically, these cases illustrated several actions by local women that set the foundation for future peacebuilding initiatives aimed at producing social, political, and economic stability.

Governance and Peacebuilding

Herein the chapter has explored the idea that natural resources act as causal variables underpinning political instability and corrupt governance. This section will refocus this negative conception to illustrate the stabilization opportunities natural resources provide. Specifically, examining how the environment and its resources could, in fact, be framed as a gateway to enhancing peacebuilding efforts.[66] The analysis will serve as an ideational bridge connecting indigenous knowledge and gender with local environmental peacebuilding and good governance practices. Environmental peacebuilding is an emerging field of research requiring continual exploration of its theoretical and explanatory powers.[67] There are numerous criticisms surrounding environmental peacebuilding efforts. First, it is argued that marginalized groups, like women, could be discriminated against during peacebuilding processes.[68] Second, a methodological critique is that the field lacks large N-supportive research.[69] Third, research in the field has yet to produce a cogent theoretical framework to advance pathways forward in resource management and sustainable peacebuilding practices.[70] The aim of this section is to address these criticisms by providing operational counter examples through a theoretical framework and its supportive explanatory mechanisms.

Three steps will be required to lay the ideational foundation for exploring the proposed field and variables of interest. The first step will be to adduce an operational case study that will serve as the basis for the environmental peacebuilding and resource governance analysis. The second step requires applying the proposed theoretical framework and its explanatory mechanisms to the case study. The third step involves connecting the case and theoretical framework with indigenous knowledge and gender. This requires specifically exploring how indigenous knowledge and gender operate as supportive explanatory variables enhancing resource governance practices. The case study selected for exploration will be the efforts of local Sudanese women who negotiated the peaceful and cooperative creation of agricultural corridors for livestock. This specific case was selected because it appears to provide provisional support for the theoretical framework. The framework selected for analysis is advanced by Krampe, Hegazi, and VanDeveer who propose three explanatory mechanisms for increasing the prospects of peacebuilding through enhanced resource governance. The three theoretical mechanisms are as follows: contact hypothesis, diffusion of international norms, and state service provision. This theoretical framework was selected because of its potential robust explanatory powers and broad application to multiple African states. Moreover, it fruitfully supports the explanatory capabilities of indigenous knowledge and gender as explanatory variables.

The inclusion of indigenous knowledge and gender as variables for analysis within the theoretical framework further connects and grounds this section with the rest of the chapter. Furthermore, identifying additional supportive and explanatory variables would strengthen the validity of the theoretical framework and its proposed mechanisms. These supportive connections are especially salient to peacebuilding efforts because they provide the opportunity for developing and implementing peacebuilding tools that are contextually sensitive. Naturally, it is important to acknowledge that this case could represent an anomaly with respect to its supportive evidence of these mechanisms and explanatory variables. It is also thoroughly possible for similar circumstances to produce completely different results and responses from both local communities and government regulators. However, with each additional case study that is explored and compiled that confirms these mechanisms and variables, the greater the opportunity for their future utilization in peacebuilding processes. Moreover, the addition of supplemental case studies compounded over time provides researchers and practitioners with the tools necessary to develop large N research projects. Therefore, if multiple case studies provide supportive evidence of these mechanisms and variables in operation, it would deliver optimism and opportunity in this promising field of research.

Sudan Case Study

Despite numerous barriers, women in western Sudan are actively engaging in peacebuilding efforts through localized resource management initiatives.

One example that illustrates this trend are the actions taken by local women in South Kordofan in the Republic of Sudan. Local women working in concert with NGOs have collaborated to promote the empowerment of youth and women through equitable resource management practices.[71] These women successfully implemented a system of agropastoral livestock corridors necessary for equitable access to vital resources, like water.[72] Bolstering local environmental peacebuilding efforts through securing amicable cooperation among numerous local stakeholders, setting a precedence for future initiatives.[73] This case provides four quintessential peacebuilding lessons. First, women played a key role in the development and implementation of sustainable resource management practices. Second, they effectively engaged multiple actors to foster agropastoral peacebuilding through equitably distributing access to resources. Third, they increased cooperative resource management efforts through an inclusive division-making process.[74] Fourth, they successfully engaged with government regulators to fortify peacebuilding opportunities.[75] As a result of their herculean effort, their efforts were ultimately legitimized by government regulators through their approval. This development is no small feat due to Sudanese women being culturally marginalized.

This case provides clear conceptual connections between indigenous knowledge, gender, resource management, and peacebuilding. The successful implementation of this initiative was a result of leveraging their indigenous knowledge of the water systems, land divisions, and cultural practices. In this context, local indigenous knowledge has proven to be an essential variable in the reduction of resource conflicts and successful policy implementation. The ability to constructively engage this with government regulators sets a positive precedence for other local communities. Opening opportunities for women to actively engage with regulators and government officials to create policy. The success of this policy is paramount to expanding local peacebuilding and equitable governance practices. Their ability to exercise social, cultural, and political sagacity led to the implementation of a cooperative and peacebuilding resource management policy. Without their contextual knowledge of local lands, culture, and agropastoral practices, this would have been improbable. Gausset concludes that agropastoral conflicts arise from systems of resource management and distribution that are not contextually sensitive.[76] In summation, this case provides an operational connection between contextual indigenous knowledge, equitable resource access, inclusive decision-making, and successful policy change. Hereunder, the three mechanisms for resource governance and their explicit connection to indigenous knowledge utilization by Sudanese women will be explored.

Explanatory Mechanisms

The first mechanism for environmental peacebuilding and resource governance that the Sudanese case provided support for was the contact hypothesis. This mechanism stipulates that intergroup cooperation is a fundamental step toward the reduction of social prejudices and biases.[77] From a social psychology perspective, contact between members of different groups reduces prejudice and fosters trust.[78] The positive interactions between these women, local stakeholders, and regulators are an example of intergroup interactions reducing bias and prejudice to secure peacebuilding activities. It also addresses concerns raised about discriminatory practices against marginalized community members. Discriminatory practices during the environmental peacebuilding process have been one major concern.[79] The salience of this development derives from the fact that socio-cultural barriers and biases are a part of everyday life for women.[80] Furthermore, this explanatory mechanism contends that intergroup interaction fosters trust that can result in cooperative resource management.[81] This case illustrated how local women engaged with multiple stakeholders through inclusive decision-making to build trust and secure equitable resource management. Moreover, their agropastoral knowledge could have enhanced their legitimacy in the eyes of the regulators. Creating policy solutions through indigenous knowledge and cooperation could be a contributing factor to removing prejudices and increasing political legitimacy in the future.

The second mechanism for environmental peacebuilding and resource governance that this case supported was the diffusion of norms. Krampe, Hegazi, and VanDeveer state that peacebuilding actors should facilitate the diffusion of transnational norms.[82] Diffusion is the result of numerous social interactions that ultimately mold intersubjective community norms. This example illustrates that the interactions between NGOs, local women, and government regulators resulted in the diffusion of political equality norms. Specifically, the ability of women to implement equitable policy practices. Moreover, Krampe, Hegazi, and VanDeveer state that international actors including non-governmental agencies play a role in the diffusion of norms.[83] In this example, NGOs and local actors worked in unison to secure political gender equality, enabling women to actively engage in the policy decision-making process. This case provides added gender research value because it represents local lived experiences with surmounting cultural and gender bias to effectuate policy change.[84] Within this context, women through their indigenous knowledge were able to provide creative solutions to complex social, political, and agricultural problems. This example particularly represents the transformation of social norms that dictate rules, standards, and behavioral expectations.[85] Naturally, over time, this could lead to a future where women are recognized socially and politically as capable of producing positive social, political, and ecological change.

The third mechanism for environmental peacebuilding and resource governance that this case supported was service provision. This mechanism emphasizes that when states provide access to services and address community needs, it increases their legitimacy in the eyes of the populace.[86] The recognition of these women by the Sudanese regulators and their willingness to address the communal agropastoral needs is in alignment with this mechanism. This action showed multiple levels of inclusive decision-making spanning international organizations, government regulators, and local populations to address community agricultural needs. Equitable state actions are imbued with numerous positive socio-political benefits; chiefly they promote the perception of state legitimacy and strengthen state-society relationships.[87] This serves as the basis for strengthening state-society relationships and political institutions. It also increases the perceived legitimacy of a state and its government officials, both locally and internationally in post-conflict regions. Finally, in a governance structure that is socio-politically representative, citizens begin to develop confidence and trust in the equitable operation of governmental institutions.[88] The ability to develop and foster trust in government actors and institutions is a direct step toward socio-political stability and the foundation for any peacebuilding initiative.

It is important to emphasize that positive changes do not occur in siloes; they frequently cascade into other facets of social and political structures. For example, positive state-society interactions increase the likelihood that other marginalized groups will actively engage and participate in governmental decision-making processes.[89] Brown argues that effort to create a political and legal environment that strengthens the management of resources is an action forming the basis of peacebuilding in post-conflict regions.[90] Therefore, these developments set the foundation for peacebuilding through cooperative and cohesive socio-political interactions. They also foster the development of inclusive governmental decision-making practices. This case further illustrated how indigenous knowledge was leveraged to produce creative policy solutions and support peacebuilding efforts that are socially, politically, and culturally sensitive. Finally, the ability of these women to strengthen state-society relationships could incline regulators and policymakers to further recognize the role of women in future policy endeavors. As a result, this would increase the likelihood that regulators would extend additional service provisions to women through state apparatuses. Through equitable access to governmental services and provisions, the perceived legitimacy of the state would increase in the eyes of both local and international communities.

This section examined three theoretical mechanisms proposed for improving governance and environmental peacebuilding through resource management. It explored supportive evidence of the theoretical framework through the practical examination of the Sudan case study. The analysis accentuated two underlying explanatory variables: indigenous knowledge and gender. Illustrating how these variables operated within each mechanism to bolster resource governance practices and increase opportunities for peacebuilding. Furthermore, the analysis addressed particular criticisms of environmental peacebuilding. Specifically addressing discrimination of marginalized groups, geographical scopes of analysis, and coherent theoretical constructs. This analysis answered the first proposed research question by exemplifying how indigenous knowledge improved resource governance and environmental peacebuilding. It answered the second research question by providing a case study with clear examples of how indigenous knowledge and gender operated cohesively within the theoretical construct to address socio-political instability. Serving as the basis for verifying the importance of indigenous knowledge and gender within future peacebuilding initiatives. This connection was highlighted in the hopes that indigenous knowledge and gender will be incorporated into the peacebuilding toolboxes of academics, practitioners, and policymakers. In summation, these variables are not silver bullet solutions to increase political stability. They appear, however, to be supportive explanatory variables that operate effectively in both theoretical constructs and practical applications.

Conclusion

The main objective of this chapter was to broaden the focus of peacebuilding by examining the relationship between natural resources and socio-political instability. It explored the historical role of religious veneration of natural resources, which led to periods of stable socio-political relations through sustainable resource consumption practices. However, over time, these sacred resources lost their significance and became material objects to be exploited for wealth. This shift in perspective coincided with the rise of elite political hierarchies that seized control of the resources. The case of Great Zimbabwe was used as an illustration of this gradual transition and its significant impact on the deterioration of socio-political relations. This historical example served as a foundation for connecting past experiences of socio-political instability with the current situations in African states. The exploration of historical experiences that connects to current African states revealed important connections between natural resources, instability, and governance practices. It is evident that poor leadership, corruption, and economic opportunities were the underlying causal variables, rather than resources themselves leading to conflict. Shifting the peacebuilding focus from international actors to local actors highlighted the role of local women as community leaders and the application of indigenous knowledge in peacebuilding initiatives. The cases of Burundi and Liberia demonstrated the potential power of local women to foster stability and enhance peacebuilding efforts through their use of indigenous knowledge. By providing examples of urban and rural cases, the analysis was sensitive to socio-political contexts that can vary greatly between these settings.

A theoretical framework was proposed for improving peacebuilding by enhancing resource governance. The Sudanese case provided insights into the framework, showcasing how local women successfully engaged with stakeholders to equitably distribute resources. Intergroup contact between stakeholders served as the foundation for developing cooperative relationships through inclusive decision-making processes. Moreover, continuous intergroup contact empowered these women to navigate cultural biases and achieve legal recognition from Sudanese regulators. The utilization of indigenous knowledge and gender as catalysts for improving peacebuilding and resource governance was evident in this context.

In conclusion, this chapter shed light on the importance of considering local actors, especially women and their indigenous knowledge, in peacebuilding efforts. The examples presented served as a starting point for further research and exploration of cases that support peacebuilding initiatives. By recognizing the significant role of local actors and their knowledge, we can enhance resource governance and contribute to sustainable peace.

Notes

1 Florian Krampe, Farah Hegazi, and Stacy D. VanDeveer, "Sustaining Peace Through Better Resource Governance: Three Potential Mechanisms for Environmental Peacebuilding," *World Development* 144 (August 2021): 105508. https://doi.org/10.1016/j.worlddev.2021.105508
2 Fred Nelson, "Introduction: The Politics of Natural Resource Governance in Africa," in *Community Rights, Conservation and Contested Land: The Politics of Natural Resource Governance in Africa*, edited by Fred Nelson (New York, NY: Earthscan, 2010): 16; Victor Ojakorotu, "Resource Control and Conflict in Africa," in *The Palgrave Handbook of African Politics, Governance and Development*, edited by Samuel O. Oloruntoba and Toyin Falola (New York, NY: Palgrave Macmillan, 2018): 367. https://doi.org/10.1057/978-1-349-95232-8_22
3 Michael Barnett, Hunjoon Kim, Madalene O'donnell, and Laura Sitea, "Peacebuilding: What Is in a Name," *Global Governance: A Review of Multilateralism and International Organizations* 13 (August 2007): 35. https://doi.org/10.1163/19426720-01301004
4 Barnett, Kim, O'donnell and Sitea, "Peacebuilding," 35.
5 Willemijn Verkoren, "Knowledge Networking: Implications for Peacebuilding Activities," *International Journal of Peace Studies* 11, no. 2 (Autumn/Winter 2006): 53. www.jstor.org/stable/41852945
6 Verkoren, "Knowledge Networking," 53.
7 Abiodun Alao, *Natural Resources and Conflict in Africa: The Tragedy of Endowment* (Rochester, NY: University of Rochester Press, 2007): 295.
8 Alao, *Natural Resources*, 295.
9 Njabulo Bruce Khumalo, and Charity Baloyi, "African Indigenous Knowledge: An Underutilized and Neglected Resource for Development," *Library Philosophy and Practice* (Summer 2017): 2. https://digitalcommons.unl.edu/libphilprac/1663/
10 Kyle Powys Whyte, "On the Role of Traditional Ecological Knowledge as a Collaborative Concept: A Philosophical Study," *Ecological Processes* 2, no. 7 (April 2013): 8. https://doi.org/10.1186/2192-1709-2-7
11 Whyte, "On the Role," 1.
12 Joost Fontein, "Silence, Destruction and Closure at Great Zimbabwe: Local Narratives of Desecration and Alienation," *Journal of Southern African Studies* 32, no. 4 (2006): 774. https://doi.org/10.1080/03057070600995723
13 Thomas Huffman, "Mapungubwe and Great Zimbabwe: The Origin and Spread of Social Complexity in Southern Africa," *Journal of Anthropological Archaeology* 28, no. 1 (2009): 52. https://doi.org/10.1016/j.jaa.2008.10.004
14 Sussy Gumo, Simon O. Gisege, Evans Raballah, and Collins Ouma, "Communicating African Spirituality Through Ecology: Challenges and Prospects for the 21st Century," *Religions* 3, no. 2 (2021): 527. https://doi.org/10.3390/rel3020523

15 Winona LaDuke, "Traditional Ecological Knowledge and Environmental Future," *Colorado Journal of International Environmental Law & Policy* 5, no. 1 (1994): 128–129.
16 Fontein, "Silence," 774.
17 Chris-Valentine Ogar Eneji, Gabriel U. Ntamu, Chibuzo C. Unwanade, Anthony B. Godwin, John E. Bassey, J. J. Willaims, and Joseph Ignatius, "Traditional African Religion in Natural Resources Conservation and Management in Cross River State, Nigeria," *Environment and Natural Resources Research* 2, no. 4 (2012): 45. https://dx.doi.org/10.5539/enrr.v2n4p45
18 Mzukisi Qobo, "Outlines of Intra-State Conflict in Zimbabwe and Regional Challenges," in *Regional Trade Integration and Conflict Resolution*, ed. Shaheen Rafi Khan (New York, NY: Routledge, 2008), 165. https://doi.org/10.4324/9780203889800
19 Shadrech Chirikure, and Innocent Pikirayi, "Inside and Outside the Dry Stone Walls: Revisiting the Material Culture of Great Zimbabwe," *Antiquity* 82, no. 318 (2008): 991. https://doi.org/10.1017/S0003598X00097726
20 Innocent Pikirayi, "The Demise of Great Zimbabwe, A.D. 1420–1550: An Environmental Re-Appraisal," in *Cities in the World: 1500–2000*, ed. Adrian Green and Rodger Leech (London: Routledge, 2006), 31. https://doi.org/10.4324/9781315095677
21 Richard Nicklin Hall, "The Great Zimbabwe," *Journal of the Royal African Society* 4, no. 15 (1905): 296. www.jstor.org/stable/714559
22 Pikirayi, "The Demise," 35.
23 Veronica Strang, "Elemental Powers: Water Beings, Nature Worship, and Long-term Trajectories in Human-Environmental Relations," *Swedish Journal of Anthropology* 4, no. 2 (2021): 15. http://urn.kb.se/resolve?urn=urn:nbn:se:uu:diva-463871
24 Courage Mlambo, "Politics and the Natural Resource Curse: Evidence from Selected African States," *Cogent Social Sciences* 8, no. 1 (2022): 2035911. https://doi.org/10.1080/23311886.2022.2035911
25 Munyae M. Mulinge, and Gwen N. Lesetedi, "Interrogating Our Past: Colonialism and Corruption in Sub-Saharan Africa," *African Journal of Political Science* 3, no. 2 (1998): 15. www.jstor.org/stable/23493651; Odi F. Nwankwo, "Impact of Corruption on Economic Growth in Nigeria," *Mediterranean Journal of Social Sciences* 5, no. 6 (2014): 41. https://dx.doi.org/10.5901/mjss.2014.v5n6p41; Paul Okojie, and Abubakar Momoh, "Corruption and Reform in Nigeria," in *Corruption and Development: The Anti-Corruption Campaigns*, ed. Sarah Bracking (Hampshire: Palgrave Macmillan, 2007), 103. https://doi.org/10.1057/9780230590625; Soma Pillay, "Corruption—The Challenge to Good Governance: A South African Perspective," *International Journal of Public Sector Management* 17, no. 7 (2004): 586. https://doi.org/10.1108/09513550410562266
26 Clionadh Raleigh, and Daniel Wigmore-Shepherd, "Elite Coalitions and Power Balance Across African Regimes: Introducing the African Cabinet and Political Elite Data Project," *Ethnopolitics* 21, no. 1 (2022): 41. https://doi.org/10.1080/17449057.2020.1771840
27 Alhaji Ahmadu Ibrahim, and Lawan Cheri, "Democracy, Political Instability and the African Crisis of Underdevelopment," *Journal of Power, Politics & Governance* 1, no. 1 (2013): 64.

28 Joseph Yav Katshung, "Greasing the Wheels of Reconciliation in the Great Lakes Region," *African Security Studies* 16, no. 3 (2007): 117. https://doi.org/10.1080/10246029.2007.9627437
29 Lars Buur, and Celso Marcos Monjane, "Elite Capture and the Development of Natural Resource Linkages in Mozambique," in *Fairness and Justice in Natural Resource Politics*, eds. Melanie Pichler, Cornelia Staritz, Karin Küblböck, Christina Plank, Werner Raza, and Fernando Ruiz Peyré (London: Routledge, 2017): 214. https://doi.org/10.4324/9781315638058
30 Matthew J. Hannaford, and David J. Nash, "Climate, History, Society Over the Last Millennium in Southeast Africa," *Wiley Interdisciplinary Reviews: Climate Change* 7, no. 3 (2016): 381. https://doi.org/10.1002/wcc.389
31 Hannaford and Nash, "Climate History," 381.
32 Roger Tangri, and Andrew Mwenda, *The Politics of Elite Corruption in Africa: Uganda in Comparative African Perspective* (London: Routledge, 2013), 4. https://doi.org/10.4324/9780203626474
33 Meike Schulte, and Cody Morris Paris, "Blood Diamonds: An Analysis of the State of Affairs and the Effectiveness of the Kimberley Process," *International Journal of Sustainable Society* 12, no. 1 (2020): 51. https://doi.org/10.1504/IJSSOC.2020.105017
34 Robert Guest, *The Shackled Continent: Power, Corruption, and African Lives* (Washington, DC: Smithsonian Institution, 2010), 61.
35 Tangri and Mwenda, *The Politics of Elite*, 5.
36 Tangri and Mwenda, *The Politics of Elite*, 6.
37 Hanna Leonardsson, and Gustav Rudd, "The 'local turn' in Peacebuilding: A Literature Review of Effective and Emancipatory Local Peacebuilding," *Third World Quarterly* 36, no. 5 (2015): 825. https://doi.org/10.1080/01436597.2015.1029905
38 Thania Paffenholz, "Unpacking the Local Turn in Peacebuilding: A Critical Assessment Towards an Agenda for Future Research," *Third World Quarterly* 36, no. 5 (2015): 858. https://doi.org/10.1080/01436597.2015.1029908
39 Kristin Ljungkvist, and Anna Jarstad, "Revisiting the Local Turn in Peacebuilding–Through the Emerging Urban Approach," *Third World Quarterly* 42, no. 10 (2021): 2210. https://doi.org/10.1080/01436597.2021.1929148
40 Chika Ezeanya-Esiobu, *Indigenous Knowledge and Curriculum in Africa* (Singapore: Springer, 2019), 6. https://doi.org/10.1007/978-981-13-6635-2
41 Louise Grenier, *Working with Indigenous Knowledge: A Guide for Researchers* (Ottawa: International Development Research Centre, 1998), 1.
42 Tony Karbo, "Peace-Building in Africa," in *Peace and Conflict in Africa*, ed. David J. Francis (New York, NY: Zed Books, 2008), 130. https://doi.org/10.5040/9781350221710
43 Emiko Noma, Dee Aker, and Jennifer Freeman, "Heeding Women's Voices: Breaking Cycles of Conflict and Deepening the Concept of Peacebuilding," *Journal of Peacebuilding & Development* 7, no. 1 (2012): 7. https://doi.org/10.1080/15423166.2012.719384
44 Noma, Aker, and Freeman, "Heeding Women's," 7.
45 John Paul Lederach, *Building Peace: Sustainable Reconciliation in Divided Societies* (Washington, DC: United States Institute of Peace Press, 1997), 87.
46 Njoki Wane, and Deborah J. Chandler, "African Women, Cultural Knowledge and Environmental Education with a Focus on Kenya's Indigenous Women," *Canadian Journal of Environmental Education* 7, no. 1 (Spring 2002): 87.

47 Jana Krause, Werner Krause, and Piia Bränfors, "Women's Participation in Peace Negotiations and the Durability of Peace," *International Interactions* 44, no. 6 (2018): 985. https://doi.org/10.1080/03050629.2018.1492386
48 Silja Halle, "Gender and Environmental Security," in *Routledge Handbook of Environmental Security*, eds. Richard Matthew, Evgenia Nizkorodov, Crystal Murphy, Kristen A. Goodrich, Ashley Hooper, Bemmy Maharramli, Maureen J. Purcell, and Paroma Wagle (New York, NY: Routledge, 2022), 290. https://doi.org/10.4324/9781315107592
49 McKay and Mazurana, "Gendering Peacebuilding," 341.
50 Grenier, *Working with Indigenous Knowledge*, 1.
51 Wole M. Olatokun and Oluyemi Folorunso Ayanbode, "Use of Indigenous Knowledge by Women in a Nigerian Rural Community," *Indian Journal of Traditional Knowledge* 8, no. 2 (2009): 287. http://nopr.niscpr.res.in/handle/123456789/3968
52 Mokua Ombati, "Women Transcending "Boundaries" in Indigenous Peacebuilding in Kenya's Sotik/Borabu Border Conflict," *Multidisciplinary Journal of Gender Studies* 4, no. 1 (2015): 637. https://doi.org/10.4471/generos.2015.50
53 United Nations Environment Programme, *Women and Natural Resources: Unlocking the Peacebuilding Potential* (New York, NY: UNEP, 2013), 32. www.unep.org/resources/report/women-and-natural-resources-unlocking-peace-building-potential
54 United Nations Environment Programme, "Women and Natural Resources," 34.
55 United Nations Environment Programme, "Women and Natural Resources," 34.
56 United Nations Environment Programme, "Women and Natural Resources," 34.
57 United Nations Environment Programme, "Women and Natural Resources," 34.
58 United Nations Environment Programme, "Women and Natural Resources," 34.
59 Christina Holder, "Growing Hope: How Urban Gardens are Empowering War-Affected Liberians and Harvesting a New Generation of City Farmers," in *Greening in the Red Zone: Disaster, Resilience and Community Greening*, eds. Keith G. Tidball, and Marianne E. Krasny (Dordrecht: Springer, 2014), 417. https://doi.org/10.1007/978-90-481-9947-1_32
60 Andrew Adam-Bradford, Ghassan El-Kahlout, Richard Byrne, Julia Wright, and Mohammed Rahman, "Stabilisation Agriculture: Reviewing an Emerging Concept with Case Studies from Afghanistan and Iraq," *CAB Reviews: Perspectives in Agriculture, Veterinary Science, Nutrition and Natural Resources* 15, no. 42 (2020): 1. https://doi.org/10.1079/PAVSNNR202015042
61 Holder, "Growing Hope," 419.
62 Holder, "Growing Hope," 424.
63 Holder, "Growing Hope," 422.
64 Masahi Soga, Daniel T. C. Cox, Yuichi Yamaura, Kevin J. Gaston, Kiyo Kurisu, and Keisuke Hanaki, "Health Benefits of Urban Allotment Gardening: Improved Physical and Psychological Well-being and Social Integration," *International Journal of Environmental Research and Public Health* 14, no. 1 (2017): 71. https://doi.org/10.3390/ijerph14010071
65 Holder, "Growing Hope," 422.
66 Ken Conca, and Michael D. Beevers, "Environmental Pathways to Peace," in *Routledge Handbook of Environmental Conflict and Peacebuilding*, eds. Ashok Swain, and Joakim Öjendal (London: Routledge, 2018), 54. https://doi.org/10.4324/9781315473772-1

67 Anaïs Dresse, et al., "Environmental Peacebuilding: Towards a Theoretical Framework," *Cooperation and Conflict* 54, no. 1 (2019): 99. https://doi.org/10.1177/0010836718808331
68 Tobias Ide, "The Dark Side of Environmental Peacebuilding," *World Development* 127 (March 2020): 15. https://doi.org/10.1016/j.worlddev.2019.104777
69 Dresse et al., "Environmental Peacebuilding," 100.
70 Krampe, Hegazi, and VanDeveer, "Sustaining Peace," 1.
71 United Nations Environment Programme, "Women and Natural Resources," 35.
72 United Nations Environment Programme, "Women and Natural Resources," 13.
73 United Nations Environment Programme, "Women and Natural Resources," 35.
74 United Nations Environment Programme, "Women and Natural Resources," 35.
75 United Nations Environment Programme, "Women and Natural Resources," 35.
76 Quentin Gausset, "Agro-Pastoral Conflicts in the Tikar Plain," in *Beyond Territory and Scarcity: Exploring Conflicts over Natural Resource Scarcities*, eds. Quentin Gausset, Michael Whyte, and Michael Birch-Thomsen (Uppsala: Nordic Africa Institute, 2005), 108.
77 Krampe, Hegazi, and VanDeveer, "Sustaining Peace," 5.
78 Oliver Christ, and Mathias Kauff, "Intergroup Contact Theory," in *Social Psychology in Action: Evidence-Based Interventions from Theory to Practice*, eds. Kai Sassenberg and Michael L. W. Vliek (Cham: Springer, 2019), 156. https://doi.org/10.1007/978-3-030-13788-5_10
79 Ide, "The Dark Side," 15.
80 United Nations Environment Programme, "Women and Natural Resources," 36.
81 Krampe, Hegazi, and VanDeveer, "Sustaining Peace," 5.
82 Krampe, Hegazi, and VanDeveer, "Sustaining Peace," 6.
83 Krampe, Hegazi, and VanDeveer, "Sustaining Peace," 6.
84 Heidi Hudson, "It Matters How You 'Do' Gender in Peacebuilding: African Approaches and Challenges," *Insight on Africa* 13, no. 2 (2021): 142. https://doi.org/10.1177/0975087820987154
85 Marijn F. Stok, and Denise T. D. de Ridder, "The Focus Theory of Normative Conduct," in *Social Psychology in Action: Evidence-Based Interventions from Theory to Practice*, eds. Kai Sassenberg and Michael L. W. Vliek (Cham: Springer, 2019), 95. https://doi.org/10.1007/978-3-030-13788-5_7
86 Krampe, Hegazi, and VanDeveer, "Sustaining Peace," 1.
87 Krampe, Hegazi, and VanDeveer, "Sustaining Peace," 5.
88 Krampe, Hegazi, and VanDeveer, "Sustaining Peace," 8.
89 Krampe, Hegazi, and VanDeveer, "Sustaining Peace," 8.
90 Oli Brown, *Encouraging Peace-Building through Better Environmental and Natural Resource Management* (London: Chatham House for the Royal Institute of International Affairs, 2013), 2.

Bibliography

Adam-Bradford, Andrew, Ghassan El-Kahlout, Richard Byrne, Julia Wright, and Mohammed Rahman. "Stabilisation Agriculture: Reviewing an Emerging Concept with Case Studies from Afghanistan and Iraq." *CAB Reviews: Perspectives in Agriculture, Veterinary Science, Nutrition and Natural Resources* 15, no. 42 (2020): 1–10. https://doi.org/10.1079/PAVSNNR202015042

Alao, Abiodun. *Natural Resources and Conflict in Africa: The Tragedy of Endowment*. Rochester, NY: University of Rochester Press, 2007.

Barnett, Michael, Hunjoon Kim, Madalene O'donnell, and Laura Sitea. "Peacebuilding: What Is in a Name." *Global Governance: A Review of Multilateralism and International Organizations* 13, no. 1 (August 2007): 35–58. https://doi.org/10.1163/19426720-01301004

Brown, Oli. *Encouraging Peace-Building through Better Environmental and Natural Resource Management*. London: Chatham House for the Royal Institute of International Affairs, 2013.

Buur, Lars, and Celso Marcos Monjane. "Elite Capture and the Development of Natural Resource Linkages in Mozambique." In *Fairness and Justice in Natural Resource Politics*, edited by Melanie Pichler, Cornelia Staritz, Karin Küblböck, Christina Plank, Werner Raza, and Fernando Ruiz Peyré, 212–229. London: Routledge, 2017. https://doi.org/10.4324/9781315638058

Chirikure, Shadrech, and Innocent Pikirayi. "Inside and Outside the Dry Stone Walls: Revisiting the Material Culture of Great Zimbabwe." *Antiquity* 82, no. 318 (2008): 976–993. https://doi.org/10.1017/S0003598X00097726

Christ, Oliver, and Mathias Kauff. "Intergroup Contact Theory." In *Social Psychology in Action: Evidence-Based Interventions from Theory to Practice*, edited by Kai Sassenberg and Michael L. W. Vliek, 145–161. Cham: Springer, 2019. https://doi.org/10.1007/978-3-030-13788-5_10

Conca, Ken, and Michael Beevers. "Environmental Pathways to Peace." In *Routledge Handbook of Environmental Conflict and Peacebuilding*, edited by Ashok Swain, and Joakim Öjendal, 54–72. London: Routledge, 2018. https://doi.org/10.4324/9781315473772-1

Dresse, Anaïs, Itay Fischhendler, Jonas Østergaard Nielsen, and Dimitrios Zikos. "Environmental Peacebuilding: Towards a Theoretical Framework." *Cooperation and Conflict* 54, no. 1 (2019): 99–119. https://doi.org/10.1177/0010836718808331

Eneji, Chris Valentine, Gabriel Ntamu, C. C. Unwanade, Anthony B. Godwin, John E. Bassey, J. J. Williams, and Joseph Ignatius. "Traditional African Religion in Natural Resources Conservation and Management in Cross River State, Nigeria." *Environment and Natural Resources Research* 2, no. 4 (2012): 45–53. https://dx.doi.org/10.5539/enrr.v2n4p45

Ezeanya-Esiobu, Chika. *Indigenous Knowledge and Curriculum in Africa*. Singapore: Springer, 2019. https://doi.org/10.1007/978-981-13-6635-2

Fontein, Joost. "Silence, Destruction and Closure at Great Zimbabwe: Local Narratives of Desecration and Alienation." *Journal of Southern African Studies* 32, no. 4 (2006): 771–794. https://doi.org/10.1080/03057070600995723

Gausset, Quentin. "Agro-Pastoral Conflicts in the Tikar Plain." In *Beyond Territory and Scarcity: Exploring Conflicts over Natural Resource Scarcities*, edited by Quentin Gausset, Michael Whyte, and Michael Birch-Thomsen, 90–111. Uppsala: Nordic Africa Institute, 2005.

Grenier, Louise. *Working with Indigenous Knowledge: A Guide for Researchers*. Ottawa: International Development Research Centre, 1998.

Guest, Robert. *The Shackled Continent: Power, Corruption, and African Lives*. Washington, DC: Smithsonian Institution, 2010.

Gumo, Sussy, Simon Gisege, Evans Raballah, and Collins Ouma. "Communicating African Spirituality Through Ecology: Challenges and Prospects for the 21st Century." *Religions* 3, no. 2 (2021): 523–543. https://doi.org/10.3390/rel3020523

Hall, Richard Nicklin. "The Great Zimbabwe." *Journal of the Royal African Society* 4, no. 15 (1905): 295–300. www.jstor.org/stable/714559

Halle, Silja. "Gender and Environmental Security." In *Routledge Handbook of Environmental Security*, edited by Richard Matthew, Evgenia Nizkorodov, Crystal Murphy, Kristen A. Goodrich, Ashley Hooper, Bemmy Maharramli, Maureen J. Purcell, and Paroma Wagle, 290–302. New York, NY: Routledge, 2022. https://doi.org/10.4324/9781315107592

Hannaford, Matthew, and David Nash. "Climate, History, Society Over the Last Millennium in Southeast Africa." *Wiley Interdisciplinary Reviews: Climate Change* 7, no. 3 (2016): 370–392. https://doi.org/10.1002/wcc.389

Holder, Christina. "Growing Hope: How Urban Gardens are Empowering War-Affected Liberians and Harvesting a New Generation of City Farmers." In *Greening in the Red Zone: Disaster, Resilience and Community Greening*, edited by Keith G. Tidball, and Marianne E. Krasny, 417–428. Dordrecht: Springer, 2014. https://doi.org/10.1007/978-90-481-9947-1_32

Hudson, Heidi. "It Matters How You 'Do' Gender in Peacebuilding: African Approaches and Challenges." *Insight on Africa* 13, no. 2 (2021): 142–159. https://doi.org/10.1177/0975087820987154

Huffman, Thomas. "Mapungubwe and Great Zimbabwe: The Origin and Spread of Social Complexity in Southern Africa." *Journal of Anthropological Archaeology* 28, no. 1 (2009): 37–54. https://doi.org/10.1016/j.jaa.2008.10.004

Ibrahim, Alhaji Ahmadu, and Lawan Cheri. "Democracy, Political Instability and the African Crisis of Underdevelopment." *Journal of Power, Politics & Governance* 1, no. 1 (2013): 59–67.

Ide, Tobias. "The Dark Side of Environmental Peacebuilding." *World Development* 127 (March 2020): 104777. https://doi.org/10.1016/j.worlddev.2019.104777

Karbo, Tony. "Peace-Building in Africa." In *Peace and Conflict in Africa*, edited by David J. Francis, 113–130. New York, NY: Zed Books, 2008. https://doi.org/10.5040/9781350221710

Katshung, Joseph Yav. "Greasing the Wheels of Reconciliation in the Great Lakes Region." *African Security Studies* 16, no. 3 (2007): 117–122. https://doi.org/10.1080/10246029.2007.9627437

Khumalo, Njabulo Bruce, and Charity Baloyi. "African Indigenous Knowledge: An Underutilized and Neglected Resource for Development." *Library Philosophy and Practice* (Summer 2017): 1–15. https://digitalcommons.unl.edu/libphilprac/1663/

Krampe, Florian, Farah Hegazi, and Stacy VanDeveer. "Sustaining Peace Through Better Resource Governance: Three Potential Mechanisms for Environmental Peacebuilding." *World Development* 144 (August 2021): 105508. https://doi.org/10.1016/j.worlddev.2021.105508

Krause, Jana, Werner Krause, and Piia Bränfors. "Women's Participation in Peace Negotiations and the Durability of Peace." *International Interactions* 44, no. 6 (2018): 985–1016. https://doi.org/10.1080/03050629.2018.1492386

LaDuke, Winona. "Traditional Ecological Knowledge and Environmental Future." *Colorado Journal of International Environmental Law & Policy* 5, no. 1 (1994): 127–148.

Lederach, John Paul. *Building Peace: Sustainable Reconciliation in Divided Societies*. Washington, DC: United States Institute of Peace Press, 1997.

Leonardsson, Hanna, and Gustav Rudd. "The 'local turn' in Peacebuilding: A Literature Review of Effective and Emancipatory Local Peacebuilding." *Third World Quarterly* 36, no. 5 (2015): 825–839. https://doi.org/10.1080/01436597.2015.1029905

Ljungkvist, Kristin, and Anna Jarstad. "Revisiting the Local Turn in Peacebuilding – Through the Emerging Urban Approach." *Third World Quarterly* 42, no. 10 (2021): 2209–2226. https://doi.org/10.1080/01436597.2021.1929148

McKay, Susan, and Dyan Mazurana. "Gendering Peacebuilding." In *Peace, Conflict, and Violence: Peace Psychology for the 21st Century*, edited by Daniel J. Christie, Richard V. Wagner, and Deborah DuNann Winter, 341–349. Englewood Cliffs, NJ: Prentice-Hall, 2001.

Mlambo, Courage. "Politics and the Natural Resource Curse: Evidence from Selected African States." *Cogent Social Sciences* 8, no. 1 (2022): 2035911. https://doi.org/10.1080/23311886.2022.2035911

Mulinge, Munyae, and Gwen Lesetedi. "Interrogating Our Past: Colonialism and Corruption in Sub-Saharan Africa." *African Journal of Political Science* 3, no. 2 (1998): 15–28. www.jstor.org/stable/23493651

Nelson, Fred. "Introduction: The Politics of Natural Resource Governance in Africa." In *Community Rights, Conservation and Contested Land: The Politics of Natural Resource Governance in Africa*, edited by Fred Nelson, 3–31. New York, NY: Earthscan, 2010.

Noma, Emiko, Dee Aker, and Jennifer Freeman. "Heeding Women's Voices: Breaking Cycles of Conflict and Deepening the Concept of Peacebuilding." *Journal of Peacebuilding & Development* 7, no. 1 (2012): 7–32. https://doi.org/10.1080/15423166.2012.719384

Nwankwo, Odi. "Impact of Corruption on Economic Growth in Nigeria." *Mediterranean Journal of Social Sciences* 5, no. 6 (2014): 41–46. https://dx.doi.org/10.5901/mjss.2014.v5n6p41

Ojakorotu, Victor. "Resource Control and Conflict in Africa." In *The Palgrave Handbook of African Politics, Governance and Development*, edited by Samuel O. Oloruntoba and Toyin Falola, 367–385. New York, NY: Palgrave Macmillan, 2018. https://doi.org/10.1057/978-1-349-95232-8_22

Okojie, Paul, and Abubakar Momoh. "Corruption and Reform in Nigeria." In *Corruption and Development: The Anti-Corruption Campaigns*, edited by Sarah Bracking, 103–120. Hampshire: Palgrave Macmillan, 2007. https://doi.org/10.1057/9780230590625

Olatokun Wole, Michael, and Oluyemi Folorunso. Ayanbode. "Use of Indigenous Knowledge by Women in a Nigerian Rural Community." *Indian Journal of Traditional Knowledge* 8, no. 2 (2009): 287–295. http://hdl.handle.net/123456789/3968

Ombati, Mokua. "Women Transcending "Boundaries" in Indigenous Peacebuilding in Kenya's Sotik/Borabu Border Conflict." *Multidisciplinary Journal of Gender Studies* 4, no. 1 (2015): 637–661. https://doi.org/10.4471/generos.2015.50

Paffenholz, Thania. "Unpacking the Local Turn in Peacebuilding: A Critical Assessment Towards an Agenda for Future Research." *Third World Quarterly* 36, no. 5 (2015): 857–874. https://doi.org/10.1080/01436597.2015.1029908

Pikirayi, Innocent. "The Demise of Great Zimbabwe, A.D. 1420–1550: An Environmental Re-Appraisal." In *Cities in the World: 1500–2000*, edited by Adrian Green and Rodger Leech, 31–47. London: Routledge, 2006. https://doi.org/10.4324/9781315095677

Pillay, Soma. "Corruption – The Challenge to Good Governance: A South African Perspective." *International Journal of Public Sector Management* 17, no. 7 (2004): 586–605. https://doi.org/10.1108/09513550410562266

Qobo, Mzukisi. "Outlines of Intra-State Conflict in Zimbabwe and Regional Challenges." In *Regional Trade Integration and Conflict Resolution*, edited by Shaheen Rafi Khan, 165–180. New York, NY: Routledge, 2008. https://doi.org/10.4324/9780203889800

Raleigh, Clionadh, and Daniel Wigmore-Shepherd. 2022. "Elite Coalitions and Power Balance Across African Regimes: Introducing the African Cabinet and Political Elite Data Project." *Ethnopolitics* 21, no. 1 (2022): 22–47. https://doi.org/10.1080/17449057.2020.1771840

Schulte, Meike, and Cody Morris Paris. "Blood Diamonds: An Analysis of the State of Affairs and the Effectiveness of the Kimberley Process." *International Journal of Sustainable Society* 12, no. 1 (2020): 51–75. https://doi.org/10.1504/IJSSOC.2020.105017

Soga, Masashi, Daniel Cox, Yuichi Yamaura, Kevin Gaston, Kiyo Kurisu, and Keisuke Hanaki. "Health Benefits of Urban Allotment Gardening: Improved Physical and Psychological Well-being and Social Integration." *International Journal of Environmental Research and Public Health* 14, no. 1 (2017): 71–83. https://doi.org/10.3390/ijerph14010071

Stok, Marijn, and Denise de Ridder. "The Focus Theory of Normative Conduct." In *Social Psychology in Action: Evidence-Based Interventions from Theory to Practice*, edited by Kai Sassenberg and Michael L. W. Vliek, 95–110. Cham: Springer, 2019. https://doi.org/10.1007/978-3-030-13788-5_7

Strang, Veronica. "Elemental Powers: Water Beings, Nature Worship, and Long-term Trajectories in Human-Environmental Relations." *Swedish Journal of Anthropology* 4, no. 2 (2021): 15–24. http://urn.kb.se/resolve?urn=urn:nbn:se:uu:diva-463871

Tangri, Roger, and Andrew Mwenda. *The Politics of Elite Corruption in Africa: Uganda in Comparative African Perspective*. London: Routledge, 2013. https://doi.org/10.4324/9780203626474.

United Nations Environment Programme, United Nations Entity for Gender Equality and the Empowerment of Women, United Nations Peacebuilding Support Office and United Nations Development Programme. *Women and Natural Resources: Unlocking the Peacebuilding Potential*. New York, NY: UNEP, 2013. http://hdl.handle.net/20.500.11822/8373

Verkoren, Willemijn. "Knowledge Networking: Implications for Peacebuilding Activities." *International Journal of Peace Studies* 11, no. 2 (Autumn/Winter 2006): 27–61. https://www.jstor.org/stable/41852945

Wane, Njoki, and Deborah Chandler. "African Women, Cultural Knowledge and Environmental Education with a Focus on Kenya's Indigenous Women." *Canadian Journal of Environmental Education* 7, no. 1 (Spring 2002): 86–98.

Whyte, Kyle Powys. "On the Role of Traditional Ecological Knowledge as a Collaborative Concept: A Philosophical Study." *Ecological Processes* 2, no. 7 (April 2013): 1–12. https://doi.org/10.1186/2192-1709-2-7

Conclusion

Ensuring a Peaceful Africa Based on the Sustainable Use of Natural Resources

Victoria R. Nalule and Obasesam Okoi

The presence of abundant natural resources within a nation is *prima facie* an indicator of wealth and potential economic growth. However, history has shown that natural resource abundance can also serve as a catalyst for the resource curse phenomenon.[1] African countries exemplify such a curse, as their abundant natural resources have failed to translate into meaningful economic growth. Instead, they find themselves among the world's poorest countries.[2] Injustices in the management of Africa's resource wealth have been prevalent, characterized by corruption, poor governance, and the misallocation of public resources. As this book has shown, economic disparities arising from poor resource governance have become a major source of conflict in many resource-rich countries across Africa.

The chapters in this book shed light on the relationship between natural resource governance, conflict, and peace in Africa, emphasizing the complexity of these issues and their implications for the continent's development and stability. The case studies and theoretical frameworks explored throughout the book provide evidence of the consequences of a resource governance deficit and underscore the need for effective governance mechanisms to achieve peace and stability on the continent. This book offers insights into potential solutions and emphasizes the importance of addressing environmental and social justice concerns in resource governance as well as improved oversight of the natural resource sector to prevent future conflicts and mitigate their impact. By incorporating chapters that utilize the theoretical framework of environmental and social justice to critically examine the mining sector in Africa, this book offers valuable insights into the social dynamics and inequalities present within that sector.

Throughout this book, the contributors raise crucial concerns about the imperative of integrating equity, justice, and the rule of law into resource governance. This integration serves as a means to unlock the potential of natural resources for sustainable development in African countries and address conflicts associated with resource exploitation. Transparency, accountability, and participatory decision-making have been identified as essential elements for effective resource governance. By addressing these concerns, African countries

DOI: 10.4324/9781003355717-14

can establish a framework that promotes responsible and inclusive governance of their natural resources. However, the chapters in this book do not aim to provide exhaustive solutions. Rather, they explore diverse approaches to natural resource governance in specific contexts, with an emphasis on addressing conflicts within those contexts. Such considerations can lay the foundation for sustainable peace by addressing inequalities, promoting inclusive development, and ensuring marginalized and disadvantaged groups that have equitable access to benefits, opportunities, and decision-making processes. Responsible resource governance should adhere to the principles of sustainability, which encompasses profits, people, and the planet. Striking a balance between these categories is crucial for promoting peace.

The contributors of this book emphasize the crucial role that land plays in the exploitation, development, and management of natural resources. The contestation between state and non-state actors over control of resource mining sites offers adeeper understanding of the complexities surrounding natural resource governance and its far-reaching implications. Moreover, injustices in accessing land for natural resource projects have contributed significantly to conflicts. The book sheds light on the importance of distributive justice in addressing land inequalities in the extractive sector, particularly to minimize conflicts that frequently arise from land-grabbing practices in many African countries. To ensure the sustainable management of natural resources and the well-being of local communities, it is imperative to integrate environmental justice principles into the frameworks of natural resource governance. This approach allows for the preservation of ecosystems, the reduction of environmental degradation, and the mitigation of negative impacts on vulnerable populations resulting from resource extraction.

Another unique perspective of this book lies in the ability of the contributors to go beyond simply acknowledging the common challenges faced in the extractive sectors across Africa to explore the role of regional institutions, such as the African Union, in providing the necessary institutional framework for conflict resolution and peacebuilding. The African Union has consistently prioritized preventive efforts in its conflict mitigation agenda. Through the examination of initiatives like the African Union Panel of Wise, the book offers valuable insights into the potential of regional cooperation to effectively address conflicts and promote sustainable resource governance throughout Africa.

Looking ahead, it is crucial to prioritize the inclusion of local communities, indigenous groups, and other relevant stakeholders in decision-making processes related to resource extraction. Gaining acceptance and approval from local communities, stakeholders, and society at large is essential for sustainable resource extraction and minimizing conflicts associated with mining activities. This forward-thinking approach recognizes the value of diverse perspectives, knowledge, and needs and seeks to incorporate them into resource governance frameworks. By engaging local communities and indigenous groups in resource-related decision-making, their sense of ownership and agency can be enhanced. This is crucial for ensuring the long-term well-being of both the communities themselves and the ecosystems they depend on.

Furthermore, this book brings to light the gender dynamics in natural resource governance. Although women play a significant role in natural resource management, they are often marginalized and excluded from decision-making processes and resource access, stressing the necessity for gender justice within the sector.[3] The book examines the contribution of women in promoting social, political, and economic stability in resource-rich countries, with a particular focus on the intersection between indigenous knowledge, gender, and peacebuilding in diverse contexts. A key solution highlighted in this book is the importance of harnessing and enhancing women's participation, representation, and leadership in resource governance, ensuring that their voices are heard and their perspectives are integrated into decision-making processes. Promoting gender-responsive practices can help overcome the barriers that hinder women's active involvement in resource governance.

It is important to address the structural inequalities and discriminatory practices that limit women's access to resources. Providing women with equal opportunities for land ownership, access to credit, and control over productive resources can empower them as key actors in sustainable resource management. Equally important is the need to recognize and value their traditional knowledge and contributions to resource governance as crucial for sustainable peace. This consideration stems from a growing understanding that women often have unique insights and perspectives, as they are directly affected by resource-related conflicts and play significant roles in the well-being of their communities. Such considerations align with the Sustainable Development Goals and the United Nations Security Council resolution 1325.

As we conclude this book, it is worth emphasizing that natural resource extraction, particularly in the mining sector, often poses significant environmental and social risks, and that inadequate regulations can result in negative impacts on ecosystems, communities, and economies. Despite the existence of various laws and regulations governing the natural resources sector in Africa, illegalities have remained prevalent, particularly in the artisanal and small-scale mining (ASM) sector. While different African countries have introduced laws and regulations to govern ASM, this book shows that persistent illegalities in the sector have led to escalating environmental, health, and social crises. Therefore, establishing robust legal frameworks is essential to ensure responsible and sustainable resource extraction practices. Mining laws should include provisions for community engagement, consultation, and consent, as well as mechanisms for environmental protection, land rehabilitation, and the equitable sharing of benefits. These measures not only safeguard the environment but also prioritize the rights and well-being of local communities. By adopting these measures, African countries can mitigate conflicts associated with natural resource exploitation, unlock the potential of their natural resources for the betterment of their societies, and strive towards sustainable peace.

Notes

1 Michael L. Ross, "What Have We Learned About the Resource Curse?" *Annual Review of Political Science* 18 (2015): 239–59.
2 Victoria R. Nalule, "Modernisation of the Mining Laws and Key Issues for Consideration in Africa."
3 Victoria N. Nalule, "Achieve Gender Equality and Empower All Women and Girls," in *Mining, Materials, and the Sustainable Development Goals (SDGs)* (CRC Press, 2020), 39–50

Index

Abeshu, Gemechu Adiamassu vii, 6, 72, 73
accountability 5, 24, 25, 28, 29, 37, 47, 48, 147–9, 158, 162, 181, 190
Adomako-kwakye viii, ix, 8, 169
Afar region 60, 63–6, 68, 70, 73
Africa 1–3, 5, 7–11, 13, 15–19, 21, 23–5, 27–48, 50, 52–8, 61, 62, 68–72, 77–83, 85–7, 89–105, 107–15, 117–42, 145–7, 149–69, 176, 181, 183, 184, 188, 189, 191–6, 199, 201, 205–8, 210–19
African Union i, viii, xviii, 1, 2, 7, 52, 121–3, 127, 129, 131, 133, 135, 136, 137, 139, 141, 145, 158, 164, 166, 167, 216
Agbaitoro, Godswill viii, ix, 7, 145, 160, 164
artisanal gold mining vii, 7, 39–41, 43–6, 48–52, 54–7, 77–9, 81, 84, 89, 94, 96, 101
artisanal miners xix, 6, 7, 39, 45, 48, 50, 51, 53, 77, 82–92, 94, 97–9, 152, 175, 176, 187
artisanal mining 6, 38–41, 45, 46, 48, 50–3, 55, 58, 77, 79–82, 85, 87, 89–92, 96, 97, 100
Auty, Richard M. 7, 9, 71

biodiversity 128, 130, 140, 145
borderlands vii, 6, 59, 60, 62, 68, 69
Botswana xv, 2, 6, 28–31, 37, 43, 44, 56, 102, 116
Burkina Faso 6, 38–40, 43–7, 49, 52–8

Cameroun 130
Carry, Inga vii, ix, 6, 77
Central Sahel i, vii, xvi, 6, 38–41, 43, 45–7, 49, 51–4, 57, 59
Civil Wars 1, 19, 21, 22, 34, 35, 123

climate change x, xiii, xx, 3, 49, 53, 55, 94, 103, 111, 118, 208, 212
Collier, Paul 9, 21, 32, 34, 35, 55, 134, 187
coltan 42, 61, 151
conflict i–iii, vii–xi, xiii, xv, xvi, 1–11, 15, 16, 19–23, 26–8, 31–6, 39, 42–4, 46–8, 50, 52–7, 61, 62, 66, 68, 71, 81, 87, 95, 100, 102, 103, 105, 116, 117, 121–4, 126–30, 132–8, 145, 146, 148–54, 157, 158, 160–63, 166–71, 173–200, 202, 204–17
conflict resolution ii–viii, 2, 5–9, 33, 53, 54, 121, 122, 124, 134, 135, 149, 157, 187, 189, 191, 193, 207, 214, 216
community engagement 180, 185, 186, 188, 190, 217
competition 1–4, 6, 16, 19, 21, 31, 43, 46, 91, 122
corruption x, 5, 15, 23, 25, 26, 28, 37, 39, 42, 47, 53, 55, 56, 61, 82, 88, 90, 133, 140, 149, 192, 194, 195, 205, 207, 208, 211, 213–15
cosmopolitan justice 102
criminal groups 48, 49, 51, 86, 88, 89
crude oil 24, 42, 104, 121, 122, 128

Dan-Woniowei, Fie David viii, 121
deforestation 84, 101, 128, 132–4, 140, 145
Democratic Republic of Congo xv, 39, 61, 145
development ix, xi, xv, xix, xx, 1, 2, 4, 8, 9, 11, 15–20, 22–6, 28, 30–8, 42, 43, 49, 53–8, 62, 71, 78, 80–2, 86, 90–8, 101, 102, 104, 108, 110–12, 114–20, 123, 124, 128, 131, 132, 134–6, 138–41, 145, 146, 149, 153–5, 157, 159–62, 164, 166, 167, 170, 172–6, 179–86, 188–90, 196–9, 202–4, 206–8, 210–18

220 *Index*

diamonds 2, 31, 42, 61, 71, 82, 121, 145, 151, 152, 161, 162, 166, 173, 176, 308, 214
displacement ix, 3, 5, 10, 73, 127, 128, 130, 132, 134, 137–40, 169, 178, 189
distributive justice vii, 6, 7, 101–3, 105, 107, 109–15, 117, 119, 159, 216
Djibouti vii, 2, 6, 60–3, 69
Dobi Salt Lake 6, 60, 63, 64
Dutch disease 16, 18, 33

economic gain 31, 41, 42, 185, 186
ecological 26, 61, 84, 87, 106, 117, 128, 140, 169, 184, 187–9, 200, 203, 206, 207, 212, 214
Ekhator, Eghosa O. viii, x, 7, 145, 158, 159, 163, 164, 167
energy justice theory 102, 110, 111, 113, 114
energy resources xiii, xv, 103
environmental degradation 3, 15, 25–7, 36, 109, 123, 127, 128, 133, 145, 154, 156, 157, 169, 174, 194, 195, 216
environmental injustice i–viii, xvi, 2, 6–8, 78, 80, 81, 94, 145–7, 149, 151–68, 184, 216
environmental justice i–viii, xvi, 2, 6–8, 78, 80, 81, 94, 145–7, 149, 151–68, 184, 216
environmental rights 25, 98, 152–4, 160, 163–5, 168
Ethiopia vii, xviii, 2, 6, 60–4, 66, 68–70, 72, 73, 103, 117, 129–31, 137, 139
extractive industries viii, 7, 28, 31, 37, 39, 40, 53, 55, 94, 95, 98–102, 109, 116, 120, 150, 151, 155, 162, 183–7
extractive industries transparency initiative 28

forests 2, 103, 109, 127, 132–4, 136, 139–41, 173, 187

gender viii, xvi, 2, 8, 21, 23, 27, 85, 88, 99, 118, 124, 147, 151, 164, 189, 191–3, 195–205, 207, 209–14, 217, 218
Ghana viii, xiii, 2, 8, 28, 36, 37, 39, 43, 53, 55, 56, 58, 71, 90, 98, 100, 125, 129, 169–71, 173–90
gold vii, xvi, xix, 2, 6, 7, 38–59, 61, 77–89, 93–101, 109, 116, 149, 151, 171, 173–7, 179, 184–9, 194
governance i, vii, ix–xi, xiii, xv, xvi, xviii, 1–10, 15–17, 19, 21, 23–33, 35–44, 47, 52, 54, 61–3, 67–9, 71, 75, 77, 78, 91, 92, 96, 102–6, 108, 110–12, 117, 121, 122, 126, 129, 133, 136, 145, 148–50, 152, 157, 160–2, 164–7, 170, 174, 184, 191–4, 200–7, 211–13, 215–17
greed and grievance 9, 32, 34, 35, 187

heterarchy 6, 62, 68
Horn of Africa i, 1
human rights x, 3, 25–7, 36, 40, 42, 57, 80, 87, 89, 93, 95, 96, 98, 99, 109, 123, 128, 137–9, 146, 148, 150, 154, 157, 158, 160, 163–9, 189, 190, 195
Humphreys, Macartan 9, 17, 33, 161, 178

illegal gold mining 41, 54, 58, 78, 83, 88, 95, 98
indigenous viii, 8, 23, 28, 91, 112, 114, 116, 117, 120, 121, 123, 127, 129–32, 134, 137, 139, 172, 175, 177, 184, 190–209, 211–13, 217
indigenous knowledge viii, 1, 8, 191–209, 211–13, 217
inequalities viii, 3, 6, 7, 15, 21, 22, 35, 77–9, 85, 87, 93, 95, 101, 107, 116, 117, 169, 170, 215–17
inequitable resource distribution 169
insecurity 1, 36, 41, 47, 48, 50, 51, 54, 57, 58, 61, 77, 131, 178, 199
instability vii, 1–6, 15, 16, 23, 30, 31, 38–43, 45–7, 49–51, 53, 55, 57, 59, 61, 68, 146, 191–5, 198–200, 205, 207, 212
institutions x, xvi, 3–5, 15, 19–21, 23, 28–32, 34, 47, 50, 55, 71, 123, 131, 133, 140, 157–9, 167, 177–9, 192, 194, 204, 216
inter-communal violence 40

jihadists 40, 46

Kimberley process xix, 152, 162, 208, 214
Kgotla 30

land vii, viii, xv, xvi, 2, 3, 5, 7, 25, 41, 42, 47, 49, 53, 60–3, 65, 67, 69, 71, 73, 80, 81, 91, 92, 96, 98, 100–21, 129–41, 145, 147, 148, 159, 169, 171, 173–9, 184, 186, 187, 194–6, 202, 206, 213, 216, 217
land grabbing 102, 117, 119, 121, 129, 131, 134, 137, 138, 216
land law reform viii, 101, 103, 105, 107–15, 117, 119

Index 221

land ownership 41, 105, 106, 118, 169, 217
law vii–ix, xi, xvi, xx, xix, 4–9, 11, 12, 23, 24, 27, 31, 41, 44, 46, 50, 55, 59, 63, 77, 80–3, 86, 87, 90, 92, 95, 96, 100–21, 124, 126, 128, 130, 132, 137–9, 145–9, 152–71, 174, 176, 179–82, 184–6, 189, 190, 207, 212, 215, 217, 218
legal framework 27, 28, 31, 36, 105, 148, 149, 176, 179, 182, 183, 217
Liberia 1, 3, 10, 34, 54, 55, 100, 121, 125, 129, 145, 151, 192, 199, 200, 205, 209, 212
liberalization 39, 153
local communities 2–4, 8, 15, 16, 23–8, 31, 49, 51, 81, 89, 109, 110, 113, 114, 126, 130, 132, 151, 169, 170, 172, 197–9, 201, 202, 217

Madagascar 102, 116, 130, 131
Mali xi, xx, 6, 38–41, 44, 46–50, 52–4, 56–60, 62, 69, 73, 78, 79, 90–2, 95, 98, 99, 122, 129, 131
marginalization 16, 21, 24, 68, 169
Mensah viii, x, 8, 169
mineral i, vii, xi, xv, xix, xx, 2, 3, 11, 15, 21, 25, 27, 28, 37, 38, 42–4, 52, 54–7, 60–5, 67, 69, 71–3, 82, 83, 88, 91, 93, 95–106, 113, 114, 116, 132, 145, 150–2, 162, 169, 172–81, 184–7, 190, 195
mine-induced poverty 196
mining i, vii, viii, xi, xv, xvi, xviii, xix, 2, 3, 6–11, 23, 25, 28, 31, 32, 37–72, 77–116, 120, 128, 132, 137, 139, 151, 162–4, 169–90, 192, 195, 200, 205, 215–18
mining companies 3, 8, 39, 48, 65, 82, 83, 88, 89, 169–84, 187, 188
mining communities 8, 53, 55, 56, 77, 80, 89, 90, 169–84, 187, 189
mining conflicts 8, 95, 173, 174, 176, 177, 184, 196
mineral resources 38, 39, 42, 44, 63–5, 69, 83, 88, 92, 95–9, 101, 145, 150, 151, 181
mismanagement of resources 193–5
Mozambique x, 86, 102, 108, 125, 130, 192, 208, 211
Müller, Melanie vii, ix, 6, 77
multinational corporations xix, 24, 26, 148, 161

Nalule, Victoria R. i–iv, viii, xi, xv, 7, 9, 95, 96, 101, 119, 120, 215, 218

natural resource conflict resolution viii, 121, 122
natural resource governance i–viii, ix, x, xiii, xv, xvi, 1–10, 15–20, 23, 24, 27–9, 31, 33, 35–7, 41–5, 47, 52, 54–6, 61, 63, 68, 101, 103, 113, 121, 122, 126, 127, 133–7, 145–8, 150–3, 158, 161, 162, 166, 169, 170, 174–6, 179–82, 185–7, 191–5, 200, 205–7, 209–11, 215–17
natural resources i, iii, viii–x, xiii, xv, xvi, 1–10, 15–20, 23, 24, 27–9, 31, 33, 35–7, 41–5, 47, 52, 54–6, 61, 63, 68, 101, 103, 113, 121, 122, 126–8, 133–7, 145–53, 158, 161, 162, 166, 169, 170, 173–6, 179–82, 185–7, 191–5, 200, 205–7, 209–11, 215–17
need creed and greed 22, 35
negotiation 170, 173, 181, 182
Niger Delta x, xix, 11, 24, 26, 27, 35, 36, 109, 119, 128, 133, 140, 146, 153, 158, 160, 161, 163, 167, 168
Nigeria viii, x, xi, xiii, 2, 3, 7, 10, 11, 18, 24, 26–8, 33, 35, 36, 39, 43, 49, 51, 55, 56, 59, 71, 95, 104, 109, 118, 119, 123, 128, 129, 133, 135, 140, 145, 146, 148, 151, 153–68, 207, 211, 213
Niger (Republic of Niger), 6, 38, 39, 40, 43, 44, 46, 49, 50, 51, 52, 53, 56, 57, 58, 59, 129, 133
norms 4, 15, 23, 29, 32, 169, 170, 201, 203
non-state actor 6, 60–3

oil xi, xix, xx, 2, 4, 9, 15–18, 21, 22, 24–7, 33, 35–7, 42, 43, 55, 56, 61, 71, 101, 102, 104, 105, 109–15, 119–23, 128–30, 132, 133, 135, 137, 145–9, 151, 153–8, 160, 161, 163–5, 167, 168, 184
Ojewale, Oluwole vii, xi, 6, 38
Ojo, John Sunday vii, xi, 6, 38
Okoi, Obasesam i–iv, vii, viii, xi, xv, 1, 6, 10, 15, 26, 36, 215
Olawari, D. J. Egbe viii, x, 7, 121

panel of the wise viii, xx, 7, 121–3, 125, 127, 129, 131, 133, 135–7, 139, 141
para-sovereign vii, xvi, 6, 60–71, 73
para-sovereign power vii, 6, 60–9, 71, 73
para-sovereignty 62, 69
peace 9, 11, 15, 17, 19, 21, 23, 25, 27, 29, 31–3, 35, 36, 58, 59, 71, 73, 123–6, 134–6, 157, 161, 162, 187, 206, 208–14

peacebuilding vii, xi, 10, 19, 36, 53, 196, 200, 206, 208–14
political stability viii, 31, 71, 91, 192, 194–7, 199, 200, 204, 205
poor governance 16, 44, 194, 215
power vii, 60, 61, 63, 65, 67, 69, 71, 73, 119, 129, 136, 207, 208, 211, 212, 214
poverty 93, 116, 119, 164, 189
privatization 39, 41, 47
procedural justice 102, 110–12, 114, 115, 159
policies 37, 120, 138, 140, 152
punctuated peace i, xi, 26, 36

revenue ix, 4, 15, 17–19, 24–8, 31, 45, 46, 48, 49, 51, 65, 82, 109, 127, 151, 179, 181, 182, 185, 186
resource curse 6, 9, 16–21, 28, 29, 33, 34, 37, 42–4, 52, 53, 55, 56, 61, 71, 149, 150, 160, 161, 166, 168, 207, 213, 215, 218
resource management ii, 3, 4, 9, 10, 27, 29, 37, 38, 92, 99, 103, 149, 150, 157, 160, 166, 170, 188, 191–3, 196–8, 200–3, 210, 211, 217
resource wealth xv, 1, 3, 15, 17, 19, 20, 23, 25, 26, 31, 33, 34, 149–51, 161, 215
restorative justice 102, 116–20
recognition justice 102
Romic, Jonathan viii, xii, 8, 191
rule of law viii, 2, 5–7, 11, 23, 145–9, 152, 153, 155–8, 160, 165, 166, 168, 215

Sachs, Jeffrey D. 17
Sahel region i, 2, 40, 44, 45
security threats i, 40, 52
Sierra Leone 1, 3, 10, 22, 34, 54, 55, 129, 130, 138, 145, 151, 176
social justice 6, 7, 23, 77, 80, 108, 120, 147, 159, 215
social legitimacy vii, xvi, 8, 169–71, 173, 175–80, 182, 183, 185, 189
small-scale mining xviii, 28, 50, 53, 55–7, 77, 78, 81–3, 94–6, 98–101, 173, 186, 187, 217

stakeholders xi, xvi, 8, 23, 24, 28, 82, 91, 117, 134, 154, 153, 156, 170, 172, 174, 175, 179, 182, 192, 193, 202, 203, 216
Stiglitz, Joseph E. 17, 200
Sudan 1, 20, 34, 109, 130, 151, 201, 202, 204
sustainable development i, xi, xv, xx, 2, 4, 11, 20, 23, 26, 28, 29, 32, 36, 55, 102, 115, 117, 120, 154, 157, 159, 160, 162, 164, 167, 180, 184, 185, 188–90, 195, 215, 217, 218
sustainable peace i–vii, xvi, 1, 2, 4–6, 8, 9, 15, 17, 19, 21, 23, 25, 27, 29, 31, 32, 35, 37, 206, 216, 217
South Africa viii–xi, xiii, xx, 2, 6, 7, 28, 29, 44, 56, 72, 77–82, 85–91, 93–102, 107, 109–14, 118, 126, 154, 183

terrorism 38, 40, 42, 46, 52, 57, 59
timber ii, 2, 15, 42, 133, 134, 136, 149, 151, 174
transnational organized crime xi, 40, 53, 54
transparency ix, xviii, 23, 24, 28, 31, 32, 37, 90, 110, 149, 158, 162, 215

unemployment 39, 79, 83, 85, 56, 93, 173, 175
Uganda viii, xiii, 2, 7, 101, 102, 105–11, 113–15, 117, 118, 120, 125, 195, 208, 214

violent conflicts 1, 15, 31, 32, 42, 43, 55, 61, 121–3, 126, 127, 129, 130, 132, 133, 148

World Bank 9, 10, 32, 38, 43, 55, 56, 58, 78, 93, 116, 131–4, 137–40, 172, 178, 185, 189

Zama zamas 82, 86, 87, 93, 95–9
Zambia 125, 130, 131
Zartman, William I 22, 32
Zimbabwe 1, 43, 86, 90, 101, 102, 116, 191, 193–5, 205–7, 212–14